GOETHE'S FAUST

Other Books by Walter Kaufmann:

Nietzsche
Critique of Religion and Philosophy
From Shakespeare to Existentialism
The Faith of a Heretic

TRANSLATOR AND EDITOR

The Portable Nietzsche
Judaism and Christianity: Essays by Leo Baeck

EDITOR

Existentialism from Dostoevsky to Sartre
Philosophic Classics: Thales to St. Thomas
Philosophic Classics: Bacon to Kant
Religion from Tolstoy to Camus

GOETHE'S
FAUST

THE ORIGINAL GERMAN
AND A NEW TRANSLATION
AND INTRODUCTION BY

WALTER KAUFMANN

PART ONE AND SECTIONS FROM PART TWO

ANCHOR BOOKS
A DIVISION OF RANDOM HOUSE, INC.
NEW YORK

Anchor Books Editions, 1963, 1990

 Published in the United States by Anchor Books, a division of Random House, Inc., New York, and simultaneously in Canada by Random House of Canada Limited, Toronto. Originally published in hardcover in the United States by Doubleday in 1961. The Anchor Books edition is published by arrangement with Doubleday, a division of Random House, Inc.

Library of Congress Cataloging-in-Publication Data
Goethe, Johann Wolfgang von, 1749–1832.
[Faust]
Goethe's Faust: the original German and a new translation and introduction by Walter Kaufmann.
p. cm.
"Part one and sections from part two."
I. Kaufmann, Walter Arnold. II. Goethe, Johann Wolfgang von, 1749–1832.
Faust. English. 1961. III. Title.
PT2026.F2K3 1989 89-18328
832'.6—dc20 CIP
ISBN 0-385-03114-9

www.anchorbooks.com

PRINTED IN THE UNITED STATES OF AMERICA
50 49

TO

FRIEDA AND EVA WUNDERLICH

in gratitude

INTRODUCTION

Goethe is generally recognized as the greatest German of all time, and *Faust* as his most important single work. Everybody has some idea of both, but few of those who don't read German really know either the poet or his play. Some associate Faust with Marlowe's tragedy or Rembrandt's etching, others with Berlioz' cantata or Thomas Mann's novel; more people with Gounod's opera. Few realize that Gounod's *Faust* is based on the First Part of Goethe's drama, and ignores the Second; fewer still that it does not give an adequate idea even of the First Part. Charles Lamb criticized Goethe, saying: "What has Margaret to do with Faust?" But there is much more to Goethe's Part One, though not to Gounod's opera, than the Gretchen tragedy. (Goethe sometimes calls her Margaret, sometimes more affectionately Gretchen.) Uncertainty about the *end* of Goethe's Faust is even more widespread, and even those who know that he is saved are frequently unsure about the details.

In 1949, when Goethe's two-hundredth birthday was widely celebrated, Webster's New Collegiate Dictionary faithfully reflected the fortunes of Faust in the English-speaking world: "Faust" rated a special entry and was defined as "The title and hero of a drama by Goethe." But the lexicographers' respect for Goethe exceeded their knowledge of his play, leading them to say of Faust's end: "After a sensual life he is carried off by the Devil, but in the final act he is regenerated and his soul is saved"—as if the last act but one were set in hell.

Perhaps the last quality which most people associate with *Faust* is its overflowing humor, which runs the whole scale from the benign to the sardonic, including in between the raw, the witty, the subtle, and Olympian malice. The old Goethe, intent on husbanding his energies for his creative work, could affect the stiff pose of a Herr Geheimrat to cut short unwelcome visits. But in his poems he is anything but stiff, and *Faust* manifests an overwhelming disrespect for etiquette and almost every thinkable propriety, including the established canons of poetic form. The play abounds in doggerel, slang, and jokes, and contains more light verse than solemn poetry.

Why, then, is it a cliché in the English-speaking world that the Germans have no sense of humor and have always been a rather pompous, saturnine, and ponderous people? It is partly because Luther's often coarse humor has been so religiously ignored, and Goethe's and Nietzsche's wit was spirited away by Victorian translators. So the tortuous inversions of the word order, the painful archaisms, and the solemn affectations of some English versions have come to be falsely imputed to the originals. But there is no warrant whatsoever in Goethe's *Faust* for the translators' incessant "ye" and "thou" with their attendant verb forms. *Faust* is one of the relatively few great books that is not only profound and inexhaustible but also readable, enjoyable, and fun.

2

Goethe. The poet was born on August 28, 1749; and by the time he was twenty-six he had finished the so-called *Urfaust*, an early version of the First Part which was not discovered until 1887. Nothing in previous German literature equals the bold conception and the concentrated power of that draft, and the final scene may well be the high point of German drama, not barring the later version which the poet deliberately made less stark.

When he wrote the *Urfaust*, Goethe was by no means unknown. His storm-and-stress drama, *Götz von Berlich-*

ingen (1773) and his novel on *Werther* (1774) were instant successes. Werther's suicide actually inspired many lovelorn young men and women, in France as well as Germany: their corpses were fished from the water with copies of the novel in their pockets.

Well before he was thirty, Goethe had proved himself a master of the drama, of the novel, and of lyric poetry as well. He needed only to repeat himself to enjoy perpetual acclaim. What distinguishes Goethe is less this early attainment of success, though his versatility is certainly unusual, than his deliberate refusal to repeat himself. No sooner had he achieved mastery in one style than he attempted another.

Late in 1775 he went to Weimar, where he joined the state cabinet and took his administrative duties very seriously. A German cartoon shows one army officer saying to another: "There's one thing about that Goethe I can't understand: how can a minister of state find time to write that many poems?" In the most complete German edition, Goethe's works, letters, and diaries fill 143 volumes. Few lives are so fully documented. Of course, by no means everything he wrote is first-rate, but—or perhaps it is because—he worked constantly and never sought the easy way out, least of all by following a formula. No other writer of equal rank had such varied interests, or scattered his contributions over such a range of fields. He made an anatomical discovery, proposed an important hypothesis in botany, worked out a theory of colors, directed a theatre for twenty-six years—the man whose works were performed most often was Mozart—and he took a lively, fruitful interest in everything that came his way. Like Nietzsche, he might well have said: *Nur wer sich wandelt, bleibt mit mir verwandt*—only those who continue to change remain my kin.

By 1790, Goethe had consummated German classicism, writing plays quite unlike the Shakespearean *Goetz.* Both his *Iphigenie* (1787) and his *Tasso* (1790) have only five *dramatis personae* and are studies in restraint. Tasso himself is, in Goethe's later words, "an intensified Werther"; but there is no longer any need to add the motto that Goethe had inserted in later editions of *Werther:* "Be a man, and do not follow me!" It is obvious that Tasso's lack of restraint is a fault, albeit associated with genius.

Having climaxed classicism, Goethe finally published, also in 1790, *Faust: A Fragment.* He omitted the stark conclusion of the *Urfaust,* revised the scenes he kept, and added a good deal of material written during the preceding fifteen years. During the following decade, he issued in installments his great *Bildungsroman,* the story of *Wilhelm Meister,* on which most of the greatest German novels are modeled, at least insofar as they, too, trace the education of the hero. In 1795, Goethe published *Roman Elegies* in praise of love and the senses; in 1796, *Venetian Epigrams* to vent some venom—not only against "smoke of tobacco, bedbugs, garlic, and cross" (#66); in 1797, an epic in hexameters, *Hermann und Dorothea;* and, also before the end of the century, some of the best German ballads and barbed satirical verses, so-called *Xenien,* to make fun of many contemporary writers.

Around the turn of the century he took up work on *Faust* again, and in 1808 he finally published Part One. The following year, he published another novel, *Elective Affinities;* another ten years later, the orientalizing poetry of his *West-Eastern Divan,* including a large number of first-rate poems in an altogether new vein. Meanwhile, between 1811 and 1814, he had issued in three parts—the fourth and last appeared posthumously—his autobiographic work, *Aus Meinem Leben: Dichtung und Wahrheit* (*From My Life: Poetry and Truth*). This work profoundly influenced not only all subsequent studies of Goethe but our whole approach to artists and the intricate relations between life and work. Before Goethe, attempts to understand an individual had not been so strongly based on the idea of development.

He continued to write scientific essays, poetry, and criticism; carried on a vast and highly interesting correspondence—his letters to his friend Zelter, a composer, are of special interest; finished a sequel to *Wilhelm Meister;* said profound things in conversations, recorded, as the poet must have realized, by his young secretary, Eckermann (others, too, wrote down their conversations with him, and eventually, long after his death, all such records were collected and published in German in five volumes); and, not least, kept working on *Faust* until a few months before he died on March 22, 1832, at the age of eighty-two. He had the satisfaction of finishing the Second Part, tied it up for posthumous publication, and refused either to open the batch of papers or to reveal how the play ended.

3

Faust. Reacting against the traditional German idolatry of Goethe's *Faust,* which began practically as soon as the *Fragment* was published in 1790, Nietzsche, in *The Wanderer and His Shadow* (1880), ridiculed "*The Faust idea.* A little seamstress is seduced and made unhappy; a great scholar in all four branches of learning is the evildoer. Surely that could not have happened without supernatural interference? No, of course not! Without the aid of the incarnate devil the great scholar could never have accomplished this. Should this really be the greatest German 'tragic idea,' as is said among the Germans? But for Goethe even this idea was still too terrible. His mild heart could not help putting the little seamstress, 'the good soul who forgot herself but once,' close to the saints after her involuntary death; indeed, by a trick played on the devil at the decisive moment, he even brought the great scholar to heaven at just the right time—'the good man' with the 'darkling aspiration'! And there, in heaven, the lovers find each other again. Goethe once said that his nature was too conciliatory for the truly tragic."*

Although Part Two bears the subtitle "The Second Part of the Tragedy," it is certainly no tragedy in the narrower, now prevalent sense of that word. Nor is Dante's *Commedia* a comedy in the sense now current. And, more to the point, many of the most renowned Greek tragedies, including Aeschylus' *Oresteia* trilogy and Sophocles' *Oedipus Coloneus,* are not "truly tragic" and end on an emphatically "conciliatory" note. But it is, of course, not merely the end of Part Two to which Nietzsche objects: Faust's crime vis-à-vis Gretchen is less imposing and unusual than Oedipus' crime or Orestes'. As Mephistopheles says of Gretchen: "She's not the first one."

Moreover—taking the word "tragedy" in its most ordinary modern sense—it is Gretchen who suffers the tragedy, which Faust takes in his stride. We never see him hunted by the furies, like Orestes: no sooner has Part Two begun than spirits "remove the burning arrows of remorse, and cleanse his mind of memories." And though he dies blind like Oedipus, he does not blind himself with clasps plucked in a passion from the corpse of his beloved, resolved to live in infamy and night. Rather, he loses his sight when he is a hundred years old, just before he dies in a moment of elation. Faust's sufferings are incidental. He is not a tragic hero like Orestes, who is called upon to kill his mother, or like Oedipus, who owes it to his city to find out who killed his predecessor and who thus discovers that he killed his father and is wedded to his mother. In *Faust,* tragedy engulfs not the hero but representatives of unheroic, non-

* Aphorism 124, pp. 69f. in *The Portable Nietzsche.* Selected and translated, with an Introduction, Prefaces, and Notes, by Walter Kaufmann; The Viking Press, New York 1954; paperback edition, with new postscript, 1958.

outstanding, suffering humanity: Gretchen, Philemon and Baucis, Gretchen's mother.

The death of Philemon and Baucis in the fifth act of Part Two involves no tragic conflict in Faust's mind: he has given different instructions; their death is a hideous surprise to him; but again he takes it in his stride. It is another episode, no more. In retrospect we realize, if it was not clear to us all along, that Gretchen's tragedy, too, was a mere episode. The drama is epic, the effect cumulative.

In all these respects *Faust* is distinctly un-Greek, non-Aristotelian, modern. It reminds us of Ibsen's *Peer Gynt*, which was modeled on it, of the epic theatre of Bertold Brecht—in the nineteen-fifties Brecht staged Goethe's *Urfaust* in East Berlin—and even of Arthur Miller's *Death of a Salesman.*

In another aphorism of *The Wanderer and His Shadow* (#109), Nietzsche rather pointedly calls "the conversations with Eckermann the best German book there is." He preferred the mature Goethe—who was untimely, unpopular, and widely resented because he was so unromantic, civilized, and humane—to *Faust,* the all-too-popular creation that was threatening to eclipse him.*

Still: are the conversations with Eckermann a greater book than *Faust?* Happily, one need not choose; but the case for *Faust* must certainly depend upon a very different conception of the drama from the one Nietzsche derided. As a nineteenth-century philosophic poem and the vehicle of "the Faust idea," the play is nearly as inadequate as it would be if considered as an attempt at a Shakespearean tragedy. But Goethe himself knew that.

Even as he realized that he was constitutionally incapable of writing anything "truly tragic"—and actually

* For his final tribute to Goethe, near the end of *Twilight of the Idols,* see *The Portable Nietzsche,* pp. 553–55; for some other pertinent quotations, see my *Nietzsche,* Meridian Books, especially pp. 131ff.

felt compelled to tone down the end of the *Urfaust*—he laughed at those who "come and ask me what idea I sought to embody in my *Faust*. As if I myself knew that and could express it! 'From heaven through the world to hell,' one might say in a pinch; but that is no idea but the course of the action. And further, that the devil loses his wager and that a human being who, out of profound aberrations, continues to strive always for the better, is to be *saved*—that is indeed an effective thought which explains a few things and is good, but it is not an idea that is the foundation of the whole and of every scene in particular. Indeed, that would have been a fine thing, had I wanted to string such a rich, variegated, and extremely versatile life, as I represented in *Faust*, on the meager thread of a single central idea! It was altogether not my manner as a poet to strive for the embodiment of something *abstract*. I received *impressions*—impressions that were sensuous, vital, lovely, motley, hundredfold—whatever a lively power of imagination offered me; and as a poet I did not have to do anything but round out and form such visions and impressions artistically, and to present them in such a live manner that others would receive the same impressions when hearing or reading what I offered. When, however, I did for once wish as a poet to represent an idea, I did it in *shorter* poems . . .; e.g., 'The Metamorphosis of Animals,' that 'of Plants,' the poem called 'Legacy,' and many others. The only creation of larger scope in which I am aware of having worked with some central idea might be my *Elective Affinities*. That made the novel comprehensible to the understanding; but I should not say that this made it *better*. My opinion is rather this: *The more incommensurable and incomprehensible for the understanding a poetic creation may be, the better.*"

These striking comments are found in Goethe's conversations with Eckermann and dated May 6, 1827. Immediately preceding the passage quoted, Goethe himself stated the moral: "The Germans are really strange people. With their profound thoughts and ideas, which they seek everywhere and project into everything, they make life harder for themselves than they should. Oh, that at long last you had the courage for once to *yield yourselves to your impressions*, to let yourselves be delighted, let yourselves be moved, let yourselves be elevated, yes, to let yourselves be taught and inspired and encouraged for something great; only do not always think that everything is vain if it is not some abstract thought or idea!"

This cutting remark about "the Germans" applies to hosts of non-German literary critics and historians and to the majority of students trained by them. Almost everybody tries to be profound; where the Germans in the nineteenth century sought ideas, the twentieth-century American seeks recurring images and symbols.

Goethe, however, was not heartless. He laughed at the scholars, but he took pity on them. In a conversation he remarked: "For thirty years almost, they have plagued themselves with the broomsticks of the Blocksberg and the monkeys' conversation in the witch's kitchen, which occur in *Faust*, and the interpreting and allegorizing of this dramatic-humorous nonsense has never gone too well. Indeed, one should indulge in such jokes more often while one is young . . ."* And on June 1, 1831, less than a year before he died, Goethe wrote Zelter that the play was all but finished, and added: "It is no trifle to put forth in one's eighty-second year what one conceived in one's twentieth, and to clothe such an internal, living skeleton with ligaments, flesh, and skin, and on top of that to wrap a few mantle folds around the finished product that it may altogether remain an evident riddle, delight men on and on, and give them something to work on."

Few writers have given the scholars so much to work

* Quoted in Otto Pniower's *Goethe's Faust: Zeugnisse und Excurse zu seiner Entstehungsgeschichte* (1899), #973.

on, and few books have elicited a literature remotely comparable to that on Goethe's *Faust*. Many of the books and articles are competent, and a few are brilliant in their way; but much of the greatness of the play can be experienced without the benefit of scholarship, without analysis of images, without any quest for central thoughts. Profundity does not depend on symbolism or ideas.

What is truly astonishing about *Faust* is its modernity and, next to that, some timeless qualities. But here scholars may interpose: the hunt for thoughts, the exegesis of symbols, the pursuit of images are possibly dispensable, but the most obvious point where erudition is needed has not even been mentioned yet.

4

Historical background. Faust is an historic figure, and a host of legends about him antedate Goethe's treatment; some of them even antedate the historic Faust. Moreover, other poets had taken up the theme before Goethe did—and many more have treated it since. A vast amount of scholarship has been devoted to those ancient and medieval legends which in time came to be associated with stories about Faust; historians are still arguing about the details of Faust's life; and research on the sixteenth-, seventeenth-, and eighteenth-century Faust books and plays and puppet shows continues. No brief summary could possibly do justice to the literature; but happily this is not necessary in order to do justice to Goethe: he was blissfully unaware of most of the lore that scholars, inspired by his play, began to adduce while he was still living.

The reason for nevertheless sketching a few high points is twofold. Some possess considerable human interest. And the claim that Goethe's play is much more modern than is usually supposed should not be based on a complete refusal to consider the historic background of his drama.

The historic Faust was born, it seems, in Knittlingen, Württemberg, about 1480. (Luther was born in 1483.) According to Melanchthon, Luther's friend, Faust studied magic at the University of Cracow, in Poland. In those days, magic was also taught at the Universities of Salamanca and Toledo. There are reports that Faust disparaged Jesus' miracles and boasted that, whatever Christ had done, he, too, could do as often as he wished. Needless to add, Luther and Melanchthon regarded Faust with horror and contempt.

Others, more impressed by him, induced him to teach school, but it is said that he molested the boys entrusted to his care and, found out, had to flee to escape punishment. Many traditions connect him with the city of Erfurt. The story goes that at the university there he lectured on Homer, and, to entertain his students, confronted them with Homer's heroes in the flesh. A Franciscan monk, Konrad Klinge, admonished Faust to return to God and threatened him with eternal damnation; but Faust is said to have replied:

"My dear sir, I realize that you are well disposed toward me, and I know myself what you have been telling me. But I have gone further than you think and have pledged myself to the devil with my own blood, to be his in eternity, body and soul. How, then, can I return? Or how could I be helped?"

Klinge replied: "That can be done if you seriously implore God's grace and mercy, truly repent and atone, renounce magic and association with devils, and neither vex nor seduce anyone: then we shall hold mass for you in our monastery that you may be rid of the devil."

"Mass, mass, mass!" retorted Faust. "My agreement ties me down irrevocably. I have deliberately despised God, have committed perjury and faithlessness against him, have believed and trusted in the devil more than in

God; so I cannot come back to him or console myself with his grace, which I have lost. Nor would it be honest or honorable if it had to be said about me that I had gone against my letter and seal, which after all I signed with my blood. The devil has kept faithfully what he promised me; so I, too, want to keep faithfully what I have promised and pledged to him."

After that, the monk had him expelled from Erfurt. Another story relates that Faust rode out of Auerbach's Keller in Leipzig on a barrel—in 1525, to be exact. Melanchthon was among those who claimed that the devil accompanied Faust in the shape of a dog. Philip von Hutten asked Faust to foretell his future before he sailed for Venezuela in 1534, and six years later, January 16, 1540, he wrote his older brother that everything had come to pass precisely as foretold by Faust. Faust is said to have died in Staufen im Breisgau in 1540.

The first "Faust Book" appeared in 1587. It was written in German, and the title page announced: "Historia of Dr. Johann Faust, the widely acclaimed magician and black artist, how he pledged himself to the devil for a certain time, what strange adventures he saw meanwhile, brought about and pursued, until he finally received his well deserved wages. Compiled and prepared for the printer in several parts out of his own literary remains, as a horrible example and sincere warning for all conceited, clever, and godless people. James 4: Submit to God, resist the devil, and he will flee from you. Cum Gratia et Privilegio. Printed in Frankfurt am Main by Johann Spies. MDLXXXVII."

The book appeared in the fall, and by year's end had been reprinted in four pirated editions. Then Spies published a second edition, a version in low German appeared in Lübeck, a rhymed version in Tübingen, a Danish translation came out in 1588, and a History of the *Damnable Life and Deserved Death of Dr. John Faustus* made its appearance in England.

Christopher Marlowe was the first great poet to take up the theme. In his *Tragical History of Doctor Faustus* the orthodox, pious moral of the German *Historia of Dr. Johann Faust* is retained, but the magnificent poetry of Faust's best lines, including his magnificent last monologue, gives him a tragic dignity.

Ah, Faustus,
Now hast thou but one bare hour to live,
And then thou must be damn'd perpetually!
Stand still, you ever-moving spheres of heaven,
That time may cease, and midnight never come;
Fair Nature's eye, rise, rise again, and make
Perpetual day; or let this hour be but
A year, a month, a week, a natural day,
That Faustus may repent and save his soul!
O lente, lente, currite noctis equi!
The stars move still, time runs, the clock will strike,
The Devil will come, and Faustus must be damn'd.
Oh, I'll leap up to my God! Who pulls me down?
See, see where Christ's blood streams in the firmament!
One drop would save my soul—half a drop: ah, my Christ!
Ah, rend not my heart for naming of my Christ!
Yet will I call on him: O, spare me, Lucifer!—
Where is it now? 'tis gone; and see where God
Stretcheth out his arm, and bends his ireful brows!
Mountains and hills come, come, and fall on me,
And hide me from the heavy wrath of God!
No! no!
Then will I headlong run into the earth;
Earth, gape! O, no, it will not harbour me!
You stars that reign'd at my nativity,
Whose influence hath allotted death and hell,
Now draw up Faustus, like a foggy mist,
Into the entrails of yon labouring clouds,
That when you vomit forth into the air,
My limbs may issue from your smoky mouths,
So that my soul may but ascend to heaven.
(The clock strikes.)
Ah, half the hour is past! 'twill all be past anon!

O God,
If thou wilt not have mercy on my soul,
Yet for Christ's sake whose blood hath ransom'd me,
Impose some end to my incessant pain;
Let Faustus live in hell a thousand years,
A hundred thousand, and at last be saved!
O, no end is limited to damned souls!
Why wert thou not a creature wanting soul?
Or why is this immortal that thou hast? . . .
(The clock strikes twelve.)
O, it strikes, it strikes! Now, body, turn to air,
Or Lucifer will bear thee quick to hell.
(Thunder and lightning.)
O soul, be changed into little water-drops,
And fall into the ocean—ne'er be found.
My God! my God! look not so fierce on me!
(Enter *Devils.*)
Adders and serpents, let me breathe awhile!
Ugly hell, gape not! come not, Lucifer!
I'll burn my books!—Ah Mephistophilis!
(Exeunt *Devils* with him. Enter *Chorus.*)

CHORUS:
Cut is the branch that might have grown full straight,
And burned is Apollo's laurel bough,
That sometime grew within this learned man.
Faustus is gone: regard his hellish fall,
Whose fiendful torture may exhort the wise
Only to wonder at unlawful things,
Whose deepness doth entice such forward wits
To practice more than heavenly power permits.

Here is a tragic ending at the price of a religious orthodoxy that Goethe found deeply repellent. If there must be tragedy, *he* would bring it about without benefit of the clergy: witness Gretchen and the Dungeon scene.

It is even arguable that Goethe's ending, at least in the *Urfaust*—in the later version he added, after Mephistopheles' "She is judged," a voice from above proclaiming "is saved"—is more tragic than Marlowe's ending. In Goethe's play, the question whether she is "judged" or "saved" is not what truly moves us: these dicta are glosses on the tragedy that we behold throughout the last scene. In Marlowe's drama, on the other hand, the question of Faust's eternal destiny is central, and Marlowe's orthodox handling of it, far from ensuring tragedy, is incompatible with real tragedy. In my *Critique of Religion and Philosophy* (section 77), I have argued that there cannot be a Christian tragedy; and Marlowe's attempt is a case in point. Mozart was profoundly perceptive when he called his (and da Ponte's) parallel effort, *Don Giovanni*, a *dramma giocoso*. There, too, comic and serious scenes alternate; there, too, the hero is in the end dragged down to hell; and a final chorus assures us that "this is the end of one who lived ill." There is a sense of tragic waste, to be sure, in Marlowe as in Mozart, but that is insufficient to make the end "truly tragic." It is therefore no accident that Marlowe's play, as it was performed on the stages of Europe, was transformed into a comedy. His ending permitted that; Goethe's Dungeon scene, hardly.

Still, "The Second Part of the Tragedy" remained to be written: eventually, Faust had to die, and the question of his posthumous fate must be faced by Goethe, too. At this point, the historic background helps us to appreciate the deliberate unorthodoxy of the end of Goethe's drama. What at first glance may seem Christian and traditional is actually the antithesis of the traditional and Christian treatment of the theme. Goethe's Faust is saved.

Goethe may not have read Marlowe's *Faustus* until relatively late in life. He certainly read a translation in 1818 and in a conversation of 1829 paid lavish tribute to the play. But soon after Marlowe was killed in a fight, at twenty-nine, in 1593, English players, traveling on the continent, introduced the story on the German stage, where it soon became as popular as the Faust books. The tragedy became a comedy, and the comedy gave way to puppet plays. It was in the form of one of these puppet shows that the young Goethe first encountered Faust.

In 1688, when the play was still performed by live actors, a bill announcing it made a great point of its buffoonery, promised such spectacles as men, dogs, cats, a dragon, and a fire-breathing raven, all of which would be seen flying through the air—and concluded that "Hell will be represented adorned with beautiful fireworks."

Goethe retained much of the traditional buffoonery, but he did not, like Marlowe, alternate serious and comic scenes. While the Greek tragedians concentrated humor in the satyr play, and the Elizabethans in special scenes, Goethe, largely by means of Mephistopheles, carried it into almost every scene—including even the Prologue in Heaven—without being the less serious for that. For it was part of Goethe's genius that he could be serious without being solemn.

He was not the first great German writer to think of turning the Faust legend into an ambitious drama. Lessing, the great critic, dramatist, and anti-theologian, who was twenty years his senior, wrote in one of his *Letters Concerning Recent Literature*, under the date of February 16, 1759:

"If Shakespeare's masterpieces had been translated for our Germans with a few modest changes, I know for sure that it would have had better consequences than their present intimate acquaintance with Corneille and Racine. . . . For a *genius* can be sparked only by a *genius;* and best of all by one who seems to owe everything to nature alone and thus does not repel by the troublesome perfections of art. Even if we invoke the ancients as models, Shakespeare is a far greater tragic poet than Corneille, although the latter knew the ancients very well and the former hardly at all. . . . After Sophocles' *Oedipus*, no play in the world has more power over our passions than *Othello*, than *King Lear*, than *Hamlet*, etc. . . . That our own old plays really had much about them that was English, I could prove to you at great length with a minimum of trouble. Merely to name the best known among them: *Doctor Faust* contains a lot of scenes which only a Shakespearean genius was capable of conceiving. And how much in love was Germany, and partly still is, with its *Doctor Faust!* One of my friends has preserved an old draft of this tragedy and he has given me a scene . . . Here it is! . . . What do you think of this scene? You wish for a German play full of such scenes? I do, too."

The scene had been written by Lessing himself.

Lessing died in 1781 without having finished his *Faust;* but his praise of Shakespeare, which in 1759 was revolutionary and a testimony to Lessing's genius, left a lasting mark on German literature and helped to inaugurate its greatest period. In his collected works, we find a letter about his lost drafts for the play from a Captain von Blankenburg, dated May 14, 1784. Of the ending, the letter says: "Enough, the hosts of hell believe that they have accomplished their work; in the fifth act they sound songs of triumph, when an apparition from the higher world interrupts them most unexpectedly and yet in the most natural and reassuring manner: 'Do not triumph!' the angel shouts at them; 'you have not vanquished humanity and science; the deity did not give man the noblest of drives to make him eternally unhappy; what you have seen and now believe to possess was nothing but a phantom.'"

Another note, signed by I. I. Engel, informs us that in the first scene of Lessing's *Faust* the devils' boasts are countered "with the solemn but gently spoken words that sound from above: 'You shall not win!' . . . The angel buries Faust in a deep sleep and puts a phantom in his place. With this the devils have their sport until, at the moment when they want to come into final possession of it, it disappears. Everything that happens to this phantom is a dream vision for the real Faust who is asleep: he awakens after the devils have withdrawn in shame and rage, and thanks providence for the warning it meant to give him with such an instructive dream."

Many of the things mentioned in this section, Goethe never knew. Told in his old age that Lord Byron had reproached him for taking this from here and that from there, Goethe said that he had not read most of the things cited by Byron, "much less thought of them when I wrote my *Faust*. But Lord Byron is great only as a poet; as soon as he reflects he is a child. Thus he does not know either how to take care of similar unperceptive attacks on himself by some of his compatriots; he should have replied in much stronger terms. Whatever is, is mine! he should have said; and whether I have taken it from life or from a book, that's all the same; what matters is merely that I should have used it well. Walter Scott utilized a scene from my *Egmont*, and he had every right to do it; and because he did it intelligently, he deserves praise. He also copied the character of my Mignon [from *Wilhelm Meister*] in one of his novels; but whether he showed equal wisdom on that occasion is another question. Lord Byron's Transformed Devil is a continuation of Mephistopheles, and that is fine. If he had tried to avoid that, owing to an eccentric desire for originality, he should have had to do worse. Thus my Mephistopheles sings a song by Shakespeare; and why shouldn't he? Why should I exert myself to invent one of my own, when Shakespeare's was just right and said just what was needed?" (Eckermann, January 18, 1825.)

The final remark refers to the scene in which Valentine appears. Goethe greatly exaggerates his debt, as any comparison with Ophelia's song (*Hamlet*, Act IV, scene 5) will show. But his attitude deserves note. And since the word "Valentine" occurs several times in Shakespeare's scene, and Gretchen's brother Valentine appears only in this scene of *Faust*, one may surmise that his name was suggested to Goethe by *Hamlet*, even as his character was influenced by Laertes'.

The question remains: historical scholarship undermines naïve expectations about originality, and Goethe himself derided the quest for philosophical ideas; what, then, makes Goethe's *Faust* world literature?

5

Goethe's characters and economy. Shakespeare, too, took many of his themes from history and from previous writers, and his greatness is emphatically not a function of abstract ideas. No doubt, in disparaging ideas, Goethe meant to associate himself with Shakespeare, although he considered the bard "a being of a higher order to whom I look up" (Eckermann, March 30, 1824). Goethe is indeed infinitely closer to Shakespeare than to Dante, not only in his impatience with philosophy and in his bold irregularities but also in his deliberate concern to entertain and to be interesting and rewarding at *every* level, including that of the untutored reader who wants little more than a sustained diversion. Much of Part Two, of course, is rather heavy going and has never attained popularity even in Germany, where it is considered the domain of scholars and commentators. These portions have been omitted in the present volume, but the first scene and the last act of Part Two, which are offered here, can be enjoyed without any commentaries, like Part One.

The marvel of *Faust* is, first of all, that in a relatively small space it reflects the poet's whole career from his twenties to his eighties—the whole range of his impressions, moods, concerns, styles, genius. Most of his other works reflect a single stage of his development, one or at most two styles, and thus give no idea of his versatility and his sustained growth. *Faust* is the whole *opus* in microcosm.

Next, the immense power of Goethe's characters should be noted. Faust leaps out of the book. He was quickly hailed as the incarnation of the German character and influenced German historiography, philosophy, and self-interpretation. Millions of young men decided they were like Faust, and some found the German destiny in boundless, ruthless, Faustian striving. Schopenhauer, in *The World as Will and Representation* (1819), considered such striving as the essence not merely of man but of the cosmos. Spengler, precisely a hundred years later, saw Faust as the representative of Western man and called Western civilization "the Faustian culture."

After all that, Faust—as who would not?—seems rather trying: one finds oneself eager to note his faults, his lack of humor, his pretentiousness, his self-deceptions. But Goethe used Faust's incurable romanticism as an effective foil for Mephistopheles. The nineteenth century thrilled to Faust's elevated cadences and put up with Mephistopheles' uninhibited sarcasm. The modern reader finds himself embarrassed by Faust's flowery phrases, and relieved by the cynical retorts that remind us continually that Goethe never wholly identified himself with his romantic hero. If Faust's poetic flights sometimes seem glib, that is not Goethe's fault but Faust's—and not his only fault either. It is, moreover, one of the devices by which Goethe makes Mephisto an engaging personality in spite of everything.

Even as Shakespeare enlists our sympathy for Lear and Coriolanus—although they behave repulsively in many ways—by wisely choosing their antagonists, Goethe forces us to sympathize with Mephistopheles. Unlike Faust, Mephisto has a sense of humor and is even capable of laughing at himself; he is a keen psychologist who sees through convention and pretense; and, though radically dishonest when it suits his purposes, he confronts us with a rarely equaled candor just when Faust's enthusiasm outsoars all scrupulous concern with truth or honesty. It may well be that Mephistopheles is Goethe's greatest single creation, and that he has come into his own only in the twentieth century, after Heine and Kierkegaard, Dostoevsky and Nietzsche, Freud and Shaw, Gide and Joyce, Mann and Sartre—who would hardly be offended at being called Mephisto's progeny—had changed our sensibilities.

Of course, Goethe's Mephistopheles is not without ancestors, and the most important of these may be found in the Bible. It is a commonplace that Goethe's Prologue in Heaven is modeled on the first two chapters of the Book of Job, but it has not been widely noted how much his Mephisto owes to the few lines spoken by Satan. After God's praise of Job, "that there is none like him on the earth, a blameless and upright man who fears God and turns away from evil, Satan answered the Lord: Does Job fear God for nothing?" And after God has taken away all that Job had and reproved Satan, saying that "still he holds fast his integrity," Satan retorts: "Skin for skin! All that a man has he will give for his life; but put forth your hand now and touch his bone and his flesh, and he will curse you to your face." This is Mephistopheles *in ovo:* a cynicism of nihilistic proportions. But what poet before Goethe realized this possibility? And it was Goethe, too, who fused this nihilism with his own inimitable sense of humor, now broad and earthy, now acidly penetrating.

Some critics still lament the fact that some of Heine's tenderest poems are punctured in the last line by a ruthless cynicism. They do not deny that this is specifically modern, but it is an aspect of modernity that they oppose. It was partly for this reason that the early twentieth-century poet Stefan George, and his very influential "Circle," considered Heine an arch-villain. (They had other reasons, too; for example, Heine's immensely witty but nasty polemic against the poet Platen, though written in 1829, was in many ways applicable to Stefan George—not only as a man but also as a poet.) George's followers, ranging all the way from the perceptive Friedrich Gundolf to some brutal Nazi hacks, lacked the deeply humane quality of Heine's irony and underestimated both his poetry and his superb prose. They considered him the ancestor of modern journalism. But it seems far more just to see him as a link between Goethe and Nietzsche (as Nietzsche himself saw Heine)—a link between *Faust* and the twentieth century.

Goethe realized the limitations of romanticism and its questionable character even before romanticism had become the style of an age. The very figure of Faust which inspired romantic poets, philosophers, and composers, and was accepted by the German people as their own ideal prototype—this poetic but unscrupulous titan who, for all his noble sentiments, becomes involved in brutal deeds—is the constant butt of Mephisto's mockery. The function of Mephistopheles resembles that of Heine's sudden sarcasms: romantic reverie is felt to be too glib, too near the cliché, too far from honesty—and hence must be exposed. It will no longer do to import comic scenes into a tragedy, as Shakespeare did: what is wanted is a device that will permit the poet a continual contrast to point up the questionable character of our feelings and conventions—what feelings hide behind conventions, and how conventional most of our feelings are —in one word: Mephistopheles. Thus Goethe's *Faust* is closer to *Ulysses* than to the *Odyssey*. It is one of the first and greatest works of modern literature. And Mephistopheles is one of the most inspired characters in the whole of world literature.

A German commentator complains that "Methistopheles is not clearly characterized; he vacillates between magnificent devilish depravity, the nature of a harmless jester, the clever conceit of one rich in experience of life, and the sublime wisdom of rich experience."* And 160 pages later, he carries his estimate to the absurd by say-

---

* *Goethe's Faust,* herausgegeben von Georg Witkowski, Zweiter Band: Kommentar und Erläuterungen, 4th ed. (1912), p. 6. The commentary is scholarly and helpful.

ing: "In and for itself, Mephistopheles, as a supernatural being, can embody only the idea of evil, of negation. Already his humor is in itself an unjustified addition; still more so, everything else that characterizes him as an individual character." In due time, of course, the commentator tries to make his peace with Goethe, but, like most commentators, he finds humor hard to pardon.

The other characters in *Faust* are of much smaller scope—and meant to be—even Gretchen. She needs no praise; she reminds us of Hegel's remark, "Phidias has no manner." The characterization is not subtle, it is perfect.

Goethe's virtuosity is at its height in the creation of some of the minor figures. Lieschen has only a single, very short scene; so does Valentine. Drafts for both scenes were included in the *Urfaust;* so was the characterization of Wagner, earlier in the play, and the delightful dialogue between Mephisto and the student. Here was a talent—a genius—Goethe possessed from the start. And in the figure of Wagner, he took care of half of his commentators before they were born. Even Shakespeare rarely, if ever, created such compelling portraits with so few strokes. What a contrast to the great lengths of Part Two in which a single notion is again and again spun out for pages—for example, Mephistopheles' invention of paper money and, also in the first act, the manner in which the women find fault with Helen's apparition, while praising Paris to the skies, and the men do just the opposite. Goethe, like Shakespeare and most great artists, was not always at his best. But in almost all of Part One and in the last act of the Second Part as well, his economy is as impressive as his wonderful array of characters.

Another feature of the play that approximates perfection is the craftsmanship of the construction. We seem to be confronted with an "epic theatre" over a hundred years before Bert Brecht. Even Part One appears loose and episodic: some of the dramatist's shorter poems could be suitably inserted, and one has the feeling that there is no limit to what could have been brought in if the poet had felt like it. There are choruses of many different kinds, some serious, some whimsical; and the variety of styles is extreme. But consider how the action is carried forward in the brilliant sequence of scenes: Martha's Garden, At the Well, City Wall, Night, and Cathedral. There are no long speeches or creaking conversations to tell us what happened: the presentation could not be simpler; what does not need to be said is left unsaid. And because Lieschen and Valentine are so superbly realized, one is scarcely aware of how they are used to carry on the action.

6

The Walpurgis Night and The Walpurgis Night's Dream. These two scenes may seem to be striking exceptions: far from carrying forward the action, they appear to interrupt it. Moreover, the saucy quatrains of the "Dream" seem completely irrelevant to the immediately preceding and succeeding scenes, and the Walpurgis Night contains words still omitted from practically all editions. Oddly, the text becomes much *less* obscene when Goethe's lines are restored from his manuscript. One gathers that the publisher balked at printing, "the witch farts," and that Goethe, very characteristically, complied —by allowing him to print "the witch f——s." The point here is exactly the same in the original German. The exchange between Mephisto and the old witch, with whom he dances, was bowdlerized in the same way: as long as "hole" could not be printed, Goethe also substituted a dash for "tremendous" and, in the next line, for "big"—and similarly in the witch's reply. Ever since, *Faust* has been printed that way, and readers have supposed that the intended text was infinitely coarser than it is in fact. But these are trifles.

Those who know Joyce's *Ulysses* will realize how much of an avant-gardist Goethe was when he published the Walpurgis Night in 1808; and those who recall that Shaw's "Don Juan in Hell" is really a dream sequence or intermezzo in his *Man and Superman* may be surprised to note that Shaw, too, followed Goethe. In this perspective, one should ask not only whether such dramatic innovations do not heighten the appeal of *Faust* but also whether both scenes are not functional.

The Walpurgis Night unquestionably belongs in its place, and it is psychologically profound. Far from interrupting the action and merely providing the poet with an opportunity to blow off steam, this scene, too, is a splendid example of Goethe's craftsmanship. Faust has fled after killing Valentine; Gretchen is alone. The play is not called "Margaret" but *Faust;* so Gretchen's agony is sketched in briefly with a few superb strokes: At the Well, City Wall, and Night have all but brought it to a climax—after Faust leaves her, the short Cathedral scene suffices. It is too early for the Dungeon scene: time must be allowed for the birth of Gretchen's child and her imprisonment, though there is no need to record her sufferings epically; the Dungeon scene can get that across, all at once, with overpowering effect. But where is Faust while Gretchen's misery passes endurance? At the Walpurgis Night, seeking forgetfulness, not quite succeeding. As the Lord told Mephistopheles, Faust, "in his darkling aspiration, remembers the right road"; he remembers it, but he does not choose it. Even insofar as Faust is a representative character and not only an individual in a play, the contrast between Gretchen's agony and Faust's Walpurgis Night bears the stamp of genius.

The Walpurgis Night's Dream is more problematic. It would not belong here if Goethe had meant to write a play about Gretchen. Clearly, he didn't; and the "Dream" helps to remind us of that. Faust is not merely Gretchen's lover but an intellectual who informs the audience in his opening words that he has studied philosophy and law, medicine and theology. So it is entirely fitting that his Walpurgis Night is not a mere orgy of sensuality but a fantastic blend of sex and satire, brilliant, rich in ideas, yet profoundly frivolous.

These two scenes contain some allusions which may stump the modern reader. None of them is important, and the reader who ignores them does not miss much.

Elend, in the initial stage direction, is the name of a real village, no less than Schierke; but *Elend* also means "misery."

Proktophantasmist means "Rump-ghostler," and the character so designated is a caricature of Friedrich Nicolai (1733–1811). Quite lacking the genius of Lessing and Moses Mendelssohn, with whom he founded a journal, he considered himself not only a spokesman for the enlightenment but also the sworn enemy of most of the more recent movements in German thought and literature. No sooner had Goethe published *The Sufferings of the Young Werther* (1774) than Nicolai countered with a parody, *Joys of the Young Werther* (1775). He denied the existence of ghosts but declared publicly, in connection with reports about a haunted house in Tegel, near Berlin, that he, too, had once been plagued by ghosts, but that he had got rid of them by applying leeches to his rump. He also published some travel books. Goethe's opinion of Nicolai as a critic requires no explanation. Whether it was fair, is another question.

The *Prater* is a famous park in Vienna.

In the Intermezzo the reference to *Mieding,* in the second line, pays tribute to J. M. Mieding of the Weimar theatre, on whose death, in 1782, Goethe had written a long poem.

The *Xenien,* who "revere Satan, our sire and singer," were polemical verses written by Goethe and Schiller, and the reference here is, of course, to Goethe himself. The *Xenien,* like the Intermezzo, can be enjoyed without erudition: instead of inquiring who it was that the poet had in mind, it is much more fruitful to ask whom in our own time the verse might fit. Two examples may show what is meant. The first was written by Schiller:

Do you desire to please the pious as well as the worldlings?
Give us a picture of lust—and the devil beside it.

The second was one of Goethe's *Xenien:*

When you blasphemed the gods of the Greeks, Apollo hurled you
From Mount Parnassus; but you are assured of heaven.

After the *Xenien* have had their say, *Hennings* appears. August Adolf von Hennings had published a journal, entitled *Genius of the Age,* and had attacked Schiller in it. In 1800, he changed the title to *Genius of the 19th Century,* but two years later it folded. Goethe's "*Ci-devant* Genius of the Age" is explained by a commentator: "because it had folded in 1802"; but it may also refer to the change of the title: "*Formerly,* Genius of the Age." *Musaget* was the title Hennings had given to a collection of his own poetry in two volumes (1798–99). Goethe evidently thought that Hennings had not been kissed by the muses and might as well have invoked witches.

That Goethe associated the *Crane* with Johann Kaspar Lavater (1741–1801) and the *Idealist* probably with Johann Gottlieb Fichte (1762–1814), matters even less. If what he derided made sense only when applied to some of his contemporaries, then the Intermezzo might indeed be out of place here. But *Orthodox* is certainly not merely Count Friedrich Leopold von Stolberg, who had attacked Schiller's poem on "The Gods of Greece." All these characters are somehow timeless.

7

Part Two. Goethe worked on Part Two until a few months before his death, and in accordance with his wishes the work appeared as the first volume of his "posthumous works" and volume 41 of *Goethe's Werke: Vollständige Ausgabe letzter Hand.* The first 40 volumes had appeared under Goethe's own editorship, beginning in 1827. Volume 41 came out in 1833, and under "Contents" listed one item only: "*Faust.* The Second Part of the Tragedy, in Five Acts. (Completed in the summer of 1831.)"

Even Part One had never been performed in public until 1829 (Goethe's eightieth year), and then it had been very severely cut. The first attempt to stage nearly the whole of Part One came in 1876, under the direction of Otto Devrient. He was also the first to try, in the same year, to stage most of Part Two. In the first six years of the 20th century, Part One was performed in Germany, respectively, 103, 110, 102, 88, 136, and 173 times; Part Two, 30, 36, 15, 11, 10, and 19 (according to Georg Witkowski's commentary). But these figures give no adequate idea of the relative popularity of the two parts: the first is exceedingly well known in Germany, while the second is not.

The relative unpopularity of Part Two is due to many factors. First, it represents a truly revolutionary feat, and a remark made by one of Edgar Allen Poe's characters (in "The Assignation") is relevant: "Properties of place, and especially of time, are the bugbears which terrify mankind from the contemplation of the magnificent." Goethe's disregard for all such proprieties accounts for some of the magnificence of Part Two; but much of it is also very difficult reading—not for those who feel thoroughly at home in classical antiquity and in Joyce's *Ulysses,* and who are able, for the most part, to read it in the original German, but for the vast majority of educated readers. That Goethe was a hundred years ahead of his time, and his Faust, alienated from his own world and from classical antiquity, too, can be understood only in terms of both and is thus related to Joyce's Stephen —that commends the Second Part to modern readers. But though it is a work of genius, most of it, except the portions offered here, is inferior to Part One in one respect: Goethe never gave it the ruthless pruning he had given to Part One.

You may say that in that way it was after all the product of failing powers; or you may say that in that respect, too, Goethe was ahead of his time: alienated from his public, writing a drama not only without any wish to see it staged but too much out of tune with his age to care for the least response. He deliberately spurned publication during his life and refused to divulge or discuss the end. Though at times he forced himself to work and commandeered the muses, so he might complete his project, he also indulged himself and did not strive for that superlative economy which some of his best poetry shares with large parts of the Old Testament.

For the translator, who must dwell carefully on every line, Part Two contains enormous lengths, and what lies between the first scene and the last act is not altogether tempting. To let Goethe speak English is one thing; to transpose into English his attempt to imitate Greek poetry in German is another. Those who wish to study Part Two but have no German should find the Victorian archaisms of existing English versions one of the lesser obstacles. It is my hope that those who would like to *enjoy* Goethe's *Faust*—as opposed to those who want to be able to say that they have read it, all of it—may find the present version readable from beginning to end, and as faithful as any.

8

Synopsis of omitted portions. Part One and the first scene of Part Two are offered without omissions. So is the final act. Some readers may appreciate a summary of the intervening scenes. Obviously, any such synopsis is bound to be almost farcical: let those who doubt that attempt a summary of the last four scenes of Part One—or of *King Lear* or *Hamlet*. The following summary begins with the second scene of Act One of Part Two.

1. *The court of the Emperor* (lines 4728–5064): The Emperor asks about his fool and is told that he collapsed, "dead or drunk, one doesn't know." Immediately, Mephistopheles appears to take the fool's place. The discussion turns to the serious shortage of money at the court. Mephistopheles points out that there is a great deal of gold under the ground, both coined and uncoined, and adds that a gifted man's "power of nature and spirit" should be able to raise it to the light of day. The Chancellor interposes:

> *Nature and spirit—Christians wish they weren't.*
> *That is why atheists are burned*
> *Because the greatest danger lies in that.*
> *Nature is sin, spirit is devil,*
> *Doubt is begotten where they revel—*
> *Malformed, hermaphroditic brat . . . .*

And Mephistopheles replies:

> *That's how the well-trained mind is known to me.*
> *What you don't grasp, you lack entirely;*
> *What you don't touch, seems miles away to you;*
> *What you don't reckon, you think can't be true;*
> *What you don't measure, that is no amount;*
> *What you don't coin, that, you think, does not count.*

The Emperor, not interested in the dispute, is eager to get money, and Mephisto tells him that whatever lies under the Emperor's land is his. Mephistopheles is told to produce money; but meanwhile, everybody is looking forward to a carnival and masked ball. Everybody leaves, except Mephisto, who speaks the often quoted words:

The way desert and fortune blend,
The fools will never comprehend.

2. *Large room, decked out for a masked ball* (lines 5065–5986): This scene is as long as Part One from Faust's opening monologue to Mephistopheles' first speech, or from "The Neighbor's House" to the "Walpurgis Night"; but it is not distinguished either by many striking lines or by any magnificent characterizations, and it contributes little to the action. Faust and Mephistopheles perform some magic and produce much gold.

3. *Pleasure garden* (lines 5987–6172): The invention of paper money is completed, with notes announcing that they are worth a thousand crowns, backed up by the security of the buried gold.

4. *Gloomy gallery* (lines 6173–6306): Faust informs Mephisto that the Emperor wants to see Helen and Paris, without delay. Mephisto explains that the ancient pagans are not his business because they dwell in a hell of their own; "but there is a way." Faust presses him, and he declares: "It is the *Mothers.*" Faust retorts, alarmed: "Mothers!" And again: "The Mothers! Mothers!—It sounds so strange!" Mephisto gives Faust a key, which grows in Faust's hand, and tells him that the key will guide him to the Mothers, where he will find a tripod. He must touch the tripod with the key, the tripod will then follow him on the way back; and once he has that, he will be able to conjure up Helen and Paris.

5. *Brightly illuminated halls* (lines 6307–6376): A blonde, a brunet, a lady, and a page boy crowd around Mephistopheles to receive his advice, in turn. In the first three cases, he relies on magic; but to the boy he says:

As long as young girls find you immature,
Look for an older paramour.

6. *Hall of knights* (lines 6377–6565): The court has assembled to see Helen and Paris, and Faust appears to conjure them up in the name of the Mothers. Paris appears first, and the women exclaim over his charm, while the men find him unmannerly. When Helen appears, Mephisto is the first to comment:

So that is she! She does not touch my feeling;
She's pretty, but I don't find her appealing.

The men are enraptured; the women find her head too small, her feet too plump—and don't consider her good enough for Paris. Paris, however, embraces her and lifts her off the ground to carry her away. Faust, consumed with jealousy, resolves to stop Paris, rushes toward him, and touches him with the key. There is an explosion, Faust falls to the ground, the spirits of Paris and Helen evaporate, and Mephistopheles picks up Faust, as the act ends in darkness and tumult.

ACT TWO

1. *High-vaulted, narrow Gothic room, once Faust's den, unchanged* (lines 6566–6818): Mephisto emerges from behind a curtain and, as he looks back, one sees Faust lying on a bed, still unconscious. Mephisto dresses up as Faust again (as he did in Part One, for his conversation with the student), and rings a bell. A Famulus enters; he has taken Wagner's place, while Wagner has taken Faust's; but Wagner has left Faust's study untouched because he is still hoping for Faust's return. Mephisto wants to see Wagner, but the Famulus hesitates to disturb him. Almost as soon as the Famulus leaves, a Baccalaureus enters—none other than the student whom Mephisto advised on his first day at the university. The young Baccalaureus is very full of himself and extremely aggressive, leading Mephisto to say:

You do not seem to know how rude you are.

In German, this line is often quoted, as is the retort:

When you're polite in German, you are lying.

At that point, Mephisto, whose chair has casters, rolls forward to the front of the stage and addresses the audience:

Up here, I fear, I'm quite unpopular;
Will you grant me asylum, if he becomes too trying?

The Baccalaureus continues to denounce the old and suggests that a man past thirty is as good as dead, and "it would be best to kill you in good time." His final speech is a parody of philosophical Idealism ("The world was not till I created it"), and commentators have argued whether Goethe was thinking of Fichte or of Schopenhauer's *The World as Will and Representation.* When the latter appeared in 1819, Schopenhauer was just over thirty, and in any case the half-baked philosophy of the Baccalaureus bears little similarity to the considerable subtlety of both philosophers. After the Baccalaureus leaves, Mephisto says:

Depart, "original" enthusiast!
How would this insight peeve you: whatsoever
A human being thinks, if dumb or clever,
Was thought before him in the past.
In a few years the young man will have changed;
There is no danger, he may turn out fine:
Although the must behaves as if deranged,
Eventually we get a wine.

(To the younger spectators in the orchestra, who do not applaud:)

My words appear to leave you cold;
You children need no reprimand:
You see, the devil is quite old—
Grow old and you will understand.

2. *Laboratory, in the medieval style, with elaborate*

and clumsy machinery for fantastic purposes (lines 6819–7004): Wagner is at work and informs Mephistopheles:

> A glorious product you shall soon be seeing.
>
> MEPHISTO:
>
> What will it be?
>
> WAGNER:
>
> We make a human being.
>
> MEPHISTO:
>
> A human? And what pair in passion
> Have you locked in the chimney pipe?
>
> WAGNER:
>
> Forbid! While procreation used to be the fashion,
> We think of that, pardon, as tripe.
> The tender point from which life used to slide,
> The gentle force that issued from inside
> And took and gave, first to become existent,
> Then to absorb the near, and then the distant,
> That is divested of its ancient rank:
> If animals still like that kind of prank,
> The human being with his gifts must win
> Henceforth a purer, nobler origin.

Soon Homunculus, the little artificial man, comes to life in his test tube, eager to be active. A side door is opened, Faust is seen on his bed, and Homunculus is asked to show what he can do. He describes Faust's dream of Leda, the mother of Helen, and the swan—

> *But suddenly a vapor cloud*
> *Envelops in a tightly woven shroud*
> *The most enchanting scene of all.*

Mephistopheles sees nothing, and Homunculus derides him because he comes from the north and lives

> *In a sad mess of knights and popery;*
> *How could your eye, my friend, be free?*
> *You are at home only in gloom.* (Looks around:)

Dingy brown stone, musty and horrid,
With pointed arches, cramped and florid!
If he awakes, surrounded by such rot,
He's sure to die right on the spot.

Faust has to be taken to surroundings similar to those which he saw in his dream, and Homunculus suddenly recalls that even now the classical Walpurgis Night is going on, "the best thing that could happen." Mephisto hesitates because he has a low opinion of the Greeks, but Homunculus lures him with a reference to Thessalian witches. They decide to leave Wagner behind, though he is afraid that he will never see Homunculus again. The scene ends as Mephisto says, *ad spectatores:*

In the end, we are dependent
Upon creatures we have made.

3. *Classical Walpurgis Night* (lines 7005–8487): Like the masked ball in Act One, and the Walpurgis Night in Part One, this scene cannot be summarized. First we see "Pharsalian Fields," and Faust's first words are: "Where is she?" Soon he leaves and the scene shifts to the Upper Peneios, where Mephisto, soon joined again by Faust, encounters sphinxes and sirens. Then we are taken to the Lower Peneios where Faust engages in a long dialogue with Chiron. Back at the Upper Peneios, we eventually encounter Thales and Anaxagoras, two pre-Socratic philosophers, arguing whether water or fire has played the decisive role in shaping the earth. Other classical characters appear; still more, after the scene shifts to the "Rocky Coves of the Aegean." The act ends as Homunculus is shattered on the shell of Galatea.

ACT THREE

1. *Before the palace of Menelaus at Sparta* (lines 8488–9126): Helen appears, and speaks:

> *Admired much but just as often censored, Helen,*
> *I come up from the beach where we first landed, still*
> *Intoxicated by the rapid rocking of*
> *The waves that carried us on their recalcitrant*
> *And lofty backs, by Euros' and Poseidon's grace,*
> *From Phrygia's plains back to our native coves . . . .*

Phrygia is Troy, Euros the southeast wind; and soon classical allusions multiply, and Helen engages in a dialogue with a chorus. Phorkyas appears, and a heated argument develops. Eventually the scene shifts to the

2. *Inner Courtyard* (lines 9127–9573): Here Faust appears at long last and addresses Helen:

> *Instead of the most festive greeting owed you,*
> *Instead of a respectful welcome, I*
> *Present in chains to you a servant who*
> *Betrayed his duty, cheating me of mine. . . .*

The servant is Lynceus, the Tower Warden, who appears again in the Fifth Act. In Act Three, too, he speaks in rhymes, while the other characters still Hellenize, and he explains movingly how Helen's beauty so stunned him that he forgot to signal her arrival. Helen forgives him, Faust offers her all he has, and soon she expresses her admiration for Lynceus' mode of speech—the way one word follows the other to caress it. And she begins to complete Faust's sentences with rhymes. Soon both abandon the Greek mode and speak in rhymes, but Phorkyas enters to warn them that Menelaus is approaching, with his army. Faust instructs his armies to repulse the attack and then changes the scene by magic into

3. *Arcadia* (lines 9574–10,038): After the chorus and Phorkyas have held the stage for a while, Helen, Faust, and their son Euphorion appear. Euphorion is generally understood as the spirit of romantic poetry, and Goethe associated him with Byron. Soon Euphorion hears thunder across the sea, perceives armies locked in battle abroad, senses their suffering, and feels the call to die.

Should I view it from a distance?
No, I share their grief and pain.

He feels as if he had suddenly grown wings and throws himself into the air; his garments bear him aloft for a moment, then "a beautiful youth falls at his parents' feet; the corpse seems to resemble a familiar form, but immediately the body vanishes, the aureole rises skyward like a comet, and clothes, cloak, and lyre remain on the ground." Euphorion's voice is heard once more "from the depth":

In the gloomy realm, mother,
Do not leave me alone!

The chorus sings a dirge, and then Helen turns to Faust:

An ancient word, alas, applies also to me:
That beauty and good fortune are not long united.
Torn into pieces is life's bond as well as love's;
Lamenting both in agony, I say farewell,
And one more time I throw myself into your arms.
Persephonia, accept thou the boy and me!

"She embraces Faust, her body vanishes, dress and veil alone remain in his arms." Phorkyas advises Faust that the dress has magic powers and, if he will only cling to it, may lift him above everything common. "Helen's clothes dissolve into clouds, surround Faust, lift him up and drift away with him." The act ends with choral odes. "The curtain falls. Phorkyas, in the proscenium, raises herself to gigantic height, steps down, takes off mask and veil, and shows herself as Mephistopheles in order to offer some commentary on the play in an epilogue, if that should prove necessary."

ACT FOUR

1. *High mountains* (lines 10,039–10,344): A cloud approaches, parts, and Faust emerges. After a fine soliloquy,

"a seven-league boot appears, another follows soon. Mephistopheles gets off. The boots stride on rapidly." Faust is impressed by the grandeur of nature, Mephisto is not. Mephisto spices his remarks with quotations from and allusions to Ephesians 6:12 and Matthew 4, the references being given in the text. Faust explains his desire to win land from the sea: he wants to defy the ocean. At that moment martial music is heard, and Mephisto explains that it will be easy to gratify Faust's wish: the Emperor is in serious trouble; they will help him win his battle, and then the Emperor will reward Faust by giving him the stretch of coast line that he wants. Mephisto summons "The Three Mighty Ones (II Samuel 23:8)," who appear again in Act Five, and informs the spectators:

Now every child likes knightly stories,
Chivalrous dress, medieval flavor;
These boys, of course, are allegories,
But that should win them even greater favor.

The three men, Faust, and Mephistopheles descend, as the scene moves to

2. *The Foothills* (lines 10,345–10,782): Here the Emperor and his generalissimo are soon joined by Faust and the Three Mighty Ones. After the three are dispatched, Mephisto enters. In the end, Faust and Mephisto win the battle by magic.

3. *The rival emperor's tent* (lines 10,783–11,042): The end of this scene may be reproduced without omission because it is the part of the play that Goethe finished last. Having been written after the end of Act Five, it leaves no doubt about Goethe's unchanged attitude toward the church. Unlike some of the romantics—and Richard Wagner fifty years later—Goethe never abandoned his hostile attitude. The point would not need laboring if the conclusion of the play had not been mis-

understood at times. The Archbishop-Arch-Chancellor speaks:

> The chancellor has left, the bishop remains here,
> Sent by the warning spirit to gain the emperor's ear.
> The Father's heart is worried because you are so weak.
>
> EMPEROR:
>
> What anxious thoughts move you in this gay hour? Speak!
>
> ARCHBISHOP:
>
> What bitter pain I feel, as I find in this hour
> Your holy head allied with Satan's evil power!
> Although your crown seems safe, it certainly is shocking.
> Both God, our Lord, and our dear father Pope you're mocking.
> And when the latter hears it, he will be sorrowful
> And smash your sinful realm with his most holy bull.
> He has not yet forgotten how at the jubilee,
> When you were crowned, you set the sinful wizard free.
> Harming Christianity, it was from your high place
> That his accursed head was first redeemed by grace.
> Therefore, beat now your breast; of your sinful delight
> Give to the sanctuary a tiny little mite.
> That wide strip of the mountains, where your tent was erected,
> Where evil spirits joined by whom you were protected,
> Where to the Prince of Lies you listened willingly,

Give, piously instructed, to our sanctuary;
The hills and the thick forest, as far as they extend,
The heights so rich in meadows and pastures without end,
Where lakes abound in fish and countless brooklets sally
In serpentine contortions, foaming, into the valley,
And the wide valley, too, and in it every place:
Thus your repentance wills it, and thus you shall find grace.

EMPEROR:

I am so frightened by my sin, I must submit:
You may decide the borders, as ever you see fit.

ARCHBISHOP:

The desecrated region where all these sins were done
Must be turned over now to serve the Holy One.
In my mind's eye, the walls leap up like flames of fire,
The sun's rays, when he rises, already hit the choir;
The church now forms a cross and grows into the sky,
The faithful are delighted, the nave grows long and high;
And through the mighty portal, they stream in pious legions,
As for the first time now the bell peals through these regions;
It sounds from the high tower, they seek God's altitude,
Repentant comes the sinner to find his life renewed.
The day of consecration—oh, that it might come soon!—

Shall from your presence, sire, receive the highest boon.

EMPEROR:

May such a glorious work proclaim my pious mind
And praise God, our Lord, while I forgiveness find.
Enough! My mind is lifted already and feels free.

ARCHBISHOP:

As chancellor I now ask a mere formality.

EMPEROR:

A formal document to give the church this treasure,
Present when you are ready, and I shall sign with pleasure.

ARCHBISHOP (*has taken leave, but turns back again on his way out*):

Then you give for the church, while it originates,
All income of the land: all tithes, interests, and rates,
In all eternity. For worthy preservation
Requires much; so, too, a good administration.
For the construction, then, on such forsaken soil
You give us some odd gold out of your bounteous spoil.
Moreover, one will need—I cannot help but say—
Wood, lime, and slate, and things that come from far away.
The people do the driving, as our priests request;
The church will bless the man who drives at her behest. (*Exit.*)

EMPEROR:

The sin that I incurred is grievous, I confess;
The fatal magic folk cause me severe distress.

ARCHBISHOP (*returning once more, with the deepest bow*):

Forgive, my Lord! You gave the ill-reputed man

The imperial beach; the church will answer with the ban,
Unless you give the church, with a repentant breast,
There, too, the tithes and taxes, and rates and interest.

EMPEROR (*disgruntled*):
The land is not yet there, it is the ocean's ground.

ARCHBISHOP:
Who has the right and patience, his time will come around.
For us your solemn word shall keep its ancient power. (*Exit.*)

EMPEROR (*alone*):
Thus I might sign away my empire in an hour.

END OF ACT FOUR

9

Poetry in Faust *and inconsistencies.* As much of the preceding implies, by no means all of the original is great poetry. Not only are there passages of rapid unpoetic dialogue, but some of the long speeches in Part Two are undistinguished, and large parts of the two long monologues at the beginning of Part One are neither lyrical nor dramatic but merely doggerel.

In the Prelude in the Theatre, one expects poetry only from the Poet—not from the Director and the Clown—and the Prelude sets the tone for the whole drama. Striking colloquialisms and slang expressions abound. Early in Faust's first monologue, where the translation rhymes "shysters" and "Christers," the original rhymes *Laffen* and *Pfaffen:* the first word is so unusual that no other literary occurrence of it comes to mind, while the second is still considered an actionable insult by some German courts. Goethe does not say "priest," or "preacher," but deliberately offends part of his audience while delighting others—and presumably introduces *Laffen* to have a rhyme on *Pfaffen.*

Occasionally, Goethe employs unrhymed lines and passages in the midst of rhymes, and sometimes these contrast very effectively with the jingles around them and convey intense emotion: for example, before the appearance of the Earth Spirit and, later, in the Cathedral scene. Goethe also often employs impure rhymes, in lyrical passages, too; and in some places in the translation pure rhymes in the first draft have been changed to come closer to the tone of the German.

Generally, the original is free of archaisms and inverted word order, but occasionally masterful inversions breathe defiance, and many a line is altogether unmetrical. But all of Part One and the portions of Part Two offered here are eminently readable and offer no great difficulties—though for anybody inclined to reflection there is surely a great deal to think about.

Edgar Allan Poe once remarked that a long poem is almost a contradiction in terms, and he explicitly denied that "there is, in extent, any advantage to counterbalance the loss of unity which attends it." And he went on to say, in "The Philosophy of Composition": "For this reason, at least one half of the Paradise Lost is essentially prose—a succession of poetical excitements interspersed, *inevitably,* with corresponding depressions." In modern literature, too, one finds time and again how a line or brief passage of great beauty is followed by what is essentially prose: "sapphires in the mud." In *Faust* the poetic peaks are also surrounded by what is, lyrically, flat land; but what helps to make the poem one of the greatest of world literature is that Goethe, though pre-eminently a lyric poet—never excelled and not often equaled in that genre—was so rich that he hardly ever needed putty, excepting perhaps a few places in Part Two. The unique range of his perception, sensitive alike to nature and psychology, his surpassing wisdom, and his uncontainable sense of humor permitted him to mount his gems in gold.

With his essentially lyric bent, Goethe composed the speeches and scenes of *Faust* as his spirit moved him, often completing first what in the drama comes later. Instead of stuffing the crevices, he let them lie and wait for future inspiration. Of course, *Faust* did not simply "grow" for sixty years: it represents a vast amount of work, and, again excepting certain portions of Part Two, the poet constantly subjected inspiration to criticism and sought improvements.

Because of this mode of composition, the drama contains some inconsistencies. Goethe did not remove them, for they mattered less to him than the effect of the individual passages. Faust's monologue in the scene "Wood and Cave," for example, implies that Mephisto was dispatched by the Earth Spirit. This is not consistent either with the Prologue in Heaven or with the appearance of the Earth Spirit in the first scene. The three scenes were written at different times, and evidently they satisfied Goethe poetically; so he had no wish to change them for the sake of consistency. That this sort of thing might give commentators trouble, only amused him. He found precedents for his disregard of consistency in Shakespeare.

10

Translations. No translation of a world-historic poem equals the original. Those who sing FitzGerald's praises do it, in effect, by insisting that the original of Omar Khayyam was no major work, and that FitzGerald's quatrains are really not translations at all. When we turn to poems with which *Faust* invites comparison, the case is clear. No translation of Dante's *Commedia* rivals the original Italian, and while August Wilhelm Schlegel's German Shakespeare and Johann Heinrich Voss's German Homer, in dactylic hexameters, represent astonishing achievements which may well surpass all kindred English efforts, they do not attain the quality of the originals. But they set a standard: while a translator cannot compete with the original poet—except occasionally in short poems—he can and should try to be faithful to the poet's meaning and form. Meter should be preserved as far as possible, and one has no right to add or subtract lines.

In English, lacking Voss and Schlegel, these standards have never been commonly accepted, and there is always talk—and not only talk—of re-creating poems altogether by adding something of one's own to make up for what is lost. Second-rate material may benefit from such generosity, but not major poems—not even when the translator himself is a good poet. Schiller's German version of *Macbeth* does not compare with Schlegel's efforts, precisely because Schiller, though a greater poet than Schlegel, was much freer and interpolated speeches and removed the Porter scene. His version, intended for a performance on the Weimar stage, antedated Schlegel's work which made the German conscience far more sensitive in matters of this sort. Some English translators of *Faust* have seen fit to add a great deal of their own. Anster's version, for example, has gone through over thirty editions, though he thought nothing of occasionally more than doubling the length of a speech.

If anybody can produce a collection of passages better than Goethe's, let him offer these creations as his own—with apologies to Goethe, if necessary. Most attempts at improvements, however, would never deserve a reading in their own right.

Shelley did not take such liberties when he translated the "Prologue in Heaven" from *Faust;* when he had something of his own to say, he did it over his own name. But his version is by no means as superior as we should have to expect if the usual talk about the translator as poet were true. Rilke did a great deal of translating, much of it superb, but never took the liberties which most translators claim as their unalienable rights. And some of Stefan George's translations of Dante and Shakespeare are marvels of fidelity.

As often as not, English and American translators render German verse that rhymes as all but prose, presumably because they feel that rhymes are too difficult, though they say that rhymes are not fashionable; but in English versions of Aeschylus and Sophocles rhymes are frequently imported though there are none in the original. The poets' epigrams are flattened out more often than not, but where the poet has no epigram one suddenly encounters startling phrases that are almost Biblical. At such points one wonders whether Paul, for example, quoted Aeschylus, or whether—to give a different illustration—Goethe quoted Scripture; but on checking the original one finds that it was only the translator who remembered something learned in Sunday school.

On the basis of such translations, however poetical or beautiful they may be, no serious discussion of a play is possible. And discussions that *are* based on versions of this nature are frequently irrelevant to the original.

While Schlegel and Voss have haunted most subsequent *German* translators, it is clearly the Authorized Version of the Bible that echoes—with a rather hollow sound—through the Victorian translations of *Faust* and *Zarathustra.* The King James Bible is not only an imposing work of English literature but also, on the whole, amazingly accurate. Even so, its style, mood, and atmosphere are often antithetical to the original. The austerity and laconic simplicity of the Hebrew gives way to a richly ornamental medium, and agonized outcries are refurbished "to be read in churches." As if Amos had wished "to be read in churches" or, for that matter, "as living literature."

There are those who feel that by giving up the original style, the translator gains greater freedom to reproduce the content faithfully—in more modern forms. This, however, is only a half-truth; and an illustration from the King James Bible may show how its magnificent rhetoric, "modern" in its time, contrasts with the original.

After selling Joseph into slavery, his brothers dipped his coat of many colors into a goat's blood and showed it to their father, saying: "This we have found; look whether it is your son's coat or not." The King James Version proceeds: "And he knew it, and said, It is my son's coat; an evil beast hath devoured him; Joseph is without doubt rent in pieces." The Hebrew reads more nearly like this—and was clearly not "appointed to be read in churches," but to express the old man's outcry: "He knew it and said: my son's coat! an evil beast devoured him! torn—torn is Joseph!"

The King James Bible minimizes the enormous difference between Isaiah's Hebrew and the highly colloquial Greek of much of the New Testament: everything comes to sound almost equally ornate and majestic; the distinction between prose and poetry is made to disappear; and the whole book creates the peculiar "holy tone" of the pulpits.

A complete change of style in a translation always changes much more, too. Imagine Genesis in doggerel, or read the Psalms in one or another verse translation, or give up the wealth of different rhyme schemes and meters in *Faust:* every time, the character of the original becomes transformed.

Goethe's disregard for conventions, his originality, and the irregularity of forms in *Faust* do not present the translator with indulgences. Goethe neither made things easy for himself nor depreciated form. On the contrary. When he published *Faust: A Fragment* in 1790, he held back the most powerful scene of the whole play, the Dungeon scene; and he refused to publish that until he had succeeded in transposing it into rhymes to modulate its effect.

In some respects, the translator's problem in the case of

Faust is the opposite of that suggested by our discussion of the Bible. Often the original seems ornate, and one is tempted to strive for greater simplicity. Yet it would be a mistake to eliminate all references to yearning, woe, bliss, rapture, and whatever else is felt deep in the breast, although such words may be used sparingly, and fewer of them will be found here than in most translations. They provide Mephisto with a foil; and the retort is, of course, doubly effective when it rhymes on Faust's words.

To substantiate the claims of this introduction regarding Goethe's modernity, the translation has to be faithful: if we transpose Goethe into the idiom of twentieth-century poetry, we simply beg the question. Also, Goethe uses different rhyme schemes and meters to vary the mood and to portray characters; and the single prose scene of Part One would lose some of its effect if some other scenes, too, were presented in prose. That the first scene of Part Two features a long speech in Dante's *terza rima*, provides a striking contrast with the end of Part One and sets the mood for the wholly different conception of the Second Part.

I have not always reproduced Goethe's many feminine (two-syllable) rhymes because English is much poorer in such rhymes than German: grammatical rhymes—ending on -ing, for example—tend to be feeble, and novel feminine rhymes are apt to sound comic in English, though not in German. Very rarely, I have shortened a line by a foot because pregnant phrasing seemed important. Faithfulness, however, was always the primary consideration. And this, too, precluded any attempt to assimilate Goethe to a contemporary poetic idiom: if we make *Faust* read like Rilke, or like Eliot, it will no longer sound like Goethe. The reader will assume in any case that Goethe's poetry in the poetic passages surpasses all the efforts of his translators: one has no right to expect anything else. But one has every right to demand that a translation should not say things that are not in the original, and that things said in the original are to be found in the translation.

In the end, some of Goethe's own remarks about translating may be quoted. To Eckermann he said, December 30, 1823: "If you render the incisive monosyllabic words of the English with polysyllabic or composite German words, all force and effect is lost immediately." On June 13, 1825, he remarked to Friedrich von Müller: "When translating foreign folk songs, incredibly much depends on maintaining the word order of the original." And in a conversation with Friedrich Förster, in May 1829, Goethe made fun of various translations of his *Faust*. He laughed at an English version of Gretchen's ballad about the king of Thule that read in part:

> *He called for his confessor,*
> *Left all to his successor . . .*

He considered the rhyme an insufficient excuse for the confessor: "the King of Thule reigned before the flood; there were no confessors at that time." And he ridiculed Madame de Staël's version of "*Misshör mich nicht, du holdes Angesicht!*" as "*Ne m'interprète pas mal, charmante créature!*"

11

Goethe versus Faust. Goethe's world view cannot be analyzed in a brief introduction, but a very few remarks may serve as a basis for reflection. Goethe should not be confounded with Faust, whose characteristic impatience he outgrew early. The poet generally liked to project himself into both of the male leads in his plays, and he cannot be identified with either of them. Unlike Faust, Goethe despised neither reason nor the present, and Mephisto's short monologue after the pact scene, before the Student appears, is worth recalling:

Have but contempt for reason and for science . . .
And, pact or no, I hold you tight.–
The spirit which he has received from fate
Sweeps ever onward with unbridled might,
Its hasty striving is so great
It leaps over the earth's delights. . . .
And were he not the devil's mate
And had not signed, he still must perish.

Yet Faust is saved. The semi-medieval heaven of the last scene does not fully explain why. Goethe's last letters show how far he was at that time from accepting, or even admiring, Catholicism; and he had no sooner finished the fifth act than he turned to the fourth, to conclude it with a diatribe against the church. As Goethe himself saw it, the elevation of Gretchen, and even Faust, into heaven was as far removed from what he once called "Dante's gruesome, often atrocious greatness,"* and from any orthodoxy, as could be. Let Dante and millions of lesser minds consign Paolo and Francesca to hell; let them exult over the torments of those who have committed theft, perjury, or murder; Goethe would not send any man to hell or even purgatory.

Was it because, like Luther, he denied the importance of good works for salvation? Unlike Luther, Goethe did not require faith either: his world picture simply contained no site of damnation. He himself called attention to the angels' chorus:

Who ever strives with all his power,
We are allowed to save.

But elsewhere, especially in *Wilhelm Meister*, Goethe distinguished sharply between the unbounded striving which Faust exemplifies—a ruthless romanticism—and another kind of striving which is quite compatible with rational self-discipline and delight in the present: Goethe's

* *"Dante's widerwärtige oft abscheuliche Grossheit."* In *Tag-und Jahres-Hefte als Ergänzung meiner sonstigen Bekenntnisse, Werke: Ausgabe letzter Hand*, vol. 32, p. 194.

own way of life. The poet knew that intense appreciation of the moment need not by any means entail the "bed of sloth" that Faust scorns. In many ways, Goethe was very different from Faust, but he let his creature be saved even so—not least from a spirit of world-embracing tolerance, the same spirit in which the Lord says of Mephisto: "I never hated those who were like you." In Goethe's world view, evil, too, is redeemed in the total design of the cosmos.

12

Faust *and philosophy*. Being a philosopher, I have leaned over backward in this introduction to suggest that *Faust* can be enjoyed and discussed without recourse to philosophy. I have emphasized Goethe's disparagement of ideas and suggested that the play is impressive and rewarding if it is read, first of all, for its magnificent character studies. Still, *Faust* represents one of the most ambitious efforts ever made in literature to impose order of a sort on the whole world of man's thought and experience, "from heaven through the world to hell." This is surely the main reason why the play has often been compared with the great epics of Homer and Dante. The significance of man's quest, efforts, and existence is part of the subject matter of the drama.

When Goethe disclaimed any central idea, he was surely ingenuous: his drama is not a device to get across a message. But the fact that it is not an allegory and that there is no theology or philosophy behind it, waiting for a commentator, is not necessarily a defect.

In his conviction that no philosophic system can do justice to the world, that man's experience is irreducible to any set of concepts, and that literature might well reflect the ambiguity of life, which always invites many differing interpretations, each of them inadequate if it is taken by itself and leaves out of account the sheer absurdity of life, Goethe invites comparison with Nietzsche, Kafka, and some existentialists. The point is not to classify him; merely to suggest that his repudiation of "ideas" and his lack of a simple message do not entail any sacrifice of scope. *Faust* can be enjoyed without going into any questions of this sort; but the perennial fascination of the play and its rank, too, are due in no small part to this dimension—to the questions which it raises in the reader's mind.

Kafka's *Castle* has sometimes been called Kafka's "Faust." It may be illuminating to turn this around and say that Goethe's *Faust* is Goethe's "Castle." To be sure, there are still interpreters who think that Kafka simply must have a theology, perhaps a variant of Kierkegaard's —as if it were so certain that the Danish writer had a theology. Those reading Kafka in this manner will not find it helpful to compare *Faust* with *The Castle*. But Kafka went out of his way to be ambiguous, and the variant beginnings of *The Castle* have in common the deliberate contrivance of an ambiguity: it is uncertain whether K. was called to the castle or not. And the Cathedral scene in Kafka's *Trial* shows at length how a simple, two-page parable can lend itself to ever-new, conflicting exegeses: surely, Kafka here gave a broad hint about the nature of both of his major novels. Even if this reading of Kafka is accepted, it does not follow, of course, that Goethe contrived ambiguity in the same way, though it is well to remember his remark about wrapping "a few mantle folds around the finished product that it may altogether remain an evident riddle" (see section 3 above). Assuredly, Goethe was very different from Kafka in a multitude of ways. But Kafka reminds us that ambiguity and the irreducibility of a literary work to one interpretation may be virtues rather than defects, compatible with literary excellence and in part responsible for the haunting quality that invites constant rereading. For that matter, Kafka's great model, the Book of Genesis, might teach us the same thing: inexhaustibility consists in large part in the possibility of ever-new interpretations. And Goethe, too, received decisive impressions from Old Testament narratives.

What makes the comparison with Kafka somewhat more appropriate than that with the Bible is Goethe's whimsical humor and his taste for the absurd—even the grotesque. Although *Faust* has no message, the drama leads us to wonder whether there is any moral world order at all, and to what extent moral judgments make sense. Goethe's opposition to the resentful bourgeois morality that would like to monopolize the word "morality" —and that comes close to having a monopoly on the term "immoral"—is quite as deep as Nietzsche's, though characteristically less vehement: Lieschen, in Part One, helps to make that clear; so does Goethe's remark, in a conversation: "I, pagan? Well, after all, I let Gretchen be executed and Ottilie [in the *Elective Affinities*] starve to death; don't people find that Christian enough? What do they want that would be more Christian?" Gretchen's execution is part of life as it is; her redemption and Faust's are projections of a way of looking at the world —an outlook which is, in Nietzsche's famous phrase, "beyond good and evil."

No absolute moral distinctions seem to remain. Goethe scholars may think of connecting this attitude with Goethe's "biologism"; others will be sure to disagree. But an Introduction is clearly not the place for trying to give final answers to questions that have perplexed great minds for well over a century—indeed for thousands of years. Suffice it here to call attention to these issues and to point out that the relevance of *Faust* to such concerns has much to do with its rank in world literature.

To suppose that *Faust* is of interest primarily to philosophers would be as wrong as the assumption that it is only a character play with a lot of wit and some fine poetry, distinguished by superlative craftsmanship and hosts of epigrams. If one begins to read for enjoyment, the play will lead one, willy-nilly, to think.

Note: Some of the questions barely touched in this Introduction are treated more fully in my *From Shakespeare to Existentialism* (Anchor Books), which contains chapters on "Shakespeare versus Goethe," "Goethe and the History of Ideas," "Goethe's Faith and Faust's Redemption," and "Goethe versus Romanticism." The problem of inconsistencies in literary masterpieces and Goethe's own remarks on this topic are discussed in Chapter 10 of my *Critique of Religion and Philosophy* (Anchor Books), and the relation of tragedy to religion and to ambiguity in section 77.

My friend and colleague Victor Lange, chairman of the German Department at Princeton University, has kindly read the Introduction in manuscript and given me the benefit of his comments. To Anne Freedgood of Anchor Books, I am more grateful than I can say.

W. K.

Princeton, N. J.
Easter Sunday, 1960

GOETHE'S FAUST: CONTENTS AND COMMENTS

to distract him with what Faust afterward calls "insipid diversions." In this scene, Goethe breaks through all current norms of decency or division of styles and merges magnificent nature poetry with satire and raw humor, while intellectualism and sensualism reach a concurrent climax.) 359

WALPURGIS NIGHT'S DREAM. Intermezzo. (A Series of quatrains, for the most part satirical.) 387

DISMAL DAY. (The sole prose scene in the drama—left that way by the poet, presumably because he felt that a really stark contrast with the preceding was entirely called for.) 399

NIGHT. Open Field. (A six-line interlude which echoes *Macbeth.*) 405

DUNGEON. (Faust would liberate Gretchen, who—Ophelia-like—has gone mad. Goethe said that he could never write a real tragedy—his outlook was essentially untragic—and Gretchen is saved in the end; but this scene is surely one of the greatest tragic scenes in world literature.) 407

THE SECOND PART OF THE TRAGEDY 423

FIRST ACT: Charming Landscape. (This is the first scene of Part Two. It accomplishes the transition between the two parts not only in terms of plot, but also in terms of style and general attitude. The Faust of Part One neither spoke in *terza rima*—the rhyme scheme of the *Divine Comedy*—nor could he have said what is here said, accepting renunciation and limitation. Later in Part Two he will forsake the German north in quest of classical antiquity. At the same time, Goethe says farewell to the forceful directness of Part One and announces that from now on he will offer something more artful: not life itself, but a "many-hued reflection." Although the remainder of Act I and all the intervening material has been

GOETHE'S FAUST

ZUEIGNUNG

Ihr naht euch wieder, schwankende Gestalten,
Die früh sich einst dem trüben Blick gezeigt.
Versuch ich wohl, euch diesmal festzuhalten?
Fühl ich mein Herz noch jenem Wahn geneigt?
5 Ihr drängt euch zu! Nun gut, so mögt ihr walten,
Wie ihr aus Dunst und Nebel um mich steigt;
Mein Busen fühlt sich jugendlich erschüttert
Vom Zauberhauch, der euren Zug umwittert.

Ihr bringt mit euch die Bilder froher Tage,
10 Und manche liebe Schatten steigen auf;
Gleich einer alten, halbverklungnen Sage
Kommt erste Lieb und Freundschaft mit herauf;
Der Schmerz wird neu, es wiederholt die Klage
Des Lebens labyrinthisch irren Lauf
15 Und nennt die Guten, die, um schöne Stunden
Vom Glück getäuscht, vor mir hinweggeschwunden.

Sie hören nicht die folgenden Gesänge,
Die Seelen, denen ich die ersten sang;
Zerstoben ist das freundliche Gedränge,

DEDICATION

You come back, wavering shapes, out of the past
In which you first appeared to clouded eyes.
Should I attempt this time to hold you fast?
Does this old dream still thrill a heart so wise?
You crowd? You press? Have, then, your way at
last.
As from the mist around me you arise;
My breast is stirred and feels with youthful pain
The magic breath that hovers round your train.

With you return pictures of joyous days,
Shadows that I once loved again draw near;
Like a primeval tale, half lost in haze,
First love and friendship also reappear;
Grief is renewed, laments retrace the maze
Of Life's strange labyrinthian career,
Recalling dear ones who, by fortune's treason
Robbed of fair hours, passed before my season.

They will not hear me as I sing these songs,
The parted souls to whom I sang the first;
Gone is that first response, in vain one longs

20 Verklungen, ach! der erste Widerklang.
Mein Leid ertönt der unbekannten Menge,
Ihr Beifall selbst macht meinem Herzen bang,
Und was sich sonst an meinem Lied erfreuet,
Wenn es noch lebt, irrt in der Welt zerstreuet.

25 Und mich ergreift ein längst entwöhntes Sehnen
Nach jenem stillen, ernsten Geisterreich,
Es schwebet nun in unbestimmten Tönen
Mein lispelnd Lied, der Äolsharfe gleich,
Ein Schauer faßt mich, Träne folgt den Tränen,
30 Das strenge Herz, es fühlt sich mild und weich;
Was ich besitze, seh ich wie im Weiten,
Und was verschwand, wird mir zu Wirklichkeiten.

For friendly crowds that have long been dispersed.
My grief resounds to strangers, unknown throngs
Applaud it, and my anxious heart would burst.
Whoever used to praise my poem's worth,
If they still live, stray scattered through the earth.

And I am seized by long forgotten yearning
For that kingdom of spirits, still and grave;
To flowing song I see my feelings turning,
As from aeolian harps, wave upon wave;
A shudder grips me, tear on tear falls burning,
Soft grows my heart, once so severe and brave;
What I possess, seems far away to me,
And what is gone becomes reality.

VORSPIEL AUF DEM THEATER

Direktor, Theaterdichter, Lustige Person.

DIREKTOR:

Ihr beiden, die ihr mir so oft,
In Not und Trübsal, beigestanden,
35 Sagt, was ihr wohl in deutschen Landen
Von unsrer Unternehmung hofft?
Ich wünschte sehr, der Menge zu behagen,
Besonders weil sie lebt und leben läßt.
Die Pfosten sind, die Bretter aufgeschlagen,
40 Und jedermann erwartet sich ein Fest.
Sie sitzen schon, mit hohen Augenbrauen,
Gelassen da und möchten gern erstaunen.
Ich weiß, wie man den Geist des Volks versöhnt;
Doch so verlegen bin ich nie gewesen:
45 Zwar sind sie an das Beste nicht gewöhnt,
Allein sie haben schrecklich viel gelesen.
Wie machen wir's, daß alles frisch und neu
Und mit Bedeutung auch gefällig sei?
Denn freilich mag ich gern die Menge sehen,
50 Wenn sich der Strom nach unsrer Bude drängt
Und mit gewaltig wiederholten Wehen
Sich durch die enge Gnadenpforte zwängt,
Bei hellem Tage, schon vor Vieren,

PRELUDE IN THE THEATRE

Director, Dramatic Poet, Clown.

DIRECTOR:

You two, that often stood by me
In former times of trouble, say:
What are the chances for our play,
If we perform in Germany?
To please crowds is what I desire most,
For they not only live, but let live, too.
The boards are up, and one sees post by post,
And everyone expects a feast from you.
I see them sit there with wide open eyes,
Relaxed and hoping for a great surprise.
I know quite well how people are impressed,
But I have never been in such a spot:
While they are not accustomed to the best,
They certainly have read a lot.
How go about it, so it will seem new,
Significant, and pleasing to them, too?
Of course, I like to see the crowded lanes
When streams of people rush to our place
And, with tremendous and recurrent pains,
Press, eager, through the narrow gate of grace;
When it is day, not even four,

Mit Stößen sich bis an die Kasse ficht
55 Und, wie in Hungersnot um Brot an Bäckertüren,
Um ein Billet sich fast die Hälse bricht.
Dies Wunder wirkt auf so verschiedne Leute
Der Dichter nur; mein Freund, o tu es heute!

DICHTER:

O sprich mir nicht von jener bunten Menge,
60 Bei deren Anblick uns der Geist entflieht!
Verhülle mir das wogende Gedränge,
Das wider Willen uns zum Strudel zieht!
Nein, führe mich zur stillen Himmelsenge,
Wo nur dem Dichter reine Freude blüht,
65 Wo Lieb und Freundschaft unsres Herzens Segen
Mit Götterhand erschaffen und erpflegen!

Ach, was in tiefer Brust uns da entsprungen,
Was sich die Lippe schüchtern vorgelallt,
Mißraten jetzt und jetzt vielleicht gelungen,
70 Verschlingt des wilden Augenblicks Gewalt.
Oft, wenn es erst durch Jahre durchgedrungen,
Erscheint es in vollendeter Gestalt.
Was glänzt, ist für den Augenblick geboren,
Das Echte bleibt der Nachwelt unverloren.

LUSTIGE PERSON:

75 Wenn ich nur nichts von Nachwelt hören sollte!
Gesetzt daß i c h von Nachwelt reden wollte,
Wer machte denn der Mitwelt Spaß?
Den will sie doch und soll ihn haben.
Die Gegenwart von einem braven Knaben
80 Ist, dächt ich, immer auch schon was.
Wer sich behaglich mitzuteilen weiß,
Den wird des Volkes Laune nicht erbittern;
Er wünscht sich einen großen Kreis,
Um ihn gewisser zu erschüttern.
85 Drum seid nur brav und zeigt euch musterhaft,
Laßt Phantasie mit allen ihren Chören,

They fight and push each other, coax and vex,
And, as in famine time, for bread at baker's door,
To get a ticket almost break their necks.
This wonder works upon such different men
The poet only—friend, do it again!

POET:

Don't speak to me of crowds at whose mere sight
The spirit flees us! That you could confine
The surging rabble that draws us with might
To compromise our every great design!
Lead me to heaven's silence, whose delight
The poet only feels; let love combine
With friendship to create and nurse
With godlike hands the gift of verse!

What deep in our breast was thus inspired,
What shy lips babbled in a quiet hour,
Clumsy perhaps, and rarely as desired,
Is swallowed by a savage moment's power.
And years may pass before it has acquired
Its perfect form and opens like a flower.
Glitter is coined to meet the moment's rage;
The genuine lives on from age to age.

CLOWN:

From age to age! What silly, fruitless chat!
Posterity! If *I* would talk of that,
Who would amuse the folks today?
That's what they want, give them their fare!
The presence of a decent lad out there
Amounts to something, I should say.
Who knows the art of pleasant self-expression
Need not resent the popular decree;
He thrives on widespread appreciation,
And moves the mass more certainly.
So be exemplary in every fashion,
Give reign to many-throated fantasy,

Vernunft, Verstand, Empfindung, Leidenschaft,
Doch merkt euch wohl, nicht ohne Narrheit hören!

DIREKTOR:

Besonders aber laßt genug geschehn!
90 Man kommt zu schaun, man will am liebsten sehn.
Wird vieles vor den Augen abgesponnen,
So daß die Menge staunend gaffen kann,
Da habt ihr in der Breite gleich gewonnen,
Ihr seid ein vielgeliebter Mann.
95 Die Masse könnt ihr nur durch Masse zwingen,
Ein jeder sucht sich endlich selbst was aus.
Wer vieles bringt, wird manchem etwas bringen;
Und jeder geht zufrieden aus dem Haus.
Gebt ihr ein Stück, so gebt es gleich in Stücken!
100 Solch ein Ragout, es muß euch glücken;
Leicht ist es vorgelegt, so leicht als ausgedacht.
Was hilft's, wenn ihr ein Ganzes dargebracht?
Das Publikum wird es euch doch zerpflücken.

DICHTER:

Ihr fühlet nicht, wie schlecht ein solches
Handwerk sei,
105 Wie wenig das dem echten Künstler zieme.
Der saubern Herren Pfuscherei
Ist, merk ich, schon bei euch Maxime.

DIREKTOR:

Ein solcher Vorwurf läßt mich ungekränkt;
Ein Mann, der recht zu wirken denkt,
110 Muß auf das beste Werkzeug halten.
Bedenkt, ihr habet weiches Holz zu spalten,
Und seht nur hin, für wen ihr schreibt!
Wenn diesen Langeweile treibt,
Kommt jener satt vom übertischten Mahle,
115 Und, was das allerschlimmste bleibt,
Gar mancher kommt vom Lesen der Journale.
Man eilt zerstreut zu uns, wie zu den
Maskenfesten,

To reason, thought, and sentiment, and passion—
But, mark it well, not without foolery!

DIRECTOR:

Above all, let us have a lot of action!
They want a show, that gives them satisfaction.
The more you can enact before their eyes,
The greater is your popular acclaim;
And if the crowd can gape in dumb surprise,
You gain a celebrated name.
The mass is overwhelmed only by masses,
Each likes some part of what has been presented.
He that gives much, gives something to all classes,
And everybody will go home contented.
You have a piece, give it in pieces then!
Write a ragout, you have a pen;
It's easy to invent, and easy to unroll.
What good is it, if you construct a whole?
The public takes it all apart again.

POET:

You do not feel how bad it is to please the rabble,
How artists spurn such craft and cheap applause.
The manner of the hacks that dabble
Has furnished you, I see, with laws.

DIRECTOR:

I am not hurt by your invective:
A man who wants to be effective
Must first make sure his tools are good.
You are like one who would split moldy wood:
Do not forget for whom you write!
They come when they are bored at night,
Or gorged on roasts and relish, spice and capers,
And—this is the most wretched plight—
Some come right after having read the papers.
They come to us distracted, as to a masquerade,
Propelled by nothing but curiosity;

Und Neugier nur beflügelt jeden Schritt;
Die Damen geben sich und ihren Putz zum besten
120 Und spielen ohne Gage mit.
Was träumet ihr auf eurer Dichterhöhe?
Was macht ein volles Haus euch froh?
Beseht die Gönner in der Nähe!
Halb sind sie kalt, halb sind sie roh.
125 Der, nach dem Schauspiel, hofft ein Kartenspiel,
Der eine wilde Nacht an einer Dirne Busen.
Was plagt ihr armen Toren viel
Zu solchem Zweck die holden Musen?
Ich sag euch, gebt nur mehr und immer, immer mehr,
130 So könnt ihr euch vom Ziele nie verirren.
Sucht nur die Menschen zu verwirren,
Sie zu befriedigen, ist schwer – –
Was fällt euch an? Entzückung oder Schmerzen?

DICHTER:

Geh hin und such dir einen andern Knecht!
135 Der Dichter sollte wohl das höchste Recht,
Das Menschenrecht, das ihm Natur vergönnt,
Um deinetwillen freventlich verscherzen!
Wodurch bewegt er alle Herzen?
Wodurch besiegt er jedes Element?
140 Ist es der Einklang nicht, der aus dem Busen dringt
Und in sein Herz die Welt zurücke schlingt?
Wenn die Natur des Fadens ewge Länge,
Gleichgültig drehend, auf die Spindel zwingt,
Wenn aller Wesen unharmon'sche Menge
145 Verdrießlich durcheinander klingt –
Wer teilt die fließend immer gleiche Reihe
Belebend ab, daß sie sich rhythmisch regt?
Wer ruft das Einzelne zur allgemeinen Weihe,
Wo es in herrlichen Akkorden schlägt?
150 Wer läßt den Sturm zu Leidenschaften wüten,
Das Abendrot im ernsten Sinne glühn?

Their dresses and their jewels, the ladies would
parade,
And act without a salary.
Why do you dream on your poetic height?
Look at your patrons without awe!
What gives a crowded house delight?
One half is cold, one half is raw.
After the play, one hopes to play at cards,
Another for an orgy in a harlot's bed.
With such an aim, you silly bards,
Why plague the muses? Go ahead,
Simply give more and more, and always something
more,
That never fails—and add some dark allusion:
Try only to create confusion;
To satisfy men is a chore.—
What seizes you? An ecstasy or pain?

POET:

Go hence and seek yourself another slave!
The noblest right the poet ought to waive?
The right of man that nature granted him,
And waste it frivolously for your gain?
How does he move all hearts, or reign
Over the elements like cherubim?
Is it not, streaming forth, the concord of his art
That carries back the world into his heart?
When nature forces the unending thread
Upon her spindle in indifferent tread,
When all the living lack the least rapport,
Each playing his disgruntled part—
Who scans the selfsame lines as they unroll,
Bestowing life, and quickening, rhythmic motion?
Who calls each single voice to celebrate the whole,
So all may blend in musical devotion?
Who creates tempests to show passion's powers?
The last red clouds, to grace the mind's repose?
Who scatters all the spring's most fragrant flowers

Wer schüttet alle schönen Frühlingsblüten
Auf der Geliebten Pfade hin?
Wer flicht die unbedeutend grünen Blätter
155 Zum Ehrenkranz Verdiensten jeder Art?
Wer sichert den Olymp, vereinet Götter?
Des Menschen Kraft, im Dichter offenbart.

LUSTIGE PERSON:

So braucht sie denn, die schönen Kräfte,
Und treibt die dichtrischen Geschäfte,
160 Wie man ein Liebesabenteuer treibt!
Zufällig naht man sich, man fühlt, man bleibt
Und nach und nach wird man verflochten;
Es wächst das Glück, dann wird es angefochten,
Man ist entzückt, nun kommt der Schmerz heran,
165 Und eh man sich's versieht, ist's eben ein Roman.
Laßt uns auch so ein Schauspiel geben!
Greift nur hinein ins volle Menschenleben!
Ein jeder lebt's, nicht vielen ist's bekannt,
Und wo ihr's packt, da ist's interessant.
170 In bunten Bildern wenig Klarheit,
Viel Irrtum und ein Fünkchen Wahrheit:
So wird der beste Trank gebraut,
Der alle Welt erquickt und auferbaut.
Dann sammelt sich der Jugend schönste Blüte
175 Vor eurem Spiel und lauscht der Offenbarung,
Dann sauget jedes zärtliche Gemüte
Aus eurem Werk sich melanchol'sche Nahrung,
Dann wird bald dies, bald jenes aufgeregt,
Ein jeder sieht, was er im Herzen trägt.
180 Noch sind sie gleich bereit, zu weinen und zu lachen,
Sie ehren noch den Schwung, erfreuen sich am Schein;
Wer fertig ist, dem ist nichts recht zu machen,

Wherever his beloved goes?
Who twines green leaves, worthless as common clods,
To wreaths of honor that stay always fresh?
Secures Olympus and unites the gods?
The strength of man, in poets become flesh.

CLOWN:

Then use your fair strength skillfully:
The business of poetry
Conduct as if it were a love affair!
One meets by chance, one feels one's way, stays there,
And by and by, one is entangled;
Happiness grows, then it is mangled,
First rapture comes, then grief and care advance:
Before you know what happened, it is a long romance. A BAD ROMANCE? RAH. RAH.
Give us a play with such emotion!
Reach into life, it is a teeming ocean!
All live in it, not many know it well,
And where you seize it, it exerts a spell.
In motley pictures little clarity,
Much error and a spark of verity—
I tell you, it is brews like these
That never fail to edify and please.
The flower of our youth will come to read
And hear whatever you may be revealing,
And every tender mind will come to feed
Upon your work its melancholy feeling;
One thrills to this, one finds that in your art,
Each sees precisely what is in his heart.
The young are still prepared to weep or show delight,
They still respect your verve, and laugh at dreamlike pranks,
Those who have ceased to grow, find nothing right;

Ein Werdender wird immer dankbar sein.

DICHTER:

So gib mir auch die Zeiten wieder,
185 Da ich noch selbst im Werden war,
Da sich ein Quell gedrängter Lieder
Ununterbrochen neu gebar,
Da Nebel mir die Welt verhüllten,
Die Knospe Wunder noch versprach,
190 Da ich die tausend Blumen brach,
Die alle Taler reichlich füllten.
Ich hatte nichts und doch genug:
Den Drang nach Wahrheit und die Lust am Trug.
Gib ungebändigt jene Triebe,
195 Das tiefe, schmerzenvolle Glück,
Des Hasses Kraft, die Macht der Liebe,
Gib meine Jugend mir zurück!

LUSTIGE PERSON:

Der Jugend, guter Freund, bedarfst du allenfalls,
Wenn dich in Schlachten Feinde drängen,
200 Wenn mit Gewalt an deinen Hals
Sich allerliebste Mädchen hängen,
Wenn fern des schnellen Laufes Kranz
Vom schwer erreichten Ziele winket,
Wenn nach dem heftgen Wirbeltanz
205 Die Nächte schmausend man vertrinket.
Doch ins bekannte Saitenspiel
Mit Mut und Anmut einzugreifen,
Nach einem selbstgesteckten Ziel
Mit holdem Irren hinzuschweifen,
210 Das, alte Herrn, ist eure Pflicht,
Und wir verehren euch darum nicht minder.
Das Alter macht nicht kindisch, wie man spricht,
Es findet uns nur noch als wahre Kinder.

DIREKTOR:

Der Worte sind genug gewechselt,
215 Laßt mich auch endlich Taten sehn!

Those who are growing still, will not spare thanks.

POET:

Then give me back, my friend, the times
When I myself was also growing
And when a well of rushing rhymes
Renewed itself as it was flowing;
The world was shrouded in a haze,
The bud still promised wondrous powers,
And I would break a thousand flowers
With which all valleys were ablaze.
Nothing I had, and yet profusion:
The lust for truth, the pleasure in illusion.
Give back the passions unabated,
That deepest joy, alive with pain,
Love's power and the strength of hatred,
Give back my youth to me again.

CLOWN:

You may need youth, my friend, in battles or in
raids,
When cannons roar and soldiers press you,
Or when adorable young maids
Put their arms round you and caress you;
Or when the wreath of honor glances
Far from the goal of a long run;
Or when, after impassioned dances,
One drinks and toasts the rising sun.
To raise the poet's well-known voice
With grace in mankind's graceless choir,
To seek the goal of one's own choice
With blessed erring—that, good sire,
Is the sweet duty of the old,
And we respect you when you play your part.
Age does not make us childish, as we're told,
It merely finds we are still young at heart.

DIRECTOR:

We have enough analyses,
Now I am eager to see deeds;

Indes ihr Komplimente drechselt,
Kann etwas Nützliches geschehn.
Was hilft es, viel von Stimmung reden?
Dem Zaudernden erscheint sie nie.
220 Gebt ihr euch einmal für Poeten,
So kommandiert die Poesie!
Euch ist bekannt, was wir bedürfen,
Wir wollen stark Getränke schlürfen;
Nun braut mir unverzüglich dran!
225 Was heute nicht geschieht, ist morgen nicht getan,
Und keinen Tag soll man verpassen,
Das Mögliche soll der Entschluß
Beherzt sogleich beim Schopfe, fassen,
Er will es dann nicht fahren lassen
230 Und wirket weiter, weil er muß.

Ihr wißt, auf unsern deutschen Bühnen
Probiert ein jeder, was er mag;
Drum schonet mir an diesem Tag
Prospekte nicht und nicht Maschinen!
235 Gebraucht das groß und kleine Himmelslicht!
Die Sterne dürfet ihr verschwenden;
An Wasser, Feuer, Felsenwänden,
An Tier und Vögeln fehlt es nicht.
So schreitet in dem engen Bretterhaus
240 Den ganzen Kreis der Schöpfung aus
Und wandelt mit bedächtger Schnelle
Vom Himmel durch die Welt zur Hölle!

While you exchange your pleasantries,
Another's useful plan succeeds.
Your talk of moods kindles no flame,
The waverer always waits and loses;
If you are poets as you claim,
Then prove that you command the muses.
You know just what we need, I think:
We want a potent brew to drink.
Concoct it now without delay!
Tomorrow we still miss what is not done today;
There is no day that one should skip,
But one should seize without distrust
The possible with iron grip;
Once grasped, one will not let it slip,
But one works on because one must.

You know, the stage in Germany
Lets each do what he wants to do;
Tonight, therefore, I say to you,
Do not spare our machinery.
Employ the sun and moon, do not hold back!
Use all the stars we have in stock;
Of water, fire, walls of rock,
And beasts and birds there is no lack.
In our narrow house of boards, bestride
The whole creation, far and wide;
Move thoughtfully, but fast as well,
From heaven through the world to hell.

PROLOG IM HIMMEL

Derr Herr. Die himmlischen Heerscharen.

Nachher Mephistopheles.

Die drei Erzengel treten vor.

RAPHAEL:

Die Sonne tönt, nach alter Weise,
In Brudersphären Wettgesang,
245 Und ihre vorgeschriebne Reise
Vollendet sie mit Donnergang.
Ihr Anblick gibt den Engeln Starke,
Wenn keiner sie ergründen mag;
Die unbegreiflich hohen Werke
250 Sind herrlich wie am ersten Tag.

GABRIEL:

Und schnell und unbegreiflich schnelle
Dreht sich umher der Erde Pracht;
Es wechselt Paradieseshelle
Mit tiefer, schauervoller Nacht;
255 Es schäumt das Meer in breiten Flüssen
Am tiefen Grund der Felsen auf,
Und Fels und Meer wird fortgerissen
In ewig schnellem Sphärenlauf.

MICHAEL:

Und Stürme brausen um die Wette,
260 Vom Meer aufs Land, vom Land aufs Meer,
Und bilden wütend eine Kette

PROLOGUE IN HEAVEN

The Lord, the heavenly hosts.

Later, Mephistopheles.

The three Archangels step forward.

RAPHAEL:

The sun intones, in ancient tourney
With brother spheres, a rival air;
And his predestinated journey,
He closes with a thundrous blare.
His sight, as none can comprehend it,
Gives strength to angels; the array
Of works, unfathomably splendid,
Is glorious as on the first day.

GABRIEL:

Unfathomably swiftly speeded,
Earth's pomp revolves in whirling flight,
As Eden's brightness is succeeded
By deep and dread-inspiring night;
In mighty torrents foams the ocean
Against the rocks with roaring song–
In ever-speeding spheric motion,
Both rock and sea are swept along.

MICHAEL:

And rival tempests roar and ravage
From sea to land, from land to sea,
And, raging, form a chain of savage,

Der tiefsten Wirkung rings umher.
Da flammt ein blitzendes Verheeren
Dem Pfade vor des Donnerschlags.
265 Doch deine Boten, Herr, verehren
Das sanfte Wandeln deines Tags.

ZU DREI:

Der Anblick gibt den Engeln Stärke,
Da keiner dich ergründen mag,
Und alle deine hohen Werke
270 Sind herrlich wie am ersten Tag.

MEPHISTOPHELES:

Da du, o Herr, dich einmal wieder nahst
Und fragst, wie alles sich bei uns befinde,
Und du mich sonst gewöhnlich gerne sahst,
So siehst du mich auch unter dem Gesinde.
275 Verzeih, ich kann nicht hohe Worte machen,
Und wenn mich auch der ganze Kreis verhöhnt;
Mein Pathos brächte dich gewiß zum Lachen,
Hätt'st du dir nicht das Lachen abgewöhnt.
Von Sonn und Welten weiß ich nichts zu sagen,
280 Ich sehe nur, wie sich die Menschen plagen.
Der kleine Gott der Welt bleibt stets von
gleichem Schlag
Und ist so wunderlich als wie am ersten Tag.
Ein wenig besser würd er leben,
Hätt'st du ihm nicht den Schein des Himmel-
slichts gegeben;
285 Er nennt's Vernunft und braucht's allein,
Nur tierischer als jedes Tier zu sein.
Er scheint mir, mit Verlaub von Euer Gnaden,
Wie eine der langbeinigen Zikaden,
Die immer fliegt und fliegend springt
290 Und gleich im Gras ihr altes Liedchen singt.
Und läg er nur noch immer in dem Grase!
In jeden Quark begräbt er seine Nase.

DER HERR:

Hast du mir weiter nichts zu sagen?

Deeply destructive energy.
There flames a flashing devastation
To clear the thunder's crashing way;
Yet, Lord, thy herald's admiration
Is for the mildness of thy day.

THE THREE:

The sight, as none can comprehend it,
Gives strength to angels; thy array
Of works, unfathomably splendid,
Is glorious as on the first day.

MEPHISTO:

Since you, oh Lord, have once again drawn near,
And ask how we have been, and are so genial,
And since you used to like to see me here,
You see me, too, as if I were a menial.
I cannot speak as nobly as your staff,
Though by this circle here I shall be spurned:
My pathos would be sure to make you laugh,
Were laughing not a habit you've unlearned.
Of suns and worlds I know nothing to say;
I only see how men live in dismay.
The small god of the world will never change his ways
And is as whimsical—as on the first of days.
His life might be a bit more fun,
Had you not given him that spark of heaven's sun;
He calls it reason and employs it, resolute
To be more brutish than is any brute.
He seems to me, if you don't mind, Your Grace,
Like a cicada of the long-legged race,
That always flies, and, flying, springs,
And in the grass the same old ditty sings;
If only it were grass he could repose in!
There is no trash he will not poke his nose in.

THE LORD:

Can you not speak but to abuse?

Kommst du nur immer anzuklagen?
295 Ist auf der Erde ewig dir nichts recht?

MEPHISTOPHELES:

Nein, Herr! Ich find es dort, wie immer, herzlich schlecht.
Die Menschen dauern mich in ihren Jammertagen,
Ich mag sogar die armen selbst nicht plagen.

DER HERR:

Kennst du den Faust?

MEPHISTOPHELES:

Den Doktor?

DER HERR:

Meinen Knecht!

MEPHISTOPHELES:

Fürwahr!
300 Er dient Euch auf besondre Weise.
Nicht irdisch ist des Toren Trank noch Speise.
Ihn treibt die Gärung in die Ferne,
Er ist sich seiner Tollheit halb bewußt;
Vom Himmel fordert er die schönsten Sterne
305 Und von der Erde jede höchste Lust,
Und alle Näh und alle Ferne
Befriedigt nicht die tiefbewegte Brust.

DER HERR:

Wenn er mir jetzt auch nur verworren dient,
So werd ich ihn bald in die Klarheit führen.
310 Weiß doch der Gärtner, wenn das Bäumchen grünt,
Daß Blüt und Frucht die künftgen Jahre zieren.

MEPHISTOPHELES:

Was wettet Ihr? Den sollt Ihr noch verlieren,
Wenn Ihr mir die Erlaubnis gebt,
Ihn meine Straße sacht zu führen.

DER HERR:

315 Solang er auf der Erde lebt,
So lange sei dir's nicht verboten;
Es irrt der Mensch, solang er strebt.

Do you come only to accuse?
Does nothing on the earth seem to you right?

MEPHISTO:

No, Lord. I find it still a rather sorry sight.
Man moves me to compassion, so wretched is his plight.
I have no wish to cause him further woe.

THE LORD:

Do you know Faust?

MEPHISTO:

The doctor?

THE LORD:

Aye, my servant.

MEPHISTO:

Lo!

He serves you most peculiarly, I think.
Not earthly are the poor fool's meat and drink.
His spirit's ferment drives him far,
And he half knows how foolish is his quest:
From heaven he demands the fairest star,
And from the earth all joys that he thinks best;
And all that's near and all that's far
Cannot soothe the upheaval in his breast.

THE LORD:

Though now he serves me but confusedly,
I shall soon lead him where the vapor clears.
The gardener knows, however small the tree,
That bloom and fruit adorn its later years.

MEPHISTO:

What will you bet? You'll lose him yet to me,
If you will graciously connive
That I may lead him carefully.

THE LORD:

As long as he may be alive,
So long you shall not be prevented.
Man errs as long as he will strive.

MEPHISTOPHELES:

Da dank ich Euch; denn mit den Toten
Hab ich mich niemals gern befangen.
320 Am meisten lieb ich mir die vollen, frischen
Wangen.
Für einen Leichnam bin ich nicht zu Haus;
Mir geht es wie der Katze mit der Maus.

DER HERR:

Nun gut, es sei dir überlassen!
Zieh diesen Geist von seinem Urquell ab
325 Und führ ihn, kannst du ihn erfassen,
Auf deinem Wege mit herab
Und steh beschämt, wenn du bekennen mußt:
Ein guter Mensch, in seinem dunklen Drange,
Ist sich des rechten Weges wohl bewußt.

MEPHISTOPHELES:

330 Schon gut! Nur dauert es nicht lange.
Mir ist für meine Wette gar nicht bange.
Wenn ich zu meinem Zweck gelange,
Erlaubt Ihr mir Triumph aus voller Brust.
Staub soll er fressen, und mit Lust,
335 Wie meine Muhme, die berühmte Schlange.

DER HERR:

Du darfst auch da nur frei erscheinen;
Ich habe deinesgleichen nie gehaßt.
Von allen Geistern, die verneinen,
Ist mir der Schalk am wenigsten zur Last.
340 Des Menschen Tatigkeit kann allzuleicht
erschlaffen,
Er liebt sich bald die unbedingte Ruh;
Drum geb ich gern ihm den Gesellen zu,
Der reizt und wirkt und muß als Teufel schaffen.
Doch ihr, die echten Göttersöhne,
345 Erfreut euch der lebendig reichen Schöne!
Das Werdende, das ewig wirkt und lebt,
Umfass euch mit der Liebe holden Schranken,
Und was in schwankender Erscheinung schwebt,

MEPHISTO:

Be thanked for that; I've never been contented
To waste my time upon the dead.
I far prefer full cheeks, a youthful curly-head.
When corpses come, I have just left the house—
I feel as does the cat about the mouse.

THE LORD:

Enough—I grant that you may try to clasp him,
Withdraw this spirit from his primal source
And lead him down, if you can grasp him,
Upon your own abysmal course—
And stand abashed when you have to attest:
A good man in his darkling aspiration
Remembers the right road throughout his quest.

MEPHISTO:

Enough—he will soon reach his station;
About my bet I have no hesitation,
And when I win, concede your stake
And let me triumph with a swelling breast:
Dust he shall eat, and that with zest,
As my relation does, the famous snake.

THE LORD:

Appear quite free on that day, too;
I never hated those who were like you:
Of all the spirits that negate.
The knavish jester gives me least to do.
For man's activity can easily abate,

He soon prefers uninterrupted rest;
To give him this companion hence seems best
Who roils and must as Devil help create.
But you, God's rightful sons, give voice
To all the beauty in which you rejoice;
And that which ever works and lives and grows
Enfold you with fair bonds that love has wrought,
And what in wavering apparition flows

Befestiget mit dauernden Gedanken!
(Der Himmel schließt, die Erzengel verteilen sich)

MEPHISTOPHELES *(allein):*

350 Von Zeit zu Zeit seh ich den Alten gern
Und hüte mich, mit ihm zu brechen.
Es ist gar hübsch von einem großen Herrn,
So menschlich mit dem Teufel selbst zu sprechen.

That fortify with everlasting thought.
(The heavens close, the Archangels disperse.)

MEPHISTO *(alone):*
I like to see the Old Man now and then
And try to be not too uncivil.
It's charming in a noble squire when
He speaks humanely with the very Devil.

KNOWS FAUSTUS WELL.

DER TRAGÖDIE ERSTER TEIL

NACHT

In einem hochgewölbten, engen gotischen Zimmer Faust, unruhig auf seinem Sessel am Pulte.

FAUST:

Habe nun, ach! Philosophie,
355 Juristerei und Medizin
Und leider auch Theologie
Durchaus studiert mit heißem Bemühn.
Da steh ich nun, ich armer Tor!
Und bin so klug als wie zuvor;
360 Heiße Magister, heiße Doktor gar,
Und ziehe schon an die zehen Jahr
Herauf, herab und quer und krumm
Meine Schüler an der Nase herum—
Und sehe, daß wir nichts wissen können!
365 Das will mir schier das Herz verbrennen.
Zwar bin ich gescheiter als alle die Laffen,
Doktoren, Magister, Schreiber und Pfaffen;
Mich plagen keine Skrupel noch Zweifel,
Fürchte mich weder vor Hölle noch Teufel—
370 Dafür ist mir auch alle Freud entrissen,

THE FIRST PART OF THE TRAGEDY

NIGHT

In a high-vaulted, narrow Gothic den, Faust, restless in his armchair at the desk.

FAUST:

I have, alas, studied philosophy,
Jurisprudence and medicine, too,
And, worst of all, theology
With keen endeavor, through and through—
And here I am, for all my lore,
The wretched fool I was before.
Called Master of Arts, and Doctor to boot,
For ten years almost I confute
And up and down, wherever it goes,
I drag my students by the nose—
And see that for all our science and art
We can know nothing. It burns my heart.
Of course, I am smarter than all the shysters,
The doctors, and teachers, and scribes, and
    Christers;
No scruple nor doubt could make me ill,
I am not afraid of the Devil or hell—

SHUT UP SHUT UP SHUT UP

Bilde mir nicht ein, was Rechts zu wissen,
Bilde mir nicht ein, ich könnte was lehren,
Die Menschen zu bessern und zu bekehren.
Auch hab ich weder Gut noch Geld,
375 Noch Ehr und Herrlichkeit der Welt.
Es möchte kein Hund so länger leben!
Drum hab ich mich der Magie ergeben,
Ob mir durch Geistes Kraft und Mund
Nicht manch Geheimnis würde kund;
380 Daß ich nicht mehr mit saurem Schweiß
Zu sagen brauche, was ich nicht weiß;
Daß ich erkenne, was die Welt
Im Innersten zusammenhält,
Schau alle Wirkenskraft und Samen
385 Und tu nicht mehr in Worten kramen.

O sähst du, voller Mondenschein,
Zum letztenmal auf meine Pein,
Den ich so manche Mitternacht
An diesem Pult herangewacht:
390 Dann über Büchern und Papier,
Trübselger Freund, erschienst du mir!
Ach, könnt ich doch auf Bergeshöhn
In deinem lieben Lichte gehn,
Um Bergeshöhle mit Geistern schweben,
395 Auf Wiesen in deinem Dämmer weben,
Von allem Wissensqualm entladen,
In deinem Tau gesund mich baden!

Weh! Steck ich in dem Kerker noch?
Verfluchtes dumpfes Mauerloch,
400 Wo selbst das liebe Himmelslicht
Trüb durch gemalte Scheiben bricht!
Beschränkt mit diesem Bücherhauf,
Den Würme nagen, Staub bedeckt,

But therefore I also lack all delight,
Do not fancy that I know anything right,
Do not fancy that I could teach or assert
What would better mankind or what might
convert.
I also have neither money nor treasures,
Nor worldly honors or earthly pleasures;
No dog would want to live longer this way!
Hence I have yielded to magic to see
Whether the spirit's mouth and might
Would bring some mysteries to light,
That I need not with work and woe
Go on to say what I don't know;
That I might see what secret force
Hides in the world and rules its course.
Envisage the creative blazes
Instead of rummaging in phrases.

Full lunar light, that you might stare
The last time now on my despair!
How often I've been waking here
At my old desk till you appeared,
And over papers, notes, and books
I caught, my gloomy friend, your looks.
Oh, that up on a mountain height
I could walk in your lovely light
And float with spirits round caves and trees,
Weave in your twilight through the leas,
Cast dusty knowledge overboard,
And bathe in dew until restored.

Still this old dungeon, still a mole!
Cursed be this moldy walled-in hole
Where heaven's lovely light must pass,
And lose its luster, through stained glass.
Confined with books, and every tome
Is gnawed by worms, covered with dust,

Den bis ans hohe Gewölb hinauf
405 Ein angeraucht Papier umsteckt;
Mit Gläsern, Büchsen rings umstellt,
Mit Instrumenten vollgepfropft,
Urväter-Hausrat drein gestopft—
Das ist deine Welt! Das heißt eine Welt!

410 Und fragst du noch, warum dein Herz
Sich bang in deinem Busen klemmt,
Warum ein unerklärter Schmerz
Dir alle Lebensregung hemmt?
Statt der lebendigen Natur,
415 Da Gott die Menschen schuf hinein,
Umgibt in Rauch und Moder nur
Dich Tiergeripp und Totenbein.

Flieh! Auf! Hinaus ins weite Land!
Und dies geheimnisvolle Buch,
420 Von Nostradamus' eigner Hand,
Ist dir es nicht Geleit genug?
Erkennest dann der Sterne Lauf,
Und wenn Natur dich unterweist,
Dann geht die Seelenkraft dir auf,
425 Wie spricht ein Geist zum andern Geist.
Umsonst, daß trocknes Sinnen hier
Die heilgen Zeichen dir erklärt:
Ihr schwebt, ihr Geister, neben mir;
Antwortet mir, wenn ihr mich hört!

(Er schlägt das Buch auf und erblickt das Zeichen des Makrokosmus.)

430 Ha! Welche Wonne fließt in diesem Blick
Auf einmal mir durch alle meine Sinnen!
Ich fühle junges, heilges Lebensglück
Neuglühend mir durch Nerv und Adern rinnen.
War es ein Gott, der diese Zeichen schrieb,

And on the walls, up to the dome,
A smoky paper, spots of rust;
Enclosed by tubes and jars that breed
More dust, by instruments and soot,
Ancestral furniture to boot—
That is your world! A world indeed!

And need you ask why in your breast
Your cramped heart throbs so anxiously?
Life's every stirring is oppressed
By an unfathomed agony?
Instead of living nature which
God made man for with holy breath,
Must stifles you, and every niche
Holds skulls and skeletons and death.

Flee! Out into the open land!
And this book full of mystery,
Written in Nostradamus' hand—
Is it not ample company?
Stars' orbits you will know; and bold,
You learn what nature has to teach;
Your soul is freed, and you behold
The spirits' words, the spirits' speech.
Though dry reflection might expound
These holy symbols, it is dreary:
You float, oh spirits, all around;
Respond to me, if you can hear me.

(He opens the book and sees the symbol of the macrocosm.)

What jubilation bursts out of this sight
Into my senses—now I feel it flowing,
Youthful, a sacred fountain of delight,
Through every nerve, my veins are glowing.
Was it a god that made these symbols be

435 Die mir das innre Toben stillen,
Das arme Herz mit Freude füllen
Und mit geheimnisvollem Trieb
Die Kräfte der Natur rings um mich her
enthüllen?

Bin ich ein Gott? Mir wird so licht!
440 Ich schau in diesen reinen Zügen
Die wirkende Natur vor meiner Seele liegen.
Jetzt erst erkenn ich, was der Weise spricht:
«Die Geisterwelt ist nicht verschlossen;
Dein Sinn ist zu, dein Herz ist tot!
445 Auf, bade, Schüler, unverdrossen
Die irdsche Brust im Morgenrot!»

(Er beschaut das Zeichen.)

Wie alles sich zum Ganzen webt,
Eins in dem andern wirkt und lebt!
Wie Himmelskräfte auf und nieder steigen
450 Und sich die goldnen Eimer reichen!
Mit segenduftenden Schwingen
Vom Himmel durch die Erde dringen,
Harmonisch all das All durchklingen!

Welch Schauspiel! Aber, ach, ein Schauspiel nur!
455 Wo faß ich dich, unendliche Natur?
Euch Brüste, wo? Ihr Quellen alles Lebens,
An denen Himmel und Erde hängt,
Dahin die welke Brust sich drängt—
Ihr quellt, ihr tränkt, und schmacht ich so
vergebens?

(Er schlägt unwillig das Buch um und erblickt das Zeichen des Erdgeistes.)

460 Wie anders wirkt dies Zeichen auf mich ein!

That soothe my feverish unrest,
Filling with joy my anxious breast,
And with mysterious potency
Make nature's hidden powers around me,
manifest?

Am I a god? Light grows this page—
In these pure lines my eye can see
Creative nature spread in front of me.
But now I grasp the meaning of the sage:
"The realm of spirits is not far away;
Your mind is closed, your heart is dead.
Rise, student, bathe without dismay
In heaven's dawn your mortal head."

(He contemplates the symbol.)

All weaves itself into the whole,
Each living in the other's soul.
How heaven's powers climb up and descend.
Passing the golden pails from hand to hand!
Bliss-scented, they are winging
Through sky and earth—their singing
Is ringing through the world.

What play! Yet but a play, however vast!
Where, boundless nature, can I hold you fast?
And where you breasts? Wells that sustain
All life—the heaven and the earth are nursed.
The wilted breast craves you in thirst—
You well, you still—and I languish in vain?

(In disgust, he turns some pages and beholds the symbol of the earth spirit.)

How different is the power of this sign!

Du, Geist der Erde, bist mir näher;
Schon fühl ich meine Kräfte höher,
Schon glüh ich wie von neuem Wein.
Ich fühle Mut, mich in die Welt zu wagen,
465 Der Erde Weh, der Erde Glück zu tragen,
Mit Stürmen mich herumzuschlagen
Und in des Schiffbruchs Knirschen nicht zu zagen.
Es wölkt sich über mir—
Der Mond verbirgt sein Licht—
470 Die Lampe schwindet!
Es dampft!—Es zucken rote Strahlen
Mir um das Haupt—Es weht
Ein Schauer vom Gewölb herab
Und faßt mich an!
475 Ich fühl's, du schwebst um mich, erflehter Geist.
Enthülle dich!
Ha! Wie's in meinem Herzen reißt!
Zu neuen Gefühlen
All meine Sinnen sich erwühlen!
480 Ich fühle ganz mein Herz dir hingegeben!
Du mußt! Du mußt! Und kostet' es mein Leben!

(Er faßt das Buch und spricht das Zeichen des Geistes geheimnisvoll aus. Es zuckt eine rötliche Flamme, der Geist erscheint in der Flamme.)

GEIST:
Wer ruft mir?

FAUST *(abgewendet)*:
Schreckliches Gesicht!

GEIST:
Du hast mich mächtig angezogen,
An meiner Sphäre lang gesogen,
485 Und nun—

FAUST:
Weh! Ich ertrag dich nicht!

You, spirit of the earth, seem close to mine:
I look and feel my powers growing,
As if I'd drunk new wine I'm glowing,
I feel a sudden courage, and should dare
To plunge into the world, to bear
All earthly grief, all earthly joy—compare
With gales my strength, face shipwreck without
care.
Now there are clouds above—
The moon conceals her light—
The lamp dies down.
It steams. Red light rays dash
About my head—a chill
Blows from the vaulting dome
And seizes me.
I feel you near me, spirit I implored.
Reveal yourself!
Oh, how my heart is gored
By never felt urges,
And my whole body surges—
My heart is yours; yours, too, am I.
You must. You must. Though I should have to die.

(He seizes the book and mysteriously pronounces the symbol of the spirit. A reddish flame flashes, and the SPIRIT *appears in the flame.)*

"EARTH SPIRIT"

SPIRIT:
Who calls me?

FAUST *(turning away):*
Vision of fright!

SPIRIT:
With all your might you drew me near
You have been sucking at my sphere,
And now—

FAUST:
I cannot bear your sight!

GEIST:

Du flehst eratmend, mich zu schauen,
Meine Stimme zu hören, mein Antlitz zu sehn;
Mich neigt dein mächtig Seelenflehn,
Da bin ich!—Welch erbärmlich Grauen
490 Faßt Übermenschen dich! Wo ist der Seele Ruf?
Wo ist die Brust, die eine Welt in sich erschuf
Und trug und hegte, die mit Freudebeben
Erschwoll, sich uns, den Geistern, gleich zu
heben?
Wo bist du, Faust, des Stimme mir erklang,
495 Der sich an mich mit allen Kräften drang?
Bist du es, der, von meinem Hauch umwittert,
In allen Lebenstiefen zittert,
Ein furchtsam weggekrümmter Wurm?

FAUST:

Soll ich dir, Flammenbildung, weichen?
500 Ich bin's, bin Faust, bin deinesgleichen!

GEIST:

In Lebensfluten, im Tatensturm
Wall ich auf und ab,
Webe hin und her.
Geburt und Grab,
505 Ein ewiges Meer,
Ein wechselnd Weben,
Ein glühend Leben:
So schaff ich am sausenden Webstuhl der Zeit
Und wirke der Gottheit lebendiges Kleid.

FAUST:

510 Der du die weite Welt umschweifst,
Geschäftiger Geist, wie nah fühl ich mich dir!

GEIST:

Du gleichst dem Geist, den du begreifst,
Nicht mir! *(Verschwindet.)*

SPIRIT:

You have implored me to appear,
Make known my voice, reveal my face;
Your soul's entreaty won my grace:
Here I am! What abject fear
Grasps you, oh superman! Where is the soul's
  impassioned
Call? And where the breast that even now had
  fashioned
A world to bear and nurse within—that trembled
  thus,
Swollen with joy that it resembled us?
Where are you, Faust, whose voice pierced my
  domain,
Who surged against me with his might and main?
Could it be you who at my breath's slight shiver
Are to the depths of life aquiver,
A miserably writhing worm?

FAUST:

Should I, phantom of fire, fly?
It's I, it's Faust; your peer am I!

"SHOULD I FLEE? NO. I STAND AS YOUR EQUAL!!" –FAUST

SPIRIT:

In the floods of life and creative storm
To and fro I wave.
Weave eternally.
And birth and grave,
An eternal sea,
A changeful strife,
A glowing life:
At the roaring loom of the ages I plod
And fashion the life-giving garment of God.

FAUST:

You that traverse worlds without end,
Sedulous spirit, I feel close to you.

SPIRIT:

Peer of the spirit that you comprehend
Not mine! *(Vanishes.)*

YOU DON'T KNOW MEEE.
(OH SNAP!)

FAUST *(zusammenstürzend):*

Nicht dir!
515 Wem denn?
Ich Ebenbild der Gottheit!
Und nicht einmal dir!

(Es klopft.)

O Tod! Ich kenn's—das ist mein Famulus—
Es wird mein schönstes Glück zunichte!
520 Daß diese Fülle der Gesichte
Der trockne Schleicher stören muß!

(Wagner im Schlafrocke und der Nachtmütze, eine Lampe in der Hand. Faust wendet sich unwillig.)

WAGNER:

Verzeiht! Ich hör Euch deklamieren;
Ihr last gewiß ein griechisch Trauerspiel?
In dieser Kunst möcht ich was profitieren,
525 Denn heutzutage wirkt das viel.
Ich hab es öfters rühmen hören,
Ein Komödiant könnt einen Pfarrer lehren.

FAUST:

Ja, wenn der Pfarrer ein Komödiant ist;
Wie das denn wohl zuzeiten kommen mag.

WAGNER:

Ach, wenn man so in sein Museum gebannt ist
530 Und sieht die Welt kaum einen Feiertag,
Kaum durch ein Fernglas, nur von weiten,
Wie soll man sie durch Überredung leiten?

FAUST:

Wenn ihr's nicht fühlt, ihr werdet's nicht erjagen,
535 Wenn es nicht aus der Seele dringt
Und mit urkräftigem Behagen

FAUST *(collapsing):*

Not yours?
Whose then?
I, image of the godhead!
And not even yours!

(A knock.)

O death! My famulus—I know it well.
My fairest happiness destroyed!
This wealth of visions I enjoyed
The dreary creeper must dispel!

*(*WAGNER *enters in a dressing gown and night cap, a light in his hand.* FAUST *turns away in disgust.)*

WAGNER:

Forgive! I hear your declamation;
Surely, you read a Grecian tragedy?
I'd profit from some work in this vocation,
These days it can be used effectively.
I have been told three times at least
That a comedian could instruct a priest.

FAUST:

Yes, when the priest is a comedian for all his
Te Deum.
As happens more often than one would own.

WAGNER:

Ah, when one is confined to one's museum
And sees the world on holidays alone,
But from a distance, only on occasion,
How can one guide it by persuasion?

FAUST:

What you don't feel, you will not grasp by art,
Unless it wells out of your soul
And with sheer pleasure takes control,

Die Herzen aller Hörer zwingt.
Sitzt ihr nur immer! Leimt zusammen,
Braut ein Ragout von andrer Schmaus
540 Und blast die kümmerlichen Flammen.
Aus eurem Aschenhäufchen 'raus!
Bewundrung von Kindern und Affen,
Wenn euch darnach der Gaumen steht—
Doch werdet ihr nie Herz zu Herzen schaffen,
545 Wenn es euch nicht von Herzen geht.

WAGNER:

Allein der Vortrag macht des Redners Glück;
Ich fühl es wohl, noch bin ich weit zurück.

FAUST:

Such Er den redlichen Gewinn!
Sei Er kein schellenlauter Tor!
550 Es trägt Verstand und rechter Sinn
Mit wenig Kunst sich selber vor;
Und wenn's euch Ernst ist, was zu sagen,
Ist's nötig, Worten nachzujagen?
Ja, eure Reden, die so blinkend sind,
555 In denen ihr der Menschheit Schnitzel kräuselt,
Sind unerquicklich wie der Nebelwind,
Der herbstlich durch die dürren Blätter säuselt.

WAGNER:

Ach Gott! Die Kunst ist lang,
Und kurz ist unser Leben.
560 Mir wird, bei meinem kritischen Bestreben,
Doch oft um Kopf und Busen bang.
Wie schwer sind nicht die Mittel zu erwerben,
Durch die man zu den Quellen steigt!
Und eh man nur den halben Weg erreicht,
565 Muß wohl ein armer Teufel sterben.

FAUST:

Das Pergament, ist das der heilge Bronnen,
Woraus ein Trunk den Durst auf ewig stillt?
Erquickung hast du nicht gewonnen,
Wenn sie dir nicht aus eigner Seele quillt.

Compelling every listener's heart.
But sit—and sit, and patch and knead,
Cook a ragout, reheat your hashes,
Blow at the sparks and try to breed
A fire out of piles of ashes!
Children and apes may think it great,
If that should titillate your gum,
But from heart to heart you will never create.
If from your heart it does not come.

WAGNER:

Yet much depends on the delivery;
I still lack much; don't you agree?

FAUST:

Oh, let him look for honest gain!
Let him not be a noisy fool!
All that makes sense you can explain
Without the tricks of any school.
If you have anything to say,
Why juggle words for a display?
Your glittering rhet'ric, subtly disciplined,
Which for mankind thin paper garlands weaves,
Is as unwholesome as the foggy wind
That blows in autumn through the wilted leaves.

WAGNER:

Oh God, art is forever,
And our life is brief.
I fear that with my critical endeavor
My head and heart may come to grief.
How hard the scholars' means are to array
With which one works up to the source;
Before we have traversed but half the course,
We wretched devils pass away.

FAUST:

Parchment—is that the sacred fount
From which you drink to still your thirst forever?
If your refreshment does not mount.
From your own soul, you gain it never.

WAGNER:

570 Verzeiht! Es ist ein groß Ergetzen,
Sich in den Geist der Zeiten zu versetzen;
Zu schauen, wie vor uns ein weiser Mann gedacht,
Und wie wir's dann zuletzt so herrlich weit
gebracht.

FAUST:

O ja, bis an die Sterne weit!
575 Mein Freund, die Zeiten der Vergangenheit
Sind uns ein Buch mit sieben Siegeln.
Was ihr den Geist der Zeiten heißt.
Das ist im Grund der Herren eigner Geist,
In dem die Zeiten sich bespiegeln.
580 Da ist's denn wahrlich oft ein Jammer!
Man läuft euch bei dem ersten Blick davon.
Ein Kehrichtfaß und eine Rumpelkammer
Und höchstens eine Haupt-und Staatsaktion
Mit trefflichen pragmatischen Maximen,
585 Wie sie den Puppen wohl im Munde ziemen!

WAGNER:

Allein die Welt! Des Menschen Herz und Geist!
Möcht jeglicher doch was davon erkennen.

FAUST:

Ja, was man so erkennen heißt!
Wer darf das Kind beim rechten Namen nennen?
590 Die wenigen, die was davon erkannt,
Die töricht gnug ihr volles Herz nicht wahrten,
Dem Pöbel ihr Gefühl, ihr Schauen offenbarten,
Hat man von je gekreuzigt und verbrannt.
Ich bitt Euch, Freund, es ist tief in der Nacht,
595 Wir müssen's diesmal unterbrechen.

WAGNER:

Ich hätte gern nur immer fortgewacht,
Um so gelehrt mit Euch mich zu besprechen.
Doch morgen, als ersten Ostertage,

WAGNER:

Forgive! It does seem so sublime,
Entering into the spirit of the time
To see what wise men, who lived long ago,
believed,
Till we at last have all the highest aims achieved.

FAUST:

Up to the stars—achieved indeed!
My friend, the times that antecede
Our own are books safely protected
By seven seals. What spirit of the time you call,
Is but the scholars' spirit, after all,
In which times past are now reflected.
In truth, it often is pathetic,
And when one sees it, one would run away:
A garbage pail, perhaps a storage attic,
At best a pompous moralistic play
With wonderfully edifying quips,
Most suitable to come from puppets' lips.

WAGNER:

And yet the world! Man's heart and spirit! Oh,
That everybody knew part of the same!

FAUST:

The things that people claim to know!
Who dares to call the child by its true name?
The few that saw something like this and, starry-
eyed
But foolishly, with glowing hearts averred
Their feelings and their visions before the
common herd
Have at all times been burned and crucified.
I beg you, friend, it is deep in the night;
We must break off this interview.

WAGNER:

Our conversation was so erudite,
I should have liked to stay awake with you.
Yet Easter comes tomorrow; then permit

Erlaubt mir ein und andre Frage.
600 Mit Eifer hab ich mich der Studien beflissen;

Zwar weiß ich viel, doch möcht ich alles wissen.
(Ab)

FAUST *(allein):*
Wie nur dem Kopf nicht alle Hoffnung schwindet,
Der immerfort an schalem Zeuge klebt,
Mit gierger Hand nach Schätzen gräbt
605 Und froh ist, wenn er Regenwürmer findet!

Darf eine solche Menschenstimme hier,
Wo Geisterfülle mich umgab, ertönen?
Doch ach, für diesmal dank ich dir,
Dem ärmlichsten von allen Erdensöhnen.
610 Du rissest mich von der Verzweiflung los,
Die mir die Sinne schon zerstören wollte.
Ach! Die Erscheinung war so riesengroß,
Daß ich mich recht als Zwerg empfinden sollte.

Ich, Ebenbild der Gottheit, das sich schon
615 Ganz nah gedünkt dem Spiegel ewger Wahrheit,
Sein selbst genoß in Himmelsglanz und Klarheit,
Und abgestreift den Erdensohn;
Ich, mehr als Cherub, dessen freie Kraft
Schon durch die Adern der Natur zu fließen
620 Und, schaffend, Götterleben zu genießen
Sich ahnungsvoll vermaß, wie muß ich's büßen!
Ein Donnerwort hat mich hinweggerafft.

Nicht darf ich dir zu gleichen mich vermessen:
Hab ich die Kraft dich anzuziehn besessen,
625 So hatt ich dich zu halten keine Kraft.
In jenem selgen Augenblicke
Ich fühlte mich so klein, so groß;
Du stießest grausam mich zurücke
Ins ungewisse Menschenlos.

That I may question you a bit.
Most zealously I've studied matters great and
small;
Though I know much, I should like to know all.
(Exit.)

FAUST *(alone)*:
Hope never seems to leave those who affirm,
The shallow minds that stick to must and mold—
They dig with greedy hands for gold
And yet are happy if they find a worm.
Dare such a human voice be sounded
Where I was even now surrounded
By spirits' might? And yet I thank you just this
once,
You, of all creatures the most wretched dunce.
You tore me from despair that had surpassed
My mind and threatened to destroy my sense.
Alas, the apparition was so vast
That I felt dwarfed in impotence.

I, image of the godhead, that began
To dream eternal truth was within reach,
Exulting on the heavens' brilliant beach
As if I had stripped off the mortal man;
I, more than cherub, whose unbounded might
Seemed even then to flow through nature's veins,
Shared the creative joys of God's domains—
Presumptuous hope for which I pay in pains:
One word of thunder swept me from my height.

I may no longer claim to be your peer:
I had the power to attract you here,
But to retain you lacked the might.
In that moment of bliss, alack,
In which I felt so small, so great,
You, cruel one, have pushed me back
Into uncertain human fate.

630 Wer lehret mich? Was soll ich meiden?
Soll ich gehorchen jenem Drang?
Ach, unsre Taten selbst, so gut als unsre Leiden,
Sie hemmen unsres Lebens Gang.

Dem Herrlichsten, was auch der Geist empfangen,
635 Drängt immer fremd und fremder Stoff sich an;
Wenn wir zum Guten dieser Welt gelangen,
Dann heißt das Bessre Trug und Wahn.
Die uns das Leben gaben, herrliche Gefühle
Erstarren in dem irdischen Gewühle.

640 Wenn Phantasie sich sonst mit kühnem Flug
Und hoffnungsvoll zum Ewigen erweitert,
So ist ein kleiner Raum ihr nun genug,
Wenn Glück auf Glück im Zeitenstrudel scheitert.
Die Sorge nistet gleich im tiefen Herzen,
645 Dort wirket sie geheime Schmerzen.
Unruhig wiegt sie sich und störet Lust und Ruh;
Sie deckt sich stets mit neuen Masken zu,
Sie mag als Haus und Hof, als Weib und Kind
erscheinen,
Als Feuer, Wasser, Dolch und Gift;
650 Du bebst vor allem, was nicht trifft,
Und was du nie verlierst, das mußt du stets
beweinen.
Den Göttern gleich ich nicht! Zu tief ist es gefühlt;
Dem Wurme gleich ich, der den Staub
durchwühlt,
Den, wie er sich im Staube nährend lebt,
655 Des Wandrers Tritt vernichtet und begräbt.
Ist es nicht Staub, was diese hohe Wand
Aus hundert Fächern mir verenget?
Der Trödel, der mit tausendfachem Tand
In dieser Mottenwelt mich dränget?
660 Hier soll ich finden, was mir fehlt?

Who teaches me? What should I shun?
Should I give in to that obsession?
Not our sufferings only, the deeds that we have
done
Inhibit our life's progression.

Whatever noblest things the mind received,
More and more foreign matter spoils the theme;
And when the good of this world is achieved,
What's better seems an idle dream.
That gave us our life, the noblest urges
Are petrified in the earth's vulgar surges.

Where fantasy once rose in glorious flight,
Hopeful and bold to capture the sublime,
It is content now with a narrow site,
Since joy on joy crashed on the rocks of time.
Deep in the heart there dwells relentless care
And secretly infects us with despair;
Restless, she sways and poisons peace and joy
She always finds new masks she can employ:
She may appear as house and home, as child and
wife,
As fire, water, poison, knife—
What does not strike, still makes you quail,
And what you never lose, for that you always wail.

I am not like the gods! That was a painful thrust;
I'm like the worm that burrows in the dust,
Who, as he makes of dust his meager meal,
Is crushed and buried by a wanderer's heel.
Is it not dust that stares from every rack
And narrows down this vaulting den?
This moths' world full of bric-a-brac
In which I live as in a pen?
Here I should find for what I care?

Soll ich vielleicht in tausend Büchern lesen,
Daß überall die Menschen sich gequält,
Daß hie und da ein Glücklicher gewesen?—
Was grinsest du mir, hohler Schädel, her?
665 Als daß dein Hirn, wie meines, einst verwirret
Den leichten Tag gesucht und in der Dämmrung schwer,
Mit Lust nach Wahrheit, jämmerlich geirret.
Ihr Instrumente freilich spottet mein
Mit Rad und Kämmen, Walz und Bügel:
670 Ich stand am Tor, ihr solltet Schlüssel sein;
Zwar euer Bart ist kraus, doch hebt ihr nicht die Riegel.
Geheimnisvoll am lichten Tag
Läß sich Natur des Schleiers nicht berauben,
Und was sie deinem Geist nicht offenbaren mag,
675 Das zwingst du ihr nicht ab mit Hebeln und mit Schrauben.
Du alt Geräte, das ich nicht gebraucht,
Du stehst nur hier, weil dich mein Vater brauchte.
Du alte Rolle, du wirst angerauchte,
Solang an diesem Pult die trübe Lampe schmauchte.
680 Weit besser hätt ich doch mein Weniges verpraßt,
Als mit dem Wenigen belastet hier zu schwitzen?
Was du ererbt von deinen Vätern hast,
Erwirb es, um es zu besitzen!
Was man nicht nützt, ist eine schwere Last;
685 Nur was der Augenblick erschafft, das kann er nützen.

Doch warum heftet sich mein Blick auf jene Stelle?
Ist jenes Fläschchen dort den Augen ein Magnet?
Warum wird mir auf einmal lieblich helle,
Als wenn im nächtgen Wald uns Mondenglanz umweht?

Should I read in a thousand books, maybe,
That men have always suffered everywhere,
Though now and then some man lived happily?—
Why, hollow skull, do you grin like a faun?
Save that your brain, like mine, once in dismay
Searched for light day, but foundered in the heavy
dawn
And, craving truth, went wretchedly astray.
You instruments, of course, can scorn and tease
With rollers, handles, cogs, and wheels:
I found the gate. you were to be the keys;
Although your webs are subtle, you cannot break
the seals.
Mysterious in the light of day,
Nature, in veils, will not let us perceive her,
And what she is unwilling to betray,
You cannot wrest from her with thumbscrews,
wheel, or lever.
You ancient tools that rest upon the rack,
Unused by me, but used once by my sire,
You ancient scroll that slowly has turned black
As my lamp on this desk gave off its smoky fire—

Far better had I squandered all of my wretched
share
Than groan under this wretched load and thus
address it!
What from your fathers you received as heir,
Acquire if you would possess it.
What is not used is but a load to bear;
But if today creates it, we can use and bless it.

Yet why does this place over there attract my
sight?
Why is that bottle as a magnet to my eyes?
Why does the world seem suddenly so bright,
As when in nightly woods one sees the moon arise?

690 Ich grüße dich, du einzige Phiole,
Die ich mit Andacht nun herunterhole.
In dir verehr ich Menschenwitz und Kunst.
Du Inbegriff der holden Schlummersäfte,
Du Auszug aller tödlich feinen Kräfte,
695 Erweise deinem Meister deine Gunst!
Ich sehe dich, es wird der Schmerz gelindert,
Ich fasse dich, das Streben wird gemindert,
Des Geistes Flutstrom ebbet nach und nach.
Ins hohe Meer werd ich hinausgewiesen,
700 Die Spiegelflut erglänzt zu meinen Füßen,
Zu neuen Ufern lockt ein neuer Tag.
Ein Feuerwagen schwebt auf leichten Schwingen
An mich heran. Ich fühle mich bereit,
Auf neuer Bahn den Äther zu durchdringen,
705 Zu neuen Sphären reiner Tätigkeit.
Dies hohe Leben, diese Götterwonne!
Du, erst noch Wurm, und die verdienest du?
Ja, kehre nur der holden Erdensonne
Entschlossen deinen Rücken zu!
710 Vermesse dich, die Pforten aufzureißen,
Vor denen jeder gern vorüberschleicht!
Hier ist es Zeit, durch Taten zu beweisen,
Daß Manneswürde nicht der Götterhöhe weicht,
Vor jener dunkeln Höhle nicht zu beben,
715 In der sich Phantasie zu eigner Qual verdammt,
Nach jenem Durchgang hinzustreben,
Um dessen engen Mund die ganze Hölle flammt;
Zu diesem Schritt sich heiter zu entschließen;
Und wär es mit Gefahr, ins Nichts dahin zu
fließen.

720 Nun komm herab, kristallne reine Schale!
Hervor aus deinem alten Futterale,
An die ich viele Jahre nicht gedacht!
Du glänztest bei der Väter Freudenfeste,
Erheitertest die ernsten Gäste,

I welcome you, incomparable potion,
Which from your place I fetch now with devotion:
In you I honor human wit and art.
You essence from all slumber-bringing flowers,
You extract of all subtly fatal powers,
Bare to your master your enticing heart!
I look upon you, soothed are all my pains,
I seize you now, and all my striving wanes,
The spirit's tidal wave now ebbs away.
Slowly I float into the open sea,
The waves beneath me now seem gay and free,
To other shores beckons another day.
A fiery chariot floats on airy pinions
Cleaving the ether—tarry and descend!
Uncharted orbits call me, new dominions
Of sheer creation, active without end.
This higher life, joys that no mortal won!
You merit this—but now a worm, despairing?
Upon the mild light of the earthly sun
Turn, bold, your back! And with undaunted daring
Tear open the eternal portals
Past which all creatures slink in silent dread.
The time has come to prove by deeds that mortals
Have as much dignity as any god,
And not to tremble at that murky cave
Where fantasy condemns itself to dwell
In agony. The passage brave
Whose narrow mouth is lit by all the flames of hell;
And take this step with cheerful resolution,
Though it involve the risk of utter dissolution.

Now you come down to me, pure crystal vase,
Emerge again out of your ancient case
Of which for many years I did not think.
You glistened at my fathers' joyous feasts
And cheered the solemn-looking guests,

725 Wenn einer dich dem andern zugebracht.
Der vielen Bilder künstlich reiche Pracht,
Des Trinkers Pflicht, sie reimweis zu erklären,
Auf einen Zug die Höhlung auszuleeren,
Erinnert mich an manche Jugendnacht.
730 Ich werde jetzt dich keinem Nachbar reichen,
Ich werde meinen Witz an deiner Kunst nicht
zeigen.
Hier ist ein Saft, der eilig trunken macht;
Mit brauner Flut erfüllt er deine Höhle.
Den ich bereitet, den ich wähle,
735 Der letzte Trunk sei nun, mit ganzer Seele,
Als festlich hoher Gruß, dem Morgen zugebracht!
(Er setzt die Schale an den Mund.)

(Glockenklang und Chorgesang.)

CHOR DER ENGEL:

Christ ist erstanden!
Freude dem Sterblichen,
Den die verderblichen,
740 Schleichenden, erblichen
Mängel umwanden.

FAUST:

Welch tiefes Summen, welch ein heller Ton
Zieht mit Gewalt das Glas von meinem Munde?
Verkündiget ihr dumpfen Glocken schon
745 Des Osterfestes erste Feierstunde?
Ihr Chöre, singt ihr schon den tröstlichen Gesang,
Der einst, um Grabes Nacht, von Engelslippen
klang,
Gewißheit einem neuen Bunde?

CHOR DER WEIBER:

Mit Spezereien
750 Hatten wir ihn gepflegt,
Wir seine Treuen
Hatten ihn hingelegt;

When you were passed around for all to drink.
The many pictures, glistening in the light,
The drinker's duty rhyming to explain them,
To scan your depths and in one draught to drain
them,
Bring back to mind many a youthful night.
There is no friend now to fulfill this duty,
Nor shall I exercise my wit upon your beauty.
Here is a juice that fast makes drunk and mute;
With its brown flood it fills this crystal bowl,
I brewed it and shall drink it whole
And offer this last drink with all my soul
Unto the morning as a festive high salute.
(He puts the bowl to his lips.)

(Chime of bells and choral song.)

CHOIR OF ANGELS:
Christ is arisen.
Hail the meek-spirited
Whom the ill-merited,
Creeping, inherited
Faults held in prison.

FAUST:
What deeply humming strokes, what brilliant tone
Draws from my lips the crystal bowl with power?
Has the time come, deep bells, when you make
known
The Easter holiday's first holy hour?
Is this already, choirs, the sweet consoling hymn
That was first sung around his tomb by cherubim,
Confirming the new covenant?

CHOIR OF WOMEN:
With myrrh, when bereaved,
We had adorned him;
We that believed
Laid down and mourned him.

Tücher und Binden
Reinlich umwanden wir,
755 Ach, und wir finden
Christ nicht mehr hier.

CHOR DER ENGEL:

Christ ist erstanden!
Selig der Liebende,
Der die betrübende,
760 Heilsam und übende
Prüfung bestanden.

FAUST:

Was sucht ihr, mächtig und gelind,
Ihr Himmelstöne, mich am Staube?
Klingt dort umher, wo weiche Menschen sind!
765 Die Botschaft hör ich wohl, allein mir fehlt der
Glaube;
Das Wunder ist des Glaubens liebstes Kind.
Zu jenen Sphären wag ich nicht zu streben,
Woher die holde Nachricht tönt;
Und doch, an diesen Klang von Jugend auf
gewöhnt,
770 Ruft er auch jetzt zurück mich in das Leben.
Sonst stürzte sich der Himmelsliebe Kuß
Auf mich herab in ernster Sabbatstille;
Da klang so ahnungsvoll des Glockentones Fülle,

Und ein Gebet war brünstiger Genuß;
775 Ein unbegreiflich holdes Sehnen
Trieb mich, durch Wald und Wiesen hinzugehn,
Und unter tausend heißen Tränen
Fühlt ich mir eine Welt entstehn.
Dies Lied verkündete der Jugend muntre Spiele,

780 Der Frühlingsfeier freies Glück;
Erinnrung hält mich nun, mit kindlichem Gefühle,
Vom letzten, ernsten Schritt zurück.
O tönet fort, ihr süßen Himmelslieder!

Linen we twined
Round the adored—
Returning, we cannot find
Christ, our Lord.

CHOIR OF ANGELS:

Christ is arisen.
Blessed be the glorious
One who victorious
Over laborious
Trials has risen.

FAUST:

Why would you, heaven's tones, compel
Me gently to rise from my dust?
Resound where tenderhearted people dwell:
Although I hear the message, I lack all faith or
trust;
And faith's favorite child is miracle.
For those far spheres I should not dare to strive,
From which these tidings come to me;
And yet these chords, which I have known since
infancy:
Call me now, too, back into life.
Once heaven's love rushed at me as a kiss
In the grave silence of the Sabbath day,
The rich tones of the bells, it seemed, had much
to say,
And every prayer brought impassioned bliss.
An unbelievably sweet yearning
Drove me to roam through wood and lea,
Crying, and as my eyes were burning,
I felt a new world grow in me.
This song proclaimed the spring feast's free
delight, appealing
To the gay games of youth—they plead:
Now memory entices me with childlike feeling
Back from the last, most solem deed.
Sound on, oh hymns of heaven, sweet and mild!

Die Träne quillt, die Erde hat mich wieder.

CHOR DER JÜNGER:

785 Hat der Begrabene
Schon sich nach oben,
Lebend Erhabene,
Herrlich erhoben;
Ist er in Werdelust
790 Schaffender Freude nah:
Ach, an der Erde Brust
Sind wir zum Leide da.
Ließ er die Seinen
Schmachtend uns hier zurück;
795 Ach, wir beweinen,
Meister, dein Glück.

CHOR DER ENGEL:

Christ ist erstanden
Aus der Verwesung Schoß.
Reißet von Banden
800 Freudig euch los!
Tätig ihn preisenden,
Liebe beweisenden,
Brüderlich speisenden,
Predigend reisenden,
805 Wonne verheißenden
Euch ist der Meister nah,
Euch ist er da!

My tears are flowing; earth, take back your child!

CHOIR OF DISCIPLES:

Has the o'ervaulted one
Burst from his prison,
The living-exalted one
Gloriously risen,
Is in this joyous birth
Zest for creation near—
Oh, on the breast of earth
We are to suffer here.
He left his own
Pining in sadness;
Alas, we bemoan,
Master, your gladness.

CHOIR OF ANGELS:

Christ is arisen
Out of corruption's womb.
Leave behind prison,
Fetters and gloom!
Those who proceed for him,
Lovingly bleed for him,
Brotherly feed for him,
Travel and plead for him,
And to bliss lead for him,
For you the Master is near,
For you he is here.

VOR DEM TOR

Spaziergänger aller Art ziehen hinaus.

EINIGE HANDWERKSBURSCHEN:
Warum denn dort hinaus?

ANDRE:
Wir gehn hinaus aufs Jägerhaus.

DIE ERSTEN:
810 Wir aber wollen nach der Mühle wandern.

EIN HANDWERKSBURSCH:
Ich rat euch, nach dem Wasserhof zu gehn.

ZWEITER:
Der Weg dahin ist gar nicht schön.

DIE ZWEITEN:
Was tust denn du?

EIN DRITTER:
Ich gehe mit den andern.

VIERTER:
Nach Burgdorf kommt herauf, gewiß dort findet ihr
815 Die schönsten Mädchen und das beste Bier
Und Händel von der ersten Sorte.

FÜNFTER:
Du überlustiger Gesell,
Juckt dich zum drittenmal das Fell?
Ich mag nicht hin, mir graut es vor dem Orte.

DIENSTMÄDCHEN:
820 Nein, nein! Ich gehe nach der Stadt zurück.

ANDRE:
Wir finden ihn gewiß bei jenen Pappeln stehen.

ERSTE:
Das ist für mich kein großes Glück;
Er wird an deiner Seite gehen,
Mit dir nur tanzt er auf dem Plan.

BEFORE THE CITY GATE

People of all kinds are walking out.

SOME APPRENTICES:
Why do you go that way?

OTHERS:
We are going to Hunter's Lodge today.

THE FIRST:
But we would rather go to the mill.

AN APPRENTICE:
Go to the River Inn, that's my advice.

ANOTHER:
I think, the way there isn't nice.

THE OTHERS:
Where are you going?

A THIRD ONE:
Up the hill.

A FOURTH ONE:
Burgdorf would be much better. Let's go there with the rest:
The girls there are stunning, their beer is the best,
And it's first-class, too, for a fight.

A FIFTH ONE:
You are indeed a peppy bird,
Twice spanked, you're itching for the third.
Let's not, the place is really a fright.

SERVANT GIRL:
No, no! I'll go back to the town again.

ANOTHER:
We'll find him at the poplars, I'm certain it is true.

THE FIRST:
What's that to me? Is it not plain,
He'll walk and dance only with you?
He thinks, you are the only one.

825 Was gehn mich deine Freuden an!

ANDRE:

Heut ist er sicher nicht allein;
Der Krauskopf, sagt er, würde bei ihm sein.

SCHÜLER:

Blitz, wie die wackern Dirnen schreiten!
Herr Bruder, komm! Wir müssen sie begleiten.
830 Ein starkes Bier, ein beizender Toback
Und eine Magd im Putz, das ist nun mein
Geschmack.

BÜRGERMÄDCHEN:

Da sieh mir nur die schönen Knaben!
Es ist wahrhaftig eine Schmach:
Gesellschaft könnten sie die allerbeste haben
835 Und laufen diesen Mägden nach!

ZWEITER SCHÜLER *(zum ersten)*:

Nicht so geschwind! Dort hinten kommen zwei,
Sie sind gar niedlich angezogen,
's ist meine Nachbarin dabei;
Ich bin dem Mädchen sehr gewogen.
840 Sie gehen ihren stillen Schritt
Und nehmen uns doch auch am Ende mit.

ERSTER:

Herr Bruder, nein! Ich bin nicht gern geniert.
Geschwind, daß wir das Wildbret nicht verlieren!
Die Hand, die samstags ihren Besen führt,
845 Wird sonntags dich am besten karessieren.

BÜRGER:

Nein, er gefällt mir nicht, der neue Burgemeister!
Nun, da er's ist, wird er nur täglich dreister.
Und für die Stadt was tut denn er?
Wird es nicht alle Tage schlimmer?
850 Gehorchen soll man mehr als immer
Und zahlen mehr als je vorher.

BETTLER *(singt)*:

Ihr guten Herrn, ihr schönen Frauen,

And why should I care for your fun?

THE OTHER ONE:

He will not be alone. He said,
Today he'd bring the curly-head.

STUDENT:

Just see those wenches over there!
Come, brother, let us help the pair.
A good strong beer, a smarting pipe,
And a maid, nicely dressed—that is my type!

CITIZEN'S DAUGHTER:

Look there and see those handsome blades!
I think it is a crying shame:
They could have any girl that meets with their
acclaim,
And chase after these silly maids.

SECOND STUDENT *(to the first)*:

Don't go so fast; behind us are two more,
And they are dressed at least as neatly.
I know one girl, she lives next door,
And she bewitches me completely.
The way they walk, they seem demure,
But won't mind company, I'm sure.

THE FIRST:

No, brother, I don't like those coy addresses.
Come on, before we lose the wilder prey.
The hand that wields the broom on Saturday
Will, comes the Sunday, give the best caresses.

CITIZEN:

No, the new mayor is no good, that's what I say.
Since he's in, he's fresher by the day.
What has he done for our city?
Things just get worse; it is a pity!
We must obey, he thinks he's clever,
And we pay taxes more than ever.

BEGGAR *(sings)*:

Good gentlemen and ladies fair,

So wohlgeputzt und backenrot,
Belieb es euch, mich anzuschauen,
855 Und seht und mildert meine Not!
Laßt hier mich nicht vergebens leiern!
Nur der ist froh, der geben mag.
Ein Tag, den alle Menschen feiern,
Er sei für mich ein Erntetag.

ANDRE BÜRGER:
860 Nichts Bessers weiß ich mir an Sonn- und Feiertagen
Als ein Gespräch von Krieg und Kriegsgeschrei,
Wenn hinten, weit, in der Türkei,
Die Völker aufeinander schlagen.
Man steht am Fenster, trinkt sein Gläschen aus
865 Und sieht den Fluß hinab die bunten Schiffe gleiten;
Dann kehrt man abends froh nach Haus
Und segnet Fried und Friedenszeiten.

DRITTER BÜRGER:
Herr Nachbar, ja! So laß ich's auch geschehn:
Sie mögen sich die Köpfe spalten,
870 Mag alles durcheinander gehn;
Doch nur zu Hause bleib's beim alten.

ALTE *(zu den Bürgermädchen)*:
Ei, wie geputzt! Das schöne junge Blut!
Wer soll sich nicht in euch vergaffen?—
Nur nicht so stolz! Es ist schon gut!
875 Und was ihr wünscht, das wüßt ich wohl zu schaffen.

BÜRGERMÄDCHEN:
Agathe, fort! Ich nehme mich in acht,
Mit solchen Hexen öffentlich zu gehen;
Sie ließ mich zwar in Sankt Andreas' Nacht
Den künftgen Liebsten leiblich sehen.

880 DIE ANDRE:
Mir zeigte sie ihn im Kristall,
Soldatenhaft, mit mehreren Verwegnen;

So red of cheek, so rich in dress,
Be pleased to look on my despair,
To see and lighten my distress.
Let me not grind here, vainly waiting!
For only those who give are gay,
And when all men are celebrating,
Then I should have my harvest day.

ANOTHER CITIZEN:

On Sun- and holidays, there is no better fun,
Than chattering of wars and warlike fray,
When off in Turkey, far away,
One people beats the other one.
We stand at the window, drink a wine that is light,
Watch the boats glide down the river, see the foam,
And cheerfully go back at night,
Grateful that we have peace at home.

THIRD CITIZEN:

Yes, neighbor, that is nicely said.
Let them crack skulls, and wound, and maim,
Let all the world stand on its head;
But here, at home, all should remain the same.

OLD WOMAN *(to the* CITIZENS' DAUGHTERS*)*:

Ah, how dressed up! So pretty and so young!
Who would not stop to stare at you?
Don't be puffed up, I'll hold my tongue.
I know your wish, and how to get it, too.

CITIZEN'S DAUGHTER:

Come quickly, Agatha! I take good heed
Not to be seen with witches; it's unwise.—
Though on St. Andrew's Night she brought indeed
My future lover right before my eyes.

THE OTHER ONE:

She showed me mine, but in a crystal ball
With other soldiers, bold and tall;

Ich seh mich um, ich such ihn überall,
Allein mir will er nicht begegnen.

SOLDATEN:

Burgen mit hohen
885 Mauern und Zinnen,
Mädchen mit stolzen
Höhnenden Sinnen
Möcht ich gewinnen!
Kühn ist das Mühen,
890 Herrlich der Lohn!
Und die Trompete
Lassen wir werben,
Wie zu der Freude,
So zum Verderben.
895 Das ist ein Stürmen!
Das ist ein Leben!
Mädchen und Burgen
Müssen sich geben.
Kühn ist das Mühen,
900 Herrlich der Lohn!
Und die Soldaten
Ziehen davon.

FAUST *und* WAGNER

FAUST:

Vom Eise befreit sind Strom und Bäche
Durch des Frühlings holden, belebenden Blick,
905 Im Tale grünet Hoffnungsglück;
Der alte Winter, in seiner Schwäche,
Zog sich in rauhe Berge zurück.
Von dorther sendet er, fliehend, nur
Ohnmächtige Schauer körnigen Eises
910 In Streifen über die grünende Flur;
Aber die Sonne duldet kein Weißes,
Uberall regt sich Bildung und Streben,
Alles will sie mit Farben beleben;
Doch an Blumen fehlt's im Revier,

I have been looking ever since,
But so far haven't found my prince.

SOLDIERS:

Castles with lofty
Towers and banners,
Maidens with haughty,
Disdainful manners
I want to capture.
Fair is the dare,
Splendid the pay.
And we let trumpets
Do our wooing,
For our pleasures
And our undoing.
Life is all storming,
Life is all splendor,
Maidens and castles
Have to surrender.
Fair is the dare,
Splendid the pay.
And then the soldiers
March on away.

FAUST *and* WAGNER.

FAUST:

Released from the ice are river and creek,
Warmed by the spring's fair quickening eye;
The valley is green with hope and joy;
The hoary winter has grown so weak
He has withdrawn to the rugged mountains.
From there he sends, but only in flight,
Impotent showers of icy hail
That streak across the greening vale;
But the sun will not suffer the white;
Everywhere stirs what develops and grows,
All he would quicken with color that glows;
Flowers are lacking, blue, yellow, and red,

915 Sie nimmt geputzte Menschen dafür.
Kehre dich um, von diesen Höhen
Nach der Stadt zurückzusehen!
Aus dem hohlen, finstren Tor
Dringt ein buntes Gewimmel hervor.
920 Jeder sonnt sich heute so gern.
Sie feiern die Auferstehung des Herrn,
Denn sie sind selber auferstanden:
Aus niedriger Häuser dumpfen Gemächern,
Aus Handwerks-und Gewerbesbanden,
925 Aus dem Druck von Giebeln und Dächern,
Aus der Straßen quetschender Enge,
Aus der Kirchen ehwürdiger Nacht
Sind sie alle ans Licht gebracht.
Sieh nur, sieh, wie behend sich die Menge
930 Durch die Gärten und Felder zerschlägt,
Wie der Fluß, in Breit und Länge,
So manchen lustigen Nachen bewegt,
Und bis zum Sinken überladen
Entfernt sich dieser letzte Kahn.
935 Selbst von des Berges fernen Pfaden
Blinken uns farbige Kleider an.
Ich höre schon des Dorfs Getümmel,
Hier ist des Volkes wahrer Himmel,
Zufrieden jauchzet groß und klein:
940 Hier bin ich Mensch, hier darf ich's sein.

WAGNER:

Mit Euch, Herr Doktor, zu spazieren
Ist ehrenvoll und ist Gewinn;
Doch würd ich nicht allein mich her verlieren,
Weil ich ein Feind von allem Rohen bin.
945 Das Fiedeln, Schreien, Kegelschieben
Ist mir ein gar verhaßter Klang;
Sie toben wie vom bösen Geist getrieben
Und nennen's Freude, nennen's Gesang.

Bauern unter der Linde
Tanz und Gesang

But he takes dressed-up people instead.
Turn around now and look down
From the heights back to the town.
Out of the hollow gloomy gate
Surges and scatters a motley horde.
All seek sunshine. They celebrate
The resurrection of the Lord.
For they themselves are resurrected
From lowly houses, musty as stables,
From trades to which they are subjected,
From the pressure of roofs and gables,
From the stifling and narrow alleys,
From the churches' reverent night
They have emerged into the light.
Look there! Look, how the crowd now sallies
Gracefully into the gardens and leas,
How on the river, all through the valley,
Frolicsome floating boats one sees,
And, overloaded beyond its fill,
This last barge now is swimming away.
From the far pathways of the hill
We can still see how their clothes are gay.
I hear the village uproar rise;
Here is the people's paradise,
And great and small shout joyously:
Here I am human, may enjoy humanity.

WAGNER:

To take a walk with you, good sir,
Is a great honor and reward,
But I myself should never so far err,
For the uncouth I always have abhorred.
This fiddling, bowling, loud delight—
I hate these noises of the throng;
They rage as if plagued by an evil sprite
And call it joy and call it song.

PEASANTS *under the linden tree.*
Dance and Song.

Der Schäfer putzte sich zum Tanz
950 Mit bunter Jacke, Band und Kranz,
Schmuck war er angezogen.
Schon um die Linde war es voll,
Und alles tanzte schon wie toll.
Juchhe! Juchhe!
955 Jucheisa! Heisa! He!
So ging der Fiedelbogen.

Er drückte hastig sich heran,
Da stieß er an ein Mädchen an
Mit seinem Ellenbogen;
960 Die frische Dirne kehrt' sich um
Und sagte: Nun, das find ich dumm!
Juchhe! Juchhe!
Juchheisa! Heisa! He!
Seid nicht so ungezogen!

965 Doch hurtig in dem Kreise ging's,
Sie tanzten rechts, sie tanzten links,
Und alle Röcke flogen.
Sie wurden rot, sie wurden warm
Und ruhten atmend Arm in Arm.
970 Juchhe! Juchhe!
Juchheisa! Heisa! He!
Und Hüft an Ellenbogen.

Und tu mir doch nicht so vertraut!
Wie mancher hat nicht seine Braut
975 Belogen und betrogen!
Er schmeichelte sie doch beiseit,
Und von der Linde scholl es weit:
Juchhe! Juchhe!
Juchheisa! Heisa! He!
980 Geschrei und Fiedelbogen.

ALTER BAUER:

Herr Doktor, das ist schön von Euch,

The shepherd wished to dance and dressed
With ribbons, wreath, and motley vest,
He was a dandy beau.
Around the linden, lass and lad
Were crowding, dancing round like mad.
Hurrah! Hurrah!
Hurrah! Hi-diddle-dee!
Thus went the fiddle bow.

He pressed into the dancing whirl
His elbow bumped a pretty girl,
And he stepped on her toe.
The lively wench, she turned and said:
"You seem to be a dunderhead!"
Hurrah! Hurrah!
Hurrah! Hi-diddle-dee!
Don't treat a poor girl so.

The circle whirled in dancing flight,
Now they danced left, now they danced right,
The skirts flow high and low.
Their cheeks were flushed and they grew warm
And rested, panting, arm in arm.
Hurrah! Hurrah!
Hurrah! Hi-diddle-dee!
With waists and elbows so.

Please do not make so free with me!
For many fool their bride-to-be
And lie, as you well know.
And yet he coaxed the girl aside,
And from the linden, far and wide:
Hurrah! Hurrah!
Hurrah! Hi-diddle-dee!
Clamor and fiddle bow.

OLD PEASANT:

Dear doctor, it is good of you

Daß Ihr uns heute nicht verschmäht
Und unter dieses Volksgedräng,
Als ein so Hochgelahrter, geht.
985 So nehmet auch den schönsten Krug,
Den wir mit frischen Trunk gefüllt,
Ich bring ihn zu und wünsche laut,
Daß er nicht nur den Durst Euch stillt:
Die Zahl der Tropfen, die er hegt,
990 Sei Euren Tagen zugelegt.

FAUST:

Ich nehme den Erquickungstrank,
Erwidr' euch allen Heil und Dank.

(Das Volk sammelt sich im Kreis umher)

ALTER BAUER:

Füwahr, es ist sehr wohl getan,
Daß Ihr am frohen Tag erscheint;
995 Habt Ihr es vormals doch mit uns
An bösen Tagen gut gemeint.
Gar mancher steht lebendig hier,
Den Euer Vater noch zuletzt
Der heißen Fieberwut entriß,
1000 Als er der Seuche Ziel gesetzt.
Auch damals Ihr, ein junger Mann,
Ihr gingt in jedes Krankenhaus,
Gar manche Leiche trug man fort,
Ihr aber kamt gesund heraus,
1005 Bestandet manche harte Proben;
Dem Helfer half der Helfer droben.

ALLE:

Gesundheit dem bewährten Mann,
Daß er noch lange helfen kann!

FAUST:

Vor jenem droben steht gebückt,
1010 Der helfen lehrt und Hilfe schickt.
(Er geht mit Wagnern weiter.)

That you don't spurn us on this day
But find into this swarming throng,
Though a great scholar, still your way.
So please accept the finest mug;
With a good drink it has been filled,
I offer it and wish aloud:
Not only may your thirst be stilled;
As many drops as it conveys
Ought to be added to your days.

FAUST:

I take the bumper and I, too,
Thank and wish health to all of you.

(The people gather around in a circle.)

OLD PEASANT:

Indeed, it is most kind of you
That you appear this happy day;
When evil days came in the past,
You always helped in every way.
And many stand here, still alive,
Whom your good father toiled to wrest
From the hot fever's burning rage
When he prevailed over the pest.
And you, a young man at that time,
Made to the sick your daily round.
While many corpses were brought out,
You always emerged safe and sound,
And took these trials in your stride:
The Helper helped the helper here.

ALL:

Health to the man so often tried!
May he yet help for many a year!

FAUST:

Bow down before Him, all of you,
Who teaches help and sends help, too.
(He walks on with WAGNER.*)*

WAGNER:

Welch ein Gefühl mußt du, o großer Mann,
Bei der Verehrung dieser Menge haben!
O glücklich, wer von seinen Gaben
Solch einen Vorteil ziehen kann!
1015 Der Vater zeigt dich seinem Knaben,
Ein jeder fragt und drängt und eilt,
Die Fiedel stockt, der Tanzer weilt,
Du gehst, in Reihen stehen sie,
Die Mützen fliegen in die Höh;
1020 Und wenig fehlt, so beugen sich die Knie,
Als käm das Venerabile.

FAUST:

Nur wenig Schritte noch hinauf zu jenim Stein;
Hier wollen wir von unsrer Wandrung rasten.
Hier saß ich oft gedankenvoll allein
1025 Und quälte mich mit Beten und mit Fasten.
An Hoffnung reich, im Glauben fest,
Mit Tränen, Seufzen, Händeringen
Dacht ich das Ende jener Pest
Vom Herrn des Himmels zu erzwingen.
1030 Der Menge Beifall tönt mir nun wie Hohn.
O könntest du in meinem Innern lesen,
Wie wenig Vater und Sohn
Solch eines Ruhmes wert gewesen!
Mein Vater war ein dunkler Ehrenmann,
1035 Der über die Natur und ihre heilgen Kreise
In Redlichkeit, jedoch auf seine Weise,
Mit grillenhafter Mühe sann;
Der, in Gesellschaft von Adepten,
Sich in die schwarze Küche schloß
1040 Und nach unendlichen Rezepten
Das Widrige zusammengoß.
Da ward ein roter Leu, ein kühner Freier,
Im lauen Bad der Lilie vermählt
Und beide dann mit offnem Flammenfeuer

WAGNER:

Oh, what a feeling you must have, great man,
When crowds revere you like a mighty lord.
Oh, blessed are all those who can
Employ their gifts for such reward.
The father shows you to his son,
They ask what gives and come and run,
The fiddle stops, the dance is done.
You walk, they stand in rows to see,
Into the air their caps will fly—
A little more, and they would bend their knee
As if the Holy Host went by.

FAUST:

Now just a few more steps uphill to the big stone,
From our wandering we can rest up there.
I often sat there, thoughtful and alone,
And vexed myself with fasting and with prayer.
In hope still rich, with faith still blessed,
I thought entreaties, tears, and sighs
Would force the Master of the Skies
To put an end to the long pest.
The crowd's applause now sounds like caustic fun.
I only wish you could read in my heart
How little father and son
Deserve such fame for their poor art.
My father was obscure, if quite genteel,
And pondered over nature and every sacred
  sphere
In his own cranky way, though quite sincere,
With ardent, though with wayward, zeal.
And with proficient devotees,
In his black kitchen he would fuse
After unending recipes,
Locked in, the most contrary brews.
They made red lions, a bold wooer came,
In tepid baths was mated to a lilly;

1045 Aus einem Brautgemach ins andere gequält.
Erschien darauf mit bunten Farben
Die junge Königin im Glas,
Hier war die Arzenei, die Patienten starben,
Und niemand fragte: wer genas?
1050 So haben wir mit höllischen Latwergen
In diesen Tälern, diesen Bergen
Weit schlimmer als die Pest getobt.
Ich habe selbst den Gift an Tausende gegeben:
Sie welkten hin, ich muß erleben,
1055 Daß man die frechen Mörder lobt.

WAGNER:
Wie könnt Ihr Euch darum betrüben!
Tut nicht ein braver Mann genug,
Die Kunst, die man ihm übertrug,
Gewissenhaft und pünktlich auszuüben?
1060 Wenn du als Jüngling deinen Vater ehrst,
So wirst du gern von ihm empfangen;
Wenn du als Mann die Wissenschaft vermehrst,
So kann dein Sohn zu höhrem Ziel gelangen.

FAUST:
O glücklich, wer noch hoffen kann,
1065 Aus diesem Meer des Irrtums aufzutauchen!
Was man nicht weiß, das eben brauchte man,
Und was man weiß, kann man nicht brauchen.
Doch laß uns dieser Stunde schönes Gut
Durch solchen Trübsinn nicht verkümmern!
1070 Betrachte, wie in Abendsonneglut
Die grünumgebnen Hütten schimmern!
Sie rückt und weicht, der Tag ist überlebt,
Dort eilt sie hin und fördert neues Leben.
O daß kein Flügel mich vom Boden hebt,
1075 Ihr nach und immer nach zu streben!

And then the pair was vexed with a wide-open flame
From one bride chamber to another, willy-nilly.
And when the queen appeared, all pied,
Within the glass after a spell,
The medicine was there, and though the patients died,
Nobody questioned: who got well?
And thus we raged fanatically
In these same mountains, in this valley,
With hellish juice worse than the pest.
Though thousands died from poison that I myself would give,
Yes, though they perished, I must live
To hear the shameless killers blessed.

WAGNER:

I cannot see why you are grieved.
What more can honest people do
Than be conscientious and pursue
With diligence the art that they received?
If you respect your father as a youth,
You'll learn from him what you desire;
If as a man you add your share of truth
To ancient lore, your son can go still higher.

FAUST:

Oh, happy who still hopes to rise
Out of this sea of errors and false views!
What one does *not* know, one could utilize,
And what one knows one cannot use.
But let the beauty offered by this hour
Not be destroyed by our spleen!
See how, touched by the sunset's parting power,
The huts are glowing in the green.
The sun moves on, the day has had its round;
He hastens on, new life greets his salute.
Oh, that no wings lift me above the ground
To strive and strive in his pursuit!

Ich säh im ewigen Abendstrahl
Die stille Welt zu meinen Füßen,
Entzündet alle Höhn, beruhigt jedes Tal,
Den Silberbach in goldne Ströme fließen.
1080 Nicht hemmte dann den göttergleichen Lauf
Der wilde Berg mit allen seinen Schluchten;
Schon tut das Meer sich mit erwärmten Buchten
Vor den erstaunten Augen auf.
Doch scheint die Göttin endlich wegzusinken;
1085 Allein der neue Trieb erwacht,
Ich eile fort, ihr ewges Licht zu trinken,
Vor mir den Tag und hinter mir die Nacht,
Den Himmel über mir und unter mir die Wellen.
Ein schöner Traum, indessen sie entweicht.
1090 Ach, zu des Geistes Flügeln wird so leicht
Kein körperlicher Flügel sich gesellen.
Doch ist es jedem eingeboren,
Daß sein Gefühl hinauf und vorwärts dringt,
Wenn über uns, im blauen Raum verloren,
1095 Ihr schmetternd Lied die Lerche singt;
Wenn über schroffen Fichtenhöhen
Der Adler ausgebreitet schwebt,
Und über Flächen, über Seen
Der Kranich nach der Heimat strebt.

WAGNER:

1100 Ich hatte selbst oft grillenhafte Stunden,
Doch solchen Trieb hab ich noch nie empfunden.
Man sieht sich leicht an Wald und Feldern satt;
Des Vogels Fittich werd ich nie beneiden.
Wie anders tragen uns die Geistesfreuden
1105 Von Buch zu Buch, von Blatt zu Blatt!
Da werden Winternächte hold und schön,
Ein selig Leben wärmet alle Glieder,
Und ach, entrollst du gar ein würdig Pergamen
So steigt der ganze Himmel zu dir nieder.

In the eternal evening light
The quiet world would lie below
With every valley tranquil, on fire every height,
The silver stream to golden rivers flow.
Nor could the mountain with its savage guise
And all its gorges check my godlike ways;
Already ocean with its glistening bays
Spreads out before astonished eyes.
At last the god sinks down, I seem forsaken;
But I feel new unrest awaken
And hurry hence to drink his deathless light,
The day before me, and behind me night,
The billows under me, and over me the sky.
A lovely dream, while he makes his escape.
The spirit's wings will not change our shape:
Our body grows no wings and cannot fly.
Yet it is innate in our race
That our feelings surge in us and long
When over us, lost in the azure space
The lark trills out her glorious song;
When over crags where fir trees quake
In icy winds, the eagle soars,
And over plains and over lakes
The crane returns to homeward shores.

WAGNER:

I, too, have spells of eccentricity,
But such unrest has never come to me.
One soon grows sick of forest, field, and brook,
And I shall never envy birds their wings.
Far greater are the joys the spirit brings—
From page to page, from book to book.
Thus winter nights grow fair and warm the soul;
Yes, blissful life suffuses every limb,
And when one opens up an ancient parchment
scroll,
The very heavens will descend on him.

FAUST:

1110 Du bist dir nur des einen Triebs bewußt,
O lerne nie den andern kennen!
Zwei Seelen wohnen, ach, in meiner Brust,
Die eine will sich von der andern trennen:
Die eine hält, in derber Liebeslust,
1115 Sich an die Welt mit klammernden Organen;
Die andre hebt gewaltsam sich vom Dunst
Zu den Gefilden hoher Ahnen.
O gibt es Geister in der Luft,
Die zwischen Erd und Himmel herrschend
weben,
1120 So steiget nieder aus dem goldnen Duft
Und führt mich weg zu neuem, buntem Leben!
Ja, wäre nur ein Zaubermantel mein,
Und trüg er mich in fremde Länder!
Mir sollt er um die köstlichsten Gewänder,
1125 Nicht feil um einen Königsmantel sein.

WAGNER:

Berufe nicht die wohlbekannte Schar,
Die strömend sich im Dunstkreis überbreitet,
Dem Menschen tausendfältige Gefahr
Von allen Enden her bereitet.
1130 Von Norden dringt der scharfe Geisterzahn
Auf dich herbei mit pfeilgespitzen Zungen;
Von Morgen ziehn vertrocknend sie heran
Und nähren sich von deinen Lungen;
Wenn sie der Mittag aus der Wüste schickt,
1135 Die Glut auf Glut um deinen Scheitel häufen,
So bringt der West den Schwarm, der erst
erquickt,
Um dich und Feld und Aue zu ersäufen.
Sie hören gern, zum Schaden froh gewandt,
Gehorchen gern, weil sie uns gern betrügen;
1140 Sie stellen wie vom Himmel sich gesandt
Und lispeln englisch, wenn sie lügen.
Doch gehen wir! Ergraut ist schon die Welt,

FAUST:

You are aware of only one unrest;
Oh, never learn to know the other!
Two souls, alas, are dwelling in my breast,
And one is striving to forsake its brother.
Unto the world in grossly loving zest,
With clinging tendrils, one adheres;
The other rises forcibly in quest
Of rarefied ancestral spheres.
If there be spirits in the air
That hold their sway between the earth and sky,
Descend out of the golden vapors there
And sweep me into iridescent life.
Oh, came a magic cloak into my hands
To carry me to distant lands,
I should not trade it for the choicest gown,
Nor for the cloak and garments of the crown.

WAGNER:

Do not invoke the well-known throng that flow
Through mists above and spread out in the haze,
Concocting danger in a thousand ways
For man wherever he may go.
From the far north the spirits' deadly fangs
Bear down on you with arrow-pointed tongues;
And from the east they come with withering pangs
And nourish themselves from your lungs.
The midday sends out of the desert those
Who pile heat upon heat upon your crown,
While evening brings the throng that spells
repose—
And then lets you, and fields and meadows, drown.
They gladly listen, but are skilled in harm,
Gladly obey, because they like deceit;
As if from heaven sent, they please and charm,
Whispering like angels when they cheat.
But let us go! The air has cooled, the world

Die Luft gekühlt, der Nebel fällt.
Am Abend schätzt man erst das Haus.—
1145 Was stehst du so und blickst erstaunt hinaus?
Was kann dich in der Dämmrung so ergreifen?

FAUST:
Sieht du den schwarzen Hund durch Saat und Stoppel streifen?

WAGNER:
Ich sah ihn lange schon, nicht wichtig schien er mir.

FAUST:
Betracht ihn recht! Für was hältst du das Tier?

WAGNER:
1150 Für einen Pudel, der auf seine Weise
Sich auf der Spur des Herren plagt.

FAUST:
Bemerkst du, wie in weitem Schneckenkreise
Er um uns her und immer näher jagt?
Und irr ich nicht, so zieht ein Feuerstrudel
1155 Auf seinen Pfaden hinterdrein.

WAGNER:
Ich sehe nichts als einen schwarzen Pudel;
Es mag bei Euch wohl Augentäuschung sein.

FAUST:
Mir scheint es, daß er magisch leise Schlingen
Ku künftgem Band um unsre Füße zieht.

WAGNER:
1160 Ich seh ihn ungewiß und furchtsam uns umspringen,
Weil er statt seines Herrn zwei Unbekannte sieht.

FAUST:
Der Kreis wird eng, schon ist er nah!

WAGNER:
Du siehst, ein Hund und kein Gespenst ist da.
Er knurrt und zweifelt, legt sich auf den Bauch,

Turned gray, mists are unfurled.
When evening comes one values home,
Why do you stand amazed? What holds your eyes?
What in the twilight merits such surprise?

FAUST:
See that black dog through grain and stubble roam?

WAGNER:
I noticed him way back, but cared not in the least.

FAUST:
Look well! For what would *you* take this strange beast?

WAGNER:
Why, for a poodle fretting doggedly
As it pursues the tracks left by its master.

FAUST:
It spirals all around us, as you see,
And it approaches, fast and faster.
And if I do not err, a fiery eddy
Whirls after it and marks the trail.

WAGNER:
I see the poodle, as I said already;
As for the rest, your eyesight seems to fail.

FAUST:
It seems to me that he winds magic snares
Around our feet, a bond of future dangers.

WAGNER:
He jumps around, unsure, and our presence scares
The dog who seeks his master, and finds instead two strangers.

FAUST:
The spiral narrows, he is near!

WAGNER:
You see, a dog and not a ghost is here.
He growls, lies on his belly, thus he waits,

1165 Er wedelt. Alles Hundebrauch.

FAUST:

Geselle dich zu uns! Komm hier!

WAGNER:

Es ist ein pudelnärrisch Tier.
Du stehest still, er wartet auf;
Du sprichst ihn an, er strebt an dir hinauf;
1170 Verliere was, er wird es bringen,
Nach deinem Stock ins Wasser springen.

FAUST:

Du hast wohl recht, ich finde nicht die Spur
Von einem Geist, und alles ist Dressur.

WAGNER:

Dem Hunde, wenn er gut gezogen,
1175 Wird selbst ein weiser Mann gewogen.
Ja, deine Gunst verdient er ganz und gar,
Er, der Studenten trefflicher Skolar.

(Sie gehen in das Stadttor.)

STUDIERZIMMER

FAUST *(mit dem Pudel hereintretend):*

Verlassen hab ich Feld und Auen,
Die eine tiefe Nacht bedeckt,
1180 Mit ahnungsvollem, heilgem Grauen
In uns die bessre Seele weckt.
Entschlafen sind nun wilde Triebe
Mit jedem ungestümen Tun,
Es reget sich die Menschenliebe,
1185 Die Liebe Gottes regt sich nun.

He wags his tail: all canine traits.

FAUST:

Come here and walk along with us!

WAGNER:

He's poodlishly ridiculous.
You stand and rest, and he waits, too;
You speak to him, and he would climb on you;
Lose something, he will bring it back again,
Jump in the lake to get your cane.

FAUST:

You seem quite right, I find, for all his skill,
No trace of any spirit: all is drill.

WAGNER:

By dogs that are expertly trained
The wisest man is entertained.
He quite deserves your favor: it is prudent
To cultivate the students' noble student.

(They pass through the City Gate.)

STUDY

FAUST *(entering with the poodle):*

The fields and meadows I have fled
As night enshrouds them and the lakes;
With apprehensive, holy dread
The better soul in us awakes.
Wild passions have succumbed to sleep,
All vehement exertions bow;
The love of man stirs in us deep,
The love of God is stirring now.

Sei ruhig, Pudel! Renne nicht hin und wider!
An der Schwelle was schnopperst du hier?
Lege dich hinter den Ofen nieder!
Mein bestes Kissen geb ich dir.
1190 Wie du draußen auf dem bergigen Wege
Durch Rennen und Springen ergetzt uns hast,
So nimm nun auch von mir die Pflege
Als ein willkommner stiller Gast!

Ach, wenn in unsrer engen Zelle
1195 Die Lampe freundlich wieder brennt,
Dann wird's in unserm Busen helle,
Im Herzen, das sich selber kennt.
Vernunft fängt wieder an zu sprechen
Und Hoffnung wieder an zu blühn,
1200 Man sehnt sich nach des Lebens Bächen,
Ach, nach des Lebens Quelle hin.

Knurre nicht, Pudel! Zu den heiligen Tönen,
Die jetzt meine ganze Seel umfassen,
Will der tierische Laut nicht passen.
1205 Wir sind gewohnt, daß die Menschen verhöhnen,
Was sie nicht verstehn,
Daß sie vor dem Guten und Schönen,
Das ihnen oft beschwerlich ist, murren;
Will es der Hund, wie sie, beknurren?

1210 Aber ach, schon fühl ich bei dem besten Willen,
Befriedigung nicht mehr aus dem Busen quillen.
Aber warum muß der Strom so bald versiegen
Und wir wieder im Dunste liegen?
Davon hab ich so viel Erfahrung.
1215 Doch dieser Mangel läßt sich ersetzen,
Wir lernen das Überirdische schätzen,
Wir sehnen uns nach Offenbarung,

Be quiet, poodle! Stop running around!
Why do you snuffle at the sill like that?
Lie down behind the stove—not on the ground:
Take my best cushion for a mat.
As you amused us on our way
With running and jumping and did your best,
Let me look after you and say:
Be quiet, please, and be my guest.

When in our narrow den
The friendly lamp glows on the shelf,
Then light pervades our breast again
And fills the heart that knows itself.
Reason again begins to speak,
Hope blooms again with ancient force,
One longs for life and one would seek
Its rivers and, alas, its source.

Stop snarling poodle! For the sacred strain
To which my soul is now submitting
Beastly sounds are hardly fitting.
We are accustomed to see *men* disdain
What they don't grasp;
When it gives trouble, they profane
Even the beautiful and the good.
Do dogs, too, snarl at what's not understood?

Even now, however, though I tried my best,
Contentment flows no longer through my
breast.
Why does the river rest so soon, and dry up,
and
Leave us to languish in the sand?
How well I know frustration!
This want, however, we can overwhelm:
We turn to the supernatural realm,
We long for the light of revelation

Die nirgends würdger und schöner brennt
Als in dem Neuen Testament.
1220 Mich drängt's den Grundtext aufzuschlagen,
Mit redlichem Gefühl einmal
Das heilige Original
In mein geliebtes Deutsch zu übertragen.

(Er schlägt ein Volum auf und schickt sich an)
Geschrieben steht: «Im Anfang war das Wort!»
1225 Hier stock ich schon! Wer hilft mir weiter fort?
Ich kann das Wort so hoch unmöglich schätzen,
Ich muß es anders übersetzen,
Wenn ich vom Geiste recht erleuchtet bin.
Geschrieben steht: Im Anfang war der Sinn.
1230 Bedenke wohl die erste Zeile,
Daß deine Feder sich nicht übereile!
Ist es der Sinn, der alles wirkt und schafft?
Es sollte stehn: Im Anfang war die Kraft!
Doch, auch indem ich dieses niederschreibe,
1235 Schon warnt mich was, daß ich dabei nicht bleibe.
Mir hilft der Geist, auf einmal seh ich Rat
Und schreibe getrost: Im Anfang war die Tat!

Soll ich mit dir das Zimmer teilen,
Pudel, so laß das Heulen,
1240 So laß das Bellen!
Solch einen störenden Gesellen
Mag ich nicht in der Nähe leiden.
Einer von uns beiden
Muß die Zelle meiden.
1245 Ungern heb ich das Gastrecht auf,
Die Tür ist offen, hast freien Lauf.
Aber was muß ich sehen?
Kann das natürlich geschehen?
Ist es Schatten? Ist's Wirklichkeit?
1250 Wie wird mein Pudel lang und breit!
Er hebt sich mit Gewalt,

Which is nowhere more magnificent
Than in our New Testament.
I would for once like to determine—
Because I am sincerely perplexed—
How the sacred original text
Could be translated into my beloved
German.

(He opens a tome and begins.)

It says: "In the beginning was the *Word.*"
Already I am stopped. It seems absurd.
The *Word* does not deserve the highest prize,
I must translate it otherwise
If I am well inspired and not blind.
It says: In the beginning was the *Mind.*
Ponder that first line, wait and see,
Lest you should write too hastily.
Is mind the all-creating source?
It ought to say: In the beginning there was *Force.*
Yet something warns me as I grasp the pen,
That my translation must be changed again.
The spirit helps me. Now it is exact.
I write: In the beginning was the *Act.*

If I am to share my room with you,
Poodle, stop moaning so!
And stop your bellow,
For such a noisy, whiny fellow
I do not like to have around.
One of us, black hound,
Will have to give ground.
With reluctance I change my mind:
The door is open, you are not confined.
But what must I see!
Can that happen naturally?
Is it a shadow? Am I open-eyed?
How grows my poodle long and wide!
He reaches up like rising fog—

Das ist nicht eines Hundes Gestalt!
Welch ein Gespenst bracht ich ins Haus!
Schon sieht er wie ein Nilpferd aus
1255 Mit feurigen Augen, schrecklichem Gebiß.
O! Du bist mir gewiß!
Für solche halbe Höllenbrut
Ist Salomonis Schlüssel gut.

GEISTER *(auf dem Gange):*

Drinnen gefangen ist einer!
1260 Bleibet haußen, folg ihm keiner!
Wie im Eisen der Fuchs
Zagt ein alter Höllenluchs.
Aber gebt acht!
Schwebet hin, schwebet wider,
1265 Auf und nieder,
Und er hat sich losgemacht.
Könnt ihr ihm nützen,
Laßt ihn nicht sitzen!
Denn er tat uns allen
1270 Schon viel zu Gefallen.

FAUST:

Erst zu begegnen dem Tiere,
Brauch ich den Spruch der Viere:

Salamander soll glühen,
Undene sich winden,
1275 Sylphe verschwinden,
Kobold sich mühen!

Wer sie nicht kennte,
Die Elemente,
Ihre Kraft
1280 Und Eigenschaft,
Wäre kein Meister
Über die Geister.

This is no longer the shape of a dog!
Oh, what a specter I brought home!
A hippopotamus of foam,
With fiery eyes; how his teeth shine!
You are as good as mine:
For such a semi-hellish brow
The Key of Solomon will do.

SPIRITS *(in the corridor):*

One has been caught inside.
Do not follow him! Abide!
As a fox in a snare,
Hell's old lynx is caught in there.
But give heed!
Float up high, float down low,
To and fro,
And he tries, and he is freed.
Can you avail him?
Then do not fail him!
For you must not forget,
We are in his debt.

FAUST:

Countering the beast, I might well
First use the fourfold spell:

Salamander shall broil,
Undene shall grieve,
Sylphe shall leave,
Kobold shall toil.

Whoever ignores
The elements' cores,
Their energy
And quality,
Cannot command
In the spirits' land.

Verschwind in Flammen,
Salamander!
1285 Rauschend fließe zusammen,
Undene!
Leucht in Meteoren-Schöne,
Sylphe!
Bring häusliche Hilfe,
1290 Incubus! Incubus!
Tritt hervor und mache den Schluß!

Keines der Viere
Steckt in dem Tiere.
Es liegt ganz ruhig und grinst mich an,
1295 Ich hab ihm noch nicht weh getan.
Du sollst mich hören
Stärker beschwören.

Bist du, Geselle,
Ein Flüchtling der Hölle?
1300 So sieh dies Zeichen,
Dem sie sich beugen,
Die schwarzen Scharen!

Schon schwillt es auf mit borstigen Haaren.

Verworfnes Wesen!
1305 Kannst du ihn lesen?
Den nie entsproßnen,
Unausgesprochnen,
Durch alle Himmel gegoßen,
Freventlich durchstochnen?

1310 Hinter den Ofen gebannt,
Schwillt es wie ein Elefant,
Den ganzen Raum füllt es an,
Es will zum Nebel zerfließen.
Steige nicht zur Decke hinan!
1315 Lege dich zu des Meisters Füßen!

Disappear flashing,
Salamander!
Flow together, splashing,
Undene!
Glow in meteoric beauty,
Sylphe!
Do your domestic duty,
Incubus! Incubus!
Step forward and finish thus.

None of the four
Is this beast's core.
It lies quite calmly there and beams;
I have not hurt it yet, it seems.
Now listen well
To a stronger spell.

If you should be
Hell's progeny,
Then see this symbol
Before which tremble
The cohorts of Hell!

Already it bristles and starts to swell.

Spirit of shame,
Can you read the name
Of the Uncreated,
Defying expression,
With whom the heavens are sated,
Who was pierced in transgression?

Behind the stove it swells
As an elephant under my spells;
It fills the whole room and quakes,
It would turn into mist and fleet.
Stop now before the ceiling breaks!
Lie down at your master's feet!

Du siehst, daß ich nicht vergebens drohe.
Ich versenge dich mit heiliger Lohe!
Erwart nicht
Das dreimal glühende Licht!
1320 Erwarte nicht
Die stärkste von meinen Künsten!

MEPHISTOPHELES *(tritt, indem der Nebel fällt, gekleidet wie ein fahrender Scholastikus hinter dem Ofen hervor):*
Wozu der Lärm? Was steht dem Herrn zu Diensten?

FAUST:
Das also war des Pudels Kern!
Ein fahrender Skolast? Der Kasus macht mich lachen.

MEPHISTOPHELES:
1325 Ich salutiere den gelehrten Herrn!
Ihr habt mich weidlich schwitzen machen.

FAUST:
Wie nennst du dich?

MEPHISTOPHELES:
Die Frage scheint mir klein
Für einen, der das Wort so sehr verachtet,
Der, weit entfernt von allem Schein,
1330 Nur in der Wesen Tiefe trachtet.

FAUST:
Bei euch, ihr Herrn, kann man das Wesen
Gewöhnlich aus dem Namen lesen,
Wo es sich allzu deutlich weist,
Wenn man euch Fliegengott, Verderber, Lügner heißt.
1335 Nun gut wer bist du denn?

MEPHISTOPHELES:
Ein Teil von jener Kraft,
Die stets das Böse will und stets das Gute schafft.

You see, I do not threaten in vain:
With holy flames I cause you pain.
Do not require
The threefold glowing fire!
Do not require
My art in its full measure!

MEPHISTO *(steps forward from behind the stove, dressed as a traveling scholar, while the mist clears away):*
Why all the noise? Good sir, what is your pleasure?

FAUST:
Then this was our poodle's core!
Simply a traveling scholar? The *casus* makes me laugh.

MEPHISTO:
Profound respects to you and to your lore:
You made me sweat with all your chaff.

FAUST:
What is your name?

MEPHISTO:
This question seems minute
For one who thinks the word so beggarly,
Who holds what seems in disrepute,
And craves only reality.

FAUST:
Your real being no less than your fame
Is often shown, sirs, by your name,
Which is not hard to analyze
When one calls you the Liar, Destroyer, God of Flies.
Enough, who are you then?

MEPHISTO:
Part of that force which would
Do evil evermore, and yet creates the good.

FAUST:

Was ist mit diesem Rätselwort gemeint?

MEPHISTOPHELES:

Ich bin der Geist, der stets verneint!
Und das mit Recht; denn alles, was entsteht,
1340 Ist wert, daß es zugrunde geht;
Drum besser wär's, daß nichts entstünde.
So ist denn alles, was ihr Sünde,
Zerstörung, kurz das Böse nennt,
Mein eigentliches Element.

FAUST:

1345 Du nennst dich einen Teil und stehst doch ganz
vor mir?

MEPHISTOPHELES:

Bescheidne Wahrheit sprech ich dir.
Wenn sich der Mensch, die kleine Narrenwelt,
Gewöhnlich für ein Ganzes hält—
Ich bin ein Teil des Teils, der anfangs alles war,
1350 Ein Teil der Finsternis, die sich das Licht gebar,
Das stolze Licht, das nun der Mutter Nacht
Den alten Rang, den Raum ihr streitig macht,
Und doch gelingt's ihm nicht, da es, soviel es
strebt,
Verhaftet an den Körpern klebt.
1355 Von Körpern strömt's, die Körper macht es schön,
Ein Körper hemmt's auf seinem Gange;
So, hoff ich, dauert es nicht lange,
Und mit den Körpern wird's zugrunde gehn.

FAUST:

Nun kenn ich deine würdgen Pflichten!
1360 Du kannst im Großen nichts vernichten
Und fängst es nun im Kleinen an.

MEPHISTOPHELES:

Und freilich ist nicht viel damit getan.
Was sich dem Nichts entegegenstellt,
Das Etwas, diese plumpe Welt,
1365 So viel als ich schon unternommen,

FAUST:

What is it that this puzzle indicates?

MEPHISTO:

I am the spirit that negates.
And rightly so, for all that comes to be
Deserves to perish wretchedly;
'Twere better nothing would begin.
Thus everything that your terms, sin,
Destruction, evil represent—
That is my proper element.

FAUST:

You call yourself a part, yet whole make your
debut?

MEPHISTO:

The modest truth I speak to you.
While man, this tiny world of fools, is droll
Enough to think himself a whole,
I am part of the part that once was everything,
Part of the darkness which gave birth to light,
That haughty light which envies mother night
Her ancient rank and place and would be king—
Yet it does not succeed: however it contend,
It sticks to bodies in the end.
It streams from bodies, it lends bodies beauty,
A body won't let it progress;
So it will not take long, I guess,
And with the bodies it will perish, too.

FAUST:

I understand your noble duty:
Too weak for great destruction, you
Attempt it on a minor scale.

MEPHISTO:

And I admit it is of slight avail.
What stands opposed to our Nought,
The some, your wretched world—for aught
That I have so far undertaken,

Ich wußte nicht, ihr beizukommen
Mit Wellen, Stürmen, Schütteln, Brand—
Geruhig bleibt an Ende Meer und Land.
Und dem verdammten Zeug, der Tier-und
Menschenbrut,
1370 Dem ist nun gar nichts anzuhaben:
Wie viele hab ich schon begraben!
Und immer zirkuliert ein neues; frisches Blut.
So geht es fort, man möchte rasend werden!
Der Luft, dem Wasser, wie der Erden
1375 Entwinden tausend Keime sich,
Im Trocknen, Feuchten, Warmen, Kalten.
Hätt ich mir nicht die Flamme vorbehalten,
Ich hätte nichts Aparts für mich.

FAUST:
So setzest du der ewig regen,
1380 Der heilsam schaffenden Gewalt
Die kalte Teufelsfaust entgegen,
Die sich vergebens tückisch ballt.
Was anders suche zu beginnen,
Des Chaos wunderlicher Sohn!

MEPHISTOPHELES:
1385 Wir wollen wirklich uns besinnen,
Die nächsten Male mehr davon!
Dürft ich wohl diesmal mich entfernen?

FAUST:
Ich sehe nicht, warum du fragst.
Ich habe jetzt dich kennen lernen,
1390 Besuche nun mich, wie du magst!
Hier ist das Fenster, hier die Türe,
Ein Rauchfang ist dir auch gewiß.

MEPHISTOPHELES:
Gesteh ich's nur! Daß ich hinausspaziere,
Verbietet mir ein kleines Hindernis,
1395 Der Drundenfuß auf Eurer Schwelle—

FAUST:
Das Pentagramma macht dir Pein?

It stands unruffled and unshaken:
With billows, fires, storms, commotion,
Calm, after all, remain both land and ocean.
And that accursed lot, the brood of beasts and
men,
One cannot hurt them anyhow.
How many have I buried now!
Yet always fresh new blood will circulate again.
Thus it goes on—I could rage in despair!
From water, earth, and even air,
A thousand seeds have ever grown
In warmth and cold and drought and mire!
If I had not reserved myself the fire,
I should have nothing of my own.

FAUST:

And thus, I see, you would resist
The ever-live creative power
By clenching your cold devil's fist
Resentfully—in vain you glower.
Try something new and unrelated,
Oh you peculiar son of chaos!

MEPHISTO:

Perchance your reasoning might sway us—
The next few times we may debate it.
But for the present, may I go?

FAUST:

I cannot see why you inquire.
Now that we met, you ought to know
That you may call as you desire.
Here is the window, here the door,
A chimney there, if that's preferred.

MEPHISTO:

I cannot leave you that way, I deplore:
By a small obstacle I am deterred:
The witch's foot on your threshold, see—

FAUST:

The pentagram distresses you?

Ei sage mir, du Sohn der Hölle,
Wenn das dich bannt, wie kamst du denn herein?
Wie ward ein solcher Geist betrogen?

MEPHISTOPHELES:

1400 Beschaut es recht! Es ist nicht gut gezogen:
Der eine Winkel, der nach außen zu,
Ist, wie du siehst, ein wenig offen.

FAUST:

Das hat der Zufall gut getroffen!
Und mein Gefangner wärst denn du?
1405 Das ist von ohngefähr gelungen!

MEPHISTOPHELES:

Der Pudel merkte nichts, als er hereingesprungen.
Die Sache sieht jetzt anders aus:
Der Teufel kann nicht aus dem Haus.

FAUST:

Doch warum gehst du nicht durchs Fenster?

MEPHISTOPHELES:

1410 's ist ein Gesetz der Teufel und Gespenster:
Wo sie hereingeschlüpft, da müssen sie hinaus.
Das erste steht uns frei, beim zweiten sind wir
Knechte.

FAUST:

Die Hölle selbst hat ihre Rechte?
Das find ich gut, da ließe sich ein Pakt,
1415 Und sicher wohl, mit euch, ihr Herren, schließen?

MEPHISTOPHELES:

Was man verspricht, das sollst du rein genießen,
Dir wird davon nichts abgezwackt.
Doch das ist nicht so kurz zu fassen,
Und wir besprechen das zunächst;
1420 Doch jetzo bitt ich hoch und höchst,
Für dieses Mal mich zu entlassen.

FAUST:

So bleibe doch noch einen Augenblick,

Then, son of hell, explain to me:
How could you enter here without ado?
And how was such a spirit cheated?

MEPHISTO:
Behold it well: It is not quite completed;
One angle—that which points outside—
Is open just a little bit.

FAUST:
That was indeed a lucky hit.
I caught you and you must abide.
How wonderful, and yet how queer!

MEPHISTO:
The poodle never noticed, when he first jumped
in here,
But now it is a different case;
The Devil cannot leave this place.

FAUST:
The window's there. Are you in awe?

MEPHISTO:
The devils and the demons have a law:
Where they slipped in, they always must
withdraw.
The first time we are free, the second time
constrained.

FAUST:
For hell, too, laws have been ordained?
Superb! Then one could surely make a pact,
And one of you might enter my employ.

MEPHISTO:
What we would promise you, you would enjoy,
And none of it we would subtract.
But that we should not hurry so,
And we shall talk about it soon;
For now I ask the single boon
That you permit me now to go.

FAUST:
For just a moment stay with me

Um mir erst gute Mär zu sagen.

MEPHISTOPHELES:

Jetzt laß mich los! Ich komme bald zurück,

1425 Dann magst du nach Belieben fragen.

FAUST:

Ich habe dir nicht nachgestellt

Bist du doch selbst ins Garn gegangen.

Den Teufel halte, wer ihn hält!

Er wird ihn nicht so bald zum zweiten Male fangen.

MEPHISTOPHELES:

1430 Wenn dir's beliebt, so bin ich auch bereit,

Dir zur Gesellschaft hier zu bleiben;

Doch mit Bedingnis, dir die Zeit

Durch meine Künste würdig zu vertreiben.

FAUST:

Ich seh es gern, steht dir frei;

1435 Nur daß die Kunst gefällig sei!

MEPHISTOPHELES:

Du wirst, mein Freund, für deine Sinnen

In dieser Stunde mehr gewinnen

Als in des Jahres Einerlei.

Was dir die zarten Geister singen,

1440 Die schönen Bilder, die sie bringen,

Sind nicht ein leeres Zauberspiel.

Auch dein Geruch wird sich ergetzen,

Dann wirst du deinen Gaumen letzen,

Und dann entzückt sich dein Gefühl.

1445 Bereitung braucht es nicht voran,

Beisammen sind wir, fangen an!

GEISTER:

Schwindet, ihr dunkeln

Wölbungen droben!

Reizender schaue

1450 Freundlich der blaue

Äther herein!

Wären die dunkeln

And let me have some happy news.

MEPHISTO:

Not now. I'll come back presently,
Then you may ask me what you choose.

FAUST:

You were not caught by my device
When you were snared like this tonight.
Who holds the Devil, hold him tight!
He can't expect to catch him twice.

MEPHISTO:

If you prefer it, I shall stay
With you, and I shall not depart,
Upon condition that I may
Amuse you with some samples of my art.

FAUST:

Go right ahead, you are quite free—
Provided it is nice to see.

MEPHISTO:

Right in this hour you will obtain
More for your senses than you gain
In a whole year's monotony.
What tender spirits now will sing,
The lovely pictures that they bring
Are not mere magic for the eye:
They will delight your sense of smell,
Be pleasing to your taste as well,
Excite your touch, and give you joy.
No preparation needs my art,
We are together, let us start.

SPIRITS:

Vanish, you darkling
Arches above him.
Friendlier beaming,
Sky should be gleaming
Down upon us.
Ah, that the darkling

Wolken zerronnen!
Sternelein funkeln,
1455 Mildere Sonnen
Scheinen darein,
Himmlischer Söhne
Geistige Schöne,
Schwankende Beugung
1460 Schwebet vorüber.
Sehnende Neigung
Folget hinüber;
Und der Gewänder
Flatternde Bänder
1465 Decken die Länder,
Decken die Laube,
Wo sich fürs Leben,
Tief in Gedanken
Liebende geben.
1470 Laube bei Laube!
Sprossende Ranken!
Lastende Traube
Stürzt ins Behälter
Drängender Kelter,
1475 Stürzen in Bächen
Schäumende Weine;
Rieseln durch reine,
Edle Gesteine,
Lassen die Höhen
1480 Hinter sich liegen,
Breiten zu Seen
Sich ums Genügen
Grünender Hügel.
Und das Geflügel
1485 Schlürfet sich Wonne,
Flieget der Sonne,
Flieget den hellen
Inseln entgegen,
Die sich auf Wellen

Clouds had departed!
Stars now are sparkling,
More tenderhearted
Suns shine on us.
Spirits aerial,
Fair and ethereal,
Wavering and bending,
Sail by like swallows.
Yearning unending
Sees them and follows.
Garments are flowing,
Ribbons are blowing,
Covering the glowing
Land and the bower
Where, in the hedges,
Thinking and dreaming,
Lovers make pledges.
Bower on bower.
Tendrils are streaming;
Heavy grapes shower
Their sweet excesses
Into the presses;
In streams are flowing
Wines that are glowing,
Foam, effervescent,
Through iridescent
Gems; they are storming
Down from the mountains;
Lakes they are forming,
Beautiful fountains
Where hills are ending,
Birds are descending,
Drink and fly onward,
Fly ever sunward,
Fly from the highlands
Toward the ocean
Where brilliant islands

1490 Gauklend bewegen;
Wo wir in Chören
Jauchzende hören,
Über den Auen
Tanzende schauen,
1495 Die sich im Freien
Alle zerstreuen.
Einige klimmen
Über die Höhen,
Andere schwimmen
1500 Über die Seen,
Andere schweben;
Alle zum Leben,
Alle zur Ferne
Liebender Sterne,
1505 Seliger Huld.

MEPHISTOPHELES:
Er schläft. So recht, ihr lustgen, zarten Jungen!
Ihr habt ihn treulich eingesungen.
Für dies Konzert bin ich in eurer Schuld.
Du bist noch nicht der Mann, den Teufel festzuhalten!
1510 Umgaukelt ihn mit süßen Traumgestalten,
Versenkt ihn in ein Meer des Wahns!
Doch dieser Schwelle Zauber zu zerspalten,
Bedarf ich eines Rattenzahns.
Nicht lange brauch ich zu beschwören,
1515 Schon raschelt eine hier und wird sogleich mich hören.
Der Herr der Ratten und der Mäuse,
Der Fliegen, Frösche, Wanzen, Läuse
Befiehlt dir, dich hervorzuwagen
Und diese Schwelle zu benagen,
1520 So wie er sie mit Öl betupft—
Da kommst du schon hervorgehupft!
Nur frisch ans Werk! Die Spitze, die mich bannte,
Sie sitzt ganz vornen an der Kante.

Sway in soft motion.
Jubilant choirs
Soothe all desires,
And are entrancing
Those who are dancing
Like whirling satyrs,
But the throng scatters.
Some now are scaling
Over the mountains,
Others are sailing
Toward the fountains,
Others are soaring,
All life adoring,
All crave the far-off
Love-spending star of
Rapturous bliss.

MEPHISTO:

He sleeps. I thank you, airy, tender throng.
You made him slumber with your song.
A splendid concert. I appreciate this.
You are not yet the man to hold the Devil fast.
Go, dazzle him with dream shapes, sweet and vast,
Plunge him into an ocean of untruth.
But now, to break the threshold's spell at last,
I have to get a rat's sharp tooth.
I need no conjuring today,
One's rustling over there and will come right away.
The lord of rats, the lord of mice,
Of flies and frogs, bedbugs and lice,
Bids you to dare now to appear
To gnaw upon this threshold here,
Where he is dabbing it with oil.
Ah, there you come. Begin your toil.
The point that stopped me like a magic hedge
Is way up front, right on the edge.

Noch einen Biß, so ist's geschehn.–
1525 Nun, Fauste, träume fort, bis wir uns wiedersehn!

FAUST *(erwachend):*
Bin ich denn abermals betrogen?
Verschwindet so der geisterreiche Drang,
Daß mir ein Traum den Teufel vorgelogen
Und daß ein Pudel mir entsprang?

STUDIERZIMMER

Faust. Mephistopheles.

FAUST:
1530 Es klopft? Herein! Wer will mich wieder plagen?
MEPHISTOPHELES:
Ich bin's.
FAUST:
Herein!
MEPHISTOPHELES:
Du mußt es dreimal sagen.
FAUST:
Herein denn!
MEPHISTOPHELES:
So gefällst du mir.
Wir werden, hoff ich, uns vertragen;
Denn dir die Grillen zu verjagen,
1535 Bin ich als edler Junker hier
In rotem, goldverbrämtem Kleide,
Das Mäntelchen von starrer Seide,
Die Hahnenfeder auf dem Hut,
Mit einem langen, spitzen Degen,

Just one more bite, and that will do.
Now, Faustus, sleep and dream, till I come back
to you.

FAUST *(awakening)*:
Betrayed again? Fooled by a scheme?
Should spirits' wealth so suddenly decay
That I behold the Devil in a dream,
And that a poodle jumps away?

STUDY

Faust. Mephistopheles.

FAUST:
A knock? Come in! Who comes to plague me now?

MEPHISTO:
It's I.

FAUST:
Come in!

MEPHISTO:
You have to say it thrice.

FAUST:
Come in, then.

MEPHISTO:
Now you're nice.
We should get along well, I vow.
To chase your spleen away, allow
That I appear a noble squire:
Look at my red and gold attire,
A little cloak of silk brocade,
The rooster's feather in my hat,
And the long, nicely pointed blade—

1540 Und rate nun dir kurz und gut,
Dergleichen gleichfalls anzulegen,
Damit du, losgebunden, frei,
Erfahrest, was das Leben sei.

FAUST:

In jedem Kleide werd ich wohl die Pein
1545 Des engen Erdelebens fühlen.
Ich bin zu alt, um nur zu spielen,
Zu jung, um ohne Wunsch zu sein.
Was kann die Welt mir wohl gewähren?
Entbehren sollst du! Sollst entbehren!
1550 Das ist der ewige Gesang,
Der jedem an die Ohren klingt,
Den unser ganzes Leben lang
Uns heiser jede Stunde singt.
Nur mit Entsetzen wach ich morgens auf,
1555 Ich möchte bittre Tränen weinen,
Den Tag zu sehn, der mir in seinem Lauf
Nicht einen Wunsch erfüllen wird, nicht einen,
Der selbst die Ahnung jeder Lust
Mit eigensinnigem Krittel mindert,
1560 Die Schöpfung meiner regen Brust
Mit tausend Lebensfratzen hindert.
Auch muß ich, wenn die Nacht sich niedersenkt,
Mich ängstlich auf das Lager strecken,
Auch da wird keine Rast geschenkt,
1565 Mich werden wilde Träume schrecken.
Der Gott, der mir im Busen wohnt,
Kann tief mein Innerstes erregen,
Der über allen meinen Kräften thront,
Er kann nach außen nichts bewegen;
1570 Und so ist mir das Dasein eine Last,
Der Tod erwünscht, das Leben mir verhaßt.

MEPHISTOPHELES:

Und doch ist nie der Tod ein ganz willkommner
Gast.

And now it is my counsel that
You, too, should be like this arrayed;
Then you would feel released and free,
And you would find what life can be.

FAUST:

I shall not cease to feel in all attires,
The pains of our narrow earthly day.
I am too old to be content to play,
Too young to be without desire.
What wonders could the world reveal?
You must renounce! You ought to yield!
That is the never-ending drone
Which we must, our life long, hear,
Which, hoarsely, all our hours intone
And grind into our weary ears.
Frightened I waken to the dismal dawn,
Wish I had tears to drown the sun
And check the day that soon will scorn
My every wish—fulfill not one.
If I but think of any pleasure,
Bright critic day is sure to chide it,
And if my heart creates itself a treasure,
A thousand mocking masks deride it.
When night descends at last, I shall recline
But anxiously upon my bed;
Though all is still, no rest is mine
As dreams enmesh my mind in dread.
The god that dwells within my heart
Can stir my depths, I cannot hide—
Rules all my powers with relentless art,
But cannot move the world outside;
And thus existence is for me a weight,
Death is desirable, and life I hate.

MEPHISTO:

And yet when death approaches, the welcome is
not great.

FAUST:

O selig der, dem er im Siegesglanze
Die blutgen Lorbeern um die Schläfe windet!
1575 Den er nach rasch durchrastem Tanze
In eines Mädchens Armen findet!
O wär ich vor des hohen Geistes Kraft
Entzückt, entseelt dahingesunken!

MEPHISTOPHELES:

Und doch hat jemand einen braunen Saft,
1580 In jener Nacht, nicht ausgetrunken.

FAUST:

Das Spionieren, scheint's, ist deine Lust.

MEPHISTOPHELES:

Allwissend bin ich nicht; doch viel ist mir bewußt.

FAUST:

Wenn aus dem schrecklichen Gewühle
Ein süß bekannter Ton mich zog,
1585 Den Rest von kindlichem Gefühle
Mit Anklang froher Zeit betrog,
So fluch ich allem, was die Seele
Mit Lock- und Gaukelwerk umspannt
Und sie in diese Trauerhöhle
1590 Mit Blend- und Schmeichelkräften bannt.
Verflucht voraus die hohe Meinung,
Womit der Geist sich selbst umfängt!
Verflucht das Blenden der Erscheinung,
Die sich an unsre Sinne drängt!
1595 Verflucht, was uns in Träumen heuchelt,
Des Ruhms, der Namensdauer Trug!
Verflucht, was als Besitz uns schmeichelt,
Als Weib und Kind, als Knecht und Pflug!
Verflucht sei Mammon, wenn mit Schätzen
1600 Er uns zu kühnen Taten regt,
Wenn er zu müßigem Ergetzen
Die Polster uns zurechte legt!
Fluch sei dem Balsamsaft der Trauben!
Fluch jener höchsten Liebeshuld!

FAUST:

Oh, blessed whom, as victory advances,
He lends the blood-drenched laurel's grace,
Who, after wildly whirling dances,
Receives him in a girl's embrace!
Oh, that before the lofty spirit's power
I might have fallen to the ground, unsouled!

MEPHISTO:

And yet someone, in that same nightly hour
Refused to drain a certain bowl.

FAUST:

You seem to eavesdrop quite proficiently.

MEPHISTO:

Omniscient I am not, but there is much I see.

FAUST:

As in that terrifying reeling
I heard the sweet familiar chimes
That duped the traces of my childhood feeling
With echoes of more joyous times,
I now curse all that would enamor
The human soul with lures and lies,
Enticing it with flattering glamour
To live on in this cave of sighs.
Cursed above all our high esteem,
The spirit's smug self-confidence,
Cursed be illusion, fraud, and dream
That flatter our guileless sense!
Cursed be the pleasing make-believe
Of fame and long posthumous life!
Cursed be possessions that deceive,
As slave and plough, and child and wife!
Cursed, too, be Mammon when with treasures
He spurs us on to daring feats,
Or lures us into slothful pleasures
With sumptuous cushions and smooth sheets!
A curse on wine that mocks our thirst!
A curse on love's last consummations!

1605 Fluch sei der Hoffnung! Fluch dem Glauben
Und Fluch vor allen der Geduld!

GEISTERCHOR *(unsichtbar)*:

Weh! Weh!
Du hast sie zerstört,
Die schöne Welt,
1610 Mit mächtiger Faust,
Sie stürzt, sie zerfällt!
Ein Halbgott hat sie zerschlagen!
Wir tragen
Die Trümmern ins Nichts hinüber
1615 Und klagen
Über die verlorne Schöne.
Mächtiger
Der Erdensöhne,
Prächtiger
1620 Baue sie wieder,
In deinem Busen baue sie auf!
Neuen Lebenslauf
Beginne
Mit hellem Sinne,
1625 Und neue Lieder
Tönen darauf!

MEPHISTOPHELES:

Dies sind die Kleinen
Von den Meinen.
Höre, wie zu Lust und Taten
1630 Altklug sie raten!
In die Welt weit,
Aus der Einsamkeit,
Wo Sinnen und Säfte stocken,
Wollen sie dich locken.

1635 Hör auf, mit deinem Gram zu spielen,
Der wie ein Geier dir am Leben frißt!
Die schlechteste Gesellschaft läßt dich fühlen,
Daß du ein Mensch mit Menschen bist.

A curse on hope! Faith, too, be cursed!
And cursed above all else be patience!

CHOIR OF SPIRITS *(invisible)*:

Alas!
You have shattered
The beautiful world
With brazen fist;
It falls, it is scattered—
By a demigod destroyed.
We are trailing
The ruins into the void
And wailing
Over beauty undone
And ended.
Earth's mighty son,
More splendid
Rebuild it, you that are strong,
Build it again within!
And begin
A new life, a new way,
Lucid and gay,
And play
New songs.

MEPHISTO:

These are the small
Ones of my thralls.
Hear how precociously they plead
For pleasure and deed!
To worldly strife
From your lonely life
Which dries up sap and sense,
They would lure you hence.

Stop playing with your melancholy
That, like a vulture, ravages your breast;
The worst of company still cures this folly,
For you are human with the rest.

Doch so ist's nicht gemeint,
1640 Dich unter das Pack zu stoßen.
Ich bin keiner von den Großen;
Doch willst du mit mir vereint
Deine Schritte durchs Leben nehmen,
So will ich mich gern bequemen,
1645 Dein zu sein auf der Stelle.
Ich bin dein Geselle
Und mach ich dir's recht,
Bin ich dein Diener, bin dein Knecht!

FAUST:
Und was soll ich dagegen dir erfüllen?

MEPHISTOPHELES:
1650 Dazu hast du noch eine lange Frist.

FAUST:
Nein, nein! Der Teufel ist ein Egoist
Und tut nicht leicht um Gottes willen,
Was einem andern nützlich ist.
Sprich die Bedingung deutlich aus!
1655 Ein solcher Diener bringt Gefahr ins Haus.

MEPHISTOPHELES:
Ich will mich h i e r zu deinem Dienst verbinden,
Auf deinen Wink nicht rasten und nicht ruhn;
Wenn wir uns d r ü b e n wiederfinden,
So sollst du mir das gleiche tun.

FAUST:
1660 Das Drüben kann mich wenig kümmern;
Schlägst du erst diese Welt zu Trümmern,
Die andre mag darnach entstehn.
Aus dieser Erde quillen meine Freuden,
Und diese Sonne scheinet meinen Leiden;
1665 Kann ich mich erst von ihnen scheiden,
Dann mag, was will und kann, geschehn.
Davon will ich nichts weiter hören,
Ob man auch künftig haßt und liebt
Und ob es auch in jenen Sphären
1670 Ein Oben oder Unten gibt.

Yet that is surely not to say
That you should join the herd you hate.
I'm not one of the great,
But if you want to make your way
Through the world with me united,
I should surely be delighted
To be yours, as of now,
Your companion, if you allow;
And if you like the way I behave,
I shall be your servant, or your slave.

FAUST:

And in return, what do you hope to take?

MEPHISTO:

There's so much time—so why insist?

FAUST:

No, no! The Devil is an egoist
And would not just for heaven's sake
Turn into a philanthropist.
Make your conditions very clear;
Where such a servant lives, danger is near.

MEPHISTO:

Here you shall be the master, I be bond,
And at your nod I'll work incessantly;
But when we meet again *beyond*,
Then you shall do the same for me.

FAUST:

Of the beyond I have no thought;
When you reduce this world to nought,
The other one may have its turn.
My joys come from this earth, and there,
That sun has burnt on my despair:
Once I have left those, I don't care:
What happens is of no concern.
I do not even wish to hear
Whether beyond they hate and love,
And whether in that other sphere
One realm's below and one above.

MEPHISTOPHELES:
In diesem Sinne kannst du's wagen.
Verbinde dich! Du sollst in diesen Tagen
Mit Freuden meine Künste sehn,
Ich gebe dir, was noch kein Mensch gesehn.

FAUST:
1675 Was willst du armer Teufel geben?
Ward eines Menschen Geist in seinem hohen
Streben
Von deinesgleichen je gefaßt?
Doch hast du Speise, die nicht sättigt, hast
Du rotes Gold, das ohne Rast,
1680 Quecksilber gleich, dir in der Hand zerrinnt,
Ein Spiel, bei dem man nie gewinnt,
Ein Mädchen, das an meiner Brust
Mit Äugeln schon dem Nachbar sich verbindet,
Der Ehre schöne Götterlust,
1685 Die wie ein Meteor verschwindet?
Zeig mir die Frucht, die fault, eh man sie bricht,
Und Bäume, die sich täglich neu begrünen!

MEPHISTOPHELES:
Ein solcher Auftrag schreckt mich nicht,
Mit solchen Schätzen kann ich dienen.
1690 Doch, guter Freund, die Zeit kommt auch heran,
Wo wir was Guts in Ruhe schmausen mögen.

FAUST:
Werd ich beruhigt je mich auf ein Faulbett legen,
So sei es gleich um mich getan!
Kannst du mich schmeichelnd je belügen,
1695 Daß ich mir selbst gefallen mag,
Kannst du mich mit Genuß betrügen—
Das sei für mich der letzte Tag!
Die Wette biet ich!

MEPHISTOPHELES:
Topp!

MEPHISTO:

So minded, dare it cheerfully.
Commit yourself and you shall see
My arts with joy. I'll give you more
Than any man has seen before.

FAUST:

What would you, wretched Devil, offer?
Was ever a man's spirit in its noble striving
Grasped by your like, devilish scoffer?
But have you food that is not satisfying,
Red gold that rolls off without rest,
Quicksilver-like, over your skin—
A game in which no man can win—
A girl who, lying at my breast,
Ogles already to entice my neighbor,
And honor—that perhaps seems best—
Though like a comet it will turn to vapor?
Show me fruit that, before we pluck them, rot,
And trees whose foliage every day makes new!

MEPHISTO:

Such a commission scares me not,
With such things I can wait on you.
But, worthy friend, the time comes when we
would
Recline in peace and feast on something good.

FAUST:

If ever I recline, calmed, on a bed of sloth,
You may destroy me then and there.
If ever flattering you should wile me
That in myself I find delight,
If with enjoyment you beguile me,
Then break on me, eternal night!
This bet I offer.

MEPHISTO:

I accept it.

FAUST:

Und Schlag auf Schlag!
Werd ich zum Augenblicke sagen:
1700 Verweile doch! Du bist so schön!
Dann magst du mich in Fesseln schlagen,
Dann will ich gern zugrunde gehn!
Dann mag die Totenglocke schallen,
Dann bist du deines Dienstes frei,
1705 Die Uhr mag stehn, der Zeiger fallen,
Es sei die Zeit für mich vorbei!

MEPHISTOPHELES:

Bedenk es wohl, wir werden's nicht vergessen.

FAUST:

Dazu hast du ein volles Recht;
Ich habe mich nicht freventlich vermessen.
1710 Wie ich beharre, bin ich Knecht,
Ob dein, was frag ich, oder wessen.

MEPHISTOPHELES:

Ich werde heute gleich beim Doktorschmaus
Als Diener meine Pflicht erfüllen.
Nur eins!—Um Lebens oder Sterbens willen
1715 Bitt ich mir ein paar Zeilen aus.

FAUST:

Auch was Geschriebnes forderst du Pedant?
Hast du noch keinen Mann, nicht Mannes-Wort gekannt?
Ist's nicht genug, daß mein gesprochnes Wort
Auf ewig soll mit meinen Tagen schalten?
1720 Rast nicht die Welt in allen Strömen fort,
Und mich soll ein Versprechen halten?
Doch dieser Wahn ist uns ins Herz gelegt,
Wer mag sich gern davon befreien?
Beglückt, wer Treue rein im Busen trägt,
17B5 Kein Opfer wird ihn je gereuen!
Allein ein Pergament, beschrieben und beprägt,
Ist ein Gespenst, vor dem sich alle scheuen.

FAUST:

Right.

If to the moment I should say:
Abide, you are so fair—
Put me in fetters on that day,
I *wish* to perish then, I swear.
Then let the death bell ever toll,
Your service done, you shall be free,
The clock may stop, the hand may fall,
As time comes to an end for me.

MEPHISTO:

Consider it, for we shall not forget it.

FAUST:

That is a right you need not waive.
I did not boast, and I shall not regret it.
As I grow stagnant I shall be a slave,
Whether or not to anyone indebted.

MEPHISTO:

At the doctor's banquet tonight I shall do
My duties as a servant without fail.
But for life's sake, or death's—just one detail:
Could you give me a line or two?

FAUST:

You pedant need it black on white?
Are man and a man's word indeed new to your
sight?
Is not my spoken word sufficient warrant
When it commits my life eternally?
Does not the world rush on in every torrent,
And a mere promise should hold me?
Yet this illusion our heart inherits,
And who would want to shirk his debt?
Blessed who counts loyalty among his merits.
No sacrifice will he regret.
And yet a parchment, signed and sealed, is an
abhorrent
Specter that haunts us, and it makes us fret.

Das Wort erstirbt schon in der Feder,
Die Herrschaft führen Wachs und Leder.
1730 Was willst du böser Geist von mir?
Erz, Marmor, Pergament, Papier?
Soll ich mit Griffel, Meißel, Feder schreiben?
Ich gebe jede Wahl dir frei.

MEPHISTOPHELES:
Wie magst du deine Rednerei
1735 Nur gleich so hitzig übertreiben?
Ist doch ein jedes Blättchen gut.
Du unterzeichnest dich mit einem Tröpfchen Blut.

FAUST:
Wenn dies dir völlig Gnüge tut,
So mag es bei der Fratze bleiben.

MEPHISTOPHELES:
1740 Blut ist ein ganz besondrer Saft.

FAUST:
Nur keine Furcht, daß ich dies Bündnis breche!
Das Streben meiner ganzen Kraft
Ist grade das, was ich verspreche.
Ich habe mich zu hoch gebläht,
1745 In deinen Rang gehör ich nur.
Der große Geist hat mich verschmäht,
Vor mir verschließt sich die Natur.
Des Denkens Faden ist zerrissen,
Mir ekelt lange vor allem Wissen.
1750 Laß in den Tiefen der Sinnlichkeit
Uns glühende Leidenschaften stillen!
In undurchdrungnen Zauberhüllen
Sei jedes Wunder gleich bereit!
Stürzen wir uns in das Rauschen der Zeit,
1755 Ins Rollen der Begebenheit!
Da mag denn Schmerz und Genuß,
Gelingen und Verdruß
Miteinander wechseln, wie es kann;
Nur rastlos betätigt sich der Mann.

The word dies when we seize the pen,
And wax and leather lord it then.
What, evil spirit, do you ask?
Paper or parchment, stone or brass?
Should I use chisel, style, or quill?
It is completely up to you.

MEPHISTO:

Why get so hot and overdo
Your rhethoric? Why must you shrill?
Use any sheet, it is the same;
And with a drop of blood you sign your name.

FAUST:

If you are sure you like this game,
Let it be done to humor you.

MEPHISTO:

Blood is a very special juice.

FAUST:

You need not fear that someday I retract.
That all my striving I unloose
Is the whole purpose of the pact.
Oh, I was puffed up all too boldly,
At your rank only is my place.
The lofty spirit spurned me coldly,
And nature hides from me her face.
Torn is the subtle thread of thought,
I loathe the knowledge I once sought.
In sensuality's abysmal land
Let our passions drink their fill!
In magic veils, not pierced by skill,
Let every wonder be at hand!
Plunge into time's whirl that dazes my sense,
Into the torrent of events!
And let enjoyment, distress,
Annoyance and success
Succeed each other as best they can;
For restless activity proves a man.

MEPHISTOPHELES:

1760 Euch ist kein Maß und Ziel gesetzt.
Beliebt's Euch, überall zu naschen,
Im Fliehen etwas zu erhaschen,
Bekomm Euch wohl, was Euch ergetzt.
Nur greift mir zu und seid nicht blöde!

FAUST:

1765 Du hörest ja, von Freud ist nicht die Rede.
Dem Taumel weih ich mich, dem schmerzlichsten Genuß,
Verliebtem Haß, erquickendem Verdruß.
Mein Busen, der vom Wissensdrang geheilt ist,
Soll keinen Schmerzen künftig sich verschließen,
1770 Und was der ganzen Menschheit zugeteilt ist,
Will ich in meinem innern Selbst genießen,
Mit meinem Geist das Höchst und Tiefste greifen,
Ihr Wohl und Weh auf meinen Busen häufen
Und so mein eigen Selbst zu ihrem Selbst erweitern
1775 Und wie sie selbst am End auch ich zerscheitern.

MEPHISTOPHELES:

O glaube mir, der manche tausend Jahre
An dieser harten Speise kaut,
Daß von der Wiege bis zur Bahre
Kein Mensch den alten Sauerteig verdaut!
1780 Glaub unsereinem, dieses Ganze
Ist nur für einen Gott gemacht!
Er findet sich in einem ewgen Glanze,
Uns hat er in die Finsternis gebracht,
Und euch taugt einzig Tag und Nacht.

FAUST:

1785 Allein ich will!

MEPHISTOPHELES:

Das läßt sich hören!
Doch nur vor einem ist mir bang:
Die Zeit ist kurz, die Kunst ist lang.
Ich dächt, ihr ließet Euch belehren.

MEPHISTO:

You are not bound by goal or measure.
If you would nibble everything
Or snatch up something on the wing,
You're welcome to what gives you pleasure.
But help yourself and don't be coy!

FAUST:

Do you not hear, I have no thought of joy!
The reeling whirl I seek, the most painful excess,
Enamored hate and quickening distress.
Cured from the craving to know all, my mind
Shall not henceforth be closed to any pain,
And what is portioned out to all mankind,
I shall enjoy deep in my self, contain
Within my spirit summit and abyss,
Pile on my breast their agony and bliss,
And thus let my own self grow into theirs,
unfettered,
Till as they are, at last I, too, am shattered.

MEPHISTO:

Believe me who for many a thousand year
Has chewed this cud and never rested,
That from the cradle to the bier
The ancient leaven cannot be digested.
Trust one like me, this whole array
Is for a God—there's no contender:
He dwells in his eternal splendor,
To darkness we had to surrender,
And you need night as well as day.

FAUST:

And yet it is my will.

MEPHISTO:

It does sound bold.
But I'm afraid, though you are clever,
Time is too brief, though art's forever.
Perhaps you're willing to be told.

Assoziiert Euch mit einem Poeten,
1790 Laßt den Herrn in Gedanken schweifen
Und alle edlen Qualitäten
Auf Euren Ehrenscheitel häufen:
Des Löwen Mut,
Des Hirsches Schnelligkeit,
Des Italieners feurig Blut,
1795 Des Nordens Dau'rbarkeit.
Laßt ihn Euch das Geheimnis finden,
Großmut und Arglist zu verbinden
Und Euch mit warmen Jugendtrieben
1800 Nach einem Plane zu verlieben.
Möchte selbst solch einen Herren kennen,
Würd ihn Herrn Mikrokosmus nennen.

FAUST:
Was bin ich denn, wenn es nicht möglich ist,
Der Menschheit Krone zu erringen,
1805 Nach der sich alle Sinne dringen?

MEPHISTOPHELES:
Du bist am Ende—was du bist.
Setz dir Perücken auf von Millionen Locken,
Setz deinen Fuß auf ellenhohe Socken,
Du bleibst doch immer, was du bist.

FAUST:
1810 Ich fühl's, vergebens hab ich alle Schätze
Des Menschengeists auf mich herbeigerafft,
Und wenn ich mich am Ende niedersetze,
Quillt innerlich doch keine neue Kraft;
Ich bin nicht um ein Haar breit höher,
1815 Bin dem Unendlichen nicht näher.

MEPHISTOPHELES:
Mein guter Herr, Ihr seht die Sachen,
Wie man die Sachen eben sieht;
Wir müssen das gescheiter machen,
Eh uns des Lebens Freude flieht.
1820 Was Henker! Freilich Händ und Füße

Why don't you find yourself a poet,
And let the gentleman ransack his dreams:
And when he finds a noble trait, let him bestow it
Upon your worthy head in reams and reams:
The lion's daring,
The swiftness of the hind,
The northerner's forbearing
And the Italian's fiery mind,
Let him resolve the mystery
How craft can be combined with magnanimity,
Or how a passion-crazed young man
Might fall in love after a plan.
If there were such a man, I'd like to meet him,
As Mr. Microcosm I would greet him.

FAUST:

Alas, what am I, if I can
Not reach for mankind's crown which merely
 mocks
Our senses' craving like a star?

MEPHISTO:

You're in the end—just what you are!
Put wigs on with a million locks
And put your foot on ell-high socks,
You still remain just what you are.

FAUST:

I feel, I gathered up and piled up high
In vain the treasures of the human mind:
When I sit down at last, I cannot find
New strength within—it is all dry.
My stature has not grown a whit,
No closer to the Infinite.

MEPHISTO:

Well, my good sir, to put it crudely,
You see matters just as they lie;
We have to look at them more shrewdly,
Or all life's pleasures pass us by.
Your hands and feet—indeed that's trite—

Und Kopf und H – –, die sind dein;
Doch alles, was ich frisch genieße,
Ist das drum weniger mein?
Wenn ich sechs Hengste zahlen kann,
1825 Sind ihre Kräfte nicht die meine?
Ich renne zu und bin ein rechter Mann,
Als hätt ich vierundzwanzig Beine.
Drum frisch! Laß alles Sinnen sein
Und grad mit in die Welt hinein!
1830 Ich sag es dir: ein Kerl, der spekuliert,
Ist wie ein Tier, auf dürrer Heide
Von einem bösen Geist im Kreis herumgeführt,
Und ringsumher liegt schöne grüne Weide.

FAUST:

Wie fangen wir das an?

MEPHISTOPHELES:

Wir gehen eben fort.
1835 Was ist das für ein Marterort?
Was heißt das für ein Leben führen,
Sich und die Jungens ennuyieren?
Laß du das dem Herrn Nachbar Wanst!
Was willst du dich das Stroh zu dreschen plagen?
1840 Das Beste, was du wissen kannst,
Darfst du den Buben doch nicht sagen.
Gleich hör ich einen auf dem Gange.

FAUST:

Mir ist's nicht möglich, ihn zu sehn.

MEPHISTOPHELES:

Der arme Knabe wartet lange,
1845 Der darf nicht ungetröstet gehn.
Komm, gib mir deinen Rock und Mütze!
Die Maske muß mir köstlich stehn. *(Er kleidet sich um.)*
Und überlaß es meinem Witze!
Ich brauche nur ein Viertelstündchen Zeit;
1850 Indessen mache dich zur schönen Fahrt bereit!
(Faust ab.)

And head and seat are yours alone;
Yet all in which I find delight,
Should they be less my own?
Suppose I buy myself six steeds:
I buy their strength; while I recline
I dash along at whirlwind speeds,
For their two dozen legs are mine.
Come on! Let your reflections rest
And plunge into the world with zest!
I say, the man that speculates
Is like a beast that in the sand,
Led by an evil spirit, round and round gyrates,
And all about lies gorgeous pasture land.

FAUST:

How shall we set about it?

MEPHISTO:

Simply leave.
What torture room is this? What site of grief?
Is this the noble life of prudence—
You bore yourself and bore your students?
Oh, let your neighbor, Mr. Paunch, live so!
Why work hard threshing straw, when it annoys?
The best that you could ever know
You may not tell the little boys.
Right now I hear one in the aisle.

FAUST:

I simply cannot face the lad.

MEPHISTO:

The poor chap waited quite a while,
I do not want him to leave sad.
Give me your cap and gown. Not bad! *(He dresses himself up.)*
This mask ought to look exquisite!
Now you can leave things to my wit.
Some fifteen minutes should be all I need;
Meanwhile get ready for our trip, and speed!
(FAUST *exit.*)

MEPHISTOPHELES *(in Fausts langem Kleide):*
Verachte nur Vernunft und Wissenschaft,
Des Menschen allerhöchste Kraft,
Laß nur in Blend- und Zauberwerken
Dich von dem Lügengeist bestärken,
1855 So hab ich dich schon unbedingt—
Ihm hat das Schicksal einen Geist gegeben,
Der ungebändigt immer vorwärts dringt
Und dessen übereiltes Streben
Der Erde Freuden überspringt.
1860 Den schlepp ich durch das wilde Leben,
Durch flache Unbedeutenheit,
Er soll mir zappeln, starren, kleben,
Und seiner Unersättlichkeit
Soll Speis und Trank vor gier'gen Lippen
schweben;
1865 Er wird Erquickung sich umsonst erflehn,
Und hätt er sich auch nicht dem Teufel
übergeben,
Er müßte doch zugrunde gehn!
(Ein Schüler tritt auf.)

SCHÜLER:
Ich bin allhier erst kurze Zeit
Und komme voll Ergebenheit,
1870 Einen Mann zu sprechen und zu kennen,
Den alle mir mit Ehrfurcht nennen.

MEPHISTOPHELES:
Eure Höflichkeit erfreut mich sehr!
Ihr seht einen Mann wie andre mehr.
Habt Ihr Euch sonst schon umgetan?

SCHÜLER:
1875 Ich bitt Euch, nehmt Euch meiner an!
Ich komme mit allem guten Mut,
Leidlichem Geld und frischem Blut;
Meine Mutter wollte mich kaum entfernen;
Möchte gern was Rechts hieraußen lernen.

MEPHISTO *(in* FAUST'S *long robe):*
Have but contempt for reason and for science,
Man's noblest force spurn with defiance,
Subscribe to magic and illusion,
The Lord of Lies aids your confusion,
And, pact or no, I hold you tight.—
The spirit which he has received from fate
Sweeps ever onward with unbridled might,
Its hasty striving is so great
It leaps over the earth's delights.
Through life I'll drag him at a rate,
Through shallow triviality,
That he shall writhe and suffocate;
And his insatiability,
With greedy lips, shall see the choicest plate
And ask in vain for all that he would cherish—
And were he not the Devil's mate
And had not signed, he still must perish.

(A STUDENT *enters.)*

STUDENT:
I have arrived quite recently
And come, full of humility,
To meet that giant intellect
Whom all refer to with respect.

MEPHISTO:
This is a charming pleasantry.
A man as others are, you see.—
Have you already called elsewhere?

STUDENT:
I pray you, take me in your care.
I am, believe me, quite sincere,
Have some odd cash and lots of cheer;
My mother scarcely let me go,
But there is much I hope to know.

MEPHISTOPHELES:

1880 Da seid Ihr eben recht am Ort.

SCHÜLER:

Aufrichtig, möchte schon wieder fort:
In diesen Mauern, diesen Hallen
Will es mir keineswegs gefallen.
Es ist ein gar beschränkter Raum,
1885 Man sieht nichts Grünes, keinen Baum,
Und in den Sälen, auf den Bänken
Vergeht mir Hören, Sehn und Denken.

MEPHISTOPHELES:

Das kommt nur auf Gewohnheit an.
So nimmt ein Kind der Mutter Brust
1890 Nicht gleich im Anfang willig an,
Doch bald ernährt es sich mit Lust.
So wird's Euch an der Weisheit Brüsten
Mit jedem Tage mehr gelüsten.

SCHÜLER:

An ihrem Hals will ich mit Freuden hangen;
1895 Doch sagt mir nur, wie kann ich hingelangen?

MEPHISTOPHELES:

Erklärt Euch, eh Ihr weiter geht,
Was wählt Ihr für eine Fakultät?

SCHÜLER:

Ich wünschte recht gelehrt zu werden
Und möchte gern, was auf der Erden
1900 Und in dem Himmel ist, erfassen,
Die Wissenschaft und die Natur.

MEPHISTOPHELES:

Da seid Ihr auf der rechten Spur;
Doch müßt Ihr Euch nicht zerstreuen lassen.

SCHÜLER:

Ich bin dabei mit Seel und Leib;
1905 Doch freilich würde mir behagen
Ein wenig Freiheit und Zeitvertreib
An schönen Sommerfeiertagen.

MEPHISTO:

This is just the place for you to stay.

STUDENT:

To be frank, I should like to run away.
I cannot say I like these walls,
These gloomy rooms and somber halls.
It seems so narrow, and I see
No patch of green, no single tree;
And in the auditorium
My hearing, sight, and thought grow numb.

MEPHISTO:

That is a question of mere habit.
The child, offered the mother's breast,
Will not in the beginning grab it;
But soon it clings to it with zest.
And thus at wisdom's copious breasts
You'll drink each day with greater zest.

STUDENT:

I'll hang around her neck, enraptured;
But tell me first: how is she captured?

MEPHISTO:

Before we get into my views—
What Department do you choose?

STUDENT:

I should like to be erudite,
And from the earth to heaven's height
Know every law and every action:
Nature and science is what I need.

MEPHISTO:

That is the way; you just proceed
And scrupulously shun distraction.

STUDENT:

Body and soul, I am a devotee;
Though, naturally, everybody prays
For some free time and liberty
On pleasant summer holidays.

MEPHISTOPHELES:

Gebraucht die Zeit, sie geht so schnell von hinnen,
Doch Ordnung lehrt Euch Zeit gewinnen.
1910 Mein teurer Freund, ich rat Euch drum
Zuerst Collegium Logicum.
Da wird der Geist Euch wohl dressiert,
In spanische Stiefeln eingeschnürt,
Daß er bedächtiger so fortan
1915 Hinschleiche die Gedankenbahn
Und nicht etwa die Kreuz und Quer
Irrlichteliere hin und her.
Dann lehret man Euch manchen Tag,
Daß, was Ihr sonst auf einen Schlag
1920 Getrieben, wie Essen und Trinken frei,
Eins! Zwei! Drei! dazu nötig sei.
Zwar ist's mit der Gedankenfabrik
Wie mit einem Weber-Meisterstück,
Wo ein Tritt tausend Fäden regt,
1925 Die Schifflein herüber hinüber schießen,
Die Fäden ungesehen fließen,
Ein Schlag tausend Verbindungen schlägt.
Der Philosoph, der tritt herein
Und beweist Euch, es müßt so sein:
1930 Das Erst wär so, das Zweite so
Und drum das Dritt und Vierte so,
Und wenn das Erst und Zweit nicht wär,
Das Dritt und Viert wär nimmermehr.
Das preisen die Schüler allerorten,
1935 Sind aber keine Weber geworden.
Wer will was Lebendigs erkennen und
beschreiben,
Sucht erst den Geist herauszutreiben,
Dann hat er die Teile in seiner Hand,
Fehlt leider nur das geistige Band.
1940 Encheiresin naturae nennt's die Chemie,
Spottet ihrer selbst und weiß nicht wie.

MEPHISTO:

Use well your time, so swiftly it runs on!
Be orderly, and time is won!
My friend, I shall be pedagogic,
And say you ought to start with Logic.
For thus your mind is trained and braced,
In Spanish boots it will be laced,
That on the road of thought maybe
It henceforth creep more thoughtfully,
And does not crisscross here and there,
Will-o'-the-wisping through the air.
Days will be spent to let you know
That what you once did at one blow,
Like eating and drinking so easy and free,
Can only be done with One, Two, Three.
Yet the web of thought has no such creases
And is more like a weaver's masterpieces:
One step, a thousand threads arise,
Hither and thither shoots each shuttle,
The threads flow on, unseen and subtle,
Each blow effects a thousand ties.
The philosoper comes with analysis
And proves it had to be like this:
The first was so, the second so,
And hence the third and fourth was so,
And were not the first and the second here,
Then the third and fourth could never appear.
That is what all the students believe,
But they have never learned to weave.
Who would study and describe the living, starts
By driving the spirit out of the parts:
In the palm of his hand he holds all the sections,
Lacks nothing, except the spirit's connections.
Encheirisis naturae the chemists baptize it,
Mock themselves and don't realize it.

SCHÜLER:

Kann Euch nicht eben ganz verstehen.

MEPHISTOPHELES:

Das wird nächstens schon besser gehen,
Wenn Ihr lernt alles reduzieren
1945 Und gehörig klassifizieren.

SCHÜLER:

Mir wird von alle dem so dumm,
Als ging mir ein Mühlrad im Kopf herum.

MEPHISTOPHELES:

Nachher, vor allen andern Sachen,
Müßt Ihr Euch an die Metaphysik machen!
1950 Da seht, daß Ihr tiefsinnig faßt,
Was in des Menschen Hirn nicht paßt;
Für was drein geht und nicht drein geht,
Ein prächtig Wort zu Diensten steht.
Doch vorerst dieses halbe Jahr
1955 Nehmt ja der besten Ordnung wahr!
Fünf Stunden habt Ihr jeden Tag;
Seid drinnen mit dem Glockenschlag!
Habt Euch vorher wohl präpariert,
Paragraphos wohl einstudiert,
1960 Damit Ihr nachher besser seht,
Daß er nichts sagt, als was in Buche steht;
Doch Euch des Schreibens ja befleißt,
Als diktiert Euch der Heilig Geist!

SCHÜLER:

Das sollt Ihr mir nicht zweimal sagen!
1965 Ich denke mir, wieviel es nützt;
Denn, was man Schwarz auf Weiß besitzt,
Kann man getrost nach Hause tragen.

MEPHISTOPHELES:

Doch wählt mir eine Fakultät!

SCHÜLER:

Zur Rechtsgelehrsamkeit kann ich mich nicht
bequemen.

STUDENT:

I did not quite get everything.

MEPHISTO:

That will improve with studying:
You will reduce things by and by
And also learn to classify.

STUDENT:

I feel so dazed by all you said
As if a mill went around in my head.

MEPHISTO:

Then, without further circumvention,
Give metaphysics your attention.
There seek profoundly to attain
What does not fit the human brain;
Whether you do or do not understand,
An impressive word is always at hand.
But now during your first half-year,
Keep above all our order here.
Five hours a day, you understand,
And when the bell peals, be on hand.
Before you come, you must prepare,
Read every paragraph with care,
Lest you, forbid, should overlook
That all he says is in the book.
But write down everything, engrossed
As if you took dictation from the Holy Ghost.

STUDENT:

Don't say that twice—I understood:
I see how useful it's to write,
For what we possess black on white
We can take home and keep for good.

MEPHISTO:

But choose a field of concentration!

STUDENT:

I have no hankering for jurisprudence.

MEPHISTOPHELES:

1970 Ich kann es Euch so sehr nicht übel nehmen,
Ich weiß, wie es um diese Lehre steht.
Es erben sich Gesetz und Rechte
Wie eine ewge Krankheit fort,
Sie schleppen von Geschlecht sich zum Geschlechte
1975 Und rücken sacht von Ort zu Ort.
Vernunft wird Unsinn, Wohltat Plage;
Weh dir, daß du ein Enkel bist!
Vom Rechte, das mit uns geboren ist,
Von dem ist leider nie die Frage.

SCHÜLER:

1980 Mein Abscheu wird durch Euch vermehrt.
O glücklich der, den Ihr belehrt!
Fast möcht ich nun Theologie studieren.

MEPHISTOPHELES:

Ich wünschte nicht, Euch irrezuführen.
Was diese Wissenschaft betrifft,
1985 Es ist so schwer, den falschen Weg zu meiden,
Es liegt in ihr so viel verborgnes Gift,
Und von der Arzenei ist's kaum zu unterscheiden.
Am besten ist's auch hier, wenn Ihr nur Einen hört
Und auf des Meisters Worte schwört.
1990 Im ganzen—haltet Euch an Worte!
Dann geht Ihr durch die sichre Pforte
Zum Tempel der Gewißheit ein.

SCHÜLER:

Doch ein Begriff muß bei dem Worte sein.

MEPHISTOPHELES:

Schon gut! Nur muß man sich nicht allzu ängstlich quälen;
1995 Denn eben, wo Begriffe fehlen,
Da stellt ein Wort zur rechten Zeit sich ein.
Mit Worten läßt sich trefflich streiten,
Mit Worten ein System bereiten,

MEPHISTO:
For that I cannot blame the students,
I know this science is a blight.
The laws and statutes of a nation
Are an inherited disease,
From generation unto generation
And place to place they drag on by degrees.
Wisdom becomes nonsense; kindness, oppression:
To be a grandson is a curse.
The right that is innate in us
Is not discussed by the profession.

STUDENT:
My scorn is heightened by your speech.
Happy the man that you would teach!
I almost think theology would pay.

MEPHISTO:
I should not wish to lead you astray.
When it comes to this discipline,
The way is hard to find, wrong roads abound,
And lots of hidden poison lies around
Which one can scarcely tell from medicine.
Here, too, it would be best you heard
One only and staked all upon your master's word.
Yes, stick to words at any rate;
There never was a surer gate
Into the temple, Certainty.

STUDENT:
Yet some idea there must be.

MEPHISTO:
All right. But do not plague yourself too anxiously;
For just where no ideas are
The proper word is never far.
With words a dispute can be won,
With words a system can be spun,

An Worte läßt sich trefflich glauben,
2000 Von einem Wort läßt sich kein Jota rauben.

SCHÜLER:

Verzeiht, ich halt Euch auf mit vielen Fragen,
Allein ich muß Euch noch bemühn.
Wollt Ihr mir von der Medizin
Nicht auch ein kräftig Wörtchen sagen?
2005 Drei Jahr ist eine kurze Zeit,
Und, Gott! das Feld ist gar zu weit.
Wenn man einen Fingerzeig nur hat,
Läßt sich's schon eher weiter fühlen.

MEPHISTOPHELES *(für sich):*

Ich bin des trocknen Tons nun satt,
2010 Muß wieder recht den Teufel spielen.
(Laut.) Der Geist der Medizin ist leicht zu fassen;
Ihr durchstudiert die groß und kleine Welt,
Um es am Ende gehn zu lassen,
Wie's Gott gefällt.
2015 Vergebens, daß Ihr ringsum wissenschaftlich
schweift,
Ein jeder lernt nur, was er lernen kann;
Doch, der den Augenblick ergreift,
Das ist der rechte Mann.
Ihr seid noch ziemlich wohl gebaut,
2020 An Kühnheit wird's Euch auch nicht fehlen,
Und wenn Ihr Euch nur selbst vertraut,
Vertrauen Euch die andern Seelen.
Besonders lernt die Weiber führen;
Es ist ihr ewig Weh und Ach
2025 So tausendfach
Aus e i n e m Punkte zu kurieren,
Und wenn Ihr halbweg ehrbar tut,
Dann habt Ihr sie all unterm Hut.
Ein Titel muß sie erst vertraulich machen,
2030 Daß Eure Kunst viel Künste übersteigt;
Zum Willkomm tappt Ihr dann nach allen
Siebensachen,

In words one can believe unshaken,
And from a word no tittle can be taken.

STUDENT:

Forgive, I hold you up with many questions,
But there is one more thing I'd like to see.
Regarding medicine, maybe,
You have some powerful suggestions?
Three years go by so very fast,
And, God, the field is all too vast.
If but a little hint is shown,
One can attempt to find one's way.

MEPHISTO *(aside)*:

I'm sick of this pedantic tone.
The Devil now again I'll play.

(loud):

The spirit of medicine is easy to know:
Through the macro–and microcosm you breeze,
And in the end you let it go
As God may please.
In vain you roam about to study science,
For each learns only what he can;
Who places on the moment his reliance,
He is the proper man.
You are quite handsome, have good sense,
And no doubt, you have courage, too,
And if you have self-confidence,
Then others will confide in you.
And give the women special care;
Their everlasting sighs and groans
In thousand tones
Are cured at *one* point everywhere.
And if you seem halfway discreet,
They will be lying at your feet.
First your degree inspires trust,
As if your art had scarcely any peers;
Right at the start, remove her clothes and touch
her bust,

Um die ein andrer viele Jahre streicht,
Versteht das Pülslein wohl zu drücken
Und fasset sie, mit feurig schlauen Blicken,
2035 Wohl um die schlanke Hüfte frei,
Zu sehn, wie fest geschnürt sie sei.

SCHÜLER:
Das sieht schon besser aus! Man sieht doch, wo und wie.

MEPHISTOPHELES:
Grau, teurer Freund, ist alle Theorie
Und grün des Lebens goldner Baum.

SCHÜLER:
2040 Ich schwör Euch zu, mir ist's als wie ein Traum.
Dürft ich Euch wohl ein andermal beschweren,
Von Eurer Weisheit auf den Grund zu hören?

MEPHISTOPHELES:
Was ich vermag, soll gern geschehn.

SCHÜLER:
Ich kann unmöglich wieder gehn,
2045 Ich muß Euch noch mein Stammbuch überreichen.
Gönn Eure Gunst mir dieses Zeichen!

MEPHISTOPHELES:
Sehr wohl. *(Er schreibt und gibt's.)*

SCHÜLER *(liest):*
Eritis sicut Deus, scientes bonum et malum.
(Macht's ehrerbietig zu und empfiehlt sich.)

MEPHISTOPHELES:
Folg nur dem alten Spruch und meiner Muhme, der Schlange!
2050 Dir wird gewiß einmal bei deiner Gottähnlichkeit bange.

(Faust tritt auf.)

FAUST:
Wohin soll es nun gehn?

MEPHISTOPHELES:
Wohin es dir gefällt.

Things for which others wait for years and years.
Learn well the little pulse to squeeze,
And with a knowing, fiery glance you seize
Her freely round her slender waist
To see how tightly she is laced.

STUDENT:

That looks much better, sir. For one sees how and where.

MEPHISTO:

Gray, my dear friend, is every theory,
And green alone life's golden tree.

STUDENT:

All this seems like a dream, I swear.
Could I impose on you sometime again
And drink more words of wisdom then?

MEPHISTO:

What I can give you, you shall get.

STUDENT:

Alas, I cannot go quite yet:
My album I must give to you;
Please, sir, show me this favor, too.

MEPHISTO:

All right. *(He writes and returns it.)*

STUDENT *(reads)*:

Eritis sicut Deus, scientes bonum et malum.
(Closes the book reverently and takes his leave.)

MEPHISTO:

Follow the ancient text and my relation, the snake;
Your very likeness to God will yet make you quiver and quake.

(FAUST *enters.)*

FAUST:

Where are we heading now?

MEPHISTO:

Wherever you may please.

Wir sehn die kleine, dann die große Welt.
Mit welcher Freude, welchem Nutzen
Wirst du den Cursum durchschmarutzen!

FAUST:

2055 Allein bei meinem langen Bart
Fehlt mir die leichte Lebensart.
Es wird mir der Versuch nicht glücken;
Ich wußte nie mich in die Welt zu schicken.
Vor andern fühl ich mich so klein;
2060 Ich werde stets verlegen sein.

MEPHISTOPHELES:

Mein guter Freund, das wird sich alles geben;
Sobald du dir vertraust, sobald weißt du zu leben.

FAUST:

Wie kommen wir denn aus dem Haus?
Wo hast du Pferde, Knecht und Wagen?

MEPHISTOPHELES:

2065 Wir breiten nur den Mantel aus,
Der soll uns durch die Lüfte tragen.
Du nimmst bei diesem kühnen Schritt
Nur keinen großen Bündel mit.
Ein bißchen Feuerluft, die ich bereiten werde,
2070 Hebt uns behend von dieser Erde.
Und sind wir leicht, so geht es schnell hinauf;
Ich gratuliere dir zum neuen Lebenslauf!

AUERBACHS KELLER IN LEIPZIG

Zeche lustiger Gesellen

FROSCH:

Will keiner trinken, keiner lachen?
Ich will euch lehren Gesichter machen!

We'll see the small world, then the larger one.
You will reap profit and have fun
As you sweep through this course with ease.

FAUST:

With my long beard I hardly may
Live in this free and easy way.
The whole endeavor seems so futile;
I always felt the world was strange and brutal.
With others, I feel small and harassed,
And I shall always be embarrassed.

MEPHISTO:

Good friend, you will become less sensitive:
Self-confidence will teach you how to live.

FAUST:

How shall we get away from here?
Where are your carriage, groom and steed?

MEPHISTO:

I rather travel through the air:
We spread this cloak—that's all we need.
But on this somewhat daring flight,
Be sure to keep your luggage light.
A little fiery air, which I plan to prepare,
Will raise us swiftly off the earth;
Without ballast we'll go up fast—
Congratulations, friend, on your rebirth!

AUERBACH'S KELLER in LEIPZIG

Jolly fellows' drinking bout.

FROSCH:

Will no one drink and no one laugh?
I'll teach you not to look so wry.

2075 Ihr seid ja heut wie nasses Stroh
Und brennt sonst immer lichterloh.

BRANDER:
Das liegt an dir; du bringst ja nichts herbei,
Nicht eine Dummheit, keine Sauerei.

FROSCH *(gießst ihm ein Glas Wein über den Kopf):*
Da hast du beides!

BRANDER:
Doppelt Schwein!

FROSCH:
2080 Ihr wollt es ja, man soll es sein!

SIEBEL:
Zur Tür hinaus, wer sich entzweit!
Mit offner Brust singt Runda, sauft und schreit!
Auf! Holla! Ho!

ALTMAYER:
Weh mir, ich bin verloren!
Baumwolle her! Der Kerl sprengt mir die Ohren.

SIEBEL:
2085 Wenn das Gewölbe widerschallt,
Fühlt man erst recht des Basses Grundgewalt.

FROSCH:
So recht, hinaus mit dem, der etwas übel nimmt!
A! Tara lara da!

ALTMAYER:
A! Tara lara da!

FROSCH:
Die Kehlen sind gestimmt.
(Singt):
2090 Das liebe heilge Röm'sche Reich,
Wie hält's nur noch zusammen?

BRANDER:
Ein garstig Lied! Pfui! Ein politisch Lied
Ein leidig Lied! Dankt Gott mit jedem Morgen,

Today you look like sodden chaff
And usually blaze to the sky.

BRANDER:
It's all your fault; you make me sick:
No joke, and not a single dirty trick.

FROSCH *(pours a glass of wine over* BRANDER'S *head)*:
There you have both.

BRANDER:
You filthy pig!

FROSCH:
You said I shouldn't be a prig.

SIEBEL:
Let those who fight, stop or get out!
With all your lungs sing chorus, swill, and shout!
Come! Holla-ho!

ALTMAYER:
Now this is where I quit.
Get me some cotton or my ears will split.

SIEBEL:
When the vault echoes and the place
Is quaking, then you can enjoy a bass.

FROSCH:
Quite right! Throw out who fusses because he is lampooned!
A! tara lara da!

ALTMAYER:
A! tara lara da!

FROSCH:
The throats seem to be tuned.
(Sings):
Dear Holy Roman Empire,
What holds you still together?

BRANDER:
A nasty song! It reeks of politics!
A wretched song! Thank God in daily prayer,

Daß ihr nicht braucht fürs Röm'sche Reich zu
sorgen!
2095 Ich halt es wenigstens für reichlichen Gewinn,
Daß ich nicht Kaiser oder Kanzler bin.
Doch muß auch uns ein Oberhaupt nicht fehlen;
Wir wollen einen Papst erwählen.
Ihr wißt, welch eine Qualität
2100 Den Ausschlag gibt, den Mann erhöht.

FROSCH *(singt)*:
Schwing dich auf, Frau Nachtigall,
Grüß mir mein Liebchen zehentausendmal!

SIEBEL:
Dem Liebchen keinen Gruß! Ich will davon
nichts hören!

FROSCH:
Dem Liebchen Gruß und Kuß! Du wirst mir's
nicht verwehren!
2105 *(Singt)*:
Riegel auf! In stiller Nacht.
Riegel auf! Der Liebste wacht.
Riegel zu! Des Morgens früh.

SIEBEL:
Ja, singe, singe nur und lob und rühme sie!
Ich will zu meiner Zeit schon lachen.
2110 Sie hat mich angeführt, dir wird sie's auch so
machen.
Zum Liebsten sei ein Kobold ihr beschert!
Der mag mit ihr auf einem Kreuzweg schäkern;
Ein alter Bock, wenn er vom Blocksberg kehrt,
Mag im Galopp noch gute Nacht ihr meckern!
2115 Ein braver Kerl von echtem Fleisch und Blut
Ist für die Dirne viel zu gut.
Ich will von keinem Gruße wissen,
Als ihr die Fenster eingeschmissen!

BRANDER *(auf den Tisch schlagend)*:
Paßt auf! Paßt auf! Gehorchet mir!

That the old Empire isn't your affair!
At least I think it is much to be grateful for
That I'm not Emperor nor Chancellor.
And yet we, too, need someone to respect—
I say, a Pope let us elect.
You know the part that elevates
And thereby proves the man who rates.

FROSCH *(sings)*:

Oh, Dame Nightingale, arise!
Bring my sweet love ten thousand sighs!

SIEBEL:

No sighs for your sweet love! I will not have such mush.

FROSCH:

A sigh and kiss for her! You cannot make me blush.

(Sings):

Ope the latch in silent night!
Ope the latch, your love invite!
Shut the latch, there is the dawn!

SIEBEL:

Go, sing and sing and sing, pay compliments and fawn!
The time will come when I shall laugh:
She led me by the nose, and you are the next calf.
Her lover should be some mischievous gnome!
He'd meet her at a crossroads and make light,
And an old billy goat that's racing home
From Blocksberg could still bleat to her "Good night!"
A decent lad of real flesh and blood
Is far too good to be her stud.
I'll stand no sighs, you silly ass,
But throw rocks through her window glass.

BRANDER *(pounding on the table)*:

Look here! Look here! Listen to me!

2120 Ihr Herrn, gesteht, ich weiß zu leben;
Verliebte Leute sitzen hier,
Und diesen muß nach Standsgebühr
Zur guten Nacht ich was zum besten geben.
Gebt acht! Ein Lied vom neusten Schnitt!
2125 Und singt den Rundreim kräftig mit!
(Er singt):

Es war eine Ratt im Kellernest,
Lebte nur von Fett und Butter,
Hatte sich ein Ränzlein angemäst't,
Als wie der Doktor Luther.
2130 Die Köchin hatt ihr Gift gestellt;
Wa ward's so eng ihr in der Welt,
Als hätte sie Lieb im Leibe.

CHORUS *(jauchzend):*

Als hätte sie Lieb im Leibe.

BRANDER:

Sie fuhr herum, sie fuhr heraus
2135 Und soff aus allen Pfützen,
Zernagt', zerkratzt' das ganze Haus,
Wollte nichts ihr Wüten nützen;
Sie tät gar manchen Ängstesprung,
Bald hatte das arme Tier genug,
2140 Als hätt es Lieb im Leibe.

CHORUS:

Als hätt es Lieb im Leibe.

BRANDER:

Sie kam für Angst am hellen Tag
Der Küche zugelaufen,
Fiel an den Herd und zuckt' und lag
2145 Und tät erbärmlich schnaufen.
Da lachte die Vergifterin noch:
Ha! Sie pfeift auf dem letzten Loch,
Als hätte sie Lieb im Leibe.

CHORUS:

Als hätte sie Lieb im Leibe.

My friends, confess I know what's right;
There are lovers here, and you'll agree
That it's only civility
That I should try to honor them tonight.
Watch out! This song's the latest fashion.
And join in the refrain with passion!

(sings):

A cellar once contained a rat
That couldn't have been uncouther,
Lived on grease and butter and grew fat—
Just like old Doctor Luther.
The cook put poison in his food,
Then he felt cramped and just as stewed,
As if love gnawed his vitals.

CHORUS *(jubilant):*

As if love gnawed his vitals.

BRANDER:

He dashed around, he dashed outdoors,
Sought puddles and swilled rain,
He clawed and scratched up walls and floors,
But his frenzy was in vain;
He jumped up in a frightful huff,
But soon the poor beast had enough,
As if love gnawed his vitals.

CHORUS:

As if love gnawed his vitals.

ANDER:

At last he rushed in open day
Into the kitchen, crazed with fear,
Dropped near the stove and writhed and lay,
And puffed out his career.
The poisoner only laughed: I hope
He's at the end now of his rope,
As if love gnawed his vitals.

ORUS:

As if love gnawed his vitals.

SIEBEL:

2150 Wie sich die platten Bursche freuen!
Es ist mir eine rechte Kunst,
Den armen Ratten Gift zu streuen!

BRANDER:

Sie stehn wohl sehr in deiner Gunst?

ALTMAYER:

Der Schmerbauch mit der kahlen Platte!
2155 Das Unglück macht ihn zahm und mild;
Er sieht in der geschwollnen Ratte
Sein ganz natürlich Ebenbild.

Faust and Mephistopheles treten auf.

MEPHISTOPHELES:

Ich muß dich nun vor allen Dingen
In lustige Gesellschaft bringen,
2160 Damit du siehst, wie leicht sich's leben läßt.
Dem Volke hier wird jeder Tag ein Fest.
Mit wenig Witz und viel Behagen
Dreht jeder sich im engen Zirkeltanz,
Wie junge Katzen mit dem Schwanz.
2165 Wenn sie nicht über Kopfweh klagen,
Solang der Wirt nur weiter borgt,
Sind sie vergnügt und unbesorgt.

BRANDER:

Die kommen eben von der Reise,
Man sieht's an ihrer wunderlichen Weise;
2170 Sie sind nicht eine Stunde hier.

FROSCH:

Wahrhaftig, du hast recht! Mein Leipzig lob ich mir!
Es ist ein klein Paris und bildet seine Leute.

SIEBEL:

Für was siehst du die Fremden an?

FROSCH:

Laß mich nur gehn! Bei einem vollen Glase
2175 Zieh ich wie einen Kinderzahn
Den Burschen leicht die Würmer aus der Nase.

SIEBEL:

How pleased these stupid chaps are! That's,
I think, indeed a proper art
To put out poison for poor rats.

BRANDER:

I see, you'd like to take their part.

ALTMAYER:

Potbelly with his shiny top!
His ill luck makes him mild and tame.
He sees the bloated rat go flop—
And sees himself: they look the same.

FAUST *and* MEPHISTOPHELES *enter.*

MEPHISTO:

Above all else, it seems to me,
You need some jolly company
To see life can be fun—to say the least:
The people here make every day a feast.
With little wit and boisterous noise,
They dance and circle in their narrow trails
Like kittens playing with their tails.
When hangovers don't vex these boys,
And while their credit's holding out,
They have no cares and drink and shout.

BRANDER:

Those two are travelers, I swear.
I tell it right off by the way they stare.
They have been here at most an hour.

FROSCH:

No doubt about it. Leipzig is a flower,
It is a little Paris and educates its people.

SIEBEL:

What may they be? Who knows the truth?

FROSCH:

Leave it to me! A drink that interposes—
And I'll pull like a baby tooth
The worms they hide, out of these fellows' noses.

Sie scheinen mir aus einem edlen Haus,
Sie sehen stolz und unzufrieden aus.

BRANDER:
Marktschreier sind's gewiß, ich wette.

ALTMAYER:
2180 Vielleicht.

FROSCH:
Gib acht, ich schraube sie!

MEPHISTOPHELES *(zu Faust):*
Den Teufel spürt das Völkchen nie,
Und wenn er sie beim Kragen hätte.

FAUST:
Seid uns gegrüßt, ihr Herrn!

SIEBEL:
Viel Dank zum Gegengruß!
(Leise, Mehpistopheles von der Seite ansehend.)
Was hinkt der Kerl auf einem Fuß?

MEPHISTOPHELES:
2185 Ist es erlaubt, uns auch zu euch zu setzen?
Statt eines guten Trunks, den man nicht haben kann,
Soll die Gesellschaft uns ergetzen.

ALTMAYER:
Ihr scheint ein sehr verwöhnter Mann.

FROSCH:
Ihr seid wohl spät von Rippach aufgebrochen?
2190 Habt ihr mit Herren Hans noch erst zu Nacht gespeist?

MEPHISTOPHELES:
Heut sind wir ihn vorbeigereist;
Wir haben ihn das letztemal gesprochen.
Von seinen Vettern wußt er viel zu sagen,
Viel Grüße hat er uns an jeden aufgetragen.
(Er neigt sich gegen Frosch.)

ALTMAYER *(leise):*
2195 Da hast du's! Der versteht's!

They seem to be of noble ancestry,
For they look proud and act disdainfully.

BRANDER:
They are mere quacks and born in squalor.

ALTMAYER:
Maybe.

FROSCH:
Watch out! We shall commence.

MEPHISTO (*to* FAUST):
The Devil people never sense,
Though he may hold them by the collar.

FAUST:
Good evening, gentlemen.

SIEBEL:
Thank you, to you the same.
(*softly, looking at* MEPHISTOPHELES *from the side*):
Look at his foot. Why is it lame?

MEPHISTO:
We'll join you, if you grant the liberty.
The drinks they have are poor, their wine not very mellow,
So we'll enjoy your company.

ALTMAYER:
You seem a most fastidious fellow.

FROSCH:
Did you leave Rippach rather late and walk?
And did you first have dinner with Master Jackass there?

MEPHISTO:
Tonight we had no time to spare.
Last time, however, we had quite a talk.
He had a lot to say of his relations
And asked us to send each his warmest salutations.
(*He bows to* FROSCH.)

ALTMAYER (*softly*):
You got it! He's all right.

SIEBEL:

Ein pfiffiger Patron!

FROSCH:

Nun, warte nur, ich krieg ihn schon!

MEPHISTOPHELES:

Wenn ich nicht irrte, hörten wir
Geübte Stimmen Chorus singen?
Gewiß, Gesang muß trefflich hier
2200 Von dieser Wölbung widerklingen.

FROSCH:

Seid Ihr wohl gar ein Virtuos?

MEPHISTOPHELES:

O nein! Die Kraft ist schwach, allein die Lust ist groß.

ALTMAYER:

Gebt uns ein Lied!

MEPHISTOPHELES:

Wenn ihr begehrt, die Menge.

SIEBEL:

Nur auch ein nagelneues Stück!

MEPHISTOPHELES:

2205 Wir kommen erst aus Spanien zurück,
Dem schönen Land des Weins und der Gesänge.
(Singt):

Es war einmal ein König,
Der hatt einen großen Floh–

FROSCH:

Horcht! Einen Floh! Habt ihr das wohl gefaßt?
2210 Ein Floh ist mir ein saubrer Gast.

MEPHISTOPHELES *(singt):*

Es war einmal ein König,
Der hatt einen großen Floh,
Den liebt' er gar nicht wenig,
Als wie seinen eignen Sohn.
2215 Da rief er seinen Schneider,
Der Schneider kam heran:
Da, miß dem Junker Kleider

SIEBEL:

A pretty repartee!

FROSCH:

I'll get him yet. Just wait and see.

MEPHISTO:

Just now we heard, if I'm not wrong,
Some voices singing without fault.
Indeed this seems a place for song;
No doubt, it echoes from the vault.

FROSCH:

Are you perchance a virtuoso?

MEPHISTO:

Oh no, the will is great, the power only so-so.

ALTMAYER:

Give us a song!

MEPHISTO:

As many as you please.

SIEBEL:

But let us have a brand-new strain!

MEPHISTO:

We have just recently returned from Spain,
The beauteous land of wine and melodies.

(sings):

A king lived long ago
Who had a giant flea—

FROSCH:

Hear, hear! A flea! That's what I call a jest.
A flea's a mighty pretty guest.

MEPHISTO *(sings):*

A king lived long ago
Who had a giant flea,
He loved him just as though
He were his son and heir.
He sent his tailor a note
And offered the tailor riches
If he would measure a coat

Und miß ihm Hosen an!

BRANDER:

Vergeßt nur nicht, dem Schneider einzuschärfen,
2220 Daß er mir aufs genauste mißt
Und daß, so lieb sein Kopf ihm ist,
Die Hosen keine Falten werfen!

MEPHISTOPHELES:

In Sammet und in Seide
War er nun angetan,
2225 Hatte Bänder auf dem Kleide,
Hatt auch ein Kreuz daran
Und war sogleich Minister
Und hatt einen großen Stern.
Da wurden seine Geschwister
2230 Bei Hof auch große Herrn.
Und Herrn und Fraun am Hofe,
Die waren sehr geplagt,
Die Königin und die Zofe
Gestochen und genagt
2235 Und durften sie nicht knicken
Und weg sie jucken nicht.
Wir knicken und ersticken
Doch gleich, wenn einer sticht.

CHORUS *(jauchzend):*

Wir knicken und ersticken
2240 Doch gleich, wenn einer sticht.

FROSCH:

Bravo! Bravo! Das war schön!

SIEBEL:

So soll es jedem Floh ergehn!

BRANDER:

Spitzt die Finger und packt sie fein!

ALTMAYER:

Es lebe die Freiheit! Es lebe der Wein!

MEPHISTOPHELES:

2245 Ich tränke gern ein Glas, die Freiheit hoch zu ehren,

And also take measure for breeches.

BRANDER:

Be sure to tell the tailor, if he twinkles,
That he must take fastidious measure;
He'll lose his head, not just the treasure,
If in the breeches there are wrinkles.

MEPHISTO:

He was in silk arrayed,
In velvet he was dressed,
Had ribbons and brocade,
A cross upon his chest,
A fancy star, great fame—
A minister, in short;
And all his kin became
Lords at the royal court.
The other lords grew lean
And suffered with their wives,
The royal maid and the queen
Were all but eaten alive,
But weren't allowed to swat them
And could not even scratch,
While we can swat and blot them
And kill the ones we catch.

CHORUS *(jubilant)*:

While we can swat and blot them
And kill the ones we catch.

FROSCH:

Bravo! Bravo! That was a treat!

SIEBEL:

That is the end all fleas should meet.

BRANDER:

Point your fingers and catch 'em fine!

ALTMAYER:

Long live our freedom! And long live wine!

MEPHISTO:

When freedom is the toast, my own voice I
should add,

Wenn eure Weine nur ein bißchen besser wären.

SIEBEL:

Wir mögen das nicht wieder hören!

MEPHISTOPHELES:

Ich fürchte nur, der Wirt beschweret sich,
Sonst gäb ich diesen werten Gästen
2250 Aus unserm Keller was zum besten.

SIEBEL:

Nur immer her! Ich nehm's auf mich.

FROSCH:

Schafft Ihr ein gutes Glas, so wollen wir Euch loben.
Nur gebt nicht gar zu kleine Proben!
Denn wenn ich judizieren soll,
2255 Verlang ich auch das Maul recht voll.

ALTMAYER *(leise)*:

Sie sind vom Rheine, wie ich spüre.

MEPHISTOPHELES:

Schafft einen Bohrer an!

BRANDER:

Was soll mit dem geschehn?
Ihr habt doch nicht die Fässer vor der Türe?

ALTMAYER:

Dahinten hat der Wirt ein Körbchen Werkzeug stehn.

MEPHISTOPHELES *(nimmt den Bohrer)*:

(Zu Frosch):

2260 Nun sagt, was wünschet Ihr zu schmecken?

FROSCH:

Wie meint Ihr das? Habt Ihr so mancherlei?

MEPHISTOPHELES:

Ich stell es einem jeden frei.

ALTMAYER *(zu* FROSCH):

Aha! Du fängst schon an, die Lippen abzulecken.

FROSCH:

Gut! Wenn ich wählen soll, so will ich Rheinwein haben.

Were your forsaken wines only not quite so bad.

SIEBEL:

You better mind your language, lad.

MEPHISTO:

I only fear the landlord might protest,
Else I should give each honored guest
From our cellar a good glass.

SIEBEL:

Let's go! The landlord is an ass.

FROSCH:

If you provide good drinks, you shall be eulogized;
But let your samples be good-sized.
When I'm to judge, I'm telling him,
I want my snout full to the brim.

ALTMAYER *(softly)*:

They're from the Rhineland, I presume.

MEPHISTO:

Bring me a gimlet.

BRANDER:

What could that be for?
You couldn't have the casks in the next room?

ALTMAYER:

The landlord keeps his tools right there behind the door.

MEPHISTO *(takes the gimlet)*:

(To FROSCH*)*:

What would you like? Something that's cool?

FROSCH:

What do you mean? You got a lot of booze?

MEPHISTO:

I let each have what he may choose.

ALTMAYER *(to* FROSCH*)*:

Oho! You lick your chops and start to drool.

FROSCH:

If it is up to me, I'll have a Rhenish brand:

2265 Das Vaterland verleiht die allerbesten Gaben.

MEPHISTOPHELES *(indem er an dem Platz, wo Frosch sitzt, ein Loch in den Tischrand bohrt):*
Verschafft ein wenig Wachs, die Pfropfen gleich zu machen!

ALTMAYER:
Ach, das sind Taschenspielersachen.

MEPHISTOPHELES *(zu Brander):*
Und Ihr?

BRANDER:
Ich will Champagner Wein,
Und recht moussierend soll er sein!

MEPHISTOPHELES *(bohrt; einer hat indessen die Wachspfropfen gemacht und verstopft):*

BRANDER:
2270 Man kann nicht stets das Fremde meiden,
Das Gute liegt uns oft so fern.
Ein echter deutscher Mann mag keinen Franzen leiden,
Doch ihre Weine trinkt er gern.

SIEBEL *(indem sich Mephistopheles seinem Platze nähert):*
Ich muß gestehn, den sauren mag ich nicht,
2275 Gebt mir ein Glas vom echten süßen!

MEPHISTOPHELES *(bohrt):*
Euch soll sogleich Tokaier fließen.

ALTMAYER:
Nein, Herren, seht mir ins Gesicht!
Ich seh es ein, ihr habt uns nur zum besten.

MEPHISTOPHELES:
Ei! Ei! Mit solchen edlen Gästen
2280 Wär es ein bißchen viel gewagt.
Geschwind! Nur gradheraus gesagt!
Mit welchem Weine kann ich dienen?

ALTMAYER:
Mit jedem! Nur nicht lang gefragt!

There's nothing that competes with our
fatherland.

MEPHISTO *(boring a hole near the edge of the table where* FROSCH *sits):*
Now let us have some wax to make a cork that
sticks.

ALTMAYER:
Oh, is it merely parlor tricks?

MEPHISTO *(to* BRANDER:)
And you?

BRANDER:
I want a good champagne—
Heady; I do not like it plain.

MEPHISTO *(bores; meanwhile someone else has made the wax stoppers and plugged the holes.)*

BRANDER:
Not all that's foreign can be banned,
For what is far is often fine.
A Frenchman is a thing no German man can
stand,
And yet we like to drink their wine.

SIEBEL *(as* MEPHISTOPHELES *approaches his place):*
I must confess, I think the dry tastes bad,
The sweet alone is exquisite.

MEPHISTO *(boring):*
Tokay will flow for you, my lad.

ALTMAYER:
I think, you might as well admit,
Good gentlemen, that these are simply jests.

MEPHISTO:
Tut, tut! With such distinguished guests
That would be quite a lot to dare.
So don't be modest, and declare
What kind of wine you would prefer.

ALTMAYER:
I like them all, so I don't care.

(Nachdem die Löcher alle gebohrt und verstopft sind.)

MEPHISTOPHELES *(mit seltsamen Gebärden):*

Trauben trägt der Weinstock,
2285 Hörner der Ziegenbock;
Der Wein ist saftig, Holz die Reben,
Der hölzerne Tisch kann Wein auch geben.
Ein tiefer Blick in die Natur:
Hier ist ein Wunder, glaubet nur!
2290 Nun zieht die Pfropfen und genießt!

ALLE *(indem sie die Pfropfen ziehen und jedem der verlangte Wein ins Glas läuft):*

O schöner Brunnen, der uns fließt!

MEPHISTOPHELES:

Nur hütet euch, daß ihr mir nichts vergießt!

(Sie trinken wiederholt.)

ALLE *(singen):*

Uns ist ganz kannibalisch wohl,
Als wie fünfhundert Säuen!

MEPHISTOPHELES:

2295 Das Volk ist frei, seht an, wie wohl's ihm geht!

FAUST:

Ich hätte Lust, nun abzufahren.

MEPHISTOPHELES:

Gib nur erst acht, die Bestialität
Wird sich gar herrlich offenbaren.

SIEBEL *(trinkt unvorsichtig, der Wein fließt auf die Erde und wird zur Flamme):*

Helft! Feuer! Helft! Die Hölle brennt!

MEPHISTOPHELES *(die Flamme besprechend):*

2300 Sei ruhig, freundlich Element!

(Zu dem Gesellen.)

Für diesmal war es nur ein Tropfen Fegefeuer.

SIEBEL:

Was soll das sein? Wart! Ihr bezahlt es teuer!
Es scheinet, daß Ihr uns nicht kennt.

(After all the holes have been bored and plugged:)

MEPHISTO *(with strange gestures):*

The grape the vine adorns,
The billy goat sports horns;
The wine is juicy, vines are wood,
The wooden table gives wine as good.
Profound insight! Now you perceive
A miracle; only believe!

Now pull the stoppers and have fun!

ALL *(as they pull out the stoppers and the wine each asked for flows into his glass):*

A gorgeous well for every one!

MEPHISTO:

Be very careful lest it overrun!

(They drink several times.)

ALL *(sing):*

We feel gigantically well,
Just like five hundred sows.

MEPHISTO:

Look there how well men are when they are free.

FAUST:

I should like to get out of here.

MEPHISTO:

First watch how their bestiality
Will in full splendor soon appear.

SIEBEL *(drinks carelessly and spills his wine on the floor where it turns into a flame):*

Help! Fire! Help! Hell blew a vent!

MEPHISTO *(conjuring the flame):*

Be quiet, friendly element!

(to the fellow):

For this time it was only a drop of purgatory.

SIEBEL:

You'll pay for it, and you can save your story!
What do you think we are, my friend?

FROSCH:
Laß Er uns das zum zweiten Male bleiben!

ALTMAYER:
2305 Ich dächt, wir hießen ihn ganz sachte seitwärts gehn.

SIEBEL:
Was, Herr? Er will sich unterstehn
Und hier sein Hokuspokus treiben?

MEPHISTOPHELES:
Still, altes Weinfaß!

SIEBEL:
Besenstiel!
Du willst uns gar noch grob begegnen?

BRANDER:
2310 Wart nur, es sollen Schläge regnen!

ALTMAYER *(zieht einen Pfropf aus dem Tisch, es springt ihm Feuer entgegen):*
Ich brenne! Ich brenne!

SIEBEL:
Zauberei!
Stoß zu! Der Kerl ist vogelfrei!
(Sie ziehen die Messer und gehn auf Mephistopheles los)

MEPHISTOPHELES *(mit ernsthafter Gebärde):*
Falsch Gebild und Wort
Verändern Sinn und Ort!
2315 Seid hier und dort!
(Sie stehn erstaunt und sehn einander an)

ALTMAYER:
Wo bin ich? Welches schöne Land!

FROSCH:
Weinberge! Seh ich recht?

SIEBEL:
Und Trauben gleich zur Hand!

BRANDES:
Hier unter dieser grünen Laube,
Seht, welch ein Stock! Seht, welche Traube!

FROSCH:

Don't dare do that a second time, you hear!

ALTMAYER:

Just let him leave in silence; that is what I say, gents!

SIEBEL:

You have the brazen impudence
To do your hocus-pocus here?

MEPHISTO:

Be still, old barrel!

SIEBEL:

Broomstick, you!
Will you insult us? Mind your prose!

BRANDER:

Just wait and see, there will be blows.

ALTMAYER *(pulls a stopper out of the table and fire leaps at him):*

I burn! I burn!

SIEBEL:

It's magic, as I said.
He is an outlaw. Strike him dead!
(They draw their knives and advance on MEPHISTOPHELES.)

MEPHISTO *(with solemn gestures):*

False images prepare
Mirages in the air.
Be here and there!
(They stand amazed and stare at each other.)

ALTMAYER:

Where am I? What a gorgeous land!

FROSCH:

And vineyards! Am I mad?

SIEBEL:

And grapes right by my hand!

BRANDER:

See in the leaves that purple shape?
I never saw that big a grape!

(Er faßt Siebeln bei der Nase. Die andern tun es wechselseitig und heben die Messer)

MEPHISTOPHELES *(wie oben):*

2320 Irrtum, laß los der Augen Band!
Und merkt euch, wie der Teufel spaße.
(Er verschwindet mit Faust, die Gesellen fahren auseinander)

SIEBEL:
Was gibt's?

ALTMAYER:
Wie?

FROSCH:
War das deine Nase?

BRANDER *(zu Siebel):*
Und deine hab ich in der Hand!

ALTMAYER:
Es war ein Schlag, der ging durch alle Glieder.
2325 Schafft einen Stuhl, ich sinke nieder!

FROSCH:
Nein, sagt mir nur, was ist geschehn?

SIEBEL:
Wo ist der Kerl? Wenn ich ihn spüre,
Er soll mir nicht lebendig gehn!

ALTMAYER:
Ich hab ihn selbst hinaus zur Kellertüre—
2330 Auf einem Fasse reiten sehn——
Es liegt mir bleischwer in den Füßen.
(Sich nach dem Tische wendend.)
Mein! Sollte wohl der Wein noch fließen?

SIEBEL:
Betrug war alles, Lug und Schein.

FROSCH:
Mir deuchte doch, als tränk ich Wein.

BRANDER:
2335 Aber wie war es mit den Trauben?

ALTMAYER:
Nun sag mir eins, man soll kein Wunder glauben!

(Grabs SIEBEL'S *nose. They all do it to each other and raise their knives.)*

MEPHISTO *(as above):*

Fall from their eyes, illusion's band!
Remember how the Devil joked.
(He disappears with FAUST, *the revelers separate.)*

SIEBEL:

What's that?

ALTMAYER:

Hah?

FROSCH:

Your nose I stroked?

BRANDER *(to* SIEBEL):

And yours is in my hand!

ALTMAYER:

The shock is more than I can bear.
I think I'll faint. Get me a chair!

FROSCH:

What was all this? Who understands?

SIEBEL:

Where is the scoundrel? I'm so sore,
If I could only get my hands—

ALTMAYER:

I saw him whiz right through the cellar door,
Riding a flying barrel. Zounds,
The fright weighs on me like a thousand pounds.
(Turning toward the table.)
Do you suppose the wine still flows?

SIEBEL:

That was a fraud! You're asinine!

FROSCH:

I surely thought that I drank wine.

BRANDER:

But what about the grapes, I say.

ALTMAYER:

Who says there are no miracles today!

HEXENKÜCHE

Auf einem niedrigen Herde steht ein großer Kessel über dem Feuer. In dem Dampfe, der davon in die Höhe steigt, zeigen sich verschiedene Gestalten. Eine Meerkatze sitzt bei dem Kessel und schäumt ihn und sorgt, daß er nicht überläuft. Der Meerkater mit den Jungen sitzt darneben und wärmt sich. Wände und Decke sind mit dem seltsamsten Hexenhausrat ausgeschmückt.

Faust. Mephistopheles.

FAUST:

Mir widersteht das tolle Zauberwesen!
Versprichst du mir, ich soll genesen
In diesem Wust von Raserei?
2340 Verlang ich Rat von einem alten Weibe?
Und schafft die Sudelköcherei
Wohl dreißig Jahre mir vom Leibe?
Weh mir, wenn du nichts Bessers weißt!
Schon ist die Hoffnung mir verschwunden.
2345 Hat die Natur und hat ein edler Geist
Nicht irgendeinen Balsam ausgefunden?

MEPHISTOPHELES:

Mein Freund, nun sprichst du wieder klug.
Dich zu verjüngen, gibt's auch ein natürlich
Mittel;
Allein es steht in einem andern Buch
2350 Und ist ein wunderlich Kapitel.

FAUST:

Ich will es wissen.

MEPHISTOPHELES:

Gut! ein Mittel, ohne Geld
Und Arzt und Zauberei zu haben:
Begib dich gleich hinaus aufs Feld,
Fang an zu hacken und zu graben,

WITCH'S KITCHEN

On a low stove, a large caldron stands over the fire. In the steam that rises from it, one can see several shapes. A long-tailed female monkey sits near the caldron, skims it, and sees to it that it does not overflow. The male monkey with the little ones sits next to her and warms himself. Walls and ceiling are decorated with the queerest implements of witchcraft.

Faust and Mephistopheles enter.

FAUST:
How I detest this crazy sorcery!
I should get well, you promise me,
In this mad frenzy of a mess?
Do I need the advice of hag fakirs?
And should this quackish sordidness
Reduce my age by thirty years?
I'm lost if that's all you could find.
My hope is drowned in sudden qualm.
Has neither nature nor some noble mind
Invented or contrived a wholesome balm?

MEPHISTO:
My friend, that was nice oratory!
Indeed, to make you young there is one way
that's apter;
But, I regret, that is another story
And forms quite an amazing chapter.

FAUST:
I want to know it.

MEPHISTO:
All right, you need no sorcery
And no physician and no dough.
Just go into the fields and see
What fun it is to dig and hoe;

2355 Erhalte dich und deinen Sinn
In einem ganz beschränkten Kreise,
Ernähre dich mit ungemischter Speise,
Leb mit dem Vieh als Vieh und acht es nicht für Raub,
Den Acker, den du erntest, selbst zu düngen!
2360 Das ist das beste Mittel, glaub,
Auf achtzig Jahr dich zu verjüngen.

FAUST:
Das bin ich nicht gewöhnt, ich kann mich nicht bequemen,
Den Spaten in die Hand zu nehmen.
Das enge Leben steht mir gar nicht an.

MEPHISTOPHELES:
2365 So muß denn doch die Hexe dran.

FAUST:
Warum denn just das alte Weib?
Kannst du den Trank nicht selber brauen?

MEPHISTOPHELES:
Das wär ein schöner Zeitvertreib!
Ich wollt indes wohl tausend Brücken bauen.
2370 Nicht Kunst und Wissenschaft allein,
Geduld will bei dem Werke sein.
Ein stiller Geist ist jahrelang geschäftig,
Die Zeit nur macht die feine Gärung kräftig.
Und alles, was dazu gehört,
2375 Es sind gar wunderbare Sachen!
Der Teufel hat sie's zwar gelehrt;
Allein der Teufel kann's nicht machen.
(Die Tiere erblickend)
Sieh, welch ein zierliches Geschlecht!
Das ist die Magd! Das ist der Knecht!
(Zu den Tieren):
2380 Es scheint, die Frau ist nicht zu Hause?

DIE TIERE:
Beim Schmause,
Aus dem Haus

Live simply and keep all your thoughts
On a few simple objects glued;
Restrict yourself and eat the plainest food;
Live with the beasts, a beast: it is no thievery
To dress the fields you work, with your own dung.
That is the surest remedy:
At eighty, you would still be young.

FAUST:
I am not used to that and can't, I am afraid,
Start now to work with hoe and spade.
For me a narrow life like that's too small.

MEPHISTO:
We need the witch then after all.

FAUST:
Why just the hag with all her grime!
Could you not brew it—with *your* head!

MEPHISTO:
A splendid way to waste my time!
A thousand bridges I could build instead.
Science is not enough, nor art;
In this work patience plays a part.
A quiet spirit plods and plods at length;
Nothing but time can give the brew its strength.
With all the things that go into it,
It's sickening just to *see* them do it.
The Devil taught them, true enough,
But he himself can't make the stuff.
(He sees the ANIMALS.*)*
Just see how delicate they look!
This is the maid, and that the cook.
(To the ANIMALS*):*
It seems the lady isn't home?

ANIMALS:
She went to roam
Away from home,

Zum Schornstein hinaus!

MEPHISTOPHELES:

Wie lange pflegt sie wohl zu schwärmen?

DIE TIERE:

2385 So lange wir uns die Pfoten wärmen.

MEPHISTOPHELES *(zu Faust):*

Wie findest du die zarten Tiere?

FAUST:

So abgeschmackt, als ich nur jemand sah.

MEPHISTOPHELES:

Nein, ein Diskurs wie dieser da
Ist grade der, den ich am liebsten führe.
(Zu den Tieren):

2390 So sagt mir doch, verfluchte Puppen,
Was quirlt ihr in dem Brei herum?

DIE TIERE:

Wir kochen breite Bettelsuppen.

MEPHISTOPHELES:

Da habt ihr ein groß Publikum.

DER KATER *(macht sich herbei und schmeichelt dem Mephistopheles):*

O würfle nur gleich
2395 Und mache mich reich
Und laß mich gewinnen!
Gar schlecht ist's bestellt,
Und wär ich bei Geld,
So wär ich bei Sinnen.

MEPHISTOPHELES:

2400 Wie glücklich würde sich der Affe schätzen,
Könnt er nur auch ins Lotto setzen!
(Indessen haben die jungen Meerkätzchen mit einer großen Kugel gespielt und rollen sie hervor.)

DER KATER:

Das ist die Welt:
Sie steigt und fällt
Und rollt beständig;

Right through the chimney in the dome.

MEPHISTO:

And how long will she walk the street?

ANIMALS:

As long as we warm our feet.

MEPHISTO (*to* FAUST):

How do you like this dainty pair?

FAUST:

They are inane beyond comparison.

MEPHISTO:

A conversation like this one
Is just the sort of thing for which I care.

(*To the* ANIMALS):

Now tell me, you accursed group,
Why do you stir that steaming mess?

ANIMALS:

We cook a watery beggars' soup.

MEPHISTO:

You should do a brisk business.

MALE MONKEY (*approaches* MEPHISTOPHELES *and fawns*):

Oh please throw the dice
And lose, and be nice
And let me get wealthy!
We are in the ditch,
And if I were rich,
Then I might be healthy.

MEPHISTO:

How happy every monkey thinks he'd be,
If he could play the lottery.
(*Meanwhile the monkey youngsters have been playing with a large ball, and now they roll it forward.*)

MALE MONKEY:

The world and ball
Both rise and fall
And roll and wallow;

2405 Sie klingt wie Glas—
Wie bald bricht das!
Ist hohl inwendig.
Hier glänzt sie sehr
Und hier noch mehr:
2410 Ich bin lebendig!
Mein lieber Sohn,
Halt dich davon!
Du mußt sterben!
Sie ist von Ton,
2415 Es gibt Scherben.

MEPHISTOPHELES:
Was soll das Sieb?

DER KATER *(holt es herunter):*
Wärst du ein Dieb,
Wollt ich dich gleich erkennen.
(Er läuft zur Kätzin und läßt sie durchsehen.)
Sieh durch das Sieb!
2420 Erkennst du den Dieb
Und darfst ihn nicht nennen?

MEPHISTOPHELES *(sich dem Feuer nähernd):*
Und dieser Topf?

KATER UND KÄTZIN:
Der alberne Tropf!
Er kennt nicht den Topf,
2425 Er kennt nicht den Kessel!

MEPHISTOPHELES:
Unhöfliches Tier!

DER KATER:
Den Wedel nimm hier
Und setz dich in Sessel!
(Er nötigt den Mephistopheles zu sitzen.)

FAUST *(welcher diese Zeit über vor einem Spiegel gestanden, sich ihm bald genähert, bald sich von ihm entfernt hat.)*
Was seh ich? Welch ein himmlisch Bild

It sounds like glass,
It bursts, alas,
The inside's hollow.
Here it is light,
There still more bright,
Life's mine to swallow!
Dear son, I say,
Please keep away!
You'll die first.
It's made of clay
It will burst.

MEPHISTO:

The sieve there, chief—?

MALE MONKEY *(gets it down):*

If you were a thief,
I'd be wise to you.

(He runs to the female monkey and lets her see through it.)

Look through, be brief!
You know the thief,
But may not say *who?*

MEPHISTO *(approaching the fire):*

And here this pot?

BOTH BIG MONKEYS:

The half-witted sot!
Does not know the pot,
Does not know the kettle!

MEPHISTO:

You impolite beast!

MALE MONKEY:

Take this brush at least
And sit down and settle!

(He makes MEPHISTOPHELES *sit down.)*

FAUST *(who has been standing before a mirror all this time, now stepping close to it, now back):*

What blissful image is revealed

2430 Zeigt sich in diesem Zauberspiegel!
O Liebe, leihe mir den schnellsten deiner Flügel
Und führe mich in ihr Gefild!
Ach, wenn ich nicht auf dieser Stelle bleibe,
Wenn ich es wage, nah zu gehn,
2435 Kann ich sie nur als wie im Nebel sehn!—
Das schönste Bild von einem Weibe!
Ist's möglich, ist das Weib so schön?
Muß ich an diesem hingestreckten Leibe
Den Inbegriff von allen Himmeln sehn?
2440 So etwas findet sich auf Erden?

MEPHISTOPHELES:
Natürlich, wenn ein Gott sich erst sechs Tage plagt
Und selbst am Ende bravo sagt,
Da muß es was Gescheites werden.
Für diesmal sieh dich immer satt!
2445 Ich weiß dir so ein Schätzchen auszuspüren,
Und selig, wer das gute Schicksal hat,
Als Bräutigam sie heimzuführen!
(Faust sieht immerfort in den Spiegel. Mephistopheles, sich in dem Sessel dehnend und mit dem Wedel spielend, fährt fort zu sprechen)
Hier sitz ich wie der König auf dem Throne,
Den Zepter halt ich hier, es fehlt nur noch die Krone.

DIE TIERE *(welche bisher allerlei wunderliche Bewegungen durcheinander gemacht haben, bringen dem Mephistopheles eine Krone mit großem Geschrei):*
2450 O sei doch so gut,
Mit Schweiß und mit Blut
Die Krone zu leimen!
(Sie gehn ungeschickt mit der Krone um und zerbrechen sie in zwei Stücke, mit welchen

To me behind this magic glass!
Lend me your swiftest pinions, love, that I
might pass
From here to her transfigured field!
When I don't stay right on this spot, but, pining,
Dare to step forward and go near
Mists cloud her shape and let it disappear.
The fairest image of a woman!
Indeed, could woman be so fair?
Or is this body which I see reclining
Heaven's quintessence from another sphere?
Is so much beauty found on earth?

MEPHISTO:

Well, if a god works hard for six whole days, my
friend,
And then says bravo in the end,
It ought to have a little worth.
For now, stare to your heart's content!
I could track down for you just such a sweet—
What bliss it would be to get her consent,
To marry her and be replete.
(FAUST *gazes into the mirror all the time.*
MEPHISTOPHELES, *stretching in the armchair and playing with the brush, goes on speaking*):
I sit here like the king upon his throne:
The scepter I hold here, I lack the crown alone.

ANIMALS (*who have so far moved around in quaint confusion, bring a crown to* MEPHISTOPHELES, *clamoring loudly*):

Oh, please be so good,
With sweat and with blood
This crown here to lime!

(*They handle the crown clumsily and break it into two pieces with which they jump around.*)

sie herumspringen)

Nun ist es geschehn!
Wir reden und sehn,
2455 Wir hören und reimen—

FAUST *(gegen den Spiegel):*
Weh mir! Ich werde schier verrückt.

MEPHISTOPHELES *(auf die Tiere deutend):*
Nun fängt mir an fast selbst der Kopf zu schwanken.

DIE TIERE:
Und wenn es uns glückt
Und wenn es sich schickt,
2460 So sind es Gedanken!

FAUST *(wie oben):*
Mein Busen fängt mir an zu brennen!
Entfernen wir uns nur geschwind!

MEPHISTOPHELES *(in obiger Stellung):*
Nun, wenigstens muß man bekennen,
Daß es aufrichtige Poeten sind.

(Der Kessel, welchen die Kätzin bisher außer acht gelassen, fängt an überzulaufen; es entsteht eine große Flamme, welche zum Schornstein hinausschlägt. Die Hexe kommt durch die Flamme mit entsetzlichem Geschrei heruntergefahren.)

DIE HEXE:
2465 Au! Au! Au! Au!
Verdammtes Tier! Verfluchte Sau!
Versäumst den Kessel, versengst die Frau!
Verfluchtes Tier!
(Faust und Mephistopheles erblickend.)
Was ist das hier?
2470 Wer seid ihr hier?
Was wollt ihr da?
Wer schlich sich ein?
Die Feuerpein
Euch ins Gebein!

It's done, let it be!
We chatter and see,
We listen and rhyme—

FAUST *(at the mirror):*
Alas, I think I'll lose my wits.

MEPHISTO *(pointing toward the* ANIMALS*):*
I fear that my head, too, begins to reel.

ANIMALS:
And if we score hits
And everything fits,
It's thoughts that we feel.

FAUST *(as above):*
My heart and soul are catching fire.
Please let us go away from here!

MEPHISTO *(in the same position as above):*
The one thing one has to admire
Is that their poetry is quite sincere.
(The caldron which the female monkey has neglected begins to run over, and a huge flame blazes up through the chimney. The WITCH *scoots down through the flame with a dreadful clamor.)*

WITCH:
Ow! Ow! Ow! Ow!
You damned old beast! You cursed old sow!
You leave the kettle and singe the frau.
You cursed old beast!
(Sees FAUST *and* MEPHISTOPHELES.*)*
What goes on here?
Why are you here?
Who are you two?
Who sneaked inside?
Come, fiery tide!
Their bones be fried!

(Sie fährt mit dem Schaumlöffel in den Kessel und spritzt Flammen nach Faust, Mephistopheles und den Tieren. Die Tiere winseln.)

MEPHISTOPHELES *(welcher den Wedel, den er in der Hand hält, umkehrt und unter die Gläser und Töpfe schlägt):*

2475 Entzwei! Entzwei!
Da liegt der Brei!
Da liegt das Glas!
Es ist nur Spaß,
Der Takt, du Aas,
2480 Zu deiner Melodei.

(Indem die Hexe voll Grimm und Entsetzen zurücktritt.)

Erkennst du mich? Gerippe! Scheusal du!
Erkennst du deinen Herrn und Meister?
Was hält mich ab, so schlag ich zu,
Zerschmettre dich und deine Katzengeister.
2485 Hast du vorm roten Wams nicht mehr Respekt?
Kannst du die Hahnenfeder nicht erkennen?
Hab ich dies Angesicht versteckt?
Soll ich mich etwa selber nennen?

DIE HEXE:

O herr, verzeiht den rohen Gruß!
2490 Seh ich doch keinen Pferdefuß.
Wo sind denn Eure beiden Raben?

MEPHISTOPHELES:

Für diesmal kommst du so davon;
Denn freilich ist es eine Weile schon,
Daß wir uns nicht gesehen haben.
2495 Auch die Kultur, die alle Welt beleckt,
Hat auf den Teufel sich erstreckt;
Das nordische Phantom ist nun nicht mehr zu schauen:
Wo siehst du Hörner, Schweif und Klauen?
Und was den Fuß betrifft, den ich nicht missen kann,

(She plunges the skimming spoon into the caldron and spatters flames at FAUST, MEPHISTOPHELES, *and the* ANIMALS. *The* ANIMALS *whine.)*

MEPHISTO *(reversing the brush he holds in his hand, and striking into the glasses and pots):*

In two! In two!
There lies the brew.
There lies the glass.
A joke, my lass,
The beat, you ass,
For melodies from you.

(As the WITCH *retreats in wrath and horror):*

You know me now? You skeleton! You shrew!
You know your master and your lord?
What holds me? I could strike at you
And shatter you and your foul monkey horde.
Does not the scarlet coat reveal His Grace?
Do you not know the rooster's feather, ma'am?
Did I perchance conceal my face?
Or must I tell you who I am?

WITCH:

Forgive the uncouth greeting, though
You have no cloven feet, you know.
And your two ravens, where are they?

MEPHISTO:

For just this once you may get by,
For it has been some time, I don't deny,
Since I have come your way,
And culture which licks out at every stew
Extends now to the Devil, too:
Gone is the Nordic phantom that former ages saw;
You see no horns, no tail or claw.
And as regards the foot with which I can't
dispense,
That does not look the least bit suave;

2500 Der würde mir bei den Leuten schaden;
Darum bedien ich mich, wie mancher junge Mann,
Seit vielen Jahren falscher Waden.

DIE HEXE *(tanzend):*
Sinn und Verstand verlier ich schier,
Seh ich den Junker Satan wieder hier!

MEPHISTOPHELES:
2505 Den Namen, Weib, verbitt ich mir!

DIE HEXE:
Warum? Was hat er Euch getan?

MEPHISTOPHELES:
Er ist schon lang ins Fabelbuch geschrieben;
Allein die Menschen sind nichts besser dran,
Den Bösen sind sie los, die Bösen sind geblieben.
2510 Du nennst mich Herr Baron, so ist die Sache gut;
Ich bin ein Kavalier wie andre Kavaliere.
Du zweifelst nicht an meinem edlen Blut;
Sieh her, das ist das Wappen, das ich führe!
(Er macht eine unanständige Gebärde)

DIE HEXE *(lacht unmäßig):*
Ha! Ha! Das ist in Eurer Art!
2515 Ihr seid ein Schelm, wie Ihr nur immer wart.

MEPHISTOPHELES *(zu Faust):*
Mein Freund, das lerne wohl verstehn!
Dies ist die Art, mit Hexen umzugehn.

DIE HEXE:
Nun sagt, ihr Herren, was ihr schafft!

MEPHISTOPHELES:
Ein gutes Glas von dem bekannten Saft!
2520 Doch muß ich Euch ums ältste bitten;
Die Jahre doppeln seine Kraft.

DIE HEXE:
Gar gern! Hier hab ich eine Flasche,
Aus der ich selbst zuweilen nasche,
Die auch nicht mehr im mindsten stinkt;
2525 Ich will euch gern ein Gläschen geben.

Like other young men nowadays, I hence
Prefer to pad my calves.

WITCH *(dancing):*
I'll lose my wits, I'll lose my brain
Since Squire Satan has come back again.

MEPHISTO:
That name is out, hag! Is that plain?

WITCH:
But why? It never gave you pain!

MEPHISTO:
It's dated, called a fable; men are clever,
But they are just as badly off as ever:
The Evil One is gone, the evil ones remain.
You call me baron, hag, and you look out:
I am a cavalier with cavalierly charms,
And my nobility don't dare to doubt!
Look here and you will see my coat of arms!
(He makes an indecent gesture.)

WITCH *(laughs immoderately):*
Ha! Ha! That is your manner, sir!
You are a jester as you always were.

MEPHISTO *(to* FAUST*):*
My friend, mark this, but don't repeat it:
This is the way a witch likes to be treated.

WITCH:
Now tell me why you came in here.

MEPHISTO:
A good glass of the famous juice, my dear!
But I must have the oldest kind:
Its strength increases with each year.

WITCH:
I got a bottle on this shelf
From which I like to nip myself;
By now it doesn't even stink.
I'll give you some, it has the power.

(Leise):

Doch wenn es dieser Mann unvorbereitet trinkt,
So kann er, wißt Ihr wohl, nicht eine Stunde leben.

MEPHISTOPHELES:

Es ist ein guter Freund, dem es gedeihen soll;
Ich gönn ihm gern das Beste deiner Küche.
2530 Zieh deinen Kreis, sprich deine Sprüche
Und gib ihm eine Tasse voll!

DIE HEXE *(mit seltsamen Gebärden, zieht einen Kreis und stellt wunderbare Sachen hinein; indessen fangen die Gläser an zu klingen, die Kessel zu tönen und machen Musik. Zuletzt bringt sie ein großes Buch, stellt die Meerkatzen in den Kreis, die ihr zum Pult dienen und die Fackel halten müssen. Sie winkt Fausten, zu ihr zu treten).*

FAUST *(zu Mephistopheles):*

Nein, sage mir, was soll das werden?
Das tolle Zeug, die rasenden Gebärden,
Der abgeschmackteste Betrug
2535 Sind mir bekannt, verhaßt genug.

MEPHISTOPHELES:

Ei Possen! Das ist nur zum Lachen;
Sei nur nicht ein so strenger Mann!
Sie muß als Arzt ein Hokuspokus machen,
Damit der Saft dir wohl gedeihen kann.

(Er nötigt Fausten, in den Kreis zu treten)

DIE HEXE *(mit großer Emphase fängt an, aus dem Buche zu deklamieren):*

2540 Du mußt verstehn!
Aus Eins mach Zehn
Und Zwei laß gehn
Und Drei mach gleich,
So bist du reich.
2545 Verlier die Vier!
Aus Fünf und Sechs,
So sagt die Hex,

(Softly):

But if, quite unprepared, this man should have a drink,
He could, as you know well, not live another hour.

MEPHISTO:

He is a friend of mine, and he will take it well.
The best you have is not too good for him.
Now draw your circle, say your spell,
And fill a bumper to the brim.

WITCH *(draws a circle with curious gestures and puts quaint objects into it, while the glasses begin to tinkle, the caldrons begin to resound and they make music. In the end, she gets a big book and puts the monkeys into the circle, and they serve her as a desk and have to hold a torch for her. She motions* FAUST *to step up).*

FAUST *(to* MEPHISTO*):*

No, tell me why these crazy antics?
The mad ado, the gestures that are frantic,
The most insipid cheat—this stuff
I've known and hated long enough.

MEPHISTO:

Relax! It's fun—a little play;
Don't be so serious, so sedate!
Such hocus-pocus is a doctor's way,
Of making sure the juice will operate.
(He makes FAUST *step into the circle.)*

WITCH *(begins to recite from the book with great emphasis):*

This you must know!
From one make ten,
And two let go,
Take three again,
Then you'll be rich.
The four you fix.
From five and six,
Thus says the witch,

Mach Sieben und Acht,
2550 So ist's vollbracht:
Und Neun ist Eins,
Und Zehn ist keins.
Das ist das Hexen-Einmal-Eins.

FAUST:

Mich dünkt, die Alte spricht im Fieber.

MEPHISTOPHELES:

2555 Das ist noch lange nicht vorüber,
Ich kenn es wohl, so klingt das ganze Buch;
Ich habe manche Zeit damit verloren,
Denn ein vollkommner Widerspruch
Bleibt gleich geheimnisvoll für Kluge wie für
Toren.
Mein Freund, die Kunst ist alt und neu.
2560 Es war die Art zu allen Zeiten,
Durch Drei und Eins und Eins und Drei
Irrtum statt Wahrheit zu verbreiten.
So schwätzt und lehrt man ungestört;
Wer will sich mit den Narrn befassen?
2565 Gewöhnlich glaubt der Mensch, wenn er nur
Worte hört,
Es müsse sich dabei doch auch was denken lassen.

DIE HEXE *(fährt fort):*

Die hohe Kraft
Der Wissenschaft,
Der ganzen Welt verborgen!
2570 Und wer nicht denkt,
Dem wird sie geschenkt,
Er hat sie ohne Sorgen.

FAUST:

Was sagt sie uns für Unsinn vor?
Es wird mir gleich den Kopf zerbrechen.
2575 Mich dünkt, ich hör ein ganzes Chor
Von hunderttausend Narren sprechen.

MEPHISTOPHELES:

Genug, genug, o treffliche Sibylle!

Make seven and eight,
That does the trick;
And nine is one,
And ten is none.
That is the witch's arithmetic.

FAUST:

It seems to me the old hag runs a fever.

MEPHISTO:

You'll hear much more before we leave her.
I know, it sounds like that for many pages.
I lost much time on this accursed affliction,
Because a perfect contradiction
Intrigues not only fools but also sages.
This art is old and new, forsooth:
It was the custom in all ages
To spread illusion and not truth
With Three in One and One in Three.
They teach it twittering like birds;
With fools there is no intervening.
Men usually believe, if only they hear words,
That there must also be some sort of meaning.

WITCH *(continues)*:

The lofty prize
Of science lies
Concealed today as ever.
Who has no thought,
To him it's brought
To own without endeavor.

FAUST:

What nonsense does she put before us?
My head aches from her stupidness.
It seems as if I heard a chorus
Of many thousand fools, no less.

MEPHISTO:

Excellent sybil, that is quite enough!

Gib deinen Trank herbei und fülle
Die Schale rasch bis an den Rand hinan!
2580 Denn meinem Freund wird dieser Trunk nicht schaden:
Er ist ein Mann von vielen Graden,
Der manchen guten Schluck getan.

DIE HEXE *(mit vielen Zeremonien, schenkt den Trank in eine Schale; wie sie Faust an den Mund bringt, ensteht eine leichte Flamme.)*

MEPHISTOPHELES:
Nur frisch hinunter! Immer zu!
Es wird dir gleich das Herz erfreuen.
2585 Bist mit dem Teufel du und du
Und willst dich vor der Flamme scheuen?
(Die Hexe löst den Kreis. Faust tritt heraus.)

MEPHISTOPHELES:
Nun frisch hinaus! Du darfst nicht ruhn.

DIE HEXE:
Mög Euch das Schlückchen wohl behagen!

MEPHISTOPHELES *(zur Hexe):*
Und kann ich dir was zu Gefallen tun,
2590 So darfst du mir's nur auf Walpurgis sagen.

DIE HEXE:
Hier ist ein Lied! Wenn Ihr's zuweilen singt,
So werdet Ihr besondre Wirkung spüren.

MEPHISTOPHELES *(zu Faust):*
Komm nur geschwind und laß dich führen!
Du mußt notwendig transpirieren,
2595 Damit die Kraft durch Inn- und Außres dringt.
Den edlen Müßiggang lehr ich hernach dich schätzen,
Und bald empfindest du mit innigem Ergetzen,
Wie sich Kupido regt und hin und wider springt.

FAUST:
Laß mich nur schnell noch in den Spiegel schauen!
2600 Das Frauenbild war gar zu schön!

Now pour the drink—just put the stuff
Into this bowl here. Fill it, sybil, pour;
My friend is safe from any injuries:
He has a number of degrees
And has had many drinks before.

WITCH *(pours the drink into a bowl with many ceremonies; as* FAUST *puts it to his lips, a small flame spurts up.)*

MEPHISTO:

What is the matter? Hold it level!
Drink fast and it will warm you up.
You are familiar with the Devil,
And shudder at a fiery cup?
(The WITCH *breaks the circle.* FAUST *steps out.)*

MEPHISTO:

Come on! Let's go! You must not rest.

WITCH:

And may this gulp give great delight!

MEPHISTO *(to the* WITCH*)*:

If there is anything that you request,
Just let me know the next Walpurgis Night.

WITCH:

Here is a song; just sing it now and then,
And you will feel a queer effect indeed.

MEPHISTO *(to* FAUST*)*:

Come quickly now before you tire,
And let me lead while you perspire
So that the force can work out through your skin.
I'll teach you later on to value noble leisure,
And soon you will perceive the most delightful pleasure,
As Cupid starts to stir and dance like jumping jinn.

FAUST:

One last look at the mirror where I stood!
So beauteous was that woman's form!

MEPHISTOPHELES:

Nein! Nein! Du sollst das Muster aller Frauen
Nun bald leibhaftig vor dir sehn.

(Leise):

Du siehst mit diesem Trank im Leibe
Bald Helenen in jedem Weibe.

STRAßE

Faust. Margarete vorubergehend.

FAUST:

2605 Mein schönes Fräulein, darf ich wagen,
Meinen Arm und Geleit Ihr anzutragen?

MARGARETE:

Bin weder Fräulein, weder schön,
Kann ungeleitet nach Hause gehn.
(Sie macht sich los und ab.)

FAUST:

Beim Himmel, dieses Kind ist schön!
2610 So etwas hab ich nie gesehn.
Sie ist so sitt- und tugendreich
Und etwas schnippisch doch zugleich.
Der Lippe Rot, der Wange Licht,
Die Tage der Welt vergess ich's nicht!
2615 Wie sie die Augen niederschlägt,
Hat tief sich in mein Herz geprägt;
Wie sie kurz angebunden war,
Das ist nun zum Entzücken gar!
(Mephistopheles tritt auf.)

FAUST:

Hör, du mußt mir die Dirne schaffen!

MEPHISTO:

No! No! The paragon of womanhood
You shall soon see alive and warm.

(Softly):

You'll soon find, with this potion's aid,
Helen of Troy in every maid.

STREET

Faust. Margaret passing by.

FAUST:

Fair lady, may I be so free
To offer my arm and company?

MARGARET:

I'm neither a lady nor am I fair,
And can go home without your care.
(She frees herself and exits.)

FAUST:

By heaven, this young girl is fair!
Her like I don't know anywhere.
She is so virtuous and pure,
But somewhat pert and not demure.
The glow of her cheeks and her lips so red
I shall not forget until I am dead.
Her downcast eyes, shy and yet smart,
Are stamped forever on my heart;
Her curtness and her brevity
Was sheer enchanting ecstasy!
(MEPHISTOPHELES *enters.)*

FAUST:

Get me that girl, and don't ask why?

MEPHISTOPHELES:

2620 Nun, welche?

FAUST:

Sie ging just vorbei.

MEPHISTOPHELES:

Da die? Sie kam von ihrem Pfaffen,
Der sprach sie aller Sünden frei;
Ich schlich mich hart am Stuhl vorbei.
Es ist ein gar unschuldig Ding,
2625 Das eben für nichts zur Beichte ging;
Über die hab ich keine Gewalt.

FAUST:

Ist über vierzehn Jahr doch alt.

MEPHISTOPHELES:

Du sprichst ja wie Hans Liederlich,
Der begehrt jede liebe Blum für sich,
2630 Und dünkelt ihm, es wär kein Ehr
Und Gunst, die nicht zu pflücken wär;
Geht aber doch nicht immer an.

FAUST:

Mein Herr Magister Lobesan,
Lass Er mich mit dem Gesetz in Frieden!
2635 Und das sag ich Ihm kurz und gut:
Wenn nicht das süße junge Blut
Heut nacht in meinen Armen ruht,
So sind wir um Mitternacht geschieden.

MEPHISTOPHELES:

Bedenkt, was gehn und stehen mag!
2640 Ich brauche wenigstens vierzehn Tag,
Nur die Gelegenheit auszuspüren.

FAUST:

Hätt ich nur sieben Stunden Ruh,
Brauchte den Teufel nicht dazu,
So ein Geschöpfchen zu verführen.

MEPHISTOPHELES:

2645 Ihr sprecht schon fast wie ein Franzos;
Doch bitt ich, laßt's Euch nicht verdrießen!

MEPHISTO:

Which one?

FAUST:

She only just went by.

MEPHISTO:

That one! She saw her priest just now,
And he pronounced her free of sin.
I stood right there and listened in.
She's so completely blemishless
That there was nothing to confess.
Over her I don't have any power.

FAUST:

She is well past her fourteenth year.

MEPHISTO:

Look at the gay Lothario here!
He would like to have every flower,
And thinks each prize or pretty trick
Just waits around for him to pick;
But sometimes that just doesn't go.

FAUST:

My Very Reverend Holy Joe,
Leave me in peace with law and right!
I tell you, if you don't comply,
And this sweet young blood doesn't lie
Between my arms this very night,
At midnight we'll have parted ways.

MEPHISTO:

Think of the limits of my might.
I need at least some fourteen days
To find a handy evening.

FAUST:

If I had peace for seven hours,
I should not need the Devil's powers
To seduce such a little thing.

MEPHISTO:

You speak just like a Frenchman. Wait,
I beg you, and don't be annoyed:

Was hilft's, nur grade zu genießen?
Die Freud ist lange nicht so groß,
Als wenn Ihr erst herauf, herum,
2650 Durch allerlei Brimborium
Das Püppchen geknetet und zugericht't,
Wie's lehret manche welsche Geschicht.

FAUST:

Hab Appetit auch ohne das.

MEPHISTOPHELES:

Jetzt ohne Schimpf und ohne Spaß:
2655 Ich sag Euch, mit dem schönen Kind
Geht's ein- für allemal nicht geschwind.
Mit Sturm ist da nichts einzunehmen;
Wir müssen uns zur List bequemen.

FAUST:

Schaff mir etwas vom Engelsschatz!
2660 Führ mich an ihren Ruheplatz!
Schaff mir ein Halstuch von ihrer Brust,
Ein Strumpfband meiner Liebeslust!

MEPHISTOPHELES:

Damit Ihr seht, daß ich Eurer Pein
Will förderlich und dienstlich sein,
2665 Wollen wir keinen Augenblick verlieren,
Will Euch noch heut in ihr Zimmer führen.

FAUST:

Und soll sie sehn? Sie haben?

MEPHISTOPHELES:

Nein!
Sie wird bei einer Nachbarin sein.
Indessen könnt Ihr ganz allein
2670 An aller Hoffnung künftger Freuden
In ihrem Dunstkreis satt Euch weiden.

FAUST:

Können wir hin?

MEPHISTOPHELES:

Es ist noch zu früh.

What have you got when it's enjoyed?
The fun is not nearly so great
As when you bit by bit imbibe it,
And first resort to playful folly
To knead and to prepare your dolly,
The way some Gallic tales describe it.

FAUST:
I've appetite without all that.

MEPHISTO:
Now without jokes or tit-for-tat:
I tell you, with this fair young child
We simply can't be fast or wild.
We'd waste our time storming and running;
We have to have recourse to cunning.

FAUST:
Get something from the angel's nest!
Or lead me to her place of rest!
Get me a kerchief from her breast,
A garter from my darling's knee.

MEPHISTO:
Just so you see, it touches me
And I would soothe your agony,
Let us not linger here and thus delay:
I'll take you to her room today.

FAUST:
And shall I see her? Have her?

MEPHISTO:
No.
To one of her neighbors she has to go.
But meanwhile you may at your leisure
Relish the hopes of future pleasure,
Till you are sated with her atmosphere.

FAUST:
Can we go now?

MEPHISTO:
It's early yet, I fear.

FAUST:
Sorg du mir für ein Geschenk für sie! *(Ab.)*

MEPHISTOPHELES:
Gleich schenken? Das ist brav! Da wird er reüssieren!

2675 Ich kenne manchen schönen Platz
Und manchen altvergrabnen Schatz,
Ich muß ein bißchen revidieren. *(Ab.)*

ABEND

Ein kleines reinliches Zimmer.

MARGARETE *(ihre Zöpfe flechtend und aufbindend):*
Ich gäb was drum, wenn ich nur wüßt,
Wer heut der Herr gewesen ist.
2680 Er sah gewiß recht wacker aus
Und ist aus einem edlen Haus;
Das konnt ich ihm an der Stirne lesen—
Er wär auch sonst nicht so keck gewesen. *(Ab.)*

MEPHISTOPHELES. FAUST.

MEPHISTOPHELES:
Herein, ganz leise, nur herein!

FAUST *(nach einigem Stillschweigen):*
2685 Ich bitte dich, laß mich allein!

MEPHISTOPHELES *(herumspürend):*
Nicht jedes Mädchen hält so rein. *(Ab.)*

FAUST *(rings aufschauend):*
Willkommen, süßer Dämmerschein,
Der du dies Heiligtum durchwebst!
Ergreif mein Herz, du süße Liebespein,
2690 Die du vom Tau der Hoffnung schmachtend lebst!

FAUST:

Get me a present for the dear! *(Exit.)*

MEPHISTO:

A present right away? Good! He will be a hit.
There's many a nice place I know
With treasures buried long ago;
I better look around a bit. *(Exit.)*

EVENING

A small neat room.

MARGARET *(braiding and binding her hair):*

I should give much if I could say
Who was that gentleman today.
He looked quite gallant, certainly,
And is of noble family;
That much even his forehead told—
How else could he have been so bold? *(Exit.)*

MEPHISTOPHELES. FAUST.

MEPHISTO:

Come in, but very quietly!

FAUST *(after a short silence):*

I beg you, leave and let me be!

MEPHISTO *(sniffing around):*

She's neater than a lot of girls I see. *(Exit.)*

FAUST *(looking up and around):*

Sweet light of dusk, guest from above
That fills this shrine, be welcome you!
Seize now my heart, sweet agony of love
That languishes and feeds on hope's clear dew!

Wie atmet rings Gefühl der Stille,
Der Ordnung, der Zufriedenheit!
In dieser Armut welche Fülle!
In diesem Kerker welche Seligkeit!
(Er wirft sich auf den ledernen Sessel am Bette.)

2695 O nimm mich auf, der du die Vorwelt schon
Bei Freud und Schmerz im offnen Arm
empfangen!
Wie oft, ach, hat an diesem Väterthron
Schon eine Schar von Kindern rings gehangen!
Vielleicht hat, dankbar für den heilgen Christ,
2700 Mein Liebchen hier mit vollen Kinderwangen
Dem Ahnherrn fromm die welke Hand geküßt.
Ich fühl, o Mädchen, deinen Geist
Der Füll und Ordnung um mich säuseln,
Der mütterlich dich täglich unterweist,
2705 Den Teppich auf dem Tisch dich reinlich breiten
heißt,
Sogar den Sand zu deinen Füßen kräuseln.
O liebe Hand! So göttergleich!
Die Hütte wird durch dich ein Himmelreich.
Und hier! *(Er hebt einen Bettvorhang auf)*
Was faßt mich für ein Wonnegraus!
2710 Hier möcht ich volle Stunden säumen.
Natur, hier bildetest in leichten Träumen
Den eingebornen Engel aus!
Hier lag das Kind, mit warmem Leben
Den zarten Busen angefüllt,
Und hier mit heilig reinem Weben
Entwirkte sich das Götterbild!

2715 Und du! Was hat dich hergeführt?
Wie innig fühl ich mich gerührt!
Was willst du hier? Was wird das Herz dir
schwer?
2720 Armselger Faust! Ich kenne dich nicht mehr.

What sense of calm embraces me,
Of order and complete content!
What bounty in this poverty!
And in this prison, ah, what ravishment!
(He throws himself into the leather armchair by the bed.)
Welcome me now, as former ages rested
Within your open arms in grief and joy!
How often was this fathers' throne contested
By eager children, prized by girl and boy!
And here, perhaps, her full cheeks flushed with
  bliss,
My darling, grateful for a Christmas toy,
Pressed on her grandsire's withered hand a kiss.
I feel your spirit, lovely maid,
Of ordered bounty breathing here
Which, motherly, comes daily to your aid
To teach you how a rug is best on tables laid
And how the sand should on the floor appear.
Oh godlike hand, to you it's given
To make a cottage, a kingdom of heaven.
And here! *(He lifts a bed curtain.)*
  What raptured shudder makes me stir?
How I should love to be immured
Where in light dreams nature matured
The angel that's innate in her.
Here lay the child, developed slowly,
Her tender breast with warm life fraught,
And here, through weaving pure and holy,
The image of the gods was wrought.

And you! Alas, what brought you here?
I feel so deeply moved, so queer!
What do you seek? Why is your heart so sore?
Poor Faust! I do not know you any more.

Umgibt mich hier ein Zauberduft?
Mich drang's, so grade zu genießen,
Und fühle mich in Liebestraum zerfließen.
Sind wir ein Spiel von jedem Druck der Luft?

2725 Und träte sie den Augenblick herein,
Wie würdest du für deinen Frevel büßen!
Der große Hans, ach, wie so klein,
Läg hingeschmolzen ihr zu Füßen.

MEPHISTOPHELES *(kommt):*
Geschwind! Ich seh sie unten kommen.

FAUST:
2730 Fort! Fort! Ich kehre nimmermehr!

MEPHISTOPHELES:
Hier ist ein Kästchen leidlich schwer,
Ich hab's wo anders hergenommen.
Stellt's hier nur immer in den Schrein!
Ich schwör Euch, ihr vergehn die Sinnen;
2735 Ich tat Euch Sächelchen hinein,
Um eine andre zu gewinnen.
Zwar Kind ist Kind, und Spiel ist Spiel.

FAUST:
Ich weiß nicht, soll ich?

MEPHISTOPHELES:
Fragt Ihr viel?
Meint Ihr vielleicht den Schatz zu wahren?
2740 Dann rat ich, Eurer Lüsternheit
Die liebe schöne Tageszeit
Und mir die weitre Müh zu sparen.
Ich hoff nicht, daß Ihr geizig seid.
Ich kratz den Kopf, reib an den Händen—
(Er stellt das Kästchen in den Schrein
und drückt das Schloß wieder zu.)
2745 Nur fort! Geschwind!—
Um Euch das süße junge Kind
Nach Herzens Wunsch und Will zu wenden;

Do magic smells surround me here?
Immediate pleasure was my bent,
But now—in dreams of love I'm all but spent.
Are we mere puppets of the atmosphere?

If she returned this instant from her call,
How for your mean transgression you would pay!
The haughty lad would be so small,
Lie at her feet and melt away.

MEPHISTO *(entering)*:
Let's go! I see her in the lane!

FAUST:
Away! I'll never come again.

MEPHISTO:
Here is a fairly decent case,
I picked it up some other place.
Just leave it in the chest up there.
She'll go out of her mind, I swear;
For I put things in it, good sir,
To win a better one than her.
But child is child and play is play.

FAUST:
I don't know—should I?

MEPHISTO:
Why delay?
You do not hope to save your jewel?
Or I'll give your lust this advice:
Don't waste fair daytime like this twice,
Nor my exertions: it is cruel.
It is not simple greed, I hope!
I scratch my head, I fret and mope—
(He puts the case into the chest and locks it again.)
Away! Let's go!—
It's just to make the child fulfil
Your heart's desire and your will;

Und Ihr seht drein,
Als solltet Ihr in den Hörsaal hinein,
2750 Als stünden grau leibhaftig vor Euch da
Physik und Metaphysika!
Nur fort! *(Ab.)*

MARGARETE *(mit einer Lampe):*
Es ist so schwül, so dumpfig hie,
(Sie macht das Fenster auf.)
Und ist doch eben so warm nicht drauß.
2755 Es wird mir so, ich weiß nicht wie—
Ich wollt, die Mutter käm nach Haus.
Mir läuft ein Schauer übern ganzen Leib—
Bin doch ein töricht furchtsam Weib!
(Sie fängt an zu singen, indem sie sich auszieht.)

Es war ein König in Thule
2760 Gar treu bis an das Grab,
Dem sterbend seine Buhle
Einen goldnen Becher gab.

Es ging ihm nichts darüber,
Er leert' ihn jeden Schmaus;
2765 Die Augen gingen ihm über,
So oft er trank daraus.

Und als er kam zu sterben,
Zählt' er seine Städt und Reich,
Gönnt' alles seinen Erben,
2770 Den Becher nicht zugleich.

Er saß beim Königsmahle,
Die Ritter um ihn her,
Auf hohem Vätersaale
Dort auf dem Schloß am Meer.

2775 Dort stand der alte Zecher,
Trank letzte Lebensglut

And you stand and frown
As if you had to lecture in cap and gown—
As if in gray there stood in front of you
Physics and Metaphysics, too.
Away! *(Exeunt.)*

MARGARET *(with a lamp):*
It seems so close, so sultry now,
(She opens the window.)
And yet outside it's not so warm.
I feel so strange, I don't know how—
I wish my mother would come home.
A shudder grips my body, I feel chilly—
How fearful I am and how silly!
(She begins to sing as she undresses.)

In Thule there was a king,
Faithful unto the grave,
To whom his mistress, dying,
A golden goblet gave.

Nothing he held more dear,
At every meal he used it;
His eyes would fill with tears
As often as he mused it.

And when he came to dying,
The towns in his realm he told,
Naught to his heir denying,
Except the goblet of gold.

He dined at evenfall
With all his chivalry
In the ancestral hall
In the castle by the sea.

The old man rose at last
And drank life's sunset glow,

Und warf den heilgen Becher
Hinunter in die Flut.

Er sah ihn stürzen, trinken
2780 Und sinken tief ins Meer,
Die Augen täten ihm sinken,
Trank nie einen Tropfen mehr.

(Sie eröffnet den Schrein, ihre Kleider einzuräumen, und erblickt das Schmuckkästchen)

Wie kommt das schöne Kästchen hier herein?
Ich schloß doch ganz gewiß den Schrein.
2785 Es ist doch wunderbar! Was mag wohl drinne sein?
Vielleicht bracht's jemand als ein Pfand,
Und meine Mutter lieh darauf.
Da hängt ein Schlüsselchen am Band—
Ich denke wohl, ich mach es auf.
2790 Was ist das? Gott im Himmel! Schau,
So was hab ich mein Tage nicht gesehn!
Ein Schmuck! Mit dem könnt eine Edelfrau
Am höchsten Feiertage gehn.
Wie sollte mir die Kette stehn?
2795 Wem mag die Herrlichkeit gehören?

(Sie putzt sich damit auf und tritt vor den Spiegel)

Wenn nur die Ohrring meine wären!
Man sieht doch gleich ganz anders drein.
Was hilft euch Schönheit, junges Blut?
Das ist wohl alles schön und gut,
2800 Allein man läßt's auch alles sein;
Man lobt euch halb mit Erbarmen.
Nach Golde drängt,
Am Golde hängt
Doch alles. Ach, wir Armen!

And the sacred goblet he cast
Into the flood below.

He saw it plunging, drinking.
And sinking into the sea;
His eyes were also sinking,
And nevermore drank he.

(She opens the chest to put away her clothes and sees the case.)

How did this lovely case get in my chest?
I locked it after I got dressed.
It certainly seems strange. And what might be in
there?
It might be a security
Left for a loan in Mother's care.
There is a ribbon with a key;
I think I'll open it and see.
What is that? God in heaven! There—
I never saw such fine array!
These jewels! Why a lord's lady could wear
These on the highest holiday.
How would this necklace look on me?
Who owns all this? It is so fine.

(She adorns herself and steps before the mirror.)

If those earrings were only mine!
One looks quite different right away.
What good is beauty, even youth?
All that may be quite good and fair,
But does it get you anywhere?
Their praise is half pity, you can be sure.
For gold contend,
On gold depend
All things. Woe to us poor!

SPAZIERGANG

Faust in Gedanken auf und ab gehend.
Zu ihm Mephistopheles.

MEPHISTOPHELES:

2805 Bei aller verschmähten Liebe! Beim höllischen Elemente!
Ich wollt, ich wüßte was Ärgers, daß ich's fluchen könnte!

FAUST:

Was hast? Was kneipt dich denn so sehr?
So kein Gesicht sah ich in meinem Leben.

MEPHISTOPHELES:

Ich möcht mich gleich dem Teufel übergeben,
2810 Wenn ich nur selbst kein Teufel wär!

FAUST:

Hat sich dir was im Kopf verschoben?
Dich kleidet's, wie ein Rasender zu toben!

MEPHISTOPHELES:

Denkt nur, den Schmuck, für Gretchen angeschafft,
Den hat ein Pfaff hinweggerafft!—
2815 Die Mutter kriegt das Ding zu schauen,
Gleich fängt's ihr heimlich an zu grauen.
Die Frau hat gar einen feinen Geruch,
Schnuffelt immer im Gebetbuch
Und riecht's einem jeden Möbel an,
2820 Ob das Ding heilig ist oder profan;
Und an dem Schmuck da spürt sie's klar,
Daß dabei nicht viel Segen war.
Mein Kind, rief sie, ungerechtes Gut
Befängt die Seele, zehrt auf das Blut.
2825 Wollen's der Mutter Gottes weihen,
Wird uns mit Himmels-Manna erfreuen!
Margretlein zog ein schiefes Maul,

PROMENADE

Faust walking up and down, lost in thought.
Mephistopheles enters.

MEPHISTO:
By the pangs of despised love! By the elements of hell!
I wish I knew something worse to curse by it as well!

FAUST:
What ails you? Steady now, keep level!
I never saw a face like yours today.

MEPHISTO:
I'd wish the Devil took me straightaway,
If I myself were not a devil.

FAUST:
Has something in your head gone bad?
It sure becomes you raving like one mad.

MEPHISTO:
Just think, the jewels got for Margaret—
A dirty priest took the whole set.
The mother gets to see the stuff
And starts to shudder, sure enough:
She has a nose to smell things out—
In prayerbooks she keeps her snout—
A whiff of anything makes plain
Whether it's holy or profane.
She sniffed the jewelry like a rat
And knew no blessings came with that.
My child, she cried, ill-gotten wealth
Will soil your soul and spoil your health.
We'll give it to the Mother of the Lord
And later get a heavenly reward.
Poor Margaret went into a pout;

Ist halt, dacht sie, ein geschenkter Gaul.
Und wahrlich! Gottlos ist nicht der,
2830 Der ihn so fein gebracht hierher.
Die Mutter ließ einen Pfaffen kommen;
Der hatte kaum den Spaß vernommen,
Ließ sich den Anblick wohl behagen.
Er sprach: So ist man recht gesinnt!
2835 Wer überwindet, der gewinnt.
Die Kirche hat einen guten Magen,
Hat ganze Länder aufgefressen
Und doch noch nie sich übergessen;
Die Kirch allein, meine lieben Frauen,
2840 Kann ungerechtes Gut verdauen.

FAUST:
Das ist ein allgemeiner Brauch,
Ein Jud und König kann es auch.

MEPHISTOPHELES:
Strich drauf ein Spange, Kett und Ring,
Als wären's eben Pfifferling,
2845 Dankt' nicht weniger und nicht mehr,
Als ob's ein Korb voll Nüsse wär,
Versprach ihnen allen himmlischen Lohn—
Und sie waren sehr erbaut davon.

FAUST:
Und Gretchen?

MEPHISTOPHELES:
Sitzt nun unruhvoll,
2850 Weiß weder, was sie will noch soll,
Denkt ans Geschmeide Tag und Nacht,
Noch mehr an den, der's ihr gebracht.

FAUST:
Des Liebchens Kummer tut mir leid.
Schaff du ihr gleich ein neu Geschmeid!
2855 Am ersten war ja so nicht viel.

MEPHISTOPHELES:
O ja, dem Herrn ist alles Kinderspiel!

She thought: a gift horse! and, no doubt,
Who brought it here so carefully
Could not be godless, certainly.
The mother called a priest at once,
He saw the gems and was no dunce;
He drooled and then said: Without question,
Your instinct is quite genuine,
Who overcomes himself will win.
The Church has a superb digestion,
Whole countries she has gobbled up,
But never is too full to sup;
The Church alone has the good health
For stomaching ill-gotten wealth.

FAUST:

Why, everybody does: a Jew
And any king can do it, too.

MEPHISTO:

So he picked up a clasp, necklace, and rings,
Like toadstools or some worthless things,
And did not thank them more nor less
Than as if it were nuts or some such mess,
And he promised them plenty after they died—
And they were duly edified.

FAUST:

And Gretchen?

MEPHISTO:

She, of course, feels blue,
She sits and doesn't know what to do,
Thinks day and night of every gem—
Still more of him who furnished them.

FAUST:

My darling's grief distresses me.
Go, get her some new jewelry.
The first one was a trifling loss.

MEPHISTO:

Oh sure, its child's play for you, boss.

FAUST:

Und mach und richt's nach meinem Sinn,
Häng dich an ihre Nachbarin!
Sei, Teufel, doch nur nicht wie Brei
2860 Und schaff einen neuen Schmuck herbei!

MEPHISTOPHELES:

Ja, gnädger Herr, von Herzen gerne.

(Faust ab):

MEPHISTOPHELES:

So ein verliebter Tor verpufft
Euch Sonne, Mond und alle Sterne
Zum Zeitvertreib dem Liebchen in die Luft.
(Ab.)

DER NACHBARIN HAUS

MARTHE *(allein):*

2865 Gott verzeih's meinem lieben Mann,
Er hat an mir nicht wohl getan!
Geht da stracks in die Welt hinein
Und läßt, mich auf dem Stroh allein.
Tät ihn doch wahrlich nicht betrügen,
2870 Tät ihn, weiß Gott, recht herzlich lieben.
(Sie weint)
Vielleicht ist er gar tot!–O Pein!—
Hätt ich nur einen Totenschein!

(Margarete kommt.)

MARGARETE:

Frau Marthe!

MARTHE:

Gretelchen, was soll's?

FAUST:

Just fix it all to suit my will;
Try on the neighbor, too, your skill.
Don't, Devil, act like sluggish paste!
Get some new jewels and make haste!

MEPHISTO:

Yes, gracious lord, it is a pleasure.

(FAUST *exits.*)

MEPHISTO:

A fool in love just doesn't care
And, just to sweeten darling's leisure,
He'd make sun, moon, and stars into thin air.
(Exit.)

THE NEIGHBOR'S HOUSE

MARTHA *(alone):*

May God forgive my husband! He
Was certainly not good to me.
He went into the world to roam
And left me on the straw at home.
God knows that I have never crossed him,
And loved him dearly; yet I lost him.
(She cries.)
Perhaps—the thought kills me—he died!—
If it were only certified!

(MARGARET *enters.*)

MARGARET:

Dame Martha!

MARTHA:

Gretchen, what could it be?

MARGARETE:

Fast sinken mir die Kniee nieder!
Da find ich so ein Kästchen wieder
In meinem Schrein, von Ebenholz,
Und Sachen herrlich ganz und gar,
Weit reicher, als das erste war.

MARTHE:

Das muß Sie nicht der Mutter sagen;
2880 Tät's wieder gleich zur Beichte tragen.

MARGARETE:

Ach seh Sie nur! Ach schau Sie nur!

MARTHE *(putzt sie auf)*:

O du glückselge Kreatur!

MARGARETE:

Darf mich leider nicht auf der Gassen,
Noch in der Kirche mit sehen lassen.

MARTHE:

2885 Komm du nur oft zu mir herüber
Und leg den Schmuck hier heimlich an!
Spazier ein Stündchen lang dem Spiegelglas vorüber,
Wir haben unsre Freude dran;
Und dann gibt's einen Anlaß, gibt's ein Fest,
2890 Wo man's so nach und nach den Leuten sehen läßt:
Ein Kettchen erst, die Perle dann ins Ohr;
Die Mutter sieht's wohl nicht, man macht ihr auch was vor.

MARGARETE:

Wer konnte nur die beiden Kästchen bringen?
Es geht nicht zu mit rechten Dingen! *(Es klopft.)*
2895 Ach Gott! Mag das meine Mutter sein?

MARTHE *(durchs Vorhängel guckend)*:

Es ist ein fremder Herr—Herein!

(Mephistopheles tritt auf.)

MEPHISTOPHELES:

Bin so frei, grad hereinzutreten,

MARGARET:

My legs feel faint, though not with pain:
I found another case, again
Right in my press, of ebony,
With things more precious all around
Than was the first case that I found.

MARTHA:

You must not show them to your mother,
She'd tell the priest as with the other.

MARGARET:

Oh look at it! Oh see! Please do!

MARTHA *(adorns her)*:

You lucky, lucky creature, you!

MARGARET:

Unfortunately, it's not meet
To wear them in the church or street.

MARTHA:

Just come here often to see me,
Put on the jewels secretly,
Walk up and down an hour before the mirror here,
And we shall have a good time, dear.
Then chances come, perhaps a holiday,
When we can bit by bit, gem after gem display,
A necklace first, then a pearl in your ear;
Your mother—we can fool her, or she may never
hear.

MARGARET:

Who bought the cases and has not appeared?
It certainly seems very weird. *(A knock.)*
Oh God, my mother—is it her?

MARTHA *(peeping through the curtain)*:

It is a stranger—come in, sir!

(MEPHISTO *enters.)*

MEPHISTO:

I'll come right in and be so free,

Muß bei den Frauen Verzeihn erbeten.
(Tritt ehrerbietig vor Margareten zurück.)
Wollte nach Frau Marthe Schwerdtlein fragen.

MARTHE:

2900 Ich bin's, was hat der Herr zu sagen?

MEPHISTOPHELES *(leise zu ihr):*

Ich kenne Sie jetzt, mir ist das genug;
Sie hat da gar vornehmen Besuch.
Verzeiht die Freiheit, die ich genommen,
Will Nachmittage wiederkommen.

MARTHE *(laut):*

2905 Denk Kind, um alles in der Welt!
Der Herr dich für ein Fräulein hält.

MARGARETE:

Ich bin ein armes junges Blut;
Ach Gott! Der Herr ist gar zu gut;
Schmuck und Geschmeide sind nicht mein.

MEPHISTOPHELES:

2910 Ach, es ist nicht der Schmuck allein;
Sie hat ein Wesen, einen Blick so scharf.
Wie freut mich's, daß ich bleiben darf.

MARTHE:

Was bringt Er denn? Verlange sehr—

MEPHISTOPHELES:

Ich wollt, ich hätt eine frohere Mär!
2915 Ich hoffe, Sie läßt mich's drum nicht büßen:
Ihr Mann ist tot und läßt Sie grüßen.

MARTHE:

Ist tot? Das treue Herz! O weh!
Mein Mann ist tot! Ach ich vegeh!

MARGARETE:

Ach, liebe Frau, verzweifelt nicht!

MEPHISTOPHELES:

2920 So hört die traurige Geschicht!

MARGARETE:

Ich möchte drum mein Tag nicht lieben,
Würde mich Verlust zu Tode betrüben.

If the ladies will grant me the liberty.
(Steps back respectfully as he sees MARGARET.)
To Martha Schwerdtlein I wished to speak.

MARTHA:
It's I. What does your honor seek?

MEPHISTO *(softly to her)*:
I know you now, that satisifies me.
You have very elegant company;
Forgive my intrusion; I shall come back soon—
If you don't mind, this afternoon.

MARTHA *(loud)*:
Oh goodness gracious! Did you hear?
He thinks you are a lady, dear!

MARGARET:
I'm nothing but a poor young maid;
You are much too kind, I am afraid;
The gems and jewels are not my own.

MEPHISTO:
It is not the jewelry alone!
Your noble eyes—indeed, it is your whole way!
How glad I am that I may stay!

MARTHA:
What is your errand? Please, good sir—

MEPHISTO:
I wish I had better news for her!
And don't get cross with your poor guest:
Your husband is dead and sends his best.

MARTHA:
Is dead? The faithful heart! Oh dear!
My husband is dead! I shall faint right here.

MARGARET:
Oh my dear woman! Don't despair!

MEPHISTO:
Let me relate the sad affair.

MARGARET:
I should sooner never be a bride:
The grief would kill me if he died.

MEPHISTOPHELES:

Freud muß Leid, Leid muß Freude haben.

MARTHE:

Erzählt mir seines Lebens Schluß!

MEPHISTOPHELES:

2925 Er liegt in Padua begraben
Beim heiligen Antonius,
An einer wohlgeweihten Stätte
Zum ewig kühlen Ruhebette.

MARTHE:

Habt Ihr sonst nichts an mich zu bringen?

MEPHISTOPHELES:

2930 Ja, eine Bitte, groß und schwer:
Laß Sie doch ja für ihn dreihundert Messen singen!
Im übrigen sind meine Taschen leer.

MARTHE:

Was! Nicht ein Schaustück? Kein Geschmeid?
Was jeder Handwerksbursch im Grund des Säckels spart,
2935 Zum Angedenken aufbewahrt,
Und lieber hungert, lieber bettelt!

MEPHISTOPHELES:

Madam, es tut mir herzlich leid;
Allein er hat sein Geld wahrhaftig nicht verzettelt.
Auch er bereute seine Fehler sehr,
2940 Ja, und bejammerte sein Unglück noch viel mehr.

MARGARETE:

Ach, daß die Menschen so unglücklich sind!
Gewiß, ich will für ihn manch Requiem noch beten.

MEPHISTOPHELES:

Ihr wäret wert, gleich in die Eh zu treten;
Ihr seid ein liebenswürdig Kind.

MARGARETE:

2945 Ach nein, das geht jetzt noch nicht an.

MEPHISTO:

Joy needs woe, woe requires joy.

MARTHA:

Tell me of the end of my sweet boy.

MEPHISTO:

In Padua, in Italy,
He is buried in St. Anthony
In ground that has been duly blessed
For such cool, everlasting rest.

MARTHA:

Surely, there is something more you bring.

MEPHISTO:

One solemn and sincere request:
For his poor soul they should three hundred
masses sing.
That's all, my purse is empty, though not of course
my breast.

MARTHA:

What? Not a gem? No work of art?
I am sure, deep in his bag the poorest wanderer
Keeps some remembrance that gives pleasure,
And sooner starves than yields this treasure.

MEPHISTO:

Madam, don't doubt it breaks my heart.
And you may rest assured, he was no squanderer.
He knew his errors well, and he repented,
Though his ill fortune was the thing he most
lamented.

MARGARET:

That men are so unfortunate and poor!
I'll say some Requiems, and for his soul I'll pray.

MEPHISTO:

You would deserve a marriage right away,
For you are charming, I am sure.

MARGARET:

Oh no! I must wait to be wed.

MEPHISTOPHELES:

Ist's nicht ein Mann, sei's derweil ein Galan.
's ist eine der größten Himmelsgaben,
So ein lieb Ding im Arm zu haben.

MARGARETE:

Das ist des Landes nicht der Brauch.

MEPHISTOPHELES:

2950 Brauch oder nicht, es gibt sich auch.

MARTHE:

Erzählt mir doch!

MEPHISTOPHELES:

Ich stand an seinem Sterbebette.
Es war was besser als von Mist,
Von halbgefaultem Stroh; allein er starb als Christ
Und fand, daß er weit mehr noch auf der Zeche hätte.
2955 Wie, rief er, muß ich mich von Grund aus hassen,
So mein Gewerb, mein Weib so zu verlassen!
Ach, die Erinnrung tötet mich.
Vergäb sie mir nur noch in diesem Leben!—

MARTHE (*weinend*):

Der gute Mann! Ich hab ihm längst vergeben.

MEPHISTOPHELES:

2960 Allein, weiß Gott, sie war mehr schuld als ich.

MARTHE:

Das lügt er! Was! Am Rand des Grabs zu lügen!

MEPHISTOPHELES:

Er fabelte gewiß in letzten Zügen,
Wenn ich nur halb ein Kenner bin.
Ich hatte, sprach er, nicht zum Zeitvertreib zu gaffen,
2965 Erst Kinder und dann Brot für sie zu schaffen,
Und Brot im allerweitsten Sinn,
Und konnte nicht einmal mein Teil in Frieden essen.

MARTHE:

Hat er so aller Treu, so aller Lieb vergessen,

MEPHISTO:

If not a husband, have a lover instead.
It is one of heaven's greatest charms
To hold such a sweetheart in one's arms.

MARGARET:

That is not the custom around here.

MEPHISTO:

Custom or not, it's done, my dear.

MARTHA:

Please tell me more!

MEPHISTO:

I stood besides the bed he died on;
It was superior to manure,
Of rotted straw, and yet he died a Christian, pure,
And found that there was more on his unsettled score.
"I'm hateful," he cried; "wicked was my life,
As I forsook my trade and also left my wife.
To think of it now makes me die.
If only she forgave me even so!"

MARTHA *(weeping)*:

The darling! I forgave him long ago.

MEPHISTO:

"And yet, God knows, she was far worse than I."

MARTHA:

He lied—alas, lied at the brink of death!

MEPHISTO:

Surely, he made up things with dying breath,
If ever I saw death before.
"To pass the time, I could not look around," he said:
"First she got children, then they needed bread—
When I say bread, I mean much more—
And she never gave peace for me to eat my share."

MARTHA:

Did he forget my love, my faithfulness and care,

Der Plackerei bei Tag und Nacht!

MEPHISTOPHELES:

2970 Nicht doch, er hat Euch herzlich dran gedacht.
Er sprach: Als ich nun weg von Malta ging,
Da betet ich für Frau und Kinder brünstig;
Uns war denn auch der Himmel günstig,
Daß unser Schiff ein türkisch Fahrzeug fing,
2975 Das einen Schatz des großen Sultans führte.
Da ward der Tapferkeit ihr Lohn,
Und ich empfing denn auch, wie sich's gebührte,
Mein wohlgemeßnes Teil davon.

MARTHE:

Ei wie? Ei wo? Hat er's vielleicht vergraben?

MEPHISTOPHELES:

2980 Wer weiß, wo nun es die vier Winde haben!
Ein schönes Fräulein nahm sich seiner an,
Als er in Napel fremd umherspazierte;
Sie hat an ihm viel Liebs und Treus getan,
Daß er's bis an sein selig Ende spürte.

MARTHE:

2985 Der Schelm! Der Dieb an seinen Kindern!
Auch alles Elend, alle Not
Konnt nicht sein schändlich Leben hindern!

MEPHISTOPHELES:

Ja seht! Dafür ist er nun tot.
Wär ich nun jetzt an Eurem Platze,
2990 Betraurt ich ihn ein züchtig Jahr,
Visierte dann unterweil nach einem neuen
Schatze.

MARTHE:

Ach Gott! Wie doch mein erster war,
Find ich nicht leicht auf dieser Welt den andern.
Es konnte kaum ein herziger Närrchen sein.
2995 Er liebte nur das allzuviele Wandern
Und fremde Weiber und fremden Wein
Und das verfluchte Würfelspiel.

And how I slaved both day and night?

MEPHISTO:

Oh no, he thought of that with all his might;
He said: "When we left Malta for another trip,
I prayed for wife and children fervently,
So heaven showed good grace to me,
And our boat soon caught a Turkish ship
That had the mighty sultan's gold on it.
Then fortitude got its reward,
And I myself was given, as was fit,
My share of the great sultan's hoard."

MARTHA:

Oh how? Oh where? Might it be buried now?

MEPHISTO:

The winds have scattered it, and who knows how?
A pretty girl in Naples, sweet and slim,
Cared for him when he was without a friend
And did so many deeds of love for him
That he could feel it till his blessed end.

MARTHA:

The rogue! He robbed children and wife!
No misery, no lack of bread
Could keep him from his shameful life!

MEPHISTO:

You see! For that he now is dead.
If I were in your place, I'd pause
To mourn him for a year, as meet,
And meanwhile I would try to find another sweet.

MARTHA:

Oh God, the way my first one was
I'll hardly find another to be mine!
How could there be a little fool that's fonder?
Only he liked so very much to wander,
And foreign women, and foreign wine,
And that damned shooting of the dice.

MEPHISTOPHELES:
Nun, nun, so konnt es gehn und stehn,
Wenn er Euch ungefähr so viel
3000 Von seiner Seite nachgesehen.
Ich schwör Euch zu, mit dem Beding
Wechselt ich selbst mit Euch den Ring!

MARTHE:
O es beliebt dem Herrn zu scherzen!

MEPHISTOPHELES *(für sich):*
Nun mach ich mich beizeiten fort!
3005 Die hielte wohl den Teufel selbst beim Wort.
(Zu Gretchen):
Wie steht es denn mit Ihrem Herzen?

MARGARETE:
Was meint der Herr damit?

MEPHISTOPHELES *(für sich):*
Du guts, unschuldigs Kind!
(Laut):
Lebt wohl, ihr Fraun!

MARGARETE:
Lebt wohl!

MARTHE:
O sagt mir doch geschwind!
Ich möchte gern ein Zeugnis haben,
3010 Wo, wie und wann mein Schatz gestorben und begraben.
Ich bin von je der Ordnung Freund gewesen,
Möcht ihn auch tot im Wochenblättchen lesen.

MEPHISTOPHELES:
Ja, gute Frau, durch zweier Zeugen Mund
Wird allerwegs die Wahrheit kund;
3015 Habe noch gar einen feinen Gesellen,
Den will ich Euch vor den Richter stellen.
Ich bring ihn her.

MARTHE:
O tut das ja!

MEPHISTO:

Well, well! It could have been quite nice,
Had he been willing to ignore
As many faults in you, or more.
On such terms, I myself would woo
And willingly change rings with you.

MARTHA:

The gentleman is pleased to jest.

MEPHISTO *(aside)*:

I better get away from here:
She'd keep the Devil to his word, I fear.
(to GRETCHEN*)*:
And how is your heart? Still at rest?

MARGARET:

What do you mean, good sir?

MEPHISTO *(aside)*:

You good, innocent child!
(loud):
Good-by, fair ladies!

MARGARET:

Good-by.

MARTHA:

Oh, not so fast and wild!
I'd like to have it certified
That my sweetheart was buried, and when and where he died.
I always hate to see things done obliquely
And want to read his death in our weekly.

MEPHISTO:

Yes, lady, what is testified by two
Is everywhere known to be true;
And I happen to have a splendid mate
Whom I'll take along to the magistrate.
I'll bring him here.

MARTHA:

Indeed, please do!

MEPHISTOPHELES:

Und hier die Jungfrau ist auch da?—
Ein braver Knab! Ist viel gereist,
3020 Fräuleins alle Höflichkeit erweist.

MARGARETE:

Müßte vor dem Herren schamrot werden.

MEPHISTOPHELES:

Vor keinem Könige der Erden.

MARTHE:

Da hinterm Haus in meinem Garten
Wollen wir der Herrn heut abend warten.

STRASSE

Faust. Mephistopheles.

FAUST:

3025 Wie ist's? Will's fördern? Will's bald gehn?

MEPHISTOPHELES:

Ah bravo! Find ich Euch in Feuer?
In kurzer Zeit ist Gretchen Euer.
Heut abend sollt Ihr sie bei Nachbar Marthen
sehn.
Das ist ein Weib wie auserlesen
3030 Zum Kuppler- und Zigeunerwesen!

FAUST:

So recht!

MEPHISTOPHELES:

Doch wird auch was von uns begehrt.

FAUST:

Ein Dienst ist wohl des andern wert.

MEPHISTOPHELES:

Wir legen nur ein gültig Zeugnis nieder,

MEPHISTO:
And will this maiden be here, too?
A gallant lad! Has traveled much with me
And shows young ladies all courtesy.

MARGARET:
I would have to blush before him, poor thing.

MEPHISTO:
Not even before a king!

MARTHA:
Behind the house, in my garden, then,
Tonight we shall expect the gentlemen.

STREET

Faust. Mephistopheles.

FAUST:
How is it? Well? Can it be soon?

MEPHISTO:
Oh bravo! Now you are on fire?
Soon Gretchen will still your desire.
At Martha's you may see her later this afternoon:
That woman seems expressly made
To ply the pimps' and gypsies' trade.

FAUST:
Oh good!

MEPHISTO:
But something's wanted from us, too.

FAUST:
One good turn makes another due.

MEPHISTO:
We merely have to go and testify

Daß ihres Ehherrn ausgereckte Glieder
3035 In Padua an heilger Stätte ruhn.

FAUST:
Sehr klug! Wir werden erst die Reise machen müssen!

MEPHISTOPHELES:
Sancta Simplicitas! Darum ist's nicht zu tun;
Bezeugt nur, ohne viel zu wissen!

FAUST:
Wenn Er nichts Bessers hat, so ist der Plan zerrissen.

MEPHISTOPHELES:
3040 O heilger Mann! Da wärt Ihr's nun!
Ist es das erstemal in Eurem Leben,
Daß Ihr falsch Zeugnis abgelegt?
Habt Ihr von Gott, der Welt und was sich drin bewegt,
Vom Menschen, was sich ihm in Kopf und Herzen regt,
3045 Definitionen nicht mit großer Kraft gegeben?
Mit frecher Stirne, kühner Brust?
Und wollt Ihr recht ins Innre gehen,
Habt Ihr davon, Ihr müßt es grad gestehen,
So viel als von Herrn Schwerdtleins Tod gewußt?

FAUST:
3050 Du bist und bleibst ein Lügner, ein Sophiste.

MEPHISTOPHELES:
Ja, wenn man's nicht ein bißchen tiefer wüßte.
Denn morgen wirst in allen Ehren
Das arme Gretchen nicht betören
Und alle Seelenlieb ihr schwören?

FAUST:
3055 Und zwar von Herzen.

MEPHISTOPHELES:
Gut und schön!
Dann wird von ewiger Treu und Liebe,

That the remains of her dear husband lie
In Padua where Anthony once sat.

FAUST:

Now we shall have to go there. Now that was smart of you!

MEPHISTO:

Sancta simplicitas! Who ever thought of that?
Just testify, and hang whether it's true!

FAUST:

If you know nothing better, this plan has fallen through.

MEPHISTO:

Oh, holy man! You are no less!
Is this the first time in your life that you
Have testified what is not true?
Of God and all the world, and every single part,
Of man and all that stirs inside his head and heart
You gave your definitions with power and finesse,
With brazen cheek and haughty breath.
And if you stop to think, I guess,
You knew as much of that, you must confess,
As you know now of Mr. Schwerdtlein's death.

FAUST:

You are and you remain a sophist and a liar.

MEPHISTO:

Yes, if one's knowledge were not just a little higher.
Tomorrow, won't you, pure as air,
Deceive poor Gretchen and declare
Your soul's profoundest love, and swear?

FAUST:

With all my heart.

MEPHISTO:

Good and fair!
Then faithfulness and love eternal

Von einzig überallmächtgem Triebe—
Wird das auch so von Herzen gehn?

FAUST:

Laß das! Es wird!—Wenn ich empfinde,
3060 Für das Gefühl, für das Gewühl
Nach Namen suche, keinen finde,
Dann durch die Welt mit allen Sinnen schweife,
Nach allen höchsten Worten greife
Und diese Glut, von der ich brenne,
3065 Unendlich, ewig, ewig nenne,
Ist das ein teuflisch Lügenspiel?

MEPHISTOPHELES:

Ich hab doch recht!

FAUST:

Hör! Merk dir dies—
Ich bitte dich, und schone meine Lunge—:
Wer recht behalten will und hat nur eine Zunge,
3070 Behält's gewiß.
Und komm, ich hab des Schwätzens Überdruß,
Denn du hast recht, vorzüglich weil ich muß.

GARTEN

Margarete an Faustens Arm, Marthe mit Mephistopheles auf und ab spazierend.

MARGARETE:

Ich fühl es wohl, daß mich der Herr nur schont,
Herab sich läßt, mich zu beschämen.
3075 Ein Reisender ist so gewohnt,
Aus Gütigkeit fürliebzunehmen;
Ich weiß zu gut, daß solch erfahrnen Mann
Mein arm Gespräch nicht unterhalten kann.

And the super-almighty urge supernal—
Will that come from your heart as well?

FAUST:

Leave off! It will.—When, lost in feeling,
For this urge, for this surge
I seek a name, find none, and, reeling
All through the world with all my senses gasping,
At all the noblest words I'm grasping
And call this blaze in which I flame,
Infinite, eternal eternally—
Is that a game or devilish jugglery?

MEPHISTO:

I am still right.

FAUST:

Listen to me,
I beg of you, and don't wear out my lung:
Whoever would be right and only has a tongue,
Always will be.
Come on! I'm sick of prating, spare your voice,
For you are right because I have no choice.

GARDEN

Margaret on Faust's arm, Martha with Mephistopheles, walking up and down.

MARGARET:

I feel it well, good sir, you're only kind to me:
You condescend—and you abash.
It is the traveler's courtesy
To put up graciously with trash.
I know too well, my poor talk never can
Give pleasure to a traveled gentleman.

FAUST:

Ein Blick von dir, ein Wort mehr unterhält
3080 Als alle Weisheit dieser Welt.

(Er küßt ihre Hand.)

MARGARETE:

Inkommodiert Euch nicht! Wie könnt Ihr sie nur küssen?
Sie ist so garstig, ist so rauh.
Was hab ich nicht schon alles schaffen müssen!
Die Mutter ist gar zu genau. *(Gehn vorüber)*

MARTHE:

3085 Und Ihr, mein Herr, Ihr reist so immer fort?

MEPHISTOPHELES:

Ach, daß Gewerb und Pflicht uns dazu treiben!
Mit wieviel Schmerz verläßt man manchen Ort
Und darf doch nun einmal nicht bleiben!

MARTHE:

In raschen Jahren geht's wohl an,
3090 So um und um frei durch die Welt zu streifen;
Doch kömmt die böse Zeit heran,
Und sich als Hagestolz allein zum Grab zu schleifen,
Das hat noch keinem wohlgetan.

MEPHISTOPHELES:

Mit Grausen seh ich das von weiten.

MARTHE:

3095 Drum, werter Herr, beratet Euch in Zeiten!
(Gehn vorüber.)

MARGARETE:

Ja, aus den Augen, aus dem Sinn!
Die Höflichkeit ist Euch geläufig;
Allein Ihr habt der Freunde häufig,
Sie sind verständiger, als ich bin.

FAUST:

One glance from you, one word gives far more pleasure
Than all the wisdom of this world.
(He kisses her hand.)

MARGARET:

Don't incommode yourself! How could you kiss it? You?
It is so ugly, is so rough.
But all the things that I have had to do!
For Mother I can't do enough. *(They pass.)*

MARTHA:

And you, sir, travel all the time, you say?

MEPHISTO:

Alas, our trade and duty keeps us going!
Though when one leaves the tears may well be flowing,
One never is allowed to stay.

MARTHA:

While it may do in younger years
To sweep around the world, feel free and suave,
There is the time when old age nears,
And then to creep alone, a bachelor, to one's grave,
That's something everybody fears.

MEPHISTO:

With dread I see it far away.

MARTHA:

Then, my dear sir, consider while you may.
(They pass.)

MARGARET:

Yes, out of sight is out of mind.
You are polite, you can't deny,
And often you have friends and find
That they are cleverer than I.

FAUST:

3100 O Beste! Glaube, was man so verständig nennt,
Ist oft mehr Eitelkeit und Kurzsinn.

MARGARETE:

Wie?

FAUST:

Ach, daß die Einfalt, daß die Unschuld nie
Sich selbst und ihren heilgen Wert erkennt!
Daß Demut, Niedrigkeit, die höchsten Gaben
3105 Der liebevoll austeilenden Natur—

MARGARETE:

Denkt Ihr an mich ein Augenblickchen nur,
Ich werde Zeit genug, an Euch zu denken, haben.

FAUST:

Ihr seid wohl viel allein?

MARGARETE:

Ja, unsre Wirtschaft ist nur klein,
3110 Und doch will sie versehen sein.
Wir haben keine Magd; muß kochen, fegen, stricken
Und nähn und laufen früh und spat;
Und meine Mutter ist in allen Stücken
So akkurat.
3115 Nicht daß sie just so sehr sich einzuschränken hat;
Wir könnten uns weit eh'r als andre regen:
Mein Vater hinterließ ein hübsch Vermögen,
Ein Häuschen und ein Gärtchen vor der Stadt.
Doch hab ich jetzt so ziemlich stille Tage:
3120 Mein Bruder ist Soldat,
Mein Schwesterchen ist tot.
Ich hatte mit dem Kind wohl meine liebe Not;
Doch übernähm ich gern noch einmal alle Plage,
So lieb war mir das Kind.

FAUST:

Oh dearest, trust me, what's called clever on this earth
Is often vain and rash rather than clever.

MARGARET:

What?

FAUST:

Oh, that the innocent and simple never
Appreciate themselves and their own worth!
That meekness and humility, supreme
Among the gifts of loving, lavish nature——

MARGARET:

If you should think of me one moment only,
I shall have time enough to think of you and dream.

FAUST:

Are you so often lonely?

MARGARET:

Yes; while our household is quite small,
You see, I have to do it all.
We have no maid, so I must cook, and sweep, and knit,
And sew, and run early and late;
And mother is in all of it
So accurate!
Not that it's necessary; our need is not so great.
We could afford much more than many another:
My father left a tidy sum to mother,
A house and garden near the city gate.
But now my days are rather plain:
A soldier is my brother,
My little sister dead.
Sore was, while she was living, the troubled life I led;
But I would gladly go through all of it again:
She was so dear to me.

FAUST:

Ein Engel, wenn dir's glich.

MARGARETE:

3125 Ich zog es auf, und herzlich liebt' es mich.
Es war nach meines Vaters Tod geboren.
Die Mutter gaben wir verloren,
So elend wie sie damals lag,
Und sie erholte sich sehr langsam, nach und nach.
3130 Da konnte sie nun nicht dran denken,
Das arme Würmchen selbst zu tränken,
Und so erzog ich's ganz allein
Mit Milch und Wasser; so ward's mein.
Auf meinem Arm, in meinem Schoß
3135 War's freundlich, zappelte, ward groß.

FAUST:

Du hast gewiß das reinste Glück empfunden.

MARGARETE:

Doch auch gewiß gar manche schwere Stunden.
Des Kleinen Wiege stand zu Nacht
An meinem Bett; es durfte kaum sich regen,
3140 War ich erwacht;
Bald mußt ich's tränken, bald es zu mir legen,
Bald, wenn's nicht schwieg, vom Bett aufstehn
Und tänzelnd in der Kammer auf und nieder gehn
Und früh am Tage schon am Waschtrog stehn;
3145 Dann auf dem Markt und an dem Herde sorgen,
Und immer fort wie heut so morgen.
Da geht's, mein Herr, nicht immer mutig zu;
Doch schmeckt dafür das Essen, schmeckt die
Ruh.
(Gehn vorüber.)

MARTHE:

Die armen Weiber sind doch übel dran:
3150 Ein Hagestolz ist schwerlich zu bekehren.

MEPHISTOPHELES:

Es käme nur auf Euresgleichen an,

FAUST:

An angel, if like you.

MARGARET:

I brought her up, and she adored me, too.
She was born only after father's death;
Mother seemed near her dying breath,
As stricken as she then would lie,
Though she got well again quite slowly, by and
by.
She was so sickly and so slight,
She could not nurse the little mite;
So I would tend her all alone,
With milk and water; she became my own.
Upon my arms and in my lap
She first grew friendly, tumbled, and grew up.

FAUST:

You must have felt the purest happiness.

MARGARET:

But also many hours of distress.
The baby's cradle stood at night
Beside my bed, and if she stirred I'd wake,
I slept so light.
Now I would have to feed her, now I'd take
Her into my bed, now I'd rise
And dandling pace the room to calm the baby's
cries.
And I would wash before the sun would rise,
Fret in the market and over the kitchen flame,
Tomorrow as today, always the same.
One's spirits, sir, are not always the best,
But one can relish meals and relish rest.
(They pass.)

MARTHA:

Poor woman has indeed a wretched fate:
A bachelor is not easy to convert.

MEPHISTO:

For one like you the job is not too great;

Mich eines Bessern zu belehren.

MARTHE:

Sagt grad, mein Herr, habt Ihr noch nichts gefunden?
Hat sich das Herz nicht irgendwo gebunden?

MEPHISTOPHELES:

3155 Das Sprichwort sagt: Ein eigner Herd,
Ein braves Weib sind Gold und Perlen wert.

MARTHE:

Ich meine, ob Ihr niemals Lust bekommen?

MEPHISTOPHELES:

Man hat mich überall recht höflich aufgenommen.

MARTHE:

Ich wollte sagen: ward's nie Ernst in Eurem Herzen?

MEPHISTOPHELES:

3160 Mit Frauen soll man sich nie unterstehn zu scherzen.

MARTHE:

Ach, Ihr versteht mich nicht!

MEPHISTOPHELES:

Das tut mir herzlich leid!
Doch ich versteh—daß Ihr sehr gütig seid.
(Gehn vorüber)

FAUST:

Du kanntest mich, o kleiner Engel, wieder,
Gleich als ich in den Garten kam?

MARGARETE:

3165 Saht Ihr es nicht? Ich schlug die Augen nieder.

FAUST:

Und du verzeihst die Freiheit, die ich nahm,
Was sich die Frechheit unterfangen,
Als du jüngst aus dem Dom gegangen?

MARGARETE:

Ich war bestürzt, mir war das nie geschehn;
3170 Es konnte niemand von mir Übles sagen.
Ach, dacht ich, hat er in deinem Betragen

You might convince me if you are alert.

MARTHA:

Be frank, dear sir, so far you have not found?
Has not your heart in some way yet been bound?

MEPHISTO:

A hearth one owns and a good wife, we're told,
Are worth as much as pearls and gold.

MARTHA:

I mean, have you not ever had a passion?

MEPHISTO:

I always was received in the most friendly fashion.

MARTHA:

Would say: weren't you ever in earnest in your
breast?

MEPHISTO:

With women one should never presume to speak
in jest.

MARTHA:

Oh, you don't understand.

MEPHISTO:

I'm sorry I'm so blind!
But I do understand—that you are very kind.
(They pass.)

FAUST:

Oh little angel, you did recognize
Me as I came into the garden?

MARGARET:

Did you not notice? I cast down my eyes.

FAUST:

My liberty you're then prepared to pardon?
What insolence presumed to say
As you left church the other day?

MARGARET:

I was upset, I did not know such daring;
And no one could have spoken ill of me.
I thought that something in my bearing

Was Freches, Unanständiges gesehn?
Es schien ihn gleich nur anzuwandeln,
Mit dieser Dirne gradehin zu handeln.
3175 Gesteh ich's doch! Ich wußte nicht, was sich
Zu Eurem Vorteil hier zu regen gleich begonnte;
Allein gewiß, ich war recht bös auf mich,
Daß ich auf Euch nicht böser werden konnte.

FAUST:
Süß Liebchen!

MARGARETE:
Laßt einmal!
(Sie pflückt eine Sternblume und zupft die Blätter ab, eins nach dem andern)

FAUST:
Was soll das? Einen Strauß?

MARGARETE:
3180 Nein, es soll nur ein Spiel.

FAUST:
Wie?

MARGARETE:
Geht! Ihr lacht mich aus.
(Sie rupft und murmelt)

FAUST:
Was murmelst du?

MARGARETE *(halblaut):*
Er liebt mich—Liebt mich nicht.

FAUST:
Du holdes Himmelsangesicht!

MARGARETE *(fährt fort):*
Liebt mich—Nicht—Liebt mich—Nicht—
(das letzte Blatt ausrupfend, mit holder Freude)
Er liebt mich!

FAUST:
Ja, mein Kind! Laß dieses Blumenwort

Must have seemed shameless and unmaidenly.
He seemed to have the sudden feeling
That this wench could be had without much
dealing.
Let me confess, I didn't know that there
Were other feelings stirring in me, and they grew;
But I was angry with myself, I swear,
That I could not get angrier with you.

FAUST:

Sweet darling!

MARGARET:

Let me do this!
(She plucks a daisy and pulls out the petals one by one.)

FAUST:

A nosegay? Or what shall it be?

MARGARET:

No, it is just a game.

FAUST:

What?

MARGARET:

Go, you will laugh at me.
(She pulls out petals and murmurs.)

FAUST:

What do you murmur?

MARGARET *(half aloud):*

He loves me—loves me not.

FAUST:

You gentle countenance of heaven!

MARGARET *(continues):*

Loves me—not—loves me—not—
(tearing out the last leaf, in utter joy:)
He loves me.

FAUST:

Yes, my child. Let this sweet flower's word

3185 Dir Götterausspruch sein! Er liebt dich!
Verstehst du, was das heißt? Er liebt dich!
(Er faßt ihre beiden Hände.)

MARGARETE:
Mich überläuft's!

FAUST:
O schaudre nicht! Laß diesen Blick,
Laß diesen Händedruck dir sagen,
3190 Was unaussprechlich ist:
Sich hinzugeben ganz und eine Wonne
Zu fühlen, die ewig sein muß!
Ewig!—Ihr Ende würde Verzweiflung sein.
Nein, kein Ende! Kein Ende!
(Margarete drückt ihm die Hände, macht sich los und läuft weg. Er steht einen Augenblick in Gedanken, dann folgt er ihr.)

MARTHE *(kommend):*
3195 Die Nacht bricht an.

MEPHISTOPHELES:
Ja, und wir wollen fort.

MARTHE:
Ich bät Euch, länger hier zu bleiben,
Allein es ist ein gar zu böser Ort.
Es ist, als hätte niemand nichts zu treiben
Und nichts zu schaffen,
3200 Als auf des Nachbarn Schritt und Tritt zu gaffen,
Und man kommt ins Gered, wie man sich immer stellt.
Und unser Pärchen?

MEPHISTOPHELES:
Ist den Gang dort aufgeflogen.
Mutwillge Sommervögel!

MARTHE:
Er scheint ihr gewogen.

MEPHISTOPHELES:
Und sie ihm auch. Das ist der Lauf der Welt.

Be as a god's word to you. He loves you.
Do you know what this means? He loves you.
(He takes both her hands.)

MARGARET:
My skin creeps.

FAUST:
Oh, shudder not! But let this glance,
And let this clasp of hands tell you
What is unspeakable:
To yield oneself entirely and feel
A rapture which must be eternal.
Eternal! For its end would be despair.
No, no end! No end!

(MARGARET *clasps his hands, frees herself, and runs away. He stands for a moment, lost in thought; then he follows her.)*

MARTHA *(entering):*
The night draws near.

MEPHISTO:
Yes, and we want to go.

MARTHA:
I should ask you to tarry even so,
But this place simply is too bad:
It is as if nobody had
Work or labor
Except to spy all day long on his neighbor,
And one gets talked about, whatever life one leads.
And our couple?

MEPHISTO:
Up that path I heard them whirr—
Frolicking butterflies.

MARTHA:
He is taking to her.

MEPHISTO:
And she to him. That's how the world proceeds.

EIN GARTENHÄUSCHEN

Margarete springt herein, steckt sich hinter die Tür, hält die Fingerspitze an die Lippe und guckt durch die Ritze

MARGARETE:
3205 Er kommt!

FAUST *(kommt):*
Ach Schelm, so neckst du mich!
Treff ich dich! *(Er küßt sie):*

MARGARETE *(ihn fassend und den Kuß zurückgebend):*
Bester Mann! Von Herzen lieb ich dich!
(Mephistopheles klopft an.)

FAUST *(stampfend):*
Wer da?

MEPHISTOPHELES:
Gut Freund!

FAUST:
Ein Tier!

MEPHISTOPHELES:
Es ist wohl Zeit, zu scheiden.

MARTHE *(kommt):*
Ja, es ist spät, mein Herr.

FAUST:
Darf ich Euch nicht geleiten?

MARGARETE:
Die Mutter würde mich–Lebt wohl!

FAUST:
Muß ich denn gehn?
3210 Lebt wohl!

MARTHE:
Ade!

MARGARETE:
Auf baldig Wiedersehn!
(Faust und Mephistopheles ab.)

A GARDEN BOWER

Margaret leaps into it, hides behind the door, puts the tip of one finger to her lips, and peeks through the crack.

MARGARET:
He comes.

FAUST *(entering):*
Oh rogue, you're teasing me.
Now I see. *(He kisses her.)*

MARGARET *(seizing him and returning the kiss):*
Dearest man! I love you from my heart.
(MEPHISTOPHELES *knocks.)*

FAUST *(stamping his foot):*
Who's there?

MEPHISTO:
A friend.

FAUST:
A beast!

MEPHISTO:
The time has come to part.

MARTHA *(entering):*
Yes, it is late, good sir.

FAUST:
May I not take you home?

MARGARET:
My mother would—Farewell!

FAUST:
Must I leave then?
Farewell.

MARTHA:
Adieu.

MARGARET:
Come soon again!
(FAUST *and* MEPHISTO *exeunt.)*

MARGARETE:

Du lieber Gott! Was so ein Mann
Nicht alles, alles denken kann!
Beschämt nur steh ich vor ihm da
Und sag zu allen Sachen ja.
3215 Bin doch ein arm unwissend Kind,
Begreife nicht, was er an mir findt. *(Ab.)*

WALD UND HÖHLE

FAUST *(allein):*

Erhabner Geist, du gabst mir, gabst mir alles,
Warum ich bat. Du hast mir nicht umsonst
Dein Angesicht im Feuer zugewendet.
3220 Gabst mir die herrliche Natur zum Königreich,
Kraft, sie zu fühlen, zu genießen. Nicht
Kalt staunenden Besuch erlaubst du nur,
Vergönnest mir, in ihre tiefe Brust
Wie in den Busen eines Freunds zu schauen.
3225 Du führst die Reihe der Lebendigen
Vor mir vorbei und lehrst mich meine Brüder
Im stillen Busch, in Luft und Wasser kennen.
Und wenn der Sturm im Walde braust und knarrt,
Die Riesenfichte, stürzend, Nachbaräste
3230 Und Nachbarstämme quetschend niederstreift
Und ihrem Fall dumpf hohl der Hügel donnert,
Dann führst du mich zur sichern Höhle, zeigst
Mich dann mir selbst, und meiner eignen Brust
Geheime tiefe Wunden öffnen sich.
3235 Und steigt vor meinem Blick der reine Mond
Besänftigend herüber, schweben mir
Von Felsenwänden, aus dem feuchten Busch

MARGARET:

Dear God, the things he thought and said!
How much goes on in a man's head!
Abashed, I merely acquiesce
And cannot answer, except Yes!
I am a poor, dumb child and cannot see
What such a man could find in me. *(Exit.)*

WOOD AND CAVE

FAUST *(alone):*

Exalted spirit, all you gave me, all
That I have asked. And it was not in vain
That amid flames you turned your face toward me.
You gave me royal nature as my own dominion,
Strength to experience her, enjoy her. Not
The cold amazement of a visit only
You granted me, but let me penetrate
Into her heart as into a close friend's.
You lead the hosts of all that is alive
Before my eyes, teach me to know my brothers
In quiet bushes and in air and water.
And when the storm roars in the wood and creaks,
The giant fir tree, falling, hits and smashes
The neighbor branches and the neighbor trunks,
And from its hollow thud the mountain thunders,
Then you lead me to this safe cave and show
Me to myself, and all the most profound
And secret wonders of my breast are opened.
And when before my eyes the pure moon rises
And passes soothingly, there float to me
From rocky cliffs and out of dewy bushes

Der Vorwelt silberne Gestalten auf
Und lindern der Betrachtung strenge Lust.
3240 O daß dem Menschen nichts Vollkommnes wird,
Empfind ich nun. Du gabst zu dieser Wonne,
Die mich den Göttern nah und näher bringt,
Mir den Gefährten, den ich schon nicht mehr
Entbehren kann, wenn er gleich kalt und frech
3245 Mich vor mir selbst erniedrigt und zu Nichts
Mit einem Worthauch deine Gaben wandelt.
Er facht in meiner Brust ein wildes Feuer
Nach jenem schönen Bild geschäftig an.
So tauml' ich von Begierde zu Genuß,
3250 Und im Genuß verschmacht ich nach Begierde.

MEPHISTOPHELES *(tritt auf):*
Habt Ihr nun bald das Leben gnug geführt?
Wie kann's Euch in die Länge freuen?
Es ist wohl gut, daß man's einmal probiert;
Dann aber wieder zu was Neuen!

FAUST:
3255 Ich wollt, du hättest mehr zu tun,
Als mich am guten Tag zu plagen.

MEPHISTOPHELES:
Nun nun! Ich lass dich gerne ruhn,
Du darfst mir's nicht im Ernste sagen.
An dir Gesellen, unhold, barsch und toll,
3260 Ist wahrlich wenig zu verlieren.
Den ganzen Tag hat man die Hände voll!
Was ihm gefällt und was man lassen soll,
Kann man dem Herrn nie an der Nase spüren.

FAUST:
Das ist so just der rechte Ton!
3265 Er will noch Dank, daß er mich ennuyiert.

MEPHISTOPHELES:
Wie hättst du, armer Erdensohn,
Dein Leben ohne mich geführt?
Vom Kribskrabs der Imagination
Hab ich dich doch auf Zeiten lang kuriert;

The silver shapes of a forgotten age,
And soften meditation's somber joy.
Alas, that man is granted nothing perfect
I now experience. With this happiness
Which brings me close and closer to the gods,
You gave me the companion whom I can
Forego no more, though with cold impudence
He makes me small in my own eyes and changes
Your gifts to nothing with a few words' breath.
He kindles in my breast a savage fire
And keeps me thirsting after that fair image.
Thus I reel from desire to enjoyment,
And in enjoyment languish for desire.

MEPHISTO (*enters*):
Have you not led this life quite long enough?
How can it keep amusing you?
It may be well for once to try such stuff
But then one turns to something new.

FAUST:
I wish that you had more to do
And would not come to pester me.

MEPHISTO:
All right. I gladly say adieu—
You should not say that seriously.
A chap like you, unpleasant, mad, and cross,
Would hardly be a serious loss.
All day long one can work and slave away.
And what he likes and what might cause dismay,
It simply isn't possible to say.

FAUST:
That is indeed the proper tone!
He wants my thanks for being such a pest.

MEPHISTO:
If I had left you wretch alone,
Would you then live with greater zest?
Was it not I that helped you to disown,
And partly cured, your feverish unrest?

3270 Und wär ich nicht, so wärst du schon
Von diesem Erdball abspaziert.
Was hast du da in Höhlen, Felsenritzen
Dich wie ein Schuhu zu versitzen?
Was schlurfst aus dumpfem Moos und triefendem
Gestein
3275 Wie eine Kröte Nahrung ein?
Ein schöner, süßer Zeitvertreib!
Dir steckt der Doktor noch im Leib.

FAUST:
Verstehst du, was für neue Lebenskraft
Mir dieser Wandel in die Öde schafft?
3280 Ja, würdest du es ahnen können,
Du wärest Teufel gnug, mein Glück mir nicht zu
gönnen.

MEPHISTOPHELES:
Ein überirdisches Vergnügen!
In Nacht und Tau auf den Gebirgen liegen
Und Erd und Himmel wonniglich umfassen,
3285 Zu einer Gottheit sich aufschwellen lassen,
Der Erde Mark mit Ahnungsdrang durchwühlen,
Alle sechs Tagewerk im Busen fühlen,
In stolzer Kraft ich weiß nicht was genießen,
Bald liebewonniglich in alles überfließen,
3290 Verschwunden ganz der Erdensohn,
Und dann die hohe Intuition—*(mit einer Gebärde)*
Ich darf nicht sagen, wie—zu schließen.

FAUST:
Pfui über dich!

MEPHISTOPHELES:
Das will Euch nicht behagen;
Ihr habt das Recht, gesittet Pfui zu sagen.
3295 Man darf das nicht vor keuschen Ohren nennen,
Was keusche Herzen nicht entbehren können.
Und kurz und gut, ich gönn Ihm das Vergnügen,
Gelegentlich sich etwas vorzulügen;
Doch lange hält Er das nicht aus.

Yes, but for me, the earthly zone
Would long be minus one poor guest.
And now, why must you sit like an old owl
In caves and rocky clefts, and scowl?
From soggy moss and dripping stones you lap
your food
Just like a toad, and sit and brood.
A fair, sweet way to pass the time!
Still steeped in your doctoral slime!

FAUST:

How this sojourn in the wilderness
Renews my vital force, you cannot guess.
And if you apprehended this,
You would be Devil enough, to envy me my bliss.

MEPHISTO:

A supernatural delight!
To lie on mountains in the dew and night,
Embracing earth and sky in raptured reeling,
To swell into a god—in one's own feeling—
To probe earth's marrow with vague divination,
Sense in your breast the whole work of creation,
With haughty strength enjoy, I know not what,
Then overflow into all things with love so hot,
Gone is all earthly inhibition,
And then the noble intuition—*(with a gesture)*
Of—need I say of what emission?

FAUST:

Shame!

MEPHISTO:

That does not meet with your acclaim;
You have the right to cry indignant: shame!
One may not tell chaste ears what, beyond doubt,
The chastest heart could never do without.
And, once for all, I don't grudge you the pleasure
Of little self-deceptions at your leisure;
But it can't last indefinitely.

3300 Du bist schon wieder abgetrieben
Und, währt es länger, aufgerieben
In Tollheit oder Angst und Graus.
Genug damit! Dein Liebchen sitzt dadrinne,
Und alles wird ihr eng und trüb.
3305 Du kommst ihr gar nicht aus dem Sinne,
Sie hat dich übermächtig lieb.
Erst kam deine Liebeswut übergeflossen,
Wie vom geschmolznen Schnee ein Bächlein übersteigt;
Du hast sie ihr ins Herz gegossen,
3310 Nun ist dein Bächlein wieder seicht.
Mich dünkt, anstatt in Wäldern zu thronen,
Ließ es dem großen Herren gut,
Das arme affenjunge Blut
Für seine Liebe zu belohnen.
3315 Die Zeit wird ihr erbärmlich lang;
Sie steht am Fenster, sieht die Wolken ziehn
Über die alte Stadtmauer hin.
Wenn ich ein Vöglein wär! so geht ihr Gesang
Tage lang, halbe Nächte lang.
3320 Einmal ist sie munter, meist betrübt,
Einmal recht ausgeweint,
Dann wieder ruhig, wie's scheint,
Und immer verliebt.

FAUST:
Schlange! Schlange!

MEPHISTOPHELES (*für sich*):
3325 Gelt! Daß ich dich fange!

FAUST:
Verruchter! Hebe dich von hinnen
Und nenne nicht das schöne Weib!
Bring die Begier zu ihrem süßen Leib
Nicht wieder vor die halb verrückten Sinnen!

MEPHISTOPHELES:
3330 Was soll es denn? Sie meint, du seist entflohn,

Already you are spent again,
And soon you will be rent again,
By madness and anxiety.
Enough of that. Your darling is distraught,
Sits inside, glum and in despair,
She can't put you out of her mind and thought
And loves you more than she can bear.
At first your raging love was past control,
As brooks that overflow when filled with melted
snow;
You poured it out into her soul,
But now your little brook is low.
Instead of posing in the wood,
It seems to me it might be good
If for her love our noble lord
Gave the poor monkey some reward.
Time seems to her intolerably long;
She stands at her window and sees the clouds in
the sky
Drift over the city wall and go by.
Were I a little bird! thus goes her song
For days and half the night long.
Once she may be cheerful, most of the time sad,
Once she has spent her tears,
Then she is calm, it appears,
And always loves you like mad.

FAUST:

Serpent! Snake!

MEPHISTO *(aside)*:

If only I catch the rake!

FAUST:

Damnable fiend! Get yourself hence,
And do not name the beautiful maid!
Let not the lust for her sweet limbs invade
And ravish once again my frenzied sense!

MEPHISTO:

What do you mean? She thinks you've run away;

Und halb und halb bist du es schon.

FAUST:

Ich bin ihr nah, und wär ich noch so fern,
Ich kann sie nie vergessen, nie verlieren;
Ja, ich beneide schon den Leib des Herrn,
3335 Wenn ihre Lippen ihn indes berühren.

MEPHISTOPHELES:

Gar wohl, mein Freund! Ich hab Euch oft beneidet
Ums Zwillingspaar, das unter Rosen weidet.

FAUST:

Entfliehe, Kuppler!

MEPHISTOPHELES:

Schön! Ihr schimpft, und ich muß lachen.
Der Gott, der Bub und Mädchen schuf,
3340 Erkannte gleich den edelsten Beruf,
Auch selbst Gelegenheit zu machen.
Nur fort, es ist ein großer Jammer!
Ihr sollt in Eures Liebchens Kammer,
Nicht etwa in den Tod.

FAUST:

3345 Was ist die Himmelsfreud in ihren Armen?
Laß mich an ihrer Brust erwarmen—
Fühl ich nicht immer ihre Not?
Bin ich der Flüchtling nicht? Der Unbehauste?
Der Unmensch ohne Zweck und Ruh,
3350 Der wie ein Wassersturz von Fels zu Felsen brauste,
Begierig wütend, nach dem Abgrund zu?
Und seitwärts sie mit kindlich dumpfen Sinnen
Im Hüttchen auf dem kleinen Alpenfeld,
Und all ihr häusliches Beginnen
3355 Umfangen in der kleinen Welt.
Und ich, der Gottverhaßte,
Hatte nicht genug,
Daß ich die Felsen faßte
Und sie zu Trümmern schlug!

And it is half-true, I must say.

FAUST:

I am near her, however far I be,
She'll never be forgotten and ignored;
Indeed, I am consumed with jealousy
That her lips touch the body of the Lord.

MEPHISTO:

I'm jealous of my friend when she exposes
The pair of twins that feed among the roses.

FAUST:

Begone, pander!

MEPHISTO:

Fine! Your wrath amuses me.
The God who fashioned man and maid
Was quick to recognize the noblest trade,
And procured opportunity.
Go on! It is a woeful pain!
You're to embrace your love again,
Not sink into the tomb.

FAUST:

What are the joys of heaven in her arms?
Let me embrace her, feel her charms—
Do I not always sense her doom?
Am I not fugitive? without a home?
Inhuman, without aim or rest,
As, like the cataract, from rock to rock I foam,
Raging with passion, toward the abyss?
And nearby, she— with childlike blunt desires
Inside her cottage on the Alpine leas,
And everything that she requires
Was in her own small world at ease.
And I, whom the gods hate and mock,
Was not satisfied
That I seized the rock
And smashed the mountainside.

3360 Sie, ihren Frieden mußt ich untergraben!
Du, Hölle, mußtest dieses Opfer haben!
Hilf, Teufel, mir die Zeit der Angst verkürzen!
Was muß geschehn, mag's gleich geschehn!
Mag ihr Geschick auf mich zusammenstürzen
3365 Und sie mit mir zugrunde gehn!

MEPHISTOPHELES:
Wie's wieder siedet, wieder glüht!
Geh ein und tröste sie, du Tor!
Wo so ein Köpfchen keinen Ausgang sieht,
Stellt er sich gleich das Ende vor.
3370 Es lebe, wer sich tapfer hält!
Du bist doch sonst so ziemlich eingeteufelt.
Nichts Abgeschmackters find ich auf der Welt
Als einen Teufel, der verzweifelt.

GRETCHENS STUBE

GRETCHEN *(am Spinnrade, allein):*
Meine Ruh ist hin,
3375 Mein Herz ist schwer,
Ich finde sie nimmer
Und nimmermehr.

Wo ich ihn nicht hab,
Ist mir das Grab,
3380 Die ganze Welt
Ist mir vergällt.

Mein armer Kopf
Ist mir verrückt,
Mein armer Sinn
3385 Ist mir zerstückt.

Her—her peace I had to undermine.
You, hell, desired this sacrifice upon your shrine.
Help, Devil, shorten this time of dread.
What must be done, come let it be.
Let then her fate come shattering on my head,
And let her perish now with me.

MEPHISTO:

How now it boils again and how you shout.
Go in and comfort her, you dunce.
Where such a little head sees no way out,
He thinks the end must come at once.
Long live who holds out undeterred!
At other times you have the Devil's airs.
In all the world there's nothing more absurd
Than is a Devil who despairs.

GRETCHEN'S ROOM

GRETCHEN *(at the spinning wheel, alone):*

My peace is gone,
My heart is sore;
I find it never
And nevermore.

Where him I not have
There is my grave.
This world is all
Turned into gall.

And my poor head
Is quite insane,
And my poor mind
Is rent with pain.

Meine Ruh ist hin,
Mein Herz ist schwer,
Ich finde sie nimmer
Und nimmermehr.

3390 Nach ihm nur schau ich
Zum Fenster hinaus,
Nach ihm nur geh ich
Aus dem Haus.

Sein hoher Gang,
3395 Sein edle Gestalt,
Seines Mundes Lächeln,
Seiner Augen Gewalt

Und seiner Rede
Zauberfluß,
3400 Sein Händedruck,
Und, ach, sein Kuß!

Meine Ruh ist hin.
Mein Herz ist schwer,
Ich finde sie nimmer
3405 Und nimmermehr.

Mein Busen drängt
Sich nach ihm hin,
Ach dürft ich fassen
Und halten ihn

3410 Und küssen ihn,
So wie ich wollt,
An seinen Küssen
Vergehen sollt!

My peace is gone,
My heart is sore;
I find it never
And nevermore.

For him only I look
From my window seat,
For him only I go
Out into the street.

His lofty gait,
His noble guise,
The smile of his mouth,
The force of his eyes,

And his words' flow—
Enchanting bliss—
The touch of his hand,
And, oh, his kiss.

My peace is gone,
My heart is sore;
I find it never
And nevermore.

My bosom surges
For him alone,
Oh that I could clasp him
And hold him so,

And kiss him
To my heart's content,
Till in his kisses
I were spent.

MARTHENS GARTEN

Margarete. Faust.

MARGARETE:
Versprich mir, Heinrich!

FAUST:
Was ich kann!

MARGARETE:
3415 Nun sag, wie hast du's mit der Religion?
Du bist ein herzlich guter Mann,
Allein ich glaub, du hältst nicht viel davon.

FAUST:
Laß das, mein Kind! Du fühlst, ich bin dir gut;
Für meine Lieben ließ' ich Leib und Blut,
3420 Will niemand sein Gefühl und seine Kirche rauben.

MARGARETE:
Das ist nicht recht, man muß dran glauben!

FAUST:
Muß man?

MARGARETE:
Ach, wenn ich etwas auf dich könnte!
Du ehrst auch nicht die heilgen Sakramente.

FAUST:
Ich ehre sie.

MARGARETE:
Doch ohne Verlangen.
3425 Zur Messe, zur Beichte bist du lange nicht gegangen.
Glaubst du an Gott?

FAUST:
Mein Liebchen, wer darf sagen:
Ich glaub an Gott?
Magst Priester oder Weise fragen,
Und ihre Antwort scheint nur Spott
3430 Über den Frager zu sein.

MARTHA'S GARDEN

Margaret. Faust.

MARGARET:
Promise me, Heinrich.

FAUST:
Whatever I can.

MARGARET:
How is it with your religion, please admit—
Your certainly are a very good man,
But I believe you don't think much of it.

FAUST:
Leave that, my child. I love you, do not fear
And would give all for those whom I hold dear,
Would not rob anyone of church or creed.

MARGARET:
That is not enough, it is faith we need.

FAUST:
Do we?

MARGARET:
Oh that I had some influence!
You don't respect the holy sacraments.

FAUST:
I do respect them.

MARGARET:
But without desire.
The mass and confession you do not require.
Do you believe in God?

FAUST:
My darling who may say
I believe in God?
Ask priests and sages, their reply
Looks like sneers that mock and prod
The one who asked the question.

MARGARETE:

So glaubst du nicht?

FAUST:

Mißhör mich nicht, du holdes Angesicht!
Wer darf ihn nennen?
Und wer bekennen:
Ich glaub ihn?
3435 Wer empfinden
Und sich unterwinden
Zu sagen: ich glaub ihn nicht?
Der Allumfasser,
Der Allerhalter,
3440 Faßt und erhält er nicht
Dich, mich, sich selbst?
Wölbt sich der Himmel nicht dadroben?
Liegt die Erde nicht hierunten fest?
Und steigen freundlich blickend
3445 Ewige Sterne nicht herauf?
Schau ich nicht Aug in Auge dir,
Und drängt nicht alles
Nach Haupt und Herzen dir
Und webt in ewigem Geheimnis
3450 Unsichtbar sichtbar neben dir?
Erfüll davon dein Herz, so groß es ist,
Und wenn du ganz in dem Gefühle selig bist,
Nenn es dann, wie du willst,
Nenn's Glück! Herz! Liebe! Gott!
3455 Ich habe keinen Namen
Dafür! Gefühl ist alles;
Name ist Schall und Rauch,
Umnebelnd Himmelsglut.

MARGARETE:

Das ist alles recht schön und gut;
3460 Ungefähr sagt das der Pfarrer auch,
Nur mit ein bißchen andern Worten.

MARGARET:

Then you deny him there?

FAUST:

Do not mistake me, you who are so fair.
Him—who may name?
And who proclaim:
I believe in him?
Who may feel,
Who dare reveal
In words: I believe him not?
The All-Embracing,
The All-Sustaining,
Does he not embrace and sustain
You, me, himself?
Does not the heaven vault above?
Is the earth not firmly based down here?
And do not, friendly,
Eternal stars rise?
Do we not look into each other's eyes,
And all in you is surging
To your head and heart,
And weaves in timeless mystery,
Unseeable, yet seen, around you?
Then let it fill your heart entirely,
And when your rapture in this feeling is complete,
Call it then as you will,
Call it bliss! heart! love! God!
I do not have a name
For this. Feeling is all;
Names are but sound and smoke
Befogging heaven's blazes.

MARGARET:

Those are very fair and noble phrases;
The priest says something, too, like what you
spoke—
Only his words are not quite so——

FAUST:

Es sagen's allerorten
Alle Herzen unter dem himmlischen Tage,
Jedes in seiner Sprache;
3465 Warum nicht ich in der meinen?

MARGARETE:

Wenn man's so hört, möcht's liedlich scheinen,
Steht aber doch immer schief darum;
Denn du hast kein Christentum.

FAUST:

Liebs Kind!

MARGARETE:

Es tut mir lang schon weh,
3470 Daß ich dich in der Gesellschaft seh.

FAUST:

Wieso?

MARGARETE:

Der Mensch, den du da bei dir hast,
Ist mir in tiefer innrer Seele verhaßt;
Es hat mir in meinem Leben
So nichts einen Stich ins Herz gegeben
3475 Als des Menschen widrig Gesicht.

FAUST:

Liebe Puppe, fürcht ihn nicht!

MARGARETE:

Seine Gegenwart bewegt mir das Blut.
Ich bin sonst allen Menschen gut;
Aber wie ich mich sehne, dich zu schauen,
3480 Hab ich vor dem Menschen ein heimlich Grauen
Und halt ihn für einen Schelm dazu.
Gott verzeih mir's, wenn ich ihm Unrecht tu!

FAUST:

Es muß auch solche Käuze geben.

MARGARETE:

Wollte nicht mit seinesgleichen leben!
3485 Kommt er einmal zur Tür herein,
Sieht er immer so spöttisch drein

FAUST:

Wherever you go,
All hearts under the heavenly day
Say it, each in its own way;
Why not I in mine?

MARGARET:

When one listens to you, one might incline
To let it pass—but I can't agree,
For you have no Christianity.

FAUST:

Dear child!

MARGARET:

It has long been a grief to me
To see you in such company.

FAUST:

Why?

MARGARET:

The man that goes around with you
Seems hateful to me through and through:
In all my life there's not a thing
That gave my heart as sharp a sting
As his repulsive eyes.

FAUST:

Sweet doll, don't fear him anywise.

MARGARET:

His presence makes me feel quite ill.
I bear all other men good will;
But just as to see you I languish,
This man fills me with secret anguish;
He seems a knave one should not trust.
May God forgive me if I am unjust.

FAUST:

There must be queer birds, too, you know.

MARGARET:

But why live with them even so?
Whenever he comes in,
He always wears a mocking grin

Und halb ergrimmt;
Man sieht, daß er an nichts keinen Anteil nimmt;
Es steht ihm an der Stirn geschrieben,
3490 Daß er nicht mag eine Seele lieben.
Mir wird's so wohl in deinem Arm,
So frei, so hingegeben warm,
Und seine Gegenwart schnürt mir das Innre zu.

FAUST:
Du ahnungsvoller Engel du!

MARGARETE:
3495 Das übermannt mich so sehr,
Daß, wo er nur mag zu uns treten,
Mein ich sogar, ich liebte dich nicht mehr.
Auch, wenn er da ist, könnt ich nimmer beten,
Und das frißt mir ins Herz hinein;
3500 Dir, Heinrich, muß es auch so sein.

FAUST:
Du hast nun die Antipathie!

MARGARETE:
Ich muß nun fort.

FAUST:
Ach, kann ich nie
Ein Stündchen ruhig dir am Busen hängen
Und Brust an Brust und Seel in Seele drängen?

MARGARETE:
3505 Ach, wenn ich nur alleine schlief!
Ich ließ' dir gern heut nacht den Riegel offen;
Doch meine Mutter schläft nicht tief,
Und würden wir von ihr betroffen,
Ich wär gleich auf der Stelle tot!

FAUST:
3510 Du Engel, das hat keine Not.
Hier ist ein Fläschchen. Drei Tropfen nur
In ihren Trank umhüllen
Mit tiefem Schlaf gefällig die Natur.

And looks half threatening:
One sees, he has no sympathy for anything;
It is written on his very face
That he thinks love is a disgrace.
In your arm I feel good and free,
Warm and abandoned as can be;
Alas, my heart and feelings are choked when he
comes, too.

FAUST:
Oh, you foreboding angel, you.

MARGARET:
It makes my heart so sore
That, when he only comes our way,
I feel I do not love you any more;
And where he is, I cannot pray.
It eats into my heart. Oh you,
Dear Heinrich, must feel that way, too.

FAUST:
That is just your antipathy.

MARGARET:
I must go.

FAUST:
Will there never be
At your sweet bosom one hour of rest
When soul touches on soul and breast on breast?

MARGARET:
Had I my own room when I sleep,
I should not bolt the door tonight;
But Mother's slumber is not deep,
And if she found us thus—oh fright,
Right then and there I should drop dead.

FAUST:
My angel, if that's what you dread,
Here is a bottle. Merely shake
Three drops into her cup,
And she won't easily wake up.

MARGARETE:

Was tu ich nicht um deinetwillen?
3515 Es wird ihr hoffentlich nicht schaden!

FAUST:

Würd ich sonst, Liebchen, dir es raten?

MARGARETE:

Seh ich dich, bester Mann, nur an,
Weiß nicht, was mich nach deinem Willen treibt;
Ich habe schon so viel für dich getan,
3520 Daß mir zu tun fast nichts mehr übrigbleibt. *(Ab)*

(Mephistopheles tritt auf)

MEPHISTOPHELES:

Der Grasaff! Ist er weg?

FAUST:

Hast wieder spioniert?

MEPHISTOPHELES:

Ich hab's ausführlich wohl vernommen,
Herr Doktor wurden da katechisiert;
Hoff, es soll Ihnen wohl bekommen.
3525 Die Mädels sind doch sehr interessiert,
Ob einer fromm und schlicht nach altem Brauch.
Sie denken: duckt er da, folgt er uns eben auch.

FAUST:

Du Ungeheuer siehst nicht ein,
Wie diese treue liebe Seele
3530 Von ihrem Glauben voll,
Der ganz allein
Ihr seligmachend ist, sich heilig quäle,
Daß sie den liebsten Mann verloren halten soll.

MEPHISTOPHELES:

Du übersinnlicher sinnlicher Freier,
3535 Ein Mägdelein nasführet dich.

FAUST:

Du Spottgeburt von Dreck und Feuer!

MARGARET:

What should I not do for your sake?
It will not harm her if one tries it?

FAUST:

Dear, if it would, would I advise it?

MARGARET:

When I but look at you, I thrill,
I don't know why, my dear, to do your will;
I have already done so much for you
That hardly anything seems left to do. *(Exit)*

(MEPHISTOPHELES *enters)*

MEPHISTO:

The monkey! Is she gone?

FAUST:

You spied?

MEPHISTO:

Are you surprised?
I listened and I understood
Our learned doctor just was catechized.
I hope that it may do you good.
The girls are quite concerned to be apprised
If one is pious and obeys tradition.
If yes, they trust they can rely on his submission.

FAUST:

You monster will not see nor own
That this sweet soul, in loyalty,
Full of her own creed
Which alone,
She trusts, can bring salvation, lives in agony
To think her lover lost, however she may plead.

MEPHISTO:

You supersensual, sensual wooer,
A maiden leads you by the nose.

FAUST:

You freak of filth and fire! Evildoer!

MEPHISTOPHELES:

Und die Physiognomie versteht sie meisterlich:
In meiner Gegenwart wird's ihr, sie weiß nicht wie,
Mein Mäskchen da weissagt verborgnen Sinn;
3540 Sie fühlt, daß ich ganz sicher ein Genie,
Vielleicht wohl gar der Teufel bin.
Nun, heute nacht—?

FAUST:

Was geht dich's an?

MEPHISTOPHELES:

Hab ich doch meine Freude dran!

AM BRUNNEN

Gretchen und Lieschen mit Krügen.

LIESCHEN:

Hast nichts von Bärbelchen gehört?

GRETCHEN:

3545 Kein Wort. Ich komm gar wenig unter Leute.

LIESCHEN:

Gewiß, Sibylle sagt' mir's heute:
Die hat sich endlich auch betört.
Das ist das Vornehmtun!

GRETCHEN:

Wieso?

LIESCHEN:

Es stinkt!

Sie füttert zwei, wenn sie nun ißt und trinkt.

GRETCHEN:

3550 Ach!

MEPHISTO:

And what a knowledge of physiognomy she shows.
She feels, she knows not what, whenever I'm about;
She finds a hidden meaning in my eyes:
I am a demon, beyond doubt,
Perhaps the Devil, that is her surmise.
Well, tonight–?

FAUST:

What's that to you?

MEPHISTO:

I have my pleasure in it, too.

AT THE WELL

Gretchen and Lieschen with Jugs.

LIESCHEN:

Of Barbara you haven't heard?

GRETCHEN:

I rarely see people–no, not a word.

LIESCHEN:

Well, Sibyl just told me in front of the school:
That girl has at last been made a fool.
That comes from having airs.

GRETCHEN:

How so?

LIESCHEN:

It stinks!
She is feeding two when she eats and drinks.

GRETCHEN:

Oh!

LIESCHEN:

So ist's ihr endlich recht ergangen.
Wie lange hat sie an dem Kerl gehangen!
Das war ein Spazieren,
Auf Dorf- und Tanzplatz Führen,
3555 Mußt überall die Erste sein,
Kurtesiert' ihr immer mit Pastetchen und Wein;
Bildt' sich was auf ihre Schönheit ein,
War doch so ehrlos, sich nicht zu schämen,
Geschenke von ihm anzunehmen.
3560 War ein Gekos und ein Geschleck;
Da ist denn auch das Blümchen weg!

GRETCHEN:

Das arme Ding!

LIESCHEN:

Bedauerst sie noch gar!
Wenn unsereins am Spinnen war,
Uns nachts die Mutter nicht hinunterließ,
3565 Stand sie bei ihrem Buhlen süß,
Auf der Türbank und im dunkeln Gang
Ward ihnen keine Stunde zu lang.
Da mag sie denn sich ducken nun,
Im Sünderhemdchen Kirchbuß tun!

GRETCHEN:

3570 Er nimmt sie gewiß zu seiner Frau.

LIESCHEN:

Er wär ein Narr! Ein flinker Jung
Hat anderwärts noch Luft genug
Er ist auch fort.

GRETCHEN:

Das ist nicht schön!

LIESCHEN:

Kriegt sie ihn, soll's ihr übel gehn!
3575 Das Kränzel reißen die Buben ihr,
Und Häckerling streuen wir vor die Tür.
(Ab)

LIESCHEN:

At last she has got what was coming to her.
She stuck to that fellow like a burr.
That was some prancing,
In the village, and dancing,
She was always the first in line;
And he flirted with her over pastries and wine;
And she thought that she looked divine—
But had no honor, no thought of her name,
And took his presents without any shame.
The way they slobbered and carried on;
But now the little flower is gone.

GRETCHEN:

Poor thing!

LIESCHEN:

That you don't say!
When girls like us would be spinning away,
And mother kept us at home every night,
She was with her lover in sweet delight
On the bench by the door, in dark alleys they
were,
And the time was never too long for her.
Now let her crouch and let her bend down
And do penance in a sinners' gown!

GRETCHEN:

He will surely take her to be his wife.

LIESCHEN:

He would be a fool! A handsome boy
Will elsewhere find more air and joy.
He's already gone.

GRETCHEN:

That is not fair!

LIESCHEN:

And if she gets him, let her beware:
Her veil the boys will throw to the floor,
And we shall strew chaff in front of her door.
(Exit)

GRETCHEN *(nach Hause gehend):*

Wie konnt ich sonst so tapfer schmälen,
Wenn tät ein armes Mägdlein fehlen!
Wie konnt ich über andrer Sünden
3580 Nicht Worte gnug der Zunge finden!
Wie schien mir's schwarz, und schwärzt's noch gar,
Mir's immer doch nicht schwarz gnug war,
Und segnet mich und tat so groß
Und bin nun selbst der Sünde bloß!
3585 Doch—alles, was dazu mich trieb,
Gott, war so gut! Ach, war so lieb!

ZWINGER

In der Mauerhohle ein Andachtsbild der Mater dolorosa, Blumenkruge davor.

GRETCHEN *(steckt frische Blumen in die Krüge):*

Ach neige,
Du Schmerzenreiche,
Dein Antlitz gnädig meiner Not!

3590 Das Schwert im Herzen,
Mit tausend Schmerzen
Blickst auf zu deines Sohnes Tod.

Zum Vater blickst du
Und Seufzer schickst du
3595 Hinauf um sein und deine Not.

GRETCHEN *(going home):*
How I once used to scold along
When some poor woman had done wrong.
How for another person's shame
I found not words enough of blame.
How black it seemed—I made it blacker still,
And yet not black enough to suit my will.
I blessed myself, would boast and grin—
And now myself am caught in sin.
Yet—everything that brought me here,
God, was so good, oh, was so dear.

CITY WALL

In a niche in the wall, an image of the Mater Dolorosa. Ewers with flowers in front of it.

GRETCHEN *(puts fresh flowers into the ewers):*
Incline,
Mother of pain,
Your face in grace to my despair.

A sword in your heart,
With pain rent apart,
Up to your son's dread death you stare.

On the Father your eyes,
You send up sighs
For your and your son's despair.

Wer fühlet,
Wie wühlet
Der Schmerz mir im Gebein?

Was mein armes Herz hier banget,
3600 Was es zittert, was verlanget,
Weißt nur du, nur du allein!

Wohin ich immer gehe,
Wie weh, wie weh, wie wehe
Wird mir im Busen hier!
3605 Ich bin, ach, kaum alleine,
Ich wein, ich wein, ich weine,
Das Herz zerbricht in mir.

Die Scherben vor meinem Fenster
Betaut ich mit Tränen, ach,
3610 Als ich am frühen Morgen
Dir diese Blumen brach.

Schien hell in meine Kammer
Die Sonne früh herauf,
Saß ich in allem Jammer
3615 In meinem Bett schon auf.

Hilf! Rette mich von Schmach und Tod!
Ach neige,
Du Schmerzenreiche,
Dein Antlitz gnädig meiner Not!

Who knows
My woes—
Despair in every bone!

How my heart is full of anguish,
How I tremble, how I languish,
Know but you, and you alone.

Wherever I may go,
What woe, what woe, what woe
Is in my bosom aching!
Scarcely alone am I,
I cry, I cry, I cry;
My heart in me is breaking.

The pots in front of my window
I watered with tears as the dew,
When early in the morning
I broke these flowers for you.

When bright into my room
The sun his first rays shed,
I sat in utter gloom
Already on my bed.

Help! Rescue me from shame and death!
Incline,
Mother of pain,
Your face in grace to my despair.

NACHT.

STRASSE VOR GRETCHENS TÜRE

VALENTIN *(Soldat, Gretchens Bruder):*

3620 Wenn ich so saß bei einem Gelag,
Wo mancher sich berühmen mag,
Und die Gesellen mir den Flor
Der Mägdlein laut gepriesen vor,
Mit vollem Glas das Lob verschwemmt—
3625 Den Ellenbogen aufgestemmt
Saß ich in meiner sichern Ruh,
Hört all dem Schwadronieren zu.
Und streiche lächelnd meinen Bart
Und kriege das volle Glas zur Hand
3630 Und sage: Alles nach seiner Art!
Aber ist Eine im ganzen Land,
Die meiner trauten Gretel gleicht,
Die meiner Schwester das Wasser reicht?
Topp! Topp! Kling! Klang! Das ging herum;
3635 Die einen schrieen: Er hat recht,
Sie ist die Zier vom ganzen Geschlecht.
Da saßen alle die Lober stumm.
Und nun!—um's Haar sich auszuraufen
Und an den Wänden hinaufzulaufen!—
3640 Mit Stichelreden, Naserümpfen
Soll jeder Schurke mich beschimpfen!
Soll wie ein böser Schuldner sitzen,
Bei jedem Zufallswörtchen schwitzen!
Und möcht ich sie zusammenschmeißen,
3645 Könnt ich sie doch nicht Lügner heißen.

Was kommt heran? Was schleicht herbei?
Irr ich nicht, es sind ihrer zwei.
Ist er's, gleich pack ich ihn beim Felle,
Soll nicht lebendig von der Stelle.

FAUST. MEPHISTOPHELES.

NIGHT.

STREET IN FRONT OF GRETCHEN'S DOOR.

VALENTINE *(soldier,* GRETCHEN'S *brother):*
When I would sit at a drinking bout
Where all had much to brag about,
And many fellows raised their voice
To praise the maidens of their choice,
Glass after glass was drained with toasting,
I listened smugly to their boasting,
My elbow propped up on the table,
And sneered at fable after fable.
I'd stroke my beard and smile and say,
Holding my bumper in my hand:
Each may be nice in her own way,
But is there one in the whole land
Like sister Gretchen to outdo her,
One that could hold a candle to her?
Hear, hear! Clink! Clink! it went around;
And some would cry: It's true, yes sir,
There is no other girl like her!
The braggarts sat without a sound.
And *now*—I could tear out my hair
And dash my brain out in despair!
His nose turned up, a scamp can face me,
With taunts and sneers he can disgrace me;
And I should sit, like one in debt,
Each chance remark should make me sweat!
I'd like to grab them all and maul them,
But liars I could never call them.

What's coming there? What sneaks in view?
If I mistake not, there are two.
If it is he, I'll spare him not,
He shall not living leave this spot.

(FAUST *and* MEPHISTOPHELES *enter.)*

FAUST:

3650 Wie von dem Fenster dort der Sakristei
Aufwärts der Schein des ewgen Lämpchens
flämmert
Und schwach und schwächer seitwärts dämmert,
Und Finsternis drängt ringsum bei!
So sieht's in meinem Busen nächtig.

MEPHISTOPHELES:

3655 Und mir ist's wie dem Kätzlein schmächtig,
Das an den Feuerleitern schleicht,
Sich leis dann um die Mauern streicht;
Mir ist's ganz tugendlich dabei,
Ein bißchen Diebsgelüst, ein bißchen Rammelei.
3660 So spukt mir schon durch alle Glieder
Die herrliche Walpurgisnacht.
Die kommt uns übermorgen wieder,
Da weiß man doch, warum man wacht.

FAUST:

Rückt wohl der Schatz indessen in die Höh,
3665 Den ich dort hinten flimmern seh?

MEPHISTOPHELES:

Du kannst die Freude bald erleben,
Das Kesselchen herauszuheben.
Ich schielte neulich so hinein,
Sind herrliche Löwentaler drein.

FAUST:

3670 Nicht ein Geschmeide, nicht ein Ring,
Meine liebe Buhle damit zu zieren?

MEPHISTOPHELES:

Ich sah dabei wohl so ein Ding,
Als wie eine Art von Perlenschnüren.

FAUST:

So ist es recht! Mir tut es weh,
3675 Wenn ich ohne Geschenke zu ihr geh.

MEPHISTOPHELES:

Es sollt Euch eben nicht verdrießen,
Umsonst auch etwas zu genießen.

FAUST:

How from the window of that sacristy
The light of the eternal lamp is glimmering,
And weak and weaker sideward shimmering,
As night engulfs it like the sea.
My heart feels like this nightly street.

MEPHISTO:

And I feel like a cat in heat,
That creeps around a fire escape
Pressing against the wall its shape.
I feel quite virtuous, I confess,
A little thievish lust, a little rammishness.
Thus I feel spooking through each vein
The wonderful Walpurgis Night.
In two days it will come again,
And waking then is pure delight.

FAUST:

And will the treasure that gleams over there
Rise in the meantime up into the air?

MEPHISTO:

Quite soon you may enjoy the pleasure
Of taking from the pot the treasure.
The other day I took a squint
And saw fine lion dollars in't.

FAUST:

Not any jewelry, not a ring
To adorn my beloved girl?

MEPHISTO:

I did see something like a string,
Or something like it, made of pearl.

FAUST:

Oh, that is fine, for it's unpleasant
To visit her without a present.

MEPHISTO:

It should not cause you such distress
When you have gratis such success.

Jetzt, da der Himmel voller Sterne glüht,
Sollt Ihr ein wahres Kunststück hören.
3680 Ich sing ihr ein moralisch Lied,
Um sie gewisser zu betören.
(Singt zur Zither)

Was machst du mir
Vor Liebchens Tür,
Kathrinchen, hier
3685 Bei frühem Tagesblicke?
Laß, laß es sein!
Er läßt dich ein,
Als Mädchen ein,
Als Mädchen nicht zurücke.

3690 Nehmt euch in acht!
Ist es vollbracht,
Dann gute Nacht,
Ihr armen, armen Dinger!
Habt ihr euch lieb,
3695 Tut keinem Dieb
Nur nichts zulieb
Als mit dem Ring am Finger!

VALENTIN *(tritt vor):*
Wen lockst du hier? Beim Element!
Vermaledeiter Rattenfänger!
3700 Zum Teufel erst das Instrument!
Zum Teufel hinterdrein den Sänger!

MEPHISTOPHELES:
Die Zither ist entzwei! An der ist nichts zu halten.

VALENTIN:
Nun soll es an ein Schädelspalten!

MEPHISTOPHELES *(zu Faust):*
Herr Doktor, nicht gewichen! Frisch!
3705 Hart an mich an, wie ich Euch führe!

Now that the sky gleams with its starry throng,
Prepare to hear a work of art:
I shall sing her a moral song
To take no chance we fool her heart.
(Sings to the cither.)[*]

It's scarcely day,
Oh, Katie, say,
Why do you stay
Before your lover's door?
Leave now, leave now!
For in you'll go
A maid, I know,
Come out a maid no more.

You ought to shun
That kind of fun;
Once it is done,
Good night, you poor, poor thing.
For your own sake
You should not make
Love to a rake
Unless you have the ring.

VALENTINE *(comes forward):*
Whom would you lure? God's element!
Rat-catching piper! Oh, perdition!
The Devil take your instrument!
The Devil then take the musician!

MEPHISTO:
The cither is all smashed. It is beyond repair.

VALENTINE:
Now let's try splitting skulls. Beware!

MEPHISTO (*to* FAUST):
Don't withdraw, doctor! Quick, don't tarry!
Stick close to me, I'll lead the way.

---

[*] Cf. Introduction, end of section 4.

Heraus mit Eurem Flederwisch!
Nur zugestoßen! Ich pariere.

VALENTIN:
Pariere den!

MEPHISTOPHELES:
Warum denn nicht?

VALENTIN:
Auch den!

MEPHISTOPHELES:
Gewiß!

VALENTIN:
Ich glaub, der Teufel ficht!
3710 Was ist denn das? Schon wird die Hand mir lahm.

MEPHISTOPHELES *(zu Faust)*:
Stoß zu!

VALENTIN *(fällt)*:
O weh!

MEPHISTOPHELES:
Nun ist der Lümmel zahm!
Nun aber fort! Wir müssen gleich verschwinden;
Denn schon entsteht ein Mörderlich Geschrei.
Ich weiß mich trefflich mit der Polizei,
3715 Doch mit dem Blutbann schlecht mich abzufinden.

MARTHE *(am Fenster)*:
Heraus! Heraus!

GRETCHEN *(am Fenster)*:
Herbei ein Licht!

MARTHE *(wie oben)*:
Man schilt und rauft, man schreit und ficht.

VOLK:
Da liegt schon einer tot!

MARTHE *(heraustretend)*:
Die Mörder, sind sie denn entflohn?

GRETCHEN *(heraustretend)*:
3720 Wer liegt hier?

VOLK:
Deiner Mutter Sohn.

Unsheathe your toothpick, don't delay;
Thrust out at him, and I shall parry.

VALENTINE:

Then parry that!

MEPHISTO:

Of course.

VALENTINE:

And that.

MEPHISTO:

All right.

VALENTINE:

I think the Devil must be in this fight.
What could that be? My hand is getting lame.

MEPHISTO (*to* FAUST):

Thrust home!

VALENTINE (*falls*):

Oh God!

MEPHISTO:

The rogue is tame.
Now hurry hence, for we must disappear:
A murderous clamor rises instantly,
And while the police does not trouble me,
The blood ban is a thing I fear.

MARTHA (*at a window*):

Come out! Come out!

GRETCHEN (*at a window*):

Quick! Bring a light.

MARTHA (*as above*):

They swear and scuffle, yell and fight.

PEOPLE:

There is one dead already, see.

MARTHA (*coming out*):

The murderers—where did they run?

GRETCHEN (*coming out*):

Who lies there?

PEOPLE:

Your own mother's son.

GRETCHEN:

Allmächtiger! Welche Not!

VALENTIN:

Ich sterbe, das ist bald gesagt
Und bälder noch getan.
Was steht ihr Weiber, heult und klagt?
3725 Kommt her und hört mich an! *(Alle treten um ihn.)*

Mein Gretchen sieh, du bist noch jung,
Bist gar noch nicht gescheit genug,
Machst deine Sachen schlecht.
Ich sag dir's im Vertrauen nur:
3730 Du bist doch nun einmal eine Hur;
So sei's auch eben recht!

GRETCHEN:

Mein Bruder! Gott! Was soll mir das?

VALENTIN:

Laß unsern Herrgott aus dem Spaß!
Geschehn ist leider nun geschehn,
3735 Und wie es gehn kann, so wird's gehn.
Du fingst mit einem heimlich an,
Bald kommen ihrer mehre dran,
Und wenn dich erst ein Dutzend hat,
So hat dich auch die ganze Stadt.

3740 Wenn erst die Schande wird geboren,
Wird sie heimlich zur Welt gebracht,
Und man zieht den Schleier der Nacht
Ihr über Kopf und Ohren;
Ja, man möchte sie gern ermorden.
3745 Wächst sie aber und macht sich groß,
Dann geht sie auch bei Tage bloß,
Und ist doch nicht schöner geworden.
Je häßlicher wird ihr Gesicht,
Je mehr sucht sie des Tages Licht.

3750 Ich seh wahrhaftig schon die Zeit,

GRETCHEN:
Almighty God! What misery!

VALENTINE:
I'm dying. That is quickly said,
And still more quickly done.
Why do you women wail in dread?
Come here, listen to me. *(All gather around him.)*

My Gretchen, you are still quite green,
Not nearly smart enough or keen,
You do not do things right.
In confidence, I should say more:
Since after all you are a whore,
Be one with all your might.

GRETCHEN:
My brother! God! What frightful shame!

VALENTINE:
Leave the Lord God out of this game.
What has been done, alas, is done,
And as it must, it now will run.
You started secretly with one,
Soon more will come to join the fun,
And once a dozen lays you down,
You might as well invite the town.

When shame is born and first appears,
It is an underhand delight,
And one drags the veil of night
Over her head and ears;
One is tempted to put her away.
But as she grows, she gets more bold,
Walks naked even in the day,
Though hardly fairer to behold.
The more repulsive grows her sight,
The more she seeks day's brilliant light.

The time I even now discern

Daß alle brave Bürgersleut
Wie von einer angesteckten Leichen
Von dir, du Metze, seitab weichen.
Dir soll das Herz im Leib verzagen,
3755 Wenn sie dir in die Augen sehn!
Sollst keine goldne Kette mehr tragen!
In der Kirche nicht mehr am Altar stehn!
In einem schönen Spitzenkragen
Dich nicht beim Tanze wohlbehagen!
3760 In eine finstre Jammerecken
Unter Bettler und Krüppel dich verstecken
Und, wenn dir dann auch Gott verzeiht,
Auf Erden sein vermaledeit!

MARTHE:
Befehlt Eure Seele Gott zu Gnaden!
3765 Wollt Ihr noch Lästrung auf Euch laden?

VALENTIN:
Könnt ich dir nur an den dürren Leib,
Du schändlich kupplerisches Weib!
Da hofft ich aller meiner Sünden
Vergebung reiche Maß zu finden.

GRETCHEN:
3770 Mein Bruder! Welche Höllenpein!

VALENTIN:
Ich sage, laß die Tränen sein!
Da du dich sprachst der Ehre los,
Gabst mir den schwersten Herzensstoß.
Ich gehe durch den Todesschlaf
3775 Zu Gott ein als Soldat und brav. *(Stirbt.)*

When honest citizens will turn,
Harlot, away from you and freeze
As from a corpse that breeds disease.
Your heart will flinch, your heart will falter
When they will look you in the face.
You'll wear no gold, you'll wear no lace,
Nor in the church come near the altar.
You will no longer show your skill
At dances, donning bow and frill,
But in dark corners on the side
With beggars and cripples you'll seek to hide;
And even if God should at last forgive,
Be cursed as long as you may live!

MARTHA:
Ask God to show your own soul grace.
Don't make it with blasphemies still more base.

VALENTINE:
That I could lay my hands on you,
You shriveled, pimping bugaboo,
Then, I hope, I might truly win
Forgiveness for my every sin.

GRETCHEN:
My brother! This is agony!

VALENTINE:
I tell you, do not bawl at me.
When you threw honor overboard,
You pierced my heart more than the sword.
Now I shall cross death's sleeping span
To God, a soldier and an honest man. *(Dies.)*

DOM

Amt, Orgel und Gesang.

Gretchen unter vielem Volke. Böser Geist hinter Gretchen.

BÖSER GEIST:

Wie anders, Gretchen, war dir's,
Als du noch voll Unschuld
Hier zum Altar tratst,
Aus dem vergriffnen Büchelchen
3780 Gebete lalltest,
Halb Kinderspiele,
Halb Gott im Herzen!
Gretchen!
Wo steht dein Kopf?
3785 In deinem Herzen
Welche Missetat?
Betst du für deiner Mutter Seele, die
Durch dich zur langen, langen Pein
hinüberschlief?
Auf deiner Schwelle wessen Blut?
3790 —Und unter deinem Herzen
Regt sich's nicht quillend schon
Und ängstet dich und sich
Mit ahnungsvoller Gegenwart?

GRETCHEN:

Weh! Weh!
3795 Wär ich der Gedanken los,
Die mir herüber und hinüber gehen
Wider mich!

CHOR:

Dies irae, dies illa
Solvet saeclum in favilla.
(Orgelton.)

BÖSER GEIST:

3800 Grimm faßt dich!

CATHEDRAL

Service, Organ, and Singing.
Gretchen among many people. Evil Spirit behind Gretchen.

EVIL SPIRIT:
How different you felt, Gretchen,
When in innocence
You came before this altar;
And from the well-worn little book
You prattled prayers,
Half childish games,
Half God in your heart!
Gretchen!
Where are your thoughts?
And in your heart
What misdeed?
Do you pray for your mother's soul that went
Because of you from sleep to lasting, lasting pain?
Upon your threshold, whose blood?
And underneath your heart,
Does it not stir and swell,
Frightened and frightening you
With its foreboding presence?

GRETCHEN:
Oh! Oh!
That I were rid of all the thoughts
Which waver in me to and fro
Against me!

CHOIR:
Dies irae, dies illa
Solvet saeclum in favilla.
(Sound of the organ.)

EVIL SPIRIT:
Wrath grips you.

Die Posaune tönt!
Die Gräber beben!
Und dein Herz,
Aus Aschenruh
3805 Zu Flammenqualen
Wieder aufgeschaffen,
Bebt auf!

GRETCHEN:

Wär ich hier weg!
Mir ist, als ob die Orgel mir
3810 Den Atem versetzte,
Gesang mein Herz
Im Tiefsten löste.

CHOR:

Judex ergo cum sedebit,
Quidquid latet adparebit,
3815 Nil inultum remanebit.

GRETCHEN:

Mir wird so eng!
Die Mauernpfeiler
Befangen mich!
Das Gewölbe
3820 Drängt mich!—Luft!

BÖSER GEIST:

Verbirg dich! Sünd und Schande
Bleibt nicht verborgen.
Luft? Licht?
Weh dir!

CHOR:

3825 Quid sum miser tunc dicturus?
Quem patronum rogaturus?
Cum vix justus sit securus.

BÖSER GEIST:

Ihr Antlitz wenden
Verklärte von dir ab.
3830 Die Hände dir zu reichen,
Schauert's den Reinen.

The great trumpet sounds.
The graves are quaking.
And your heart,
Resurrected
From ashen calm
To flaming tortures,
Flares up.

GRETCHEN:

Would I were far!
I feel as if the organ had
Taken my breath,
As if the song
Dissolved my heart!

CHOIR:

Judex ergo cum sedebit,
Quidquid latet adparebit,
Nil inultum remanebit.

GRETCHEN:

I feel so close.
The stony pillars
Imprison me.
The vault above
Presses on me.—Air!

EVIL SPIRIT:

Hide yourself. Sin and shame
Do not stay hidden.
Air? Light?
Woe unto you!

CHOIR:

Quid sum miser tunc dicturus?
Quem patronum rogaturus?
Cum vix justus sit securus.

EVIL SPIRIT:

The transfigured turn
Their countenance from you.
To hold out their hands to you
Makes the pure shudder.

Weh!

CHOR:

Quid sum miser tunc dicturus?

GRETCHEN:

Nachbarin! Euer Fläschchen!—

(Sie fällt in Ohnmacht.)

WALPURGISNACHT

Harzgebirg. Gegend von Schierke und Elend
Faust. Mephistopheles.

MEPHISTOPHELES:

3835 Verlangst du nicht nach einem Besenstiele?
Ich wünschte mir den allerderbsten Bock.
Auf diesem Weg sind wir noch weit vom Ziele.

FAUST:

Solang ich mich noch frisch auf meinen Beinen fühle,
Genügt mir dieser Knotenstock.
3840 Was hilft's, daß man den Weg verkürzt?—
Im Labyrinth der Täler hinzuschleichen,
Dann diesen Felsen zu ersteigen,
Von dem der Quell sich ewig sprudelnd stürzt,
Das ist die Lust, die solche Pfade würzt!
3845 Der Frühling webt schon in den Birken,
Und selbst die Fichte fühlt ihn schon;
Sollt er nicht auch auf unsre Glieder wirken?

MEPHISTOPHELES:

Fürwahr, ich spüre nichts davon!
Mir ist es winterlich im Leibe,

Woe!

CHOIR:

Quid sum miser tunc dicturus?

GRETCHEN:

Neighbor! Your smelling salts!

(She faints.)

*WALPURGIS NIGHT**

Harz mountains. Region of Schierke and Elend.
Faust and Mephistopheles.

MEPHISTO:

How would you like a broomstick now to fly?
I wish I had a billy goat that's tough.
For on this road we still have to climb high.

FAUST:

As long as I feel fresh, and while my legs are spry,
This knotted staff seems good enough.
Why should we shun each stumbling block?
To creep first through the valleys' lovely maze,
And then to scale this wall of rock
From which the torrent foams in silver haze—
There is the zest that spices our ways.
Around the birches weaves the spring,
Even the fir tree feels its spell:
Should it not stir in our limbs as well?

MEPHISTO:

Of all that I don't feel a thing.
In me the winter is still brisk,

* For some explanatory remarks, see section 6 of the Introduction.

3850 Ich wünschte Schnee und Frost auf meiner Bahn.
Wie traurig steigt die unvollkommne Scheibe
Des roten Monds mit später Glut heran
Und leuchtet schlecht, daß man bei jedem Schritte
Vor einen Baum, vor einen Felsen rennt!
3855 Erlaub, daß ich ein Irrlicht bitte!
Dort seh ich eins, das eben lustig brennt.
He da, mein Freund, darf ich dich zu uns fordern?
Was willst du so vergebens lodern?
Sei doch so gut und leucht uns da hinauf!

IRRLICHT:

3860 Aus Ehrfurcht, hoff ich, soll es mir gelingen,
Mein leichtes Naturell zu zwingen;
Nur zickzack geht gewöhnlich unser Lauf.

MEPHISTOPHELES:

Ei! Ei! Er denkt's den Menschen nachzuahmen.
Geh Er nur grad in 's Teufels Namen!
3865 Sonst blas ich Ihm Sein Flackerleben aus.

IRRLICHT:

Ich merke wohl, Ihr seid der Herr vom Haus,
Und will mich gern nach Euch bequemen.
Allein bedenkt, der Berg ist heute zaubertoll,
Und wenn ein Irrlicht Euch die Wege weisen soll,
3870 So müßt Ihr's so genau nicht nehmen.

FAUST, MEPHISTOPHELES, IRRLICHT
(im Wechselgesang).

In die Traum- und Zaubersphäre
Sind wir, scheint es, eingegangen.
Führ uns gut und mach dir Ehre,
Daß wir vorwärts bald gelangen
3875 In den weiten, öden Räumen!

Seh die Bäume hinter Bäumen,
Wie sie schnell vorüberrücken,
Und die Klippen, die sich bücken,

I wish my path were graced with frost and snow.
How wretchedly the moon's imperfect disk
Arises now with its red, tardy glow,
And is so dim that one could bump one's head
At every step against a rock or tree!
Let's use a will-o'-the-wisp instead!
I see one there that burns quite merrily.
Hello there! Would you come and join us, friend?
Why blaze away to no good end?
Please be so kind and show us up the hill!

WILL-O'-THE-WISP:

I hope my deep respect will help me force
My generally flighty will;
For zigzag is the rule in our course.

MEPHISTO:

Hear! Hear! It's man you like to imitate!
Now, in the Devil's name, go straight—
Or I shall blow your flickering life span out.

WILL-O'-THE-WISP:

You are the master of the house, no doubt,
And I shall try to serve you nicely.
But don't forget, the mountain is magic-mad
today,
And if Will-o'-the-wisp must guide you on your
way,
You must not take things too precisely.

FAUST, MEPHISTOPHELES, and WILL-O'-THE-WISP
(in alternating song):

In the sphere of dream and spell
We have entered now indeed.
Have some pride and guide us well
That we get ahead with speed
In the vast deserted spaces!

See the trees behind the trees,
See how swiftly they change places,
And the cliffs that bow with ease,

Und die langen Felsennasen,
3880 Wie sie schnarchen, wie sie blasen!

Durch die Steine, durch den Rasen
Eilet Bach und Bächlein nieder.
Hör ich Rauschen? Hör ich Lieder?
Hör ich holde Liebesklage,
3885 Stimmen jener Himmelstage?
Was wir hoffen, was wir lieben!
Und das Echo, wie die Sage
Alter Zeiten, hallet wider.

Uhu! Schuhu! tönt es näher,
3890 Kauz und Kiebitz und der Häher,
Sind sie alle wach geblieben?
Sind das Molche durchs Gesträuche?
Lange Beine, dicke Bäuche!
Und die Wurzeln wie die Schlangen
3895 Winden sich aus Fels und Sande,
Strecken wunderliche Bande,
Uns zu schrecken, uns zu fangen;
Aus belebten derben Masern
Strecken sie Polypenfasern
3900 Nach dem Wandrer. Und die Mäuse
Tausendfärbig, scharenweise,
Durch das Moos und durch die Heide!
Und die Funkenwürmer fliegen
Mit gedrängten Schwärmezügen
3905 Zum verwirrenden Geleite.

Aber sag mir, ob wir stehen
Oder ob wir weitergehen?
Alles, alles scheint zu drehen,
Fels und Bäume, die Gesichter
3910 Schneiden, und die irren Lichter,
Die sich mehren, die sich blähen.

Craggy noses, long and short,
How they snore and how they snort!

Through the stones and through the leas
Tumble brooks of every sort.
Is it splash or melodies?
Is it love that wails and prays,
Voices of those heavenly days?
What we hope and what we love!
Echoes and dim memories
Of forgotten times come back.

Oo-hoo! Shoo-hoo! Thus they squawk,
Screech owl, plover, and the hawk;
Did they all stay up above?
Are those salamanders crawling?
Bellies bloated, long legs sprawling!
And the roots, as serpents, coil
From the rocks through sandy soil,
With their eerie bonds would scare us,
Block our path and then ensnare us;
Hungry as a starving leech,
Their strong polyp's tendrils reach
For the wanderer. And in swarms
Mice of myriad hues and forms
Storm through moss and heath and lea.
And a host of fireflies
Throng about and improvise
The most maddening company.

Tell me: do we now stand still,
Or do we go up the hill?
Everything now seems to mill,
Rocks and trees and faces blend,
Will-o'-the-wisps grow and extend
And inflate themselves at will.

MEPHISTOPHELES:

Fasse wacker meinen Zipfel!
Hier ist so ein Mittelgipfel,
Wo man mit Erstaunen sieht,
3915 Wie im Berg der Mammon glüht.

FAUST:

Wie seltsam glimmert durch die Gründe
Ein morgenrötlich trüber Schein!
Und selbst bis in die tiefen Schlünde
Des Abgrunds wittert er hinein.
3920 Da steigt ein Dampf, dort ziehen Schwaden,
Hier leuchtet Glut aus Dunst und Flor,
Dann schleicht sie wie ein zarter Faden,
Dann bricht sie wie ein Quell hervor.

Hier schlingt sie eine ganze Strecke
3925 Mit hundert Adern sich durchs Tal,
Und hier in der gedrängten Ecke
Vereinzelt sie sich auf einmal.
Da sprühen Funken in der Nähe
Wie ausgestreuter goldner Sand.
3930 Doch schau! In ihrer ganzen Höhe
Entzündet sich die Felsenwand.

MEPHISTOPHELES:

Erleuchtet nicht zu diesem Feste
Herr Mammon prächtig den Palast?
Ein Glück, daß du's gesehen hast;
3935 Ich spüre schon die ungestümen Gäste.

FAUST:

Wie rast die Windsbraut durch die Luft!
Mit welchen Schlägen trifft sie meinen Nacken!

MEPHISTOPHELES:

Du mußt des Felsens alte Rippen packen,
Sonst stürzt sie dich hinab in dieser Schlünde
Gruft.
3940 Ein Nebel verdichtet die Nacht.
Höre, wie's durch die Wälder kracht!

MEPHISTO:

Grip my coat and hold on tight!
Here is such a central height
Where one sees, and it amazes,
In the mountain, Mammon's blazes.

FAUST:

How queer glimmers a dawnlike sheen
Faintly beneath this precipice,
And plays into the dark ravine
Of the near bottomless abyss.
Here mists arise, there vapors spread,
And here it gleams deep in the mountain,
Then creeps along, a tender thread,
And gushes up, a glistening fountain.

Here it is winding in a tangle,
With myriad veins the gorges blaze,
And here in this congested angle
A single stream shines through the haze.
There sparks are flying at our right,
As plentiful as golden sand.
But look! In its entire height
The rock becomes a firebrand.

MEPHISTO:

Sir Mammon never spares the light
To hold the feast in proper fashion.
How lucky that you saw this sight!
I hear the guests approach in wanton passion.

FAUST:

The tempests lash the air and rave,
And with gigantic blows they hit my shoulders.

MEPHISTO:

You have to clutch the ribs of those big hoary
boulders,
Or they will hurtle you to that abysmal grave.
A fog blinds the night with its hood.
Do you hear the crashes in the wood?

Aufgescheucht fliegen die Eulen.
Hör, es splittern die Säulen
Ewig grüner Paläste.
3945 Girren und Brechen der Äste!
Der Stämme mächtiges Dröhnen!
Der Wurzeln Knarren und Gähnen!
Im fürchterlich verworrenen Falle
Übereinander krachen sie alle,
3950 Und durch die übertrümmerten Klüfte
Zischen und heulen die Lüfte.
Hörst du die Stimmen in der Höhe?
In der Ferne, in der Nähe?
Ja, den ganzen Berg entlang
3955 Strömt ein wütender Zaubergesang!

HEXEN IM CHOR:

Die Hexen zu dem Brocken ziehn,
Die Stoppel ist gelb, die Saat ist grün.
Dort sammelt sich der große Hauf,
Herr Urian sitzt oben auf.
3960 So geht es über Stein und Stock,
Es f–t die Hexe, es st–t der Bock.

STIMME:

Die alte Baubo kommt allein,
Sie reitet auf einem Mutterschwein.

CHOR:

So Ehre denn, wem Ehre gebührt!
3965 Frau Baubo vor! Und angeführt!
Ein tüchtig Schwein und Mutter drauf,
Da folgt der ganze Hexenhauf.

STIMME:

Welchen Weg kommst du her?

STIMME:

Übern Ilsenstein!
Da guckt ich der Eule ins Nest hinein.
3970 Die macht' ein Paar Augen!

STIMME:

O fahre zur Hölle!

Frightened, the owls are scattered.
Hear how the pillars
Of ever green castles are shattered.
Quaking and breaking of branches!
The trunks' overpowering groaning!
The roots' creaking and moaning!
In a frightfully tangled fall
They crash over each other, one and all,
And through the ruin-covered abysses
The frenzied air howls and hisses.
Do you hear voices up high?
In the distance and nearby?
The whole mountain is afire
With a furious magic choir.

WITCHES' CHORUS:

The witches ride to Blocksberg's top,
The stubble is yellow, and green the crop.
They gather on the mountainside,
Sir Urian comes to preside.
We are riding over crag and brink,
The witches fart, the billy goats stink.

VOICE:

Old Baubo comes alone right now,
She is riding on a mother sow.

CHORUS:

Give honor to whom honor's due!
Dame Baubo, lead our retinue!
A real swine and mother, too,
The witches' crew will follow you.

VOICE:

Which way did you come?

VOICE:

By the Ilsenstone.

I peeped at the owl who was roosting alone.
Did she ever makes eyes!

VOICE:

Oh, go to hell!

Was reitst du so schnelle?

STIMME:

Mich hat sie geschunden,
Da sieh nur die Wunden!

HEXEN. CHOR:

Der Weg ist breit, der Weg ist lang,
3975 Was ist das für ein toller Drang?
Die Gabel sticht, der Besen kratzt.
Das Kind erstickt, die Mutter platzt.

HEXENMEISTER. HALBES CHOR:

Wir schleichen wie die Schneck im Haus,
Die Weiber alle sind voraus.
3980 Denn, geht es zu des Bösen Haus,
Das Weib hat tausend Schritt voraus.

ANDRE HÄLFTE:

Wir nehmen das nicht so genau:
Mit tausend Schritten macht's die Frau;
Doch, wie sie auch sich eilen kann,
3985 Mit einem Sprunge macht's der Mann.

STIMME *(oben)*:

Kommt mit, kommt mit, vom Felsensee!

STIMMEN *(von unten)*:

Wir möchten gerne mit in die Höh.
Wir waschen, und blank sind wir ganz und gar;
Aber auch ewig unfruchtbar.

BEIDE CHÖRE:

3990 Es schweigt der Wind, es flieht der Stern,
Der trübe Mond verbirgt sich gern.
Im Sausen sprüht das Zauberchor
Viel tausend Feuerfunken hervor.

STIMME *(von unten)*:

Halte! Halte!

STIMME *(von oben)*:

3995 Wer ruft da aus der Felsenspalte?

STIMME *(unten)*:

Nehmt mich mit! Nehmt mich mit!
Ich steige schon dreihundert Jahr

Why ride so pell-mell?

VOICE:

See how she has flayed me!
The wounds she made me!

WITCHES' CHORUS:

The way is wide, the way is long;
Just see the frantic pushing throng!
The broomstick pokes, the pitchfork thrusts
The infant chokes, the mother bursts.

WIZARDS' HALF CHORUS:

Slow as the snail's is our pace,
The women are ahead and race;
When it goes to the Devil's place,
By a thousand steps they win the race.

OTHER HALF:

If that is so, we do not mind it:
With a thousand steps the women find it;
But though they rush, we do not care:
With one big jump the men get there.

VOICE *(above)*:

Come on, come on from Rocky Lake!

VOICES *(from below)*:

We'd like to join you and partake.
We wash, but though we are quite clean,
We're barren as we've always been.

BOTH CHORUSES:

The wind is hushed, the star takes flight,
The dreary moon conceals her light.
As it whirls by, the wizards' choir
Scatters a myriad sparks of fire.

VOICE *(from below)*:

Halt, please! Halt, ho!

VOICE *(from above)*:

Who calls out of the cleft below?

VOICE *(below)*:

Take me along! Take me along!
I've been climbing for three hundred years,

Und kann den Gipfel nicht erreichen.
Ich wäre gern bei meinesgleichen.

BEIDE CHÖRE:

4000 Es trägt der Besen, trägt der Stock,
Die Gabel trägt, es trägt der Bock;
Wer heute sich nicht heben kann,
Ist ewig ein verlorner Mann.

HALBHEXE *(unten)*:

Ich tripple nach, so lange Zeit,
4005 Wie sind die andern schon so weit!
Ich hab zu Hause keine Ruh
Und komme hier doch nicht dazu.

CHOR DER HEXEN:

Die Salbe gibt den Hexen Mut,
Ein Lumpen ist zum Segel gut,
4010 Ein gutes Schiff ist jeder Trog;
Der flieget nie, der heut nicht flog.

BEIDE CHÖRE:

Und wenn wir um den Gipfel ziehn,
So streichet an dem Boden hin
Und deckt die Heide weit und breit
4015 Mit eurem Schwarm der Hexenheit!

(Sie lassen sich nieder)

MEPHISTOPHELES:

Das drängt und stößt, das ruscht und klappert!
Das zischt und quirlt, das zieht und plappert!
Das leuchtet, sprüht und stinkt und brennt!
Ein wahres Hexenelement!
Nur fest an mir, sonst sind wir gleich getrennt!
Wo bist du?

FAUST *(in der Ferne)*:

Hier!

MEPHISTOPHELES:

Was! Dort schon hingerissen?
Da werd ich Hausrecht brauchen müssen.
Platz! Junker Voland kommt. Platz! Süßer Pöbel, Platz!

And yet the peak I cannot find.
But I would like to join my kind.

BOTH CHORUSES:

The stick and broom can make you float,
So can pitchfork and billy goat;
Who cannot rise today to soar,
That man is doomed for evermore.

HALF-WITCH *(below)*:

I move and move and try and try;
How did the others get so high?
At home I'm restless through and through,
And now shall miss my chance here, too.

WITCHES' CHORUS:

The salve gives courage to the witch,
For sails we use a rag and switch,
A tub's a ship, if you know how;
If you would ever fly, fly now!

BOTH CHORUSES:

We near the peak, we fly around,
Now sweep down low over the ground,
And cover up the heath's vast regions
With witches' swarms and wizards' legions.

(They alight.)

MEPHISTO:

They throng and push, they rush and clatter.
They hiss and whirl, they pull and chatter.
It glistens, sparks, and stinks and flares;
Those are indeed the witches' airs!
Stay close to me, or we'll be solitaires!
Where are you?

FAUST *(far away)*:

Here.

MEPHISTO:

So far? Almost a loss!
Then I must show them who is boss.
Back! Squire Nick is coming! Back, sweet rabble!
Slump!

Hier, Doktor, fasse mich! Und nun, in einem Satz
4025 Laß uns aus dem Gedräng entweichen!
Es ist zu toll, sogar für meinesgleichen.
Dortneben leuchtet was mit ganz besondrem
Schein,
Es zieht mich was nach jenen Sträuchen.
Komm, komm! Wir schlupfen da hinein.

FAUST:

4030 Du Geist des Widerspruchs! Nur zu! Du magst
mich führen.
Ich denke doch, das war recht klug gemacht:
Zum Brocken wandeln wir in der Walpurgisnacht,
Um uns beliebig nun hieselbst zu isolieren.

MEPHISTOPHELES:

Da sieh nur, welche bunten Flammen!
4035 Es ist ein muntrer Klub beisammen.
Im Kleinen ist man nicht allein.

FAUST:

Doch droben möcht ich lieber sein!
Schon seh ich Glut und Wirbelrauch.
Dort strömt die Menge zu dem Bösen;
4040 Da muß sich manches Rätsel lösen.

MEPHISTOPHELES:

Doch manches Rätsel knüpft sich auch.
Laß du die große Welt nur sausen,
Wir wollen hier im Stillen hausen.
Es ist doch lange hergebracht,
4045 Daß in der großen Welt man kleine Welten macht.
Da seh ich junge Hexchen nackt und bloß
Und alte, die sich klug verhüllen.
Seid freundlich, nur um meinetwillen;
Die Müh ist klein, der Spaß ist groß.
4050 Ich höre was von Instrumenten tönen.
Verflucht Geschnarr! Man muß sich dran
gewöhnen.
Komm mit! Komm mit! Es kann nicht anders sein,
Ich tret heran und führe dich herein

Here, Doctor, take a hold! And now in one big
 jump
Let's leave behind this noisy crowd;
Even for me it's much too loud.
On that side is a light with quite a special flare,
Let's penetrate the bushes' shroud;
Come, come! Now let us slink in there!

FAUST:
Spirit of Contradiction! Go on! I'll follow him.
I must say, it's exceptionally bright
To wander to the Blocksberg in the Walpurgis
 Night,
To isolate ourselves to follow out some whim.

MEPHISTO:
You see that multicolored flare?
A cheerful club is meeting there:
In small groups one is not alone.

FAUST:
I'd rather be up there: around that stone
The fires blaze, they have begun;
The crowds throng to the Evil One
Where many riddles must be solved.

MEPHISTO:
But many new ones are evolved.
Leave the great world, let it run riot,
And let us stay where it is quiet.
It's something that has long been done,
To fashion little worlds within the bigger one.
I see young witches there, completely nude,
And old ones who are veiled as shrewdly.
Just for my sake, don't treat them rudely;
It's little effort and great fun!
There are some instruments that grind and grit.
Damnable noise! One must get used to it.
Come on! Come on! Please do not fret!
I'll lead the way and take you to this place,

Und ich verbinde dich aufs neue.
4055 Was sagst du, Freund? Das ist kein kleiner Raum.
Da sieh nur hin! Du siehst das Ende kaum.
Ein Hundert Feuer brennen in der Reihe;
Man tanzt, man schwatzt, man kocht, man trinkt, man liebt;
Nun sage mir, wo es was Bessers gibt!

FAUST:

4060 Willst du dich nun, um uns hier einzuführen,
Als Zaubrer oder Teufel produzieren?

MEPHISTOPHELES:

Zwar bin ich sehr gewohnt, inkognito zu gehn,
Doch läßt am Galatag man seinen Orden sehn.
Ein Knieband zeichnet mich nicht aus,
4065 Doch ist der Pferdefuß hier ehrenvoll zu Haus.
Siehst du die Schnecke da? Sie kommt herangekrochen;
Mit ihrem tastenden Gesicht
Hat sie mir schon was abgerochen.
Wenn ich auch will, verleugn' ich hier mich nicht.
4070 Komm nur! Von Feuer gehen wir zu Feuer,
Ich bin der Werber, und du bist der Freier.
(Zu einigen, die um verglimmende Kohlen sitzen)
Ihr alten Herrn, was macht ihr hier am Ende?
Ich lobt euch, wenn ich euch hübsch in der Mitte fände,
Von Saus umzirkt und Jugendbraus;
4075 Genug allein ist jeder ja zu Haus.

GENERAL:

Wer mag auf Nationen trauen,
Man habe noch so viel für sie getan!
Denn bei dem Volk wie bei den Frauen
Steht immerfort die Jugend oben an.

MINISTER:

4080 Jetzt ist man von dem Rechten allzu weit,

And you will be quite grateful yet!
What do you say? There isn't enough space?
Just look! You barely see the other end.
A hundred fires in a row, my friend!
They dance, they chat, they cook, they drink, they
court;
Now you just tell me where there's better sport!

FAUST:

When you will introduce us at this revel,
Will you appear a sorcerer or devil?

MEPHISTO:

I generally travel, without showing my station,
But on a gala day one shows one's decoration.
I have no garter I could show,
But here the cloven foot is honored, as you know.
Do you perceive that snail? It comes, though it
seems stiff;
For with its eager, groping face
It knows me with a single whiff.
Though I'd conceal myself, they'd know me in
this place.
Come on! From flame to flame we'll make our tour,
I am the go-between, and you the wooer.
(To some who sit around dying embers):
Old gentlemen, why tarry outside? Enter!
I'd praise you if I found you in the center,
Engulfed by youthful waves and foam;
You are alone enough when you are home.

GENERAL:

Who ever thought nations were true,
Though you have served them with your hands
and tongue;
For people will, as women do,
Reserve their greatest favors for the young.

STATESMAN:

Now they are far from what is sage;

Ich lobe mir die guten Alten;
Denn freilich, da wir alles galten,
Da war die rechte goldne Zeit.

PARVENÜ:

Wir waren wahrlich auch nicht dumm
4085 Und taten oft, was wir nicht sollten;
Doch jetzo kehrt sich alles um und um,
Und eben da wir's fest erhalten wollten.

AUTOR:

Wer mag wohl überhaupt jetzt eine Schrift
Von mäßig klugem Inhalt lesen!
4090 Und was das liebe junge Volk betrifft,
Das ist noch nie so naseweis gewesen.

MEPHISTOPHELES *(der auf einmal sehr alt erscheint):*

Zum Jüngsten Tag fühl ich das Volk gereift,
Da ich zum letzten Mal den Hexenberg ersteige,
Und weil mein Fäßchen trübe läuft,
4095 So ist die Welt auch auf der Neige.

TRÖDELHEXE:

Ihr Herren, geht nicht so vorbei!
Laßt die Gelegenheit nicht fahren!
Aufmerksam blickt nach meinen Waren!
Es steht dahier gar mancherlei.
4100 Und doch ist nichts in meinem Laden,
Dem keiner auf der Erde gleicht,
Das nicht einmal zum tüchtgen Schaden
Der Menschen und der Welt gereicht.
Kein Dolch ist hier, von dem nicht Blut geflossen,
4105 Kein Kelch, aus dem sich nicht in ganz gesunden
Leib
Verzehrend heißes Gift ergossen,
Kein Schmuck, der nicht ein liebenswürdig Weib
Verführt, kein Schwert, das nicht den Bund
gebrochen,
Nicht etwa hinterrücks den Gegenmann
durchstochen.

The old ones should be kept in awe;
For, truly, when our word was law,
Then was indeed the golden age.

PARVENU:

We, too, had surely ample wits,
And often did things that we shouldn't;
But now things are reversed and go to bits,
Just when we changed our mind and wished they
  wouldn't.

AUTHOR:

Today, who even looks at any book
That makes some sense and is mature?
And our younger generation—look,
You never saw one that was so cocksure.

MEPHISTO *(who suddenly appears very old):*

I think the Judgment Day must soon draw nigh,
For this is the last time I can attend this shrine;
And as my little cask runs dry,
The world is certain to decline.

HUCKSTER-WITCH:

Please, gentlemen, don't pass like that!
Don't miss this opportunity!
Look at my goods attentively:
There is a lot to marvel at.
And my shop has a special charm—
You will not find its peer on earth:
All that I sell has once done harm
To man and world and what has worth.
There is no dagger here which has not gored;
No golden cup from which, to end a youthful life,
A fatal poison was not poured;
No gems that did not help to win another's wife;
No sword but broke the peace with sly attack,
By stabbing, for example, a rival in the back.

MEPHISTOPHELES:

4110 Frau Muhme! Sie versteht mir schlecht die Zeiten.
Getan, geschehn! Geschehn, getan!
Verleg Sie sich auf Neuigkeiten!
Nur Neuigkeiten ziehn uns an.

FAUST:

Daß ich mich nur nicht selbst vergesse!
4115 Heiß ich mir das doch eine Messe!

MEPHISTOPHELES:

Der ganze Strudel strebt nach oben;
Du glaubst zu schieben, und du wirst geschoben.

FAUST:

Wer ist denn das?

MEPHISTOPHELES:

Betrachte sie genau!
Lilith ist das.

FAUST:

Wer?

MEPHISTOPHELES:

Adams erste Frau.
4120 Nimm dich in acht vor ihren schönen Haaren,
Vor diesem Schmuck, mit dem sie einzig prangt!
Wenn sie damit den jungen Mann erlangt,
So läßt sie ihn so bald nicht wieder fahren.

FAUST:

Da sitzen zwei, die Alte mit der Jungen;
4125 Die haben schon was Rechts gesprungen!

MEPHISTOPHELES:

Das hat nun heute keine Ruh.
Es geht zum neuen Tanz, nun komm! Wir
greifen zu.

FAUST *(mit der Jungen tanzend):*

Einst hatt ich einen schönen Traum;
Da sah ich einen Apfelbaum,
4130 Zwei schöne Äpfel glänzten dran,
Sie reizten mich, ich stieg hinan.

MEPHISTO:

Dear cousin, that's no good in times like these!
What's done is done; what's done is trite.
You better switch to novelties,
For novelties alone excite.

FAUST:

I must not lose my head, I swear;
For this is what I call a fair.

MEPHISTO:

This eddy whirls to get above,
And you are shoved, though you may think you
shove.

FAUST:

And who is that?

MEPHISTO:

That little madam?
That's Lilith.

FAUST:

Lilith?

MEPHISTO:

The first wife of Adam.
Watch out and shun her captivating tresses:
She likes to use her never-equaled hair
To lure a youth into her luscious lair,
And he won't lightly leave her lewd caresses.

FAUST:

There two sit, one is young, one old;
They certainly have jumped and trolled!

MEPHISTO:

They did not come here for a rest.
There is another dance. Come, let us do our best.

FAUST *(dancing with the young one):*

A pretty dream once came to me
In which I saw an apple tree;
Two pretty apples gleamed on it,
They lured me, and I climbed a bit.

DIE SCHÖNE:

Der Äpfelchen begehrt ihr sehr,
Und schon vom Paradiese her.
Von Freuden fühl ich mich bewegt,
4135 Daß auch mein Garten solche trägt.

MEPHISTOPHELES *(mit der Alten):*

Einst hatt ich einen wüsten Traum;
Da sah ich einen gespaltnen Baum,
Der hatt ein — — —;
So—es war, gefiel mir's doch.

DIE ALTE:

4140 Ich biete meinen besten Gruß
Dem Ritter mit dem Pferdefuß!
Halt Er einen — — bereit,
Wenn Er — — — nicht scheut.

PROKTOPHANTASMIST:

Verfluchtes Volk! Was untersteht ihr euch?
4145 Hat man euch lange nicht bewiesen:
Ein Geist steht nie auf ordentlichen Füßen?
Nun tanzt ihr gar, uns andern Menschen gleich!

DIE SCHÖNE *(tanzend):*

Was will denn der auf unserm Ball?

FAUST *(tanzend):*

Ei! Der ist eben überall.
4150 Was andre tanzen, muß er schätzen.
Kann er nicht jeden Schritt beschwätzen,
So ist der Schritt so gut als nicht geschehn.
Am meisten ärgert ihn, sobald wir vorwärts gehn.
Wenn ihr euch so im Kreise drehen wolltet,
4155 Wie er's in seiner alten Mühle tut,
Das hieß er allenfalls noch gut;
Besonders wenn ihr ihn darum begrüßen solltet.

PROKTOPHANTASMIST:

Ihr seid noch immer da? Nein, das ist unerhört.
Verschwindet doch! Wir haben ja aufgeklärt!
4160 Das Teufelspack, es fragt nach keiner Regel.

THE FAIR ONE:

You find the little apples nice
Since first they grew in Paradise.
And I am happy telling you
That they grow in my garden, too.

MEPHISTO *(with the old one):*

A wanton dream once came to me
In which I saw a cloven tree.
It had the most tremendous hole;
Though it was big, it pleased my soul.

THE OLD ONE:

I greet you with profound delight,
My gentle, cloven-footed knight!
Provide the proper grafting-twig,
If you don't mind the hole so big.

PROKTOPHANTASMIST:

Damnable folk! How dare you make such fuss!
Have we not often proved to you
That tales of walking ghosts cannot be true?
And now you dance just like the rest of us!

THE FAIR ONE *(dancing):*

What does he want at our fair?

FAUST *(dancing):*

Oh, he! You find him everywhere.
What others dance, he must assess;
No step has really occurred, unless
His chatter has been duly said.
And what annoys him most, is when we get ahead.
If you would turn in circles, in endless repetition,
As he does all the time in his old mill,
Perhaps he would not take it ill,
Especially if you would first get his permission.

PROKTOPHANTASMIST:

You still are there! Oh no! That's without
precedent.
Please go! Have we not brought enlightenment?
By our rules these devils are not daunted;

Wir sind so klug, und dennoch spukt's in Tegel.
Wie lange hab ich nicht am Wahn hinausgekehrt,
Und nie wird's rein; das ist doch unerhört!

DIE SCHÖNE:
So hört doch auf, uns hier zu ennuyieren!

PROKTOPHANTASMIST:
4165 Ich sag's euch Geistern ins Gesicht:
Den Geistesdespotismus leid ich nicht;
Mein Geist kann ihn nicht exerzieren.
(Es wird fortgetanzt.)

Heut, seh ich, will mir nichts gelingen;
Doch eine Reise nehm ich immer mit
4170 Und hoffe, noch vor meinem letzten Schritt
Die Teufel und die Dichter zu bezwingen.

MEPHISTOPHELES:
Er wird sich gleich in eine Pfütze setzen,
Das ist die Art, wie er sich soulagiert,
Und wenn Blutegel sich an seinem Steiß ergetzen,
4175 Ist er von Geistern und von Geist kuriert.
(Zu Faust, der aus dem Tanz getreten ist.)
Was lässest du das schöne Mädchen fahren,
Das dir zum Tanz so lieblich sang?

FAUST:
Ach, mitten im Gesange sprang
Ein rotes Mäuschen ihr aus dem Munde.

MEPHISTOPHELES:
4180 Das ist was Rechts! Das nimmt man nicht genau.
Genug, die Maus war doch nicht grau.
Wer fragt darnach in einer Schäferstunde?

FAUST:
Dann sah ich—

MEPHISTOPHELES:
Was?

FAUST:
Mephisto, siehst du dort

We are so smart, but Tegel is still haunted.
To sweep illusion out, my energies were spent,
But things never get clean; that's without
precedent.

THE FAIR ONE:

Why don't you stop annoying us and quit!

PROKTOPHANTASMIST:

I tell you spirits to your face,
The spirit's despotism's a disgrace:
My spirit can't make rules for it.

(The dancing goes on.)

Today there's nothing I can do;
But traveling is always fun,
And I still hope, before my final step is done,
I'll ban the devils, and the poets, too.

MEPHISTO:

He'll sit down in a puddle and unbend:
That is how his condition is improved;
For when the leeches prosper on his fat rear end,
The spirits and his spirit are removed.
(To FAUST, *who has left the dance):*
Why did you let that pretty woman go
Who sang so nicely while you danced?

FAUST:

She sang, and suddenly there pranced
Out of her mouth a little mouse, all red.

MEPHISTO:

That is a trifle and no cause for dread!
Who cares? At least it was not gray.
Why bother on this glorious lovers' day?

FAUST:

Then I saw——

MEPHISTO:

What?

FAUST:

Mephisto, do you see

Ein blasses, schönes Kind allein und ferne stehen?
4185 Sie schiebt sich langsam nur vom Ort,
Sie scheint mit geschloßnen Füßen zu gehen.
Ich muß bekennen, daß mir deucht,
Daß sie dem guten Gretchen gleicht.

MEPHISTOPHELES:
Laß das nur stehn! Dabei wird's niemand wohl.
4190 Es ist ein Zauberbild, ist leblos, ein Idol.
Ihm zu begegnen, ist nicht gut;
Vom starren Blick erstarrt des Menschen Blut,
Und er wird fast in Stein verkehrt;
Von der Meduse hast du ja gehört.

FAUST:
4195 Fürwahr, es sind die Augen eines Toten,
Die eine liebende Hand nicht schloß.
Das ist die Brust, die Gretchen mir geboten,
Das ist der süße Leib, den ich genoß.

MEPHISTOPHELES:
Das ist die Zauberei, du leicht verführter Tor!
4200 Denn jedem kommt sie wie sein Liebchen vor.

FAUST:
Welch eine Wonne! Welch ein Leiden!
Ich kann von diesem Blick nicht scheiden.
Wie sonderbar muß diesen schönen Hals
Ein einzig rotes Schnürchen schmücken,
4205 Nicht breiter als ein Messerrücken!

MEPHISTOPHELES:
Ganz recht! Ich seh es ebenfalls.
Sie kann das Haupt auch unterm Arme tragen;
Denn Perseus hat's ihr abgeschlagen.
Nur immer diese Lust zum Wahn!
4210 Komm doch das Hügelchen heran!
Hier ist's so lustig wie im Prater;
Und hat man mir's nicht angetan,
So seh ich wahrlich ein Theater.
Was gibt's denn da?

That pale, beautiful child, alone there on the
heather?
She moves slowly but steadily,
She seems to walk with her feet chained together.
I must confess that she, forbid,
Looks much as my good Gretchen did.

MEPHISTO:

That does nobody good; leave it alone!
It is a magic image, a lifeless apparition.
Encounters are fraught with perdition;
Its icy stare turns human blood to stone
In truth, it almost petrifies;
You know the story of Medusa's eyes.

FAUST:

Those are the eyes of one that's dead I see,
No loving hand closed them to rest.
That is the breast that Gretchen offered me,
And that is the sweet body I possessed.

MEPHISTO:

That is just sorcery; you're easily deceived!
All think she is their sweetheart and are grieved.

FAUST:

What rapture! Oh, what agony!
I cannot leave her, cannot flee.
How strange, a narrow ruby band should deck,
The sole adornment, her sweet neck,
No wider than a knife's thin blade.

MEPHISTO:

I see it, too; it is quite so.
Her head under her arm she can parade,
Since Perseus lopped it off, you know.–
Illusion holds you captive still.
Come, let us climb that little hill,
The Prater's not so full of glee;
And if they're not bewitching me,
There is a theatre I see.
What will it be?

SERVIBILIS:

Gleich fängt man wieder an.

4215 Ein neues Stück, das letzte Stück von sieben;
So viel zu geben, ist allhier der Brauch.
Ein Dilettant hat es geschrieben,
Und Dilettanten spielen's auch.
Verzeiht, ihr Herrn, wenn ich verschwinde;
4220 Mich dilettiert's, den Vorhang aufzuziehn.

MEPHISTOPHELES:

Wenn ich euch auf dem Blocksberg finde,
Das find ich gut; denn da gehört ihr hin.

WALPURGISNACHTSTRAUM
oder
OBERONS UND TITANIAS GOLDNE HOCHZEIT

Intermezzo.

THEATERMEISTER:

Heute ruhen wir einmal,
Miedings wackre Söhne.
4225 Alter Berg und feuchtes Tal,
Das ist die ganze Szene.

HEROLD:

Daß die Hochzeit golden sei,
Soll'n fünfzig Jahr sein vorüber;
Aber ist der Streit vorbei,
4230 Das golden ist mir lieber.

OBERON:

Seid ihr Geister, wo ich bin,

SERVIBILIS:

They'll resume instantly.
We'll have the seventh play, a brand-new hit;
We do not think, so many are exacting.
An amateur has written it,
And amateurs do all the acting.
Forgive, good sirs, if now I leave you;
It amateurs me to draw up the curtain.

MEPHISTO:

When it's on Blocksberg I perceive you,
I'm glad; for that's where you belong for certain.

WALPURGIS NIGHT'S DREAM
OR
THE GOLDEN WEDDING OF OBERON AND TITANIA*

Intermezzo

STAGE MANAGER:

This time we can keep quite still,
Mieding's progeny;
Misty vale and hoary hill,
That's our scenery.

HERALD:

To make a golden wedding day
Takes fifty years to the letter;
But when their quarrels pass away,
That gold I like much better.

OBERON:

If you spirits can be seen,

* For some explanatory remarks, see section 6 of the Introduction.

So zeigt's in diesen Stunden;
König und die Königin,
Sie sind aufs neu verbunden.

PUCK:

4235 Kommt der Puck und dreht sich quer
Und schleift den Fuß im Reihen,
Hundert kommen hinterher,
Sich auch mit ihm zu freuen.

ARIEL:

Ariel bewegt den Sang
4240 In himmlisch reinen Tönen,
Viele Fratzen lockt sein Klang,
Doch lockt er auch die Schönen.

OBERON:

Gatten, die sich vertragen wollen,
Lernen's von uns beiden!
4245 Wenn sich zwie lieben sollen,
Braucht man sie nur zu scheiden.

TITANIA:

Schmollt der Mann und grillt die Frau,
So faßt sie nur behende,
Führt mir nach dem Mittag sie,
4250 Und ihn an Nordens Ende.

ORCHESTER TUTTI *(fortissimo)*:

Fliegenschnauz und Mückennas
Mit ihren Anverwandten,
Frosch im Laub und Grill im Gras,
Das sind die Musikanten!

SOLO:

4255 Seht, da kommt der Dudelsack!
Es ist die Seifenblase.
Hört den Schneckeschnickeschnack
Durch seine stumpfe Nase.

GEIST, DER SICH ERST BILDET:

Spinnenfuß und Krötenbauch
4260 Und Flügelchen dem Wichtchen!
Zwar ein Tierchen gibt es nicht,

Show yourselves tonight;
Fairy king and fairy queen
Now will reunite.

PUCK:

Puck is coming, turns about,
And drags his feet to dance;
Hundreds come behind and shout
And join with him and prance.

ARIEL:

Ariel stirs up a song,
A heavenly pure air;
Many gargoyles come along,
And many who are fair.

OBERON:

You would get along, dear couple?
Learn from us the art;
If you want to keep love supple,
You only have to part.

TITANIA:

He is sulky, sullen she,
Grab them, upon my soul;
Take her to the Southern Sea,
And him up to the pole.

ORCHESTRA TUTTI *(fortissimo):*

Snout of Fly, Mosquito Nose,
With family additions,
Frog O'Leaves and Crick't O'Grass,
Those are the musicians.

SOLO:

Now the bagpipe's joining in,
A soap bubble it blows;
Hear the snicker-snacking din
Come through his blunted nose.

SPIRIT IN PROCESS OF FORMATION:

Spider feet, belly of toad,
And little wings, he'll grow 'em;
There is no animal like that,

Doch gibt es ein Gedichtchen.

EIN PÄRCHEN:

Kleiner Schritt und hoher Sprung
Durch Honigtau und Düfte;
4265 Zwar du trippelst mir genung,
Doch geht's nicht in die Lüfte.

NEUGIERIGER REISENDER:

Ist das nicht Maskeraden-Spott?
Soll ich den Augen trauen,
Oberon, den schönen Gott,
4270 Auch heute hier zu schauen?

ORTHODOX:

Keine Klauen, keinen Schwanz!
Doch bleibt es außer Zweifel:
So wie die Götter Griechenlands,
So ist auch er ein Teufel.

NORDISCHER KÜNSTLER:

4275 Was ich ergreife, das ist heut
Fürwahr nur skizzenweise;
Doch ich bereite mich beizeit
Zur italienschen Reise.

PURIST:

Ach, mein Unglück führt mich her:
4280 Wie wird nicht hier geludert!
Und von dem ganzen Hexenheer
Sind zweie nur gepudert.

JUNGE HEXE:

Der Puder ist so wie der Rock
Für alt und graue Weibchen,
4285 Drum sitz ich nackt auf meinem Bock
Und zeig ein derbes Leibchen.

MATRONE:

Wir haben zu viel Lebensart,
Um hier mit euch zu maulen;
Doch hoff ich, sollt ihr jung und zart,
4290 So wie ihr seid, verfaulen.

But it's a little poem.

A LITTLE COUPLE:

Mighty leaps and nimble feet,
Through honey scent up high;
While you bounce enough, my sweet,
Still you cannot fly.

INQUISITIVE TRAVELER:

Is that not mummery right there?
Can that be what I see?
Oberon who is so fair
Amid this company!

ORTHODOX:

No claws or tail or satyr's fleece!
And yet you cannot cavil:
Just like the gods of ancient Greece,
He, too, must be a devil.

NORDIC ARTIST:

What I do in the local clime,
Are sketches of this tourney;
But I prepare, while it is time,
For my Italian journey.

PURIST:

Bad luck brought me to these regions:
They could not be much louder;
And in the bawdy witches' legions
Two only have used powder.

YOUNG WITCH:

White powder, just like dresses, serves
Old hags who are out of luck;
I want to show my luscious curves,
Ride naked on my buck.

MATRON:

Our manners, dear, are far too neat
To argue and to scold;
I only hope that young and sweet,
Just as you are, you mold.

KAPELLMEISTER:

Fliegenschnauz und Mückennas,
Umschwärmt mir nicht die Nackte!
Frosch im Laub und Grill im Gras,
So bleibt doch auch im Takte!

WINDFAHNE *(nach der einen Seite):*

4295 Gesellschaft, wie man wünschen kann.
Wahrhaftig lauter Bräute!
Und Junggesellen, Mann für Mann
Die hoffnungsvollsten Leute!

WINDFAHNE *(nach der andern Seite):*

Und tut sich nicht der Boden auf,
4300 Sie alle zu verschlingen,
So will ich mit behendem Lauf
Gleich in die Hölle springen.

XENIEN:

Als Insekten sind wir da,
Mit kleinen scharfen Scheren
4305 Satan, unsern Herrn Papa,
Nach Würden zu verehren.

HENNINGS:

Seht, wie sie in gedrängter Schar
Naiv zusammen scherzen!
Am Ende sagen sie noch gar,
4310 Sie hätten gute Herzen.

MUSAGET:

Ich mag in diesem Hexenheer
Mich gar zu gern verlieren;
Denn freilich diese wüßt ich eh'r
Als Musen anzuführen.

CI-DEVANT GENIUS DER ZEIT:

4315 Mit rechten Leuten wird man was.
Komm, fasse meinen Zipfel!
Der Blocksberg wie der deutche Parnaß
Hat gar einen breiten Gipfel.

NEUGIERIGER REISENDER:

Sagt, wie heißt der steife Mann?

CONDUCTOR:

Snout of Fly, Mosquito Nose,
Leave off the naked sweet;
Frog O'Leaves and Crick't O'Grass
Get back into the beat!

WEATHERCOCK *(to one side):*

The most exquisite company!
Each girl should be a bride;
The bachelors, grooms; for one can see
How well they are allied.

WEATHERCOCK *(to the other side):*

The earth should open up and gape
To swallow this young revel,
Or I will make a swift escape
To hell to see the Devil.

XENIEN:

We appear as insects here,
Each with a little stinger,
That we may fittingly revere
Satan, our sire and singer.

HENNINGS:

Look at their thronging legions play,
Naïve, with little art;
The next thing they will dare to say
Is that they're good at heart.

MUSAGET:

To dwell among the witches' folk
Seems quite a lot of fun;
They are the ones I should invoke,
Not Muses, as I've done.

CI-DEVANT GENIUS OF THE AGE:

Choose your friends well and you will zoom,
Join in and do not pass us!
Blocksberg has almost as much room
As Germany's Parnassus.

INQUISITIVE TRAVELER:

Say, who is that haughty man

4320 Er geht mit stolzen Schritten.
Er schnopert, was er schnopern kann. –
«Er spürt nach Jesuiten.»

KRANICH:

In dem Klaren mag ich gern
Und auch im Trüben fischen,
Darum seht ihr den frommen Herrn
4325 Sich auch mit Teufeln mischen.

WELTKIND:

Ja für die Frommen, glaubet mir,
Ist alles ein Vehikel,
Sie bilden auf dem Blocksberg hier
4330 Gar manches Konventikel.

TÄNZER:

Da kommt ja wohl ein neues Chor?
Ich höre ferne Trommeln. –
«Nur ungestört! Es sind im Rohr
Die unisonen Dommeln.»

TANZMEISTER:

4335 Wie jeder doch die Beine lupft,
Sich, wie er kann, herauszieht!
Der Krumme springt, der Plumpe hupft
Und fragt nicht, wie es aussieht.

FIEDLER:

Das haßt sich schwer, das Lumpenpack,
4340 Und gäb sich gern das Restchen;
Es eint sie hier der Dudelsack,
Wie Orpheus' Leier die Bestien.

DOGMATIKER:

Ich lasse mich nicht irre schrein,
Nicht durch Kritik noch Zweifel.
4345 Der Teufel muß doch etwas sein;
Wie gäb's denn sonst auch Teufel?

IDEALIST:

Die Phantasie in meinem Sinn
Ist diesmal gar zu herrisch.

Who walks as if he sits?
He sniffs and snuffles as best he can:
"He smells out Jesuits."

CRANE:

I like to fish where it is clear,
Also in muddy brew;
That's why the pious man is here
To mix with devils, too.

CHILD OF THE WORLD:

The pious need no fancy prop,
All vehicles seem sound:
Even up here on Blocksberg's top
Conventicles abound.

DANCERS:

It seems, another choir succeeds,
I hear the drums resuming.
"That dull sound comes out of the reeds,
It is the bitterns' booming."

BALLET MASTER:

How each picks up his legs and toddles,
And comes by hook or crook!
The stooped one jumps, the plump one
waddles;
They don't know how they look!

FIDDLER:

They hate each other, wretched rabble,
And each would kill the choir;
They're harmonized by bagpipe babble,
As beasts by Orpheus' lyre.

DOGMATIST:

I am undaunted and resist
Both skeptic and critique;
The Devil simply must exist,
Else *what* would he be? Speak!

IDEALIST:

Imagination is in me
Today far too despotic;

Fürwahr, wenn ich das alles bin,
4350 So bin ich heute närrisch.

REALIST:

Das Wesen ist mir recht zur Qual
Und muß mich baß verdrießen;
Ich stehe hier zum ersten Mal
Nicht fest auf meinen Füßen.

SUPERNATURALIST:

4355 Mit viel Vergnügen bin ich da
Und freue mich mit diesen;
Denn von den Teufeln kann ich ja
Auf gute Geister schließen.

SKEPTIKER:

Sie gehn den Flämmchen auf der Spur
4360 Und glaub'n sich nah dem Schatze.
Auf Teufel reimt der Zweifel nur,
Da bin ich recht am Platze.

KAPELLMEISTER:

Frosch im Laub und Grill im Gras,
Verfluchte Dilettanten!
4365 Fliegenschnauz und Mückennas,
Ihr seid doch Musikanten!

DIE GEWANDTEN:

Sanssouci, so heißt das Heer
Von lustigen Geschöpfen;
Auf den Füßen geht's nicht mehr,
4370 Drum gehn wir auf den Köpfen.

DIE UNBEHILFLICHEN:

Sonst haben wir manchen Bissen erschranzt,
Nun aber Gott befohlen!
Unsere Schuhe sind durchgetanzt,
Wir laufen auf nackten Sohlen.

IRRLICHTER:

4375 Von dem Sumpfe kommen wir,
Woraus wir erst entstanden;
Doch sind wir gleich im Reihen hier
Die glänzenden Galanten.

If I am everything I see,
Then I must be idiotic.

REALIST:

The spirits' element is vexing,
I wish it weren't there;
I never saw what's so perplexing,
It drives me to despair.

SUPERNATURALIST:

I am delighted by this whir,
And glad that they persist;
For from the devils I infer,
Good spirits, too, exist.

SKEPTIC:

They follow little flames about,
And think they're near the treasure;
Devil alliterates with doubt
So I am here with pleasure.

CONDUCTOR:

Snout of Fly, Mosquito Nose,
Damnable amateurs!
Frog O'Leaves and Crick't O'Grass
You are musicians, sirs!

ADEPTS:

Sansouci, that is the name
Of our whole caboodle;
Walking meets with ill acclaim,
So we move on our noodle.

NE'ER-DO-WELLS:

We used to be good hangers-on
And sponged good wine and meat;
We danced till our shoes were gone,
And now walk on bare feet.

WILL-O'-THE-WISPS:

We come out of the swamps where we
Were born without a penny;
But now we join the revelry,
As elegant as any.

STERNSCHNUPPE:

Aus der Höhe schoß ich her
4380 Im Stern- und Feuerscheine,
Liege nun im Grase quer —
Wer hilft mir auf die Beine?

DIE MASSIVEN:

Platz und Platz! Und ringsherum!
So gehn die Gräschen nieder.
4385 Geister kommen, Geister auch
Sie haben plumpe Glieder.

PUCK:

Tretet nicht so mastig auf
Wie Elefantenkälber!
Und der plumpst' an diesem Tag,
4390 Sei Puck, der derbe, selber.

ARIEL:

Gab die liebende Natur,
Gab der Geist euch Flügel,
Folget meiner leichten Spur,
Auf zum Rosenhügel!

ORCHESTER: *(Pianissimo.)*

4395 Wolkenzug und Nebelflor
Erhellen sich von oben.
Luft im Laub und Wind im Rohr,
Und alles ist zerstoben.

TRÜBER TAG.

Feld.

Faust. Mephistopheles

FAUST:

Im Elend! Verzweifelnd! Erbärmlich auf der Erde lange verirrt und nun gefangen! Als Missetäterin

SHOOTING STAR:

I shot down from starry height
With brilliant, fiery charm;
But I lie in the grass tonight:
Who'll proffer me his arm?

MASSIVE MOB:

All around, give way! Give way!
Trample down the grass!
Spirits come, and sometimes they
Form a heavy mass.

PUCK:

Please don't walk like elephants,
And do not be so rough;
Let no one be as plump as Puck,
For he is plump enough.

ARIEL:

If nature gave with lavish grace,
Or Spirit, wings and will,
Follow in my airy trace
Up to the roses' hill!

ORCHESTRA *(Pianissimo)*:

Floating clouds and wreaths of fog
Dawn has quickly banished;
Breeze in leaves, wind in the bog,
And everything has vanished.

DISMAL DAY.

Field.
Faust. Mephistopheles.

FAUST:

In misery! Despairing! Long lost wretchedly on the earth, and now imprisoned! As a felon locked

im Kerker zu entsetzlichen Qualen eingesperrt, das holde unselige Geschöpf! Bis dahin, dahin!– Verrätrischer, nichtswürdiger Geist, und das hast du mir verheimlicht!–Steh nur, steh! Wälze die teuflischen Augen ingrimmend im Kopf herum! Steh und trutze mir durch deine unerträgliche Gegenwart! Gefangen! Im unwiederbringlichen Elend! Bösen Geistern übergeben und der richtenden gefühllosen Menschheit! Und mich wiegst du indes in abgeschmackten Zerstreuungen, verbirgst mir ihren wachsenden Jammer und lässest sie hilflos verderben!

MEPHISTOPHELES:

Sie ist die erste nicht.

FAUST:

Hund! Abscheuliches Untier! – Wandle ihn, du unendlicher Geist! Wandle den Wurm wieder in seine Hundsgestalt, wie er sich oft nächtlicherweile gefiel, vor mir herzutrotten, dem harmlosen Wandrer vor die Füße zu kollern und sich dem niederstürzenden auf die Schultern zu hängen. Wandl' ihn wieder in seine Lieblingsbildung, daß er vor mir im Sand auf dem Bauch krieche, ich ihn mit Füßen trete, den Verworfnen! – Die erste nicht! – Jammer! Jammer! Von keiner Menschenseele zu fassen, daß mehr als ein Geschöpf in die Tiefe dieses Elends versank, daß nicht das erste genugtat für die Schuld aller übrigen in seiner windenden Todesnot vor den Augen des ewig Verzeihenden! Mir wühlt es Mark und Leben durch, das Elend dieser einzigen – du grinsest gelassen über das Schicksal von Tausenden hin!

MEPHISTOPHELES:

Nun sind wir schon wieder an der Grenze unsres Witzes, da, wo euch Menschen der Sinn überschnappt. Warum machst du Gemeinschaft mit uns, wenn du sie nicht durchführen kannst? Willst

up in a dungeon with horrible torments, the fair ill-fated creature! It's come to that! To that!—Treacherous, despicable Spirit—and that you have kept from me!—Keep standing there, stand! Roll your devilish eyes wrathfully in your face! Stand and defy me with your intolerable presence! Imprisoned! In irreparable misery! Handed over to evil spirits and judging, unfeeling mankind! And meanwhile you soothe me with insipid diversions; hide her growing grief from me, and let her perish helplessly!

MEPHISTO:

She's not the first one.

FAUST:

Dog! Abominable monster!—Change him, oh infinite spirit! Change back this worm into his dog-shape, as he used to amuse himself in the night when he trotted along before me, rolled in front of the feet of the harmless wanderer and, when he stumbled, clung to his shoulders. Change him again to his favorite form that he may crawl on his belly in the sand before me and I may trample on him with my feet, the caitiff!—Not the first one! —Grief! Grief! past what a human soul can grasp, that more than one creature has sunk into the depth of this misery, that the first one did not enough for the guilt of all the others, writhing in the agony of death before the eyes of the ever-forgiving one! The misery of this one woman surges through my heart and marrow, and you grin imperturbed over the fate of thousands!

MEPHISTO:

Now we're once again at our wit's end where your human minds snap. Why do you seek fellowship with us if you can't go through with it? You would fly, but get dizzy? Did we impose on you, or you

fliegen und bist vorm Schwindel nicht sicher? Drängen wir uns dir auf oder du dich uns?

FAUST:

Fletsche deine gefräßigen Zähne mir nicht so entgegen! Mir ekelt's! – Großer, herrlicher Geist, der du mir zu erscheinen würdigtest, der du mein Herz kennest und meine Seele, warum, an den Schandgesellen mich schmieden, der sich am Schaden weidet und am Verderben sich lechzt?

MEPHISTOPHELES:

Endigst du?

FAUST:

Rette sie! Oder weh dir! Den gräßlichsten Fluch über dich auf Jahrtausende!

MEPHISTOPHELES:

Ich kann die Bande des Rächers nicht lösen, seine Riegel nicht öffnen. – Rette sie! – Wer war's, der sie ins Verderben stürzte? Ich oder du? *(Faust blickt wild umher.)* Greifst du nach dem Donner? Wohl, daß er euch elenden Sterblichen nicht gegeben ward! Den unschuldig Entgegnenden zu zerschmettern, das ist so Tyrannenart, sich in Verlegenheiten Luft zu machen.

FAUST:

Bringe mich hin! Sie soll frei sein!

MEPHISTOPHELES:

Und die Gefahr, der du dich aussetzest? Wisse, noch liegt auf der Stadt Blutschuld von deiner Hand. Über des Erschlagenen Stätte schweben rächende Geister und lauern auf den wiederkehrenden Mörder.

FAUST:

Noch das von dir? Mord und Tod einer Welt über dich Ungeheuer! Führe mich hin, sag ich, und befrei sie!

MEPHISTOPHELES:

Ich führe dich, und was ich tun kann, höre! Habe

on us?

FAUST:

Don't bare your greedy teeth at me like that! It sickens me! — Great, magnificent spirit that deigned to appear to me, that know my heart and soul—why forge me to this monster who gorges himself on harm, and on corruption—feasts.

MEPHISTO:

Have you finished?

FAUST:

Save her! or woe unto you! The most hideous curse upon you for millenniums!

MEPHISTO:

I cannot loosen the avenger's bonds, nor open his bolts.—Save her!—Who was it that plunged her into ruin? I or you? (FAUST *looks around furiously.*) Are you reaching for thunder? Well that it was not given to you wretched mortals! Shattering those who answer innocently, is the tyrant's way of easing his embarrassment.

FAUST:

Take me there! She shall be freed!

MEPHISTO:

And the dangers you risk? Know that blood-guilt from your hand still lies on the town. Over the slain man's site avenging spirits hover, waiting for the returning murderer.

FAUST:

That, too, from you? A world's murder and death upon you, monster! Guide me to her, I say, and free her!

MEPHISTO:

I shall guide you; hear what I can do. Do I have

ich alle Macht im Himmel und auf Erden? Des Türners Sinne will ich umnebeln, bemächtige dich der Schlüssel und führe sie heraus mit Menschenhand! Ich wache, die Zauberpferde sind bereit, ich entführe euch. Das vermag ich.

FAUST:

Auf und davon!

NACHT, OFFEN FELD

Faust, Mephistopheles, auf schwarzen Pferden daherbrausend.

FAUST:

Was weben die dort um den Rabenstein?

MEPHISTOPHELES:

4400 Weiß nicht, was sie kochen und schaffen.

FAUST:

Schweben auf, schweben ab, neigen sich, beugen sich.

MEPHISTOPHELES:

Eine Hexenzunft.

FAUST:

Sie streuen und weihen.

MEPHISTOPHELES:

Vorbei! Vorbei!

all the power in the heaven and on the earth? I shall make the jailer's senses foggy, and you may get the keys and lead her out with human hands. I shall stand guard, magic horses shall be prepared, and I shall carry you away. That I can do.

FAUST:

Up and away!

NIGHT, OPEN FIELD.

Faust and Mephistopheles, storming along on black horses.

FAUST:

What are they weaving around the Ravenstone?

MEPHISTO:

I do not know what they do and brew.

FAUST:

Floating to, floating fro, bowing and bending.

MEPHISTO:

A witches' guild.

FAUST:

They strew and dedicate.

MEPHISTO:

Go by! Go by!

KERKER

FAUST *(mit einem Bund Schlüssel und einer Lampe, vor einem eisernen Türchen):*

4405 Mich faßt ein längst entwohnter Schauer,
Der Menschheit ganzer Jammer faßt mich an.
Hier wohnt sie, hinter dieser feuchten Mauer,
Und ihr Verbrechen war ein guter Wahn!
Du zauderst, zu ihr zu gehen?
4410 Du fürchtest, sie wieder zu sehen?
Fort! Dein Zagen zögert den Tod heran.
(Er ergreift das Schloß.)
(Es singt inwendig.)

Meine Mutter, die Hur,
Die mich umgebracht hat!
Mein Vater, der Schelm,
4415 Der mich gessen hat!
Mein Schwesterlein klein
Hub auf die Bein
An einem kühlen Ort;
Da ward ich ein schönes Waldvögelein.
4420 Fliege fort, fliege fort!

FAUST *(aufschließend):*
Sie ahnet nicht, daß der Geliebt lauscht,
Die Ketten klirren hört, das Stroh, das rauscht.
(Er tritt ein.)

MARGARETE *(sich auf dem Lager verbergend):*
Weh! Weh! Sie kommen. Bitter Tod!

FAUST *(leise):*
Still! Still! Ich komme, dich zu befreien.

MARGARETE *(sich vor ihn hinwälzend):*
4425 Bist du ein Mensch, so fühle meine Not!

FAUST:
Du wirst die Wächter aus dem Schlafe schreien!
(Er faßt die Ketten, sie aufzuschließen)

DUNGEON.

FAUST *(with a bunch of keys and a lamp before a small iron gate):*

A long unwonted shudder grips,
Mankind's entire grief grips me.
She's here, behind this wall that drips,
And all her crime was a fond fantasy.
You hesitate to go in?
You dread to see her again?
On! Your wavering waves on death's decree.
(He seizes the lock.)

(Song from within):

My mother, the whore,
Who has murdered me—
My father, the rogue,
Who has eaten me—
My little sister alone
Picked up every bone,
In a cool place she put them away;
Into a fair bird I now have grown;
Fly away, fly away!

FAUST *(unlocking):*

She does not dream how her lover at the door
Hears the clanking chains and the rustling straw.
(Enters.)

MARGARET *(hiding on her pallet):*

Oh! Oh! They come. Death's bitterness!

FAUST *(softly):*

Still! Still! I come to set you free.

MARGARET *(groveling toward his feet):*

If you are human, pity my distress.

FAUST:

You'll awaken the guards. Speak quietly.
(He seizes the chains to unlock them.)

MARGARETE *(auf den Knien):*
Wer hat dir, Henker, diese Macht
Über mich gegeben?
Du holst mich schon um Mitternacht.
4430 Erbarme dich und laß mich leben!
Ist's morgen früh nicht zeitig genug?

(Sie steht auf)

Bin ich doch noch so jung, so jung!
Und soll schon sterben!
Schön war ich auch, und das war mein Verderben.
4435 Nah war der Freund, nun ist er weit,
Zerrissen liegt der Kranz, die Blumen zerstreut.
Fasse mich nicht so gewaltsam an!
Schone mich! Was hab ich dir getan?
Laß mich nicht vergebens flehen,
4440 Hab ich dich doch mein Tage nicht gesehen!

FAUST:
Werd ich den Jammer überstehen?

MARGARETE:
Ich bin nun ganz in deiner Macht.
Laß mich nur erst das Kind noch tränken.
Ich herzt es diese ganze Nacht;
4445 Sie nahmen mir's, um mich zu kränken,
Und sagen nun, ich hätt es umgebracht.
Und niemals werd ich wieder froh.
Sie singen Lieder auf mich! Es ist bös von den
Leuten!
Ein altes Märchen endigt so,
4450 Wer heißt sie's deuten?

FAUST *(wirft sich nieder):*
Ein Liebender liegt dir zu Füßen,
Die Jammerknechtschaft aufzuschließen.

MARGATETE *(wirft sich zu ihm):*
O laß uns knien, die Heilgen anzurufen!
Sieh, unter diesen Stufen,
4455 Unter der Schwelle

MARGARET *(on her knees):*
Who, hangman, could give
You over me this might?
You come for me in the middle of the night.
Have pity on me, let me live!
Is it not time when the morning chimes have
rung?
(She gets up.)
I am still so young, so very young.
And must already die.
I was beautiful, too, and that was why.
Near was the friend, now he is away.
Torn lies the wreath, the flowers decay.
Do not grip me so brutally. What shall I do?
Spare me. What have I done to you?
Let me not in vain implore.
After all, I have never seen you before.

FAUST:
After such grief, can I live any more?

MARGARET:
Now I am entirely in your might.
Only let me nurse the baby again.
I fondled it all through the night;
They took it from me to give me pain,
And now they say I put it away.
And I shall never again be gay.
They sing songs about me. The people are wicked.
An ancient fairy tale ends that way,
Who made them pick it?

FAUST *(casts himself down):*
One loving you lies at your feet
To end your bondage. Listen, sweet!

MARGARET *(casts herself down beside him):*
Ah, let us kneel, send to the saints our prayers!
See, underneath these stairs,
Underneath the sill

Siedet die Hölle!
Der Böse
Mit furchtbarem Grimme
Macht ein Getöse!

FAUST *(laut):*

4460 Gretchen! Gretchen!

MARGARETE *(aufmerksam):*

Das war des Freundes Stimme!
(Sie springt auf. Die Ketten fallen ab.)
Wo ist er? Ich hab ihn rufen hören.
Ich bin frei! Mir soll niemand wehren.
An seinen Hals will ich fliegen,
4465 An seinem Busen liegen!
Er rief: Gretchen! Er stand auf der Schwelle.
Mitten durchs Heulen und Klappen der Hölle,
Durch den grimmigen, teuflischen Hohn
Erkannt ich den süßen, den liebenden Ton.

FAUST:

4470 Ich bin's!

MARGARETE:

Du bist's! O sag es noch einmal!
(Ihn fassend)
Er ist's! Er ist's! Wohin ist alle Qual?
Wohin die Angst des Kerkers? Der Ketten?
Du bist's! Kommst, mich zu retten!
Ich bin gerettet! –
4475 Schon ist die Straße wieder da,
Auf der ich dich zum ersten Male sah,
Und der heitere Garten,
Wo ich und Marthe deiner warten.

FAUST *(fortstrebend):*

Komm mit! Komm mit!

MARGARETE:

O weile!
4480 Weil' ich doch so gern, wo du weilest.
(Liebkosend)

There seethes hell.
The Devil
Makes a thundering noise
With his angry revel.

FAUST *(loud)*:
Gretchen! Gretchen!

MARGARET *(attentively)*:
That was my lover's voice!
(She jumps up. The chains drop off.)
Where is he? I heard him call. I am free.
No one shall hinder me.
To his neck I shall fly,
On his bosom lie.
He called Gretchen. He stood on the sill.
Amid the wailing and howling of hell,
Through the angry and devilish jeers
The sweet and loving tone touched my ears.

FAUST:
It is I.

MARGARET:
It is you. Oh, do say it again.
(She seizes him.)
It is he. It is he. Where, then, is all my pain?
Where the fear of the dungeon? the chain?
It is you. Come to save me.
I am saved!
Now I see the road again, too,
Where, for the first time, I laid eyes on you—
And the garden and the gate
Where I and Martha stand and wait.

FAUST *(striving away)*:
Come on! Come on!

MARGARET:
O Stay!
Because I am so happy where you are staying.
(Caresses him.)

FAUST:

Eile!
Wenn du nicht eilest,
Werden wir's teuer büßen müssen.

MARGARETE:

Wie? Du kannst nicht mehr küssen?
4485 Mein Freund, so kurz von mir entfernt,
Und hast's Küssen verlernt
Warum wird mir an deinem Halse so bang?
Wenn sonst von deinen Worten, deinen Blicken

Ein ganzer Himmel mich überdrang
4490 Und du mich küßtest, als wolltest du mich
ersticken –
Küsse mich!
Sonst küß ich dich! *(Sie umfaßt ihn)*
O weh! Deine Lippen sind kalt,
Sind stumm.
4495 Wo ist dein Lieben
Geblieben?
Wer brachte mich drum?
(Sie wendet sich von ihm.)

FAUST:

Komm! Folge mir! Liebchen, fasse Mut!
Ich herze dich mit tausendfacher Glut,
4500 Nur folge mir! Ich bitte dich nur dies!

MARGARETE *(zu ihm gewendet)*:

Und bist du's denn? Und bist du's auch gewiß?

FAUST:

Ich bin's! Komm mit!

MARGARETE:

Du machst die Fesseln los,
Nimmst wieder mich in deinen Schoß.
Wie kommt es, daß du dich vor mir nicht
scheust? –
4505 Und weißt du denn, mein Freund, wen du
befreist?

FAUST:

Do not delay.
If you keep on delaying,
We shall have to pay dearly therefor.

MARGARET:

What? You cannot kiss any more?
My friend, you were not gone longer than this—
And forgot how to kiss?
Why, at your neck, do I feel such dread,
When once from your eyes and from what you said
A whole heaven surged down to fill me,
And you would kiss me as if you wanted to kill me?
Kiss me!
Else I'll kiss you. *(She embraces him.)*
Oh, grief! Your lips are cold,
Are mute.
Where
Is your loving air?
Who took it from me?
(She turns away from him.)

FAUST:

Come, follow me, dearest, and be bold!
I shall caress you a thousandfold;
Only follow me! That is all I plead.

MARGARET *(turning toward him):*

And is it you? Is it you indeed?

FAUST:

It is I. Come along!

MARGARET:

You take off the chain,
And take me into your lap again.
How is it that you do not shrink from me?—
Do you know at all, my friend, whom you make free?

FAUST:

Komm! Komm! Schon weicht die tiefe Nacht.

MARGARETE:

Meine Mutter hab ich umgebracht,
Mein Kind hab ich ertränkt.
War es nicht dir und mir geschenkt?
4510 Dir auch – Du bist's! Ich glaub es kaum.
Gib deine Hand! Es ist kein Traum!
Deine liebe Hand! – Ach, aber sie ist feucht!
Wische sie ab! Wie mich deucht,
Ist Blut dran.
4515 Ach Gott Was hast du getan?
Stecke den Degen ein,
Ich bitte dich drum!

FAUST:

Laß das Vergangne vergangen sein!
Du bringst mich um.

MARGARETE:

4520 Nein, du mußt übrigbleiben!
Ich will dir die Gräber beschreiben,
Für die mußt du sorgen
Gleich morgen;
Der Mutter den besten Platz geben,
4525 Meinen Bruder sogleich darneben,
Mich ein wenig beiseit,
Nur nicht gar zu weit!
Und das Kleine mir an die rechte Brust.
Niemand wird sonst bei mir liegen. –
4530 Mich an deine Seite zu schmiegen,
Das wer ein süßes, ein holdes Glück!
Aber es will mir nicht mehr gelingen,
Mir ist's, als müßt ich mich zu dir zwingen,
Als stießest du mich von dir zurück.
4535 Und doch bist du's und blickst so gut, so fromm.

FAUST:

Fühlst, du, daß ich es bin, so komm!

FAUST:

Come! Come! Soon dawns the light of day.

MARGARET:

I've put my mother away,
I've drowned my child, don't you see?
Was it not given to you and to me?
You, too—it is you! Could it merely seem?
Give me your hand! It is no dream.
Your dear hand!—But alas, it is wet.
Wipe it off! There is yet
Blood on this one.
Oh God! What have you done!
Sheathe your sword;
I am begging you.

FAUST:

Let the past be forever past—oh Lord,
You will kill me, too.

MARGARET:

Oh no, you must outlive us!
I'll describe the graves you should give us.
Care for them and sorrow
Tomorrow:
Give the best place to my mother,
And next to her lay my brother;
Me, a little aside,
Only don't make the space too wide!
And the little one at my right breast.
Nobody else will lie by my side.—
Oh, to lie with you and to hide
In your arms, what happiness!
Now it is more than I can do;
I feel, I must force myself on you,
And you, it seems, push back my caress;
And yet it is you, and look so pure, so devout.

FAUST:

If you feel, it is I, come out!

MARGARETE:

Dahinaus?

FAUST:

Ins Freie!

MARGARETE:

Ist das Grab drauß,
Lauert der Tod, so komm!
4540 Von hier ins ewige Ruhebett
Und weiter keinen Schritt –
Du gehst nun fort? O Heinrich, könnt ich mit!

FAUST:

Du kannst! So wolle nur! Die Tür steht offen.

MARGARETE:

Ich darf nicht fort; für mich ist nichts zu hoffen.
4545 Was hilft es, fliehn? Sie lauern doch mir auf.
Es ist so elend, betteln zu müssen,
Und noch dazu mit bösem Gewissen!
Es ist so elend, in der Fremde schweifen,
Und sie werden mich doch ergreifen!

FAUST:

4550 Ich bleibe bei dir.

MARGARETE:

Geschwind! Geschwind!
Rette dein armes Kind!
Fort! Immer den Weg
Am Bach hinauf,
4555 Über den Steg
In den Wald hinein,
Links, so die Planke steht,
Im Teich!
Fass es nur gleich!
4560 Es will sich heben,
Es zappelt noch,
Rette! Rette!

FAUST:

Besinne dich doch!

MARGARET:
Out where?

FAUST:
Into the open.

MARGARET:
If the grave is there,
If death awaits us, then come!
From here to the bed of eternal rest,
And not a step beyond—no!
You are leaving now? Oh, Heinrich, that I could go!

FAUST:
You can! If only you would! Open stands the door.

MARGARET:
I may not go; for me there is no hope any more.
What good to flee? They lie in wait for me.
To have to go begging is misery,
And to have a bad conscience, too.
It is misery to stray far and forsaken,
And, anyhow, I would be taken.

FAUST:
I stall stay with you.

MARGARET:
Quick! Quick! I pray.
Save your poor child.
On! Follow the way
Along the brook,
Over the bridge,
Into the wood,
To the left where the planks stick
Out of the pond.
Seize it—oh, quick!
It wants to rise,
It is still struggling.
Save! Save!

FAUST:
Can you not see,

Nur einen Schritt, so bist du frei!

MARGARETE:

4565 Wären wir nur den Berg vorbei!
Da sitzt meine Mutter auf einem Stein,
Es faßt mich kalt beim Schopfe;
Da sitzt meine Mutter auf einem Stein
Und wackelt mit dem Kopfe.
4570 Sie winkt nicht, sie nickt nicht, der Kopf ist ihr schwer,
Sie schlief so lange, sie wacht nicht mehr.
Sie schlief, damit wir uns freuten.
Es waren glückliche Zeiten!

FAUST:

Hilft hier kein Flehen, hilft kein Zagen,
4575 So wag' ich's, dich hinwegzutragen.

MARGARETE:

Laß mich! Nein, ich leide keine Gewalt!
Fasse mich nicht so mörderich an!
Sonst hab ich dir ja alles zulieb getan.

FAUST:

Der Tag graut! Liebchen! Liebchen!

MARGARETE:

4580 Tag! Ja, es wird Tag! Der letzte Tag dringt herein!
Mein Hochzeitstag sollt es sein!
Sag niemand, daß du schon bei Gretchen warst.
Weh meinem Kranze!
Es ist eben geschehn!
4585 Wir werden uns wiedersehn;
Aber nicht beim Tanze.
Die Menge drängt sich, man hört sie nicht.
Der Platz, die Gassen
Können sie nicht fassen.
4590 Die Glocke ruft, das Stäbchen bricht.
Wie sie mich binden und packen!
Zum Blutstuhl bin ich schon entrückt.
Schon zuckt nach jedem Nacken

It takes *one* step, and you are free.

MARGARET:

If only we were past the hill!
My mother sits there on a stone,
My scalp is creeping with dread!
My mother sits there on a stone
And wags and wags her head;
She becks not, she nods not, her head is heavy and sore,
She has slept so long, she awakes no more.
She slept that we might embrace.
Those were the days of grace.

FAUST:

In vain is my pleading, in vain what I say;
What can I do but bear you away?

MARGARET:

Leave me! No, I shall suffer no force!
Do not grip me so murderously!
After all, I did everything else you asked.

FAUST:

The day dawns. Dearest! Dearest!

MARGARET:

Day. Yes, day is coming. The last day breaks;
It was to be my wedding day.
Tell no one that you have already been with Gretchen.
My veil! Oh pain!
It just happened that way.
We shall meet again,
But not dance that day.
The crowd is pushing, no word is spoken.
The alleys below
And the streets overflow.
The bell is tolling, the wand is broken.
How they tie and grab me, now one delivers
Me to the block and gives the sign,
And for every neck quivers

Die Schärfe, die nach meinem zückt.
4595 Stumm liegt die Welt wie das Grab.

FAUST:

O wär ich nie geboren!

MEPHISTOPHELES *(erscheint draußen):*

Auf! Oder ihr seid verloren.
Unnützes Zagen! Zaudern und Plaudern!
Meine Pferde schaudern,
4600 Der Morgen dämmert auf.

MARGARETE:

Was steigt aus dem Boden herauf?
Der! Der! Schicke ihn fort!
Was will der an dem heiligen Ort?
Er will mich!

FAUST:

Du sollst leben!

MARGARETE:

4605 Gericht Gottes! Dir hab ich mich übergeben!

MEPHISTOPHELES *(zu Faust):*

Komm! Komm! Ich lasse dich mit ihr im Stich.

MARGARETE:

Dein bin ich, Vater! Rette mich!
Ihr Engel! Ihr heiligen Scharen,
Lagert euch umher, mich zu bewahren!
4610 Heinrich! Mir graut's vor dir.

MEPHISTOPHELES:

Sie ist gerichtet!

STIMME *(von oben):*

Ist gerettet!

MEPHISTOPHELES *(zu Faust):*

Her zu mir!

(Verschwindet mit Faust)

STIMME *(von innen, verhallend):*

Heinrich! Heinrich!

The blade that quivers for mine.
Mute lies the world as a grave.

FAUST:
That I had never been born!

MEPHISTO *(appears outside):*
Up! Or you are lost.
Prating and waiting and pointless wavering.
My horses are quavering,
Over the sky creeps the dawn.

MARGARET:
What did the darkness spawn?
He! He! Send him away!
What does he want in this holy place?
He wants me!

FAUST:
You shall live.

MARGARET:
Judgment of God! I give
Myself to you.

MEPHISTO *(to* FAUST*):*
Come! Come! I shall abandon you with her.

MARGARET:
Thine I am, father. Save me!
You angels, hosts of heaven, stir,
Encamp about me, be my guard.
Heinrich! I quail at thee.

MEPHISTO:
She is judged.

VOICE *(from above):*
Is saved.

MEPHISTO *(to* FAUST*):*
Hither to me!
(Disappears with FAUST.*)*

VOICE *(from within, fading away):*
Heinrich! Heinrich!

DER ZWEITE TEIL DER TRAGÖDIE

ERSTER AKT
ANMUTIGE GEGEND

Faust auf blumigen Rasen gebettet, ermüdet, unruhig, schlafsuchend. Dämmerung. Geisterkreis schwebend bewegt, anmutige kleine gestalten.

ARIEL *(Gesang, von Äolsharfen begleitet):*
Wenn der Blüten Frühlingsregen
Über alle schwebend sinkt,
4615 Wenn der Felder grüner Segen
Allen Erdgebornen blinkt,
Kleiner Elfen Geistergröße
Eilet, wo sie helfen kann;
Ob er heilig, ob er böse,
4620 Jammert sie der Unglücksmann.

Die ihr dies Haupt umschwebt im luftgen Kreise,
Erzeigt euch hier nach edler Elfen Weise,
Besänftiget des Herzens grimmen Strauß,
Entfernt des Vorwurfs glühend bittre Pfeile,
4625 Sein Innres reinigt von erlebtem Graus!
V i e r sind die Pausen nächtiger Weile,
Nun ohne Säumen füllt sie freundlich aus!
Erst senkt sein Haupt aufs kühle Polster nieder,
Dann badet ihn im Tau aus Lethes Flut;
4630 Gelenk sind bald die krampferstarrten
Glieder,

THE SECOND PART OF THE TRAGEDY

FIRST ACT
CHARMING LANDSCAPE

Faust, reclining on a lawn with flowers, weary,
restless, seeking twilight sleep.
A circle of spirits, moving in the air: charming little figures.

ARIEL *(chant, accompanied by Aeolian harps):*

When the vernal blossom showers
Sink down to embrace the earth,
When green fields, alive with flowers,
Fill all human hearts with mirth,
Then great spirits, looking lowly,
Rush to help those whom they can;
Whether wicked, whether holy,
They would heal the wretched man.

You who surround his head in airy beauty,
Prepare to do the elfins' noblest duty:
Relieve the bitter conflict in his heart,
Remove the burning arrows of remorse,
And cleanse his mind of memories that smart.
Four watches mark the nightly course,
Without delay fill them with friendly art.
First let his head recline on a cool pillow,
Then bathe him in the dew of Lethe's spray;
The limbs, stiffened by cramps, grow lithe as
willow,

Wenn er gestärkt dem Tag entgegenruht;
Vollbringt der Elfen schönste Pflicht,
Gebt ihn zurück dem heiligen Licht!

CHOR *(einzeln, zu zweien und vielen, abwechselnd und gesammelt):*

Wenn sich lau die Lüfte füllen
4635 Um den grünumschränkten Plan,
Süße Düfte, Nebelhüllen
Senkt die Dämmerung heran;
Lispelt leise süßen Frieden,
Wiegt das Herz in Kindesruh;
4640 Und den Augen dieses Müden
Schließt des Tages Pforte zu.

Nacht ist schon hereingesunken,
Schließt sich heilig Stern an Stern,
Große Lichter, kleine Funken
4645 Glitzern nah und glänzen fern;
Glitzern hier im See sich spiegelnd,
Glänzen droben klarer Nacht,
Tiefsten Ruhens Glück besiegelnd
Herrscht des Mondes volle Pracht.

4650 Schon verloschen sind die Stunden,
Hingeschwunden Schmerz und Glück;
Fühl es vor! Du wirst gesunden;
Traue neuem Tagesblick!
Täler grünen, Hügel schwellen,
4655 Buschen sich zu Schattenruh;
Und in schwanken Silberwellen
Wogt die Saat der Ernte zu.

Wunsch um Wünsche zu erlangen,
Schaue nach dem Glanze dort!
4660 Leise bist du nur umfangen,
Schlaf ist Schale, wirf sie fort!
Säume nicht, dich zu erdreisten,
Wenn die Menge zaudernd schweift;

When rest has made him strong to meet the day.
Perform the elfins' fairest rite:
Restore him to the holy light!

CHORUS *(singly, by two or more, alternately and together):*

When the green-encircled meadow
Bears a cool, ethereal crown,
When sweet scents and misty shadows
Show that twilight settles down—
Sing of peace and, thus inspired,
Rock his heart as cradles sway;
For his eyes that are so tired
Close the portals of the day!

Night succeeds the twilight's glimmer,
Star is linked to holy star,
Brilliant light and faintest shimmer
Glisten near and gleam afar,
Glisten, in the lake reflected,
Gleam above in the clear night;
And his deep sleep is perfected
In the full moon's splendid light.

What occured is dead and ended,
Pain and joy have passed away;
You are healed—oh, apprehend it,
Trust the newborn light of day!
Greening valleys, swelling mountains
Full of bushes, offer shadow;
Silver-waved from unseen fountains,
Wheat fields ripple in the meadow.

To have wish on wish fulfilled,
See the splendor of the day!
Lightly only you are held:
Sleep is shell, cast it away!
Do not waver even when
Many falter and stand back:

Alles kann der Edle leisten,
4665 Der versteht und rasch ergreift.

(Ungeheures Getöse verkündet das Herannahen der Sonne.)

ARIEL:

Horchet! Horcht dem Sturm der Horen!
Tönend wird für Geistesohren
Schon der neue Tag geboren.
Felsentore knarren rasselnd,
4670 Phöbus' Räder rollen prasselnd,
Welch Getöse bringt das Licht!
Es trompetet, es posaunet,
Auge blinzt und Ohr erstaunet,
Unerhörtes hört sich nicht.
4675 Schlüpfet zu den Blumenkronen,
Tiefer, tiefer, still zu wohnen,
In die Felsen, unters Laub;
Trifft es euch, so seid ihr taub.

FAUST:

Des Lebens Pulse schlagen frisch lebendig,
4680 Ätherische Dämmerung milde zu begrüßen;
Du, Erde, warst auch diese Nacht beständig
Und atmest neu erquickt zu meinen Füßen,
Beginnest schon mit Lust mich zu umgeben,
Du regst und rührst ein kräftiges Beschließen,
4685 Zum höchsten Dasein immerfort zu streben. –
In Dämmerschein liegt schon die Welt erschlossen,
Der Wald ertönt von tausendstimmigem Leben;
Tal aus, Tal ein ist Nebelstreif ergossen,
Doch senkt sich Himmelsklarheit in die Tiefen,
4690 Und Zweig und Äste, frisch erquickt, entsprossen
Dem duftgen Abgrund, wo versenkt sie schliefen;
Auch Farb an Farbe klärt sich los vom Grunde,
Wo Blum und Blatt von Zitterperle triefen –
Ein Paradies wird um mich her die Runde.

All things can be done by men
Who are quick to see and act.

(A tremendous tumult announces the approach of the sun.)

ARIEL:

Listen! how the Horae near.
Thundering for the spirit's ear,
We can feel the day appear.
Rocky portals open chattering,
Phoebus' wheels are rolling, clattering,
Tumult rends the atmosphere.
Light approaches, trumps are sounded,
Eyes are blinded, ears astounded,
The Unheard one cannot hear.
Slip into a flower bell,
Deeper, deeper, there to dwell,
In the rocks beneath a leaf;
If it strikes you, you are deaf.

FAUST:

Enlivened once again, life's pulses waken
To greet the kindly dawn's ethereal vision;
You, earth, outlasted this night, too, unshaken,
And at my feet you breathe, renewed Elysian,
Surrounding me with pleasure-scented flowers,
And deep within you prompt a stern decision:
To strive for highest life with all my powers.—
Touched by the dawn's soft sheen, the world is
glowing,
A thousand voices fill the forest's bowers;
All through the valley misty streaks are flowing,
But light descends, the deeps, too, are unsealed,
And I see twigs and branches growing
From the ravine where they could sleep
concealed.
Color on color rises from the ground
Where dewy leaves and blossoms stand revealed,
And I behold a paradise around.

4695 Hinaufgeschaut! – Der Berge Gipfelriesen
Verkünden schon die feierlichste Stunde;
Sie dürfen früh des ewigen Lichts genießen,
Das später sich zu uns hernieder wendet.
Jetzt zu der Alpe grüngesenkten Wiesen
4700 Wird neuer Glanz und Deutlichkeit gespendet,
Und stufenweis herab ist es gelungen –
Sie tritt hervor! – und, leider schon geblendet,
Kehr ich mich weg, vom Augenschmerz
durchdrungen.

So ist es also, wenn ein sehnend Hoffen
4705 Dem höchsten Wunsch sich traulich zugerungen,
Erfüllungspforten findet flügeloffen;
Nun aber bricht aus jenen ewigen Gründen
Ein Flammenübermaß, wir stehn betroffen;
Des Lebens Fackel wollten wir entzünden,
4710 Ein Feuermeer umschlingt uns, welch ein Feuer!
Ist's Lieb! Ist's Haß? die glühend uns umwinden,
Mit Schmerz und Freuden wechselnd ungeheuer,
So daß wir wieder nach der Erde blicken,
Zu bergen uns in jugendlichstem Schleier.

4715 So bleibe denn die Sonne mir im Rücken!
Der Wassersturz, das Felsenriff durchbrausend,
Ihn schau ich an mit wachsendem Entzücken.
Von Sturz zu Sturzen wälzt er jetzt in tausend,
Dann abertausend Strömen sich ergießend,
4720 Hoch in die Lüfte Schaum an Schäume sausend.
Allein wie herrlich, diesem Sturm ersprießend,
Wölbt sich des bunten Bogens Wechseldauer,
Bald rein gezeichnet, bald in Luft zerfließend,
Umher verbreitend duftig kühle Schauer.
4725 D e r spiegelt ab das menschliche Bestreben.
Ihm sinne nach, und du begreifst genauer:
Am farbigen Abglanz haben wir das Leben.

Look up! Where the snow-covered mountains
tower,
The giant peaks, graced early, crimson-crowned,
Announce already the most sacred hour
That soon will reach us in the low terrain.
And now a burst of light, a radiant shower
Falls on the Alpine leas like golden rain,
Speeds down, and the long pathway lies behind it.
Then he steps forth!—My eyes are pierced with
pain,
And I must turn away, my vision blinded.

Thus it is always when a keen desire
Has neared its highest hope and strains to find it:
Fulfillment's portals gape—but sudden fire
Breaks oceanlike out of eternal gorges,
Engulfing us—and we stand petrified.
We dreamed we would ignite life's torches,
But floods of flame embrace us without measure;
We do not know if love or hatred scorch us
And alternate with monstrous pain and pleasure,
So that we look again upon the green
And hide in morning's youthful mist and leisure.

Let then the sun stay in my back, unseen!
The waterfall I now behold with growing
Delight as it roars down to the ravine.
From fall to fall a thousand streams are flowing,
A thousand more are plunging, effervescent,
And high up in the air the spray is glowing.
Out of this thunder rises, iridescent,
Enduring through all change the motley bow,
Now painted clearly, and now evanescent,
Spreading a fragrant, cooling spray below.
The rainbow mirrors human love and strife;
Consider it and you will better know:
In many-hued reflection we have life.

FUNFTER AKT

OFFENE GEGEND.

WANDRER:

Ja! Sie sind's, die dunkeln Linden
Dort in ihres Alters Kraft.
11045 Und ich soll sie wiederfinden
Nach so langer Wanderschaft!
Ist es doch die alte Stelle,
Jene Hütte, die mich barg,
Als die sturmeregte Welle
11050 Mich an jene Dünen warf!
Meine Wirte möcht ich segnen,
Hilfsbereit, ein wackres Paar,
Das, um heut mir zu begegnen,
Alt schon jener Tage war.
11055 Ach, das waren fromme Leute!
Poch ich? Ruf ich?—Seid gegrüßt,
Wenn gastfreundlich auch noch heute
Ihr des Wohltuns Glück genießt!

BAUCIS *(Mütterchen, sehr alt):*

Lieber Kömmling! Leise! Leise!
11060 Ruhe! Laß den Gatten ruhn!
Langer Schlaf, verleiht dem Greise
Kurzen Wachens rasches Tun.

WANDRER:

Sage, Mutter, bist du's eben,
Meinen Dank noch zu empfahn,
11065 Was du für des Jünglings Leben
Mit dem Gatten einst getan?
Bist du Baucis, die geschäftig

FIFTH ACT*

OPEN COUNTRY

WANDERER:

Yes, this is the linden trees'
Peaceful dark that I behold;
Gratefully, the wanderer sees
Them again, now strong and old.
There's the cottage that once gave
Shelter to me, years before,
When the raging, storm-whipped wave
Thrust me on the dune-lined shore.
Are my helpful hosts still there?
How I'd like to see again
And to bless the valiant pair
Who were aged even then.
They were pious, good, and kind.
Should I knock? call?—Welcome me,
If today, as once, you find
Joy in hospitality.

BAUCIS *(a little grandam, very old):*

Soft, dear stranger! Not so bold!
Let my husband rest, dear neighbor!
Sleeping long, permits the old
A brief day of rapid labor.

WANDERER:

Is it you indeed, the wife
Who once saved me with her spouse?
That I thank you for my life,
You still live here in this house?
Are you Baucis whose kind care

* For a synopsis of the preceding portions of Part Two, which are omitted here, see Section 8 of the Introduction.

Halberstorbnen Mund erquickt?
(Der gatte tritt auf.)

Du Philemon, der so kräftig
11070 Meinen Schatz der Flut entrückt?
Eures Flammen raschen Feuers
Eures Glöckchens Silberlaut,
Jenes grausen Abenteuers
Lösung war euch anvertraut.

11075 Und nun laßt hervor mich treten,
Schaun das grenzenlose Meer;
Laßt mich knieen, laßt mich beten,
Mich bedrängt die Brust so sehr.
(Er schreitet vorwärts auf der Düne.)

PHILEMON *(zu Baucis):*
Eile nur, den Tisch zu decken,
11080 Wo's im Gärtchen munter blüht.
Laß ihn rennen, ihn erschrecken,
Denn er glaubt nicht, was er sieht.
(Neben dem Wandrer stehend.)

Das Euch grimmig mißgehandelt,
Wog auf Woge, schäumend wild,
11085 Seht als Garten Ihr behandelt,
Seht ein paradiesisch Bild.
Älter, war ich nicht zuhanden,
Hilfreich nicht wie sonst bereit,
Und wie meine Kräfte schwanden,
11090 War auch schon die Woge weit.
Kluger Herren kühne Knechte
Gruben Gräben, dämmten ein,
Schmälerten des Meeres Rechte,
Herrn an seiner Statt zu sein.
11095 Schaue grünend Wies an Wiese,
Anger, Garten, Dorf und Wald.
Komm nun aber und genieße,

Filled the half-dead mouth with food?
(The husband enters.)

You, Philemon, whose quick dare
Saved my treasure from the flood?
Is it your hearth's rapid flame?
Is it your bell's silver tone?
And my dread adventure came
To an end through you alone?

Let me walk up and survey
Once again the boundless ocean!
Let me kneel and let me pray!
For my breast bursts with emotion.
(He walks forward on the dune.)

PHILEMON *(to* BAUCIS):
Hurry on, and set the table
In the garden, by the trees!
Let him stand amazed, unable
to believe the things he sees!
(Standing next to the wanderer.)

Where the wildly foaming breakers
Tortured you with cruel spite,
You see gardens now and acres
Of a paradisiac sight.
Older now, I could not play
My part, helping as before;
As my powers ebbed away,
Ebbed the breakers and the shore.
Clever masters' daring slaves
Toiled till dams and trenches spread,
Pruned the power of the waves
To be masters in their stead.
See the thriving meadows meet
Pastures, gardens, wood, and town.—
But now come and let us eat,

Denn die Sonne scheidet bald.
Dort im Fernsten ziehen Segel,
11100 Suchen nächtlich sichern Port.
Kennen doch ihr Nest die Vögel,
Denn jetzt ist der Hafen dort.
So erblickst du in der Weite
Erst des Meeres blauen Saum,
11105 Rechts und links, in aller Breite,
Dichtgedrängt bewohnten Raum.

Am Tische zu drei, im Gärtchen.

BAUCIS:

Bleibst du stumm? Und keinen Bissen
Bringst du zum verlechzten Mund?

PHILEMON:

Möcht er doch vom Wunder wissen;
11110 Sprichst so gerne, tu's ihm kund.

BAUCIS:

Wohl, ein Wunder ist's gewesen!
Läßt mich heut noch nicht in Ruh;
Denn es ging das ganze Wesen
Nicht mit rechten Dingen zu.

PHILEMON:

11115 Kann der Kaiser sich versündgen,
Der das Ufer ihm verliehn?
Tät's ein Herold nicht verkündgen
Schmetternd im Vorüberziehn?

Nicht entfernt von unsern Dünen
11120 Ward der erste Fuß gefaßt,
Tags umsonst die Knechte lärmten,
Hack und Schaufel, Schlag um Schlag;

BAUCIS:

Zelte, Hütten! – Doch im Grünen
Richtet bald sich ein Palast.
11125 Wo die Flämmchen nächtig schwärmten,

For the sun will soon go down.—
Far away, the sails seek rest,
To their port the boats repair;
For, like birds, they know their nest,
And the harbor now is there.
You can see the ocean gleaming
Only in the azure distance;
Right and left, the land is teeming,
Offering men a new existence.

The Three at a Table in the Little Garden.

BAUCIS:
You stay silent and, my dear,
Eat no bite? You sit and balk?

PHILEMON:
Of the wonder he would hear;
Tell him, for you like to talk!

BAUCIS:
Yes, we saw a wonder there!
Even now it troubles me,
For it was a strange affair,
As uncanny as can be.

PHILEMON:
Could the Emperor have sinned, too,
When he gave him our strand?
For it was his herald who
First proclaimed it in the land.

Near our dunes they were first seen,
Tents and huts of every size;
And, soon after, in the green
We could see a palace rise.

BAUCIS:
Daily they would vainly storm,
Pick and shovel, stroke for stroke;
Where the flames would nightly swarm,

Stand ein Damm den andern Tag.
Menschenopfer mußten bluten,
Nachts erscholl des Jammers Qual;
Meerab flossen Feuergluten,
11130 Morgens war es ein Kanal.
Gottlos ist er, ihn gelüstet
Unsre Hütte, unser Hain;
Wie er sich als Nachbar brüstet,
Soll man untertänig sein.

PHILEMON:

11135 Hat er uns doch angeboten
Schönes Gut im neuen Land!

BAUCIS:

Traue nicht dem Wasserboden,
Halt auf deiner Höhe stand!

PHILEMON:

Laßt uns zur Kapelle treten,
11140 Letzten Sonnenblick zu schaun!
Laßt uns läuten, knieen, beten
Und dem alten Gott Vertraun!

PALAST.

Weiter Ziergarten, großer, gradgeführter Kanal.
Faust im höchsten Alter, wandelnd, nachdenkend.

LYNCEUS DER TÜRMER *(durchs Sprachrohr):*

Die Sonne sinkt, die letzten Schiffe,
Sie ziehen munter hafenein.
11145 Ein großer Kahn ist im Begriffe,
Auf dem Kanale hier zu sein.
Die bunten Wimpel wehen fröhlich,

Was a dam when we awoke.
Human sacrifices bled,
Tortured yells would pierce the night,
And where blazes seaward sped
A canal would greet the light.
He is godless, covets our
Cottage and our wooded fringe;
As the neighbor swells with power,
We should crouch, and we should cringe.

PHILEMON:

But he offered—you are harsh!—
Fair estate in his new land!

BAUCIS:

Do not trust the swampy marsh,
On your height maintain your stand!

PHILEMON:

Now, to see the sun's last ray,
To the chapel let us plod,
Ring the bell, and kneel and pray,
Trusting in the ancient God!

PALACE

Spacious ornamental garden and large straight canal.
Faust, extremely old, walking and thinking.

LYNCEUS THE TOWER WARDEN *(through a speaking trumpet):*

The sun goes down, and the last barges
Glide toward the haven, full of cheer.
A big boat nears; soon it discharges
Its load of brilliant treasures here.
The motley flags are flying gaily,

Die starren Masten stehn bereit;
In dir preist sich der Bootsmann selig,
11150 Dich grüßt das Glück zur höchsten Zeit.
(Das Glöcklein läutet auf der Düne.)

FAUST *(auffahrend):*
Verdammtes Läuten! Allzuschändlich
Verwundet's wie ein tückischer Schuß;
Vor Augen ist mein Reich unendlich,
Im Rücken neckt mich der Verdruß,
11155 Erinnert mich durch neidische Laute:
Mein Hochbesitz, er ist nicht rein,
Der Lindenraum, die braune Baute,
Das morsche Kirchlein ist nicht mein.
Und wünscht ich, dort mich zu erholen,
11160 Vor fremdem Schatten schaudert mir,
Ist Dorn den Augen, Dorn den Sohlen;
O, wär ich weit hinweg von hier!

TÜRMER *(wie oben):*
Wie segelt froh der bunte Kahn
Mit frischem Abendwind heran!
11165 Wie türmt sich sein behender Lauf
In Kisten, Kasten, Säcken auf!
(Prächtiger Kahn, reich und bunt beladen mit Erzeugnissen fremder Weltgegenden.)

MEPHISTOPHELES. DIE DREI GEWALTIGEN GESELLEN.

CHORUS:
Da landen wir,
Da sind wir schon.
Glücken dem Herren,
11170 Dem Patron!
(Sie stiegen aus, die Güter werden ans Land geschafft.)

MEPHISTOPHELES:
So haben wir uns wohl erprobt,
Vergnügt, wenn der Patron es lobt.
Nur mit zwei Schiffen ging es fort,
Mit zwanzig sind wir nun im Port.

The rigid masts reach up, sublime;
Through you the seamen succeed daily,
And fortune hails you in your prime.
(The chapel bell rings on the dune.)

FAUST *(starting)*:
Damned ringing! It is all too sly,
Wounds me like a perfidious shot.
My realm is endless for the eye;
Behind my back I hear it mock,
Reminding me with jealous sounds
That my possessions bear a smirch:
The cottage and the linden grounds
Are not mine, nor that moldy church.
And if I'd rest there from the heat,
Their shadows would fill me with fear,
Thorns in my eyes, thorns in my feet;
Oh, would that I were far from here!

TOWER WARDEN *(as above)*:
How, swept on by the evening breeze,
The gay and motley cargo sails!
How the boat glides toward us with ease
And carries crates and chests and bales!
(A magnificent boat with a rich and motley load of products of foreign countries.)
MEPHISTOPHELES. THE THREE MIGHTY FELLOWS.

CHORUS:
Now here we land,
Now come off board.
Hail our patron,
Our lord!
(They debark, the goods are brought ashore.)

MEPHISTO:
We proved ourselves and came back here,
Content with our patron's cheer.
With just two ships we went away,
With twenty we come back today.

11175 Was große Dinge wir getan,
Das sieht man unsrer Ladung an.
Das freie Meer befreit den Geist,
Wer weiß da, was Besinnen heißt!
Da fördert nur ein rascher Griff,
11180 Man fängt den Fisch, man fängt ein Schiff,
Und ist man erst der Herr zu drei,
Dann hakelt man das vierte bei;
Da geht es denn dem fünften schlecht,
Man hat Gewalt, so hat man Recht.
11185 Man fragt ums W a s und nicht ums W i e.
Ich müßte keine Schiffahrt kennen:
Krieg, Handel und Piraterie,
Dreieinig sind sie, nicht zu trennen.

DIE DREI GEWALTIGEN GESELLEN:

Nicht Dank und Gruß!
11190 Nicht Gruß und Dank!
Als brächten wir
Dem Herrn Gestank.
Er macht ein
Widerlich Gesicht;
11195 Das Königsgut
Gefällt ihm nicht.

MEPHISTOPHELES:

Erwartet weiter
Keinen Lohn!
Nahmt ihr doch
11200 Euren Teil davon.

DIE GESELLEN:

Das ist nur für
Die Langeweil;
Wir alle fordern
Gleichen Teil.

MEPHISTOPHELES:

11205 Erst ordnet oben
Saal an Saal
Die Kostbarkeiten

We did great things—you see how great
By simply looking at our freight.
The ocean's freedom frees the mind,
So who would try to be refined!
What matters is a sudden grip,
You catch a fish, you catch a ship;
And once you are the lord of three,
You hook the fourth one easily;
The fifth is in a sorry plight;
One has the power, hence the right,
One cares for What, not How—you see.
If I know how the sea is charted,
Then commerce, war, and piracy
Are three in one and can't be parted.

THE THREE MIGHTY FELLOWS:

He does not greet,
He does not thank!
As if the gifts
We brought him stank!
He makes a most
Disgusted face;
He deems the royal
Wealth disgrace.

MEPHISTO:

Do not expect more;
Leave and go!
For your share
You took long ago.

THE THREE MIGHTY MEN:

Then we were bored,
So that was fair;
We all demand
An equal share.

MEPHISTO:

First you arrange,
Hall upon hall,
The precious things here,

Allzumal!
Und tritt er zu
11210 Der reichen Schau,
Berechnet er alles
Mehr genau,
Er sich gewiß
Nicht lumpen läßt
11215 Und gibt der Flotte
Fest nach Fest.
Die bunten Vögel kommen morgen,
Für die werd ich zum besten sorgen.
(Die Ladung wird weggeschafft.)

MEPHISTOPHELES *(zu Faust):*
Mit ernster Stirn, mit düsterm Blick
11220 Vernimmst du dein erhaben Glück.
Die hohe Weisheit wird gekrönt,
Das Ufer ist dem Meer versöhnt;
Vom Ufer nimmt zu rascher Bahn
Das Meer die Schiffe willig an;
11225 So sprich, daß hier, hier vom Palast
Dein Arm die ganze Welt umfaßt.
Von dieser Stelle ging es aus,
Hier stand das erste Bretterhaus;
Ein Gräbchen ward hinabgeritzt,
11230 Wo jetzt das Ruder emsig spritzt.
Dein hoher Sinn, der Deinen Fleiß
Erwarb des Meers, der Erde Preis.
Von hier aus —

FAUST:
Das verfluchte H i e r!
Das eben leidig lastet's mir.
11235 Dir Vielgewandten muß ich's sagen,
Mir gibt's im Herzen Stich um Stich,
Mir ist's unmöglich zu ertragen!
Und wie ich's sage, schäm ich mich.
Die Alten droben sollten weichen,
11240 Die Linden wünscht ich mir zum Sitz,

One and all.
And when he sees
Sights without price,
Makes his appraisal
More precise,
Then he will change
And give at least
For our fleet
Feast upon feast.
At dawn, our motley birds will glide
Into the port, and I'll provide.
(The cargo is carried away.)

MEPHISTO (*to* FAUST):
With somber brow, with gloomy eye,
You spurn good fortune without joy.
Your noble wisdom now bears fruit,
As shore and sea end their dispute;
And from the shore, for their swift trips,
The friendly sea accepts the ships:
Confess that here, here from this place,
The whole world is in your embrace.
At this spot we began: here stood
The first mean shanty, made of wood;
A ditch was scratched into the shore
Where one now sees the splashing oar.
Your noble mind and your men's toil
Have won the prize of sea and soil.
From here, too——

FAUST:
Damn the accursèd *here!*
That is the thorn, the mocking sneer!
Need I tell *you,* so rich in lore,
It stings my heart? Could you not guess it?
I cannot bear it any more–
And am ashamed as I confess it.
The old folks there ought to resign
Their linden trees, so dark and tall;

Die wenig Bäume, nicht mein eigen,
Verderben mir den Weltbesitz.
Dort wollt ich, weit umher zu schauen,
Von Ast zu Ast Gerüste bauen,
11245 Dem Blick eröffnen weite Bahn,
Zu sehn, was alles ich getan,
Zu überschaun mit einem Blick
Des Menschengeistes Meisterstück,
Betätigend mit klugem Sinn
11250 Der Völker breiten Wohngewinn.
So sind am härtsten wir gequält,
Im Reichtum fühlend, was uns fehlt.
Des Glöckchens Klang, der Linden Duft
Umfängt mich wie in Kirch und Gruft.
11255 Des allgewaltigen Willens Kür
Bricht sich an diesem Sande hier.
Wie schaff ich mir es vom Gemüte!
Das Glöcklein läutet, und ich wüte.

MEPHISTOPHELES:

Natürlich! Daß ein Hauptverdruß
11260 Das Leben dir vergällen muß.
Wer leugnet's! Jedem edlen Ohr
Kommt das Geklingel widrig vor.
Und das verfluchte Bim-Baum-Bimmel,
Umnebelnd heitern Abendhimmel,
11265 Mischt sich in jegliches Begebnis
Vom ersten Bad bis zum Begräbnis,
Als wäre zwischen Bim und Baum
Das Leben ein verschollner Traum.

FAUST:

Das Widerstehn, der Eigensinn
11270 Verkümmern herrlichsten Gewinn,
Daß man zu tiefer, grimmiger Pein
Ermüden muß, gerecht zu sein.

MEPHISTOPHELES:

Was willst du dich denn hier genieren?

The few trees there that are not mine
Reduce the world I own to gall.
There I would build, better to see,
A scaffolding from tree to tree,
And thus a vision might be won
Of all the things that I have done;
A single glance could then impart
The masterpiece of human art;
Securing with good sense and grace
The peoples' spacious dwelling place.
For this is the most cruel rack,
To feel in riches what we lack.
The bell, the lindens' sweet perfume
Enfold me as a church or tomb.
My otherwise almighty will
Breaks down before that sandy hill.
What could relieve me or assuage!
The little bell rings, and I rage.

MEPHISTO:

Too bad that such a great distress
Should turn your life to bitterness.
Of course, for every noble ear
Bells are a thing one hates to hear.
And those damnable dingdong sighs,
Befogging cheerful evening skies,
Fill every happening with their gloom,
From the first bath down to the tomb,
As if, between the ding and dong,
Life were a dream or faded song.

FAUST:

Resistance and such stubbornness
Thwart the most glorious success,
Till in the end, to one's disgust,
One would as soon no more be just.

MEPHISTO:

Why hesitate or temporize?

Mußt du nicht längst kolonisieren?

FAUST:

11275 So geht und schafft sie mir zur Seite! –
Das schöne Gütchen kennst du ja,
Das ich den Alten ausersah.

MEPHISTOPHELES:

Man trägt sie fort und setzt sie nieder,
Eh man sich umsieht, stehn sie wieder;
11280 Nach überstandener Gewalt
Versöhnt ein schöner Aufenthalt.
(Er pfeift gellend. die drei treten auf.)

MEPHISTOPHELES:

Kommt, wie der Herr gebieten läßt!
Und morgen gibt's ein Flottenfest.

DIE DREI:

Der alte Herr empfing uns schlecht,
11285 Ein flottes Fest ist uns zu Recht.

MEPHISTOPHELES *(ad Spectatores):*

Auch hier geschieht, was längst geschah,
Denn Naboths Weinberg war schon da.
(Regum I, 21.)

TIEFE NACHT.

LYNCEUS DER TÜRMER *(auf der Schloßwarte singend):*

Zum Sehen geboren,
Zum Schauen bestellt,
11290 Dem Turme geschworen,
Gefällt mir die Welt.
Ich blick in die Ferne,

Are you not used to colonize?

FAUST:

Go then, get them out of the way!—
You know the small but fair estate
I offered them at any rate.

MEPHISTO:

First carried off and landed then,
Before you look, they stand again.
And after violence and wiles,
A pleasant sojourn reconciles.
(He whistles shrilly. THE THREE *enter.)*

MEPHISTO:

Do what he wants once more at least!
Tomorrow you shall have a feast.

THE THREE:

The ancient gent was very curt;
A boisterous feast is our desert.

MEPHISTO *(ad spectatores):*

Here, too, occurs what long occurred:
Of Naboth's vineyard you have heard.
(I Kings 21)

DEEP NIGHT

LYNCEUS THE TOWER WARDEN *(singing on the watch tower of the castle):*

To see I was born,
To look is my call,
To the tower sworn,
I delight in all.
I glance out far

Ich seh in der Näh
Den Mond und die Sterne,
11295 Den Wald und das Reh.
So seh ich in allen
Die ewige Zier,
Und wie mir's gefallen,
Gefall ich auch mir.
11300 Ihr glücklichen Augen,
Was je ihr gesehn,
Es sei, wie es wolle,
Es war doch so schön! *(Pause.)*

Nicht allein mich zu ergetzen,
11305 Bin ich hier so hoch gestellt;
Welch ein greuliches Entsetzen
Droht mir aus der finstern Welt!
Funkenblicke seh ich sprühen
Durch der Linden Doppelnacht;
11310 Immer stärker wühlt ein Glühen,
Von der Zugluft angefacht.
Ach! Die innre Hütte lodert,
Die bemoost und feucht gestanden;
Schnelle Hilfe wird gefodert,
11315 Keine Rettung ist vorhanden.
Ach, die guten alten Leute,
Sonst so sorglich um das Feuer,
Werden sie dem Qualm zur Beute!
Welch ein schrecklich Abenteuer!
11320 Flamme flammet, rot in Gluten
Steht das schwarze Moosgestelle;
Retteten sich nur die Guten
Aus der wildentbrannten Hölle!
Züngelnd lichte Blitze steigen
11325 Zwischen Blättern, zwischen Zweigen;
Äste dürr, die flackernd brennen,
Glühen schnell und stürzen ein.
Sollt ihr Augen dies erkennen!

And see what is near,
The moon and the stars,
The wood and the deer.
In all things I see
The eternally bright,
And as they please me,
In myself I delight.
You blessèd eyes,
What you saw everywhere,
It be as it may,
It was, oh, so fair! *(Pause.)*

But not for my joy alone
I am placed at such a height;
What a hideous threat has grown
Under me out of the night!
Flashing, I see spark on spark
In the lindens' double dark;
Strong and stronger grows their glow,
As the drafty breezes blow.
Now the cottage is aflame,
Though its mossy walls seemed wet;
Help is lacking—if it came,
Maybe, they could save it yet!
Oh, the good old people there,
Always careful with their fire,
Will be lost in smoke and flare!
Dread event! The flames leap higher;
Now the scarlet core stands lonely
In the black moss-covered shell.
If the good old folks could only
Save themselves out of this hell!
Now a tongue of fire lashes
At the foliage, lightning flashes;
Branches blazing in the night
Flare and fall like shooting stars.
Eyes, must you behold this sight!

Muß ich so weitsichtig sein!
11330 Das Kapellchen bricht zusammen
Von der Äste Sturz und Last.
Schlängelnd sind mit spitzen Flammen
Schon die Gipfel angefaßt.
Bis zur Wurzel glühn die hohlen
11335 Stämme, purpurrot im Glühn.–
(Lange Pause, Gesang.)

Was sich sonst dem Blick empfohlen,
Mit Jahrhunderten ist hin.

FAUST *(auf dem Balkon, gegen die Dünen):*
Von oben welch ein singend
Wimmern?
Das Wort ist hier, der Ton zu spat.
11340 Mein Türmer jammert; mich im Innern
Verdrießt die ungeduldge Tat.
Doch sei der Lindenwuchs vernichtet
Zu halbverkohlter Stämme Graun,
Ein Luginsland ist bald errichtet,
11345 Um ins Unendliche zu schaun.
Da seh ich auch die neue Wohnung,
Die jenes alte Paar umschließt,
Das im Gefühl großmütiger Schonung
Der späten Tage froh genießt.

MEPHISTOPHELES UND DIE DREIE *(unten):*
11350 Da kommen wir mit vollem Trab;
Verzeiht! Es ging nicht gütlich ab.
Wir klopften an, wir pochten an,
Und immer ward nicht aufgetan;
Wir rüttelten, wir pochten fort,
11355 Da lag die morsche Türe dort;
Wir riefen laut und drohten schwer,
Allein wir fanden kein Gehör.
Und wie's in solchem Fall geschicht,
Sie hörten nicht, sie wollten nicht;
11360 Wir aber haben nicht gesäumt,

Must you see so very far!
Now the falling branches crash
Through the chapel, it falls down,
As the flames, like serpents, dash
To embrace the lindens' crown.
To their roots the hollow trees
Have turned crimson.
(Long pause. Song.)

What for many centuries
Pleased all eyes—now is gone.

FAUST *(on the balcony, facing the dunes):*
From up there, what a whining squeal?
It is too late to speak or plead.
My warden wails; at heart I feel
Annoyed at this impatient deed.
The lindens are part of the past,
Charred trunks are of no benefit;
Yet a good lookout is built fast
To gaze into the infinite.
The new estate I also see
Where the old couple has been sent:
Glad of my generosity
They'll spend their last years there content.

MEPHISTO AND THE THREE *(below):*
Here we come, racing like a horse.
Forgive, but we had to use force.
We banged and knocked and raised a din,
But they just would not let us in;
We shook a bit and banged some more,
And there it lay, that rotten door.
We shouted and we made a threat,
But did not get a hearing yet.
It was as often with this pair, too:
They did not hear, they did not care to:
But we did not make much ado,

Behende dir sie weggeräumt.
Das Paar hat sich nicht viel gequält,
Vor Schrecken fielen sie entseelt.
Ein Fremder, der sich dort versteckt
11365 Und fechten wollte, ward gestreckt.
In wilden Kampfes kurzer Zeit
Von Kohlen, ringsumher gestreut,
Entflammte Stroh. Nun lodert's frei
Als Scheiterhaufen dieser drei.

FAUST:
11370 Wart ihr für meine Worte taub?
Tausch wollt ich, wollte keinen Raub.
Dem unbesonnenen wilden Streich,
Ihm fluch ich; teilt es unter euch!

CHORUS:
Das alte Wort, das Wort erschallt:
11375 Gehorche willig der Gewalt!
Und bist du kühn und hältst du Stich,
So wage Haus und Hof und–dich.
(Ab.)

FAUST *(auf dem Balkon):*
Die Sterne bergen Blick und Schein,
Das Feuer sinkt und lodert klein;
11380 Ein Schauerwindchen fächelt's an,
Bringt Rauch und Dunst zu mir heran.
Geboten schnell, zu schnell getan!–
Was schwebet schattenhaft heran?

MITTERNACHT.

Vier graue Weiber treten auf.

ERSTE:
Ich heiße der Mangel.

And quickly cleared them out for you.
The couple did not suffer much,
Fright stopped their hearts with scarce a touch.
A stranger who had been concealed
Fought and was left upon the field.
And as we fought, he stood his ground,
And coals were lying all around,
The straw flared up. It burns, you see,
A pretty pyre for those three.

FAUST:
Did you not hear me that I bade
Not robbery but simply trade?
The ill-considered, savage blow
I curse herewith; share it, and go!

CHORUS:
The ancient word still makes good sense:
Succumb at once to violence!
If you are bold and don't give in,
Then risk your house and home and—skin.
(Exeunt.)

FAUST *(on the balcony)*:
The stars conceal their light and glow,
The fire flickers and ebbs low;
A little breeze blows toward the bog,
And brings me clouds of smoke and fog.
Commanded fast, too fast obeyed!—
What hovers toward me like a shade?

MIDNIGHT

Four gray women enter.

FIRST:
I am called Want.

ZWEITE:

Ich heiße die Schuld.

DRITTE:

11385 Ich heiße die Sorge.

VIERTE:

Ich heiße die Not.

ZU DREI:

Die Tür ist verschlossen, wir können nicht ein;
Drin wohnet ein Reicher, wir mögen nicht 'nein.

MANGEL:

Da werd ich zum Schatten.

SCHULD:

Da werd ich zunicht.

NOT:

Man wendet von mir das verwöhnte Gesicht.

SORGE:

11390 Ihr Schwestern, ihr könnt nicht und dürft nicht hinein.
Die Sorge, sie schleicht sich durchs Schlüsselloch ein.

(Sorge verschwindet.)

MANGEL:

Ihr, graue Geschwister, entfernt euch von hier!

SCHULD:

Ganz nah an der Seite verbind ich mich dir.

NOT:

Ganz nah an der Ferse begleitet die Not.

ZU DREI:

11395 Es ziehen die Wolken, es schwinden die Sterne!
Dahinten, dahinten! Von ferne, von ferne,
Da kommt er, der Bruder, da kommt er, der – – –
Tod.

FAUST *(im Palast):*

Vier sah ich kommen, drei nur gehn;
Den Sinn der Rede konnt ich nicht verstehn.
11400 Es klang so nach, als hieß es–Not,
Ein düstres Reimwort folgte–Tod.

SECOND:

I am called Guilt.

THIRD:

I am called Care.

FOURTH:

I am called Need.

THREE OF THEM:

The door has been locked, we cannot get in;
A rich man lives in there, we would not go in.

WANT:

I am turned a shadow.

GUILT:

I am out of place.

NEED:

From me he would turn his pampered face.

CARE:

My sisters, you cannot and may not go there.

But in through the key hole, there sneaks in Care.

(CARE *disappears.*)

WANT:

My sisters in gray, you must vanish from here.

GUILT:

I join you; where you are, there I am near.

NEED:

Need follows; where you are, one feels my breath.

THE THREE:

The clouds are drifting and hide every star.
Behind there, behind there, from far, from far,
Comes our brother; there comes, there comes—
Death.

FAUST *(in the palace)*:

Four I saw coming, three only go hence;
I heard them speak, but grasped not the sense.
They spoke of Need and of her breath.
A gloomy rhyme word followed—Death.

Es tönte hohl, gespensterhaft gedämpft.
Noch hab ich mich ins Freie nicht gekämpft.
Könnt ich Magie von meinem Pfad entfernen,
11405 Die Zaubersprüche ganz und gar verlernen,
Stünd ich, Natur, vor dir ein Mann allein,
Da wär's der Mühe wert, ein Mensch zu sein.

Das war ich sonst, eh ich's im Düstern suchte,
Mit Frevelwort mich und die Welt verfluchte.
11410 Nun ist die Luft von solchem Spuk so voll,
Daß niemand weiß, wie er ihn meiden soll.
Wenn auch ein Tag uns klar vernünftig lacht,
In Traumgespinst verwickelt uns die Nacht;
Wir kehren froh von junger Flur zurück,
11415 Ein Vogel krächzt; was krächzt er? Mißgeschick.
Von Aberglauben früh und spat umgarnt,
Es eignet sich, es zeigt sich an, es warnt.
Und so verschüchtert, stehen wir allein.
Die Pforte knarrt, und niemand kommt herein.
(Erschüttert.)
11420 Ist jemand hier?

SORGE:
Die Frage fordert Ja!

FAUST:
Und du, wer bist denn du?

SORGE:
Bin einmal da.

FAUST:
Entferne dich!

SORGE:
Ich bin am rechten Ort.

FAUST *(erst ergrimmt, dann besänftigt, für sich).*
Nimm dich in acht und sprich kein Zauberwort!

SORGE:
Würde mich kein Ohr vernehmen,
11425 Müßt es doch im Herzen dröhnen;
In verwandelter Gestalt

It sounded hollow, ghostlike, as a threat.
I have not fought my way to freedom yet.
Could I but banish witchcraft from my road,
Unlearn all magic spells—oh, if I stood
Before you, Nature, human without guile,
The toil of being man might be worthwhile.

Once I was that, before I searched the night,
Damning myself and life with words of spite:
But now the air is so full of these ghosts
That no one knows how to escape their hosts.
And if one day smiles, rational and bright,
We are yet caught in dreamy webs at night;
We come home happy from the green young lea,
A bird will croak; croak what? Calamity.
Enmeshed by superstition, we're forlorn:
For things will happen, and forebode, and warn.
Frightened, we stand alone; our blood runs thin.
The portal creaks, but no one has come in.

(Deeply agitated):

Is someone there?

CARE:

The question calls for Yes.

FAUST:

And you, who might you be?

CARE:

I found access.

FAUST:

Leave me!

CARE:

This is where I should be.

FAUST *(first irate, then calmer, to himself):*

Beware and speak no word of sorcery.

CARE:

Though no ear perceived a sound,
Yet the heart would hear and pound;
In all forms, at every hour,

Üb ich grimmige Gewalt.
Auf den Pfaden, auf der Welle,
Ewig ängstlicher Geselle,
11430 Stets gefunden, nie gesucht,
So geschmeichelt wie verflucht.–
Hast du die Sorge nie gekannt?

FAUST:

Ich bin nur durch die Welt gerannt;
Ein jed Gelüst ergriff ich bei den Haaren,
11435 Was nicht genügte, ließ ich fahren,
Was mir entwischte, ließ ich ziehn.
Ich habe nur begehrt und nur vollbracht
Und abermals gewünscht und so mit Macht
Mein Leben durchgestürmt; erst groß und mächtig,
11440 Nun aber geht es weise, geht bedächtig.
Der Erdenkreis ist mir genug bekannt.
Nach drüben ist die Aussicht uns verrannt;
Tor, wer dorthin die Augen blinzelnd richtet,
Sich über Wolken seinesgleichen dichtet!
11445 Er stehe fest und sehe hier sich um;
Dem Tüchtigen ist diese Welt nicht stumm.
Was braucht er in die Ewigkeit zu schweifen!
Was er erkennt, läßt sich ergreifen.
Er wandle so den Erdentag entlang;
11450 Wenn Geister spuken, geh er seinen Gang,
Im Weiterschreiten find er Qual und Glück,
Er, unbefriedigt jeden Augenblick!

SORGE:

Wen ich einmal mir besitze,
Dem ist alle Welt nichts nütze;
11455 Ewiges Düstre steigt herunter,
Sonne geht nicht auf noch unter,
Bei vollkommen äußern Sinnen
Wohnen Finsternisse drinnen,
Und er weiß von allen Schätzen
11460 Sich nicht in Besitz zu setzen.

I wield the most cruel power.
On the road and on the sea,
Ever-anxious company,
Always found and always nursed,
Never sought, and always cursed.
Is Care a force you never faced?

FAUST:

Through all the world I only raced:
Whatever I might crave, I laid my hand on,
What would not do, I would abandon,
And what escaped, I would let go.
I only would desire and attain,
And wish for more, and thus with might and main
I stormed through life; first powerful and great,
But now with calmer wisdom, and sedate.
The earthly sphere I know sufficiently,
But into the beyond we cannot see;
A fool, that squints and tries to pierce those
shrouds,
And would invent his like above the clouds!
Let him survey this life, be resolute,
For to the able this world is not mute.
Why fly into eternities?
What man perceives, that he can seize.
Thus he may wander through his earthly day;
Heedless of ghosts, let him pursue his way,
In his progression agony and joy,
At every moment still dissatisfied.

CARE:

He whom I have conquered could
Own the world and not feel good:
Gloom surrounds him without end,
Sun shall not rise nor descend;
Though his senses all abide,
Darknesses now dwell inside,
And though he owned every treasure,
None should give him any pleasure;

Glück und Unglück wird zur Grille,
Er verhungert in der Fülle;
Sei es Wonne, sei es Plage,
Schiebt er's zu dem andern Tage,
11465 Ist der Zukunft nur gewärtig,
Und so wird es niemals fertig.

FAUST:

Hör auf! So kommst du mir nicht bei!
Ich mag nicht solchen Unsinn hören.
Fahr hin! Die schlechte Litanei,
11470 Sie könnte selbst den klügsten Mann betören.

SORGE:

Soll er gehen, soll er kommen?
Der Entschluß ist ihm genommen;
Auf gebahnten Weges Mitte
Wankt er tastend halbe Schritte,
11475 Er verliert sich immer tiefer,
Siehet alle Dinge schiefer,
Sich und andre lästig drückend,
Atem holend und erstickend;
Nicht erstickt und ohne Leben,
11480 Nicht verzweifelnd, nicht ergeben.
So ein unaufhaltsam Rollen,
Schmerzlich Lassen, widrig Sollen,
Bald Befreien, bald Erdrücken,
Halber Schlaf und schlecht Erquicken
11485 Heftet ihn an seine Stelle
Und bereitet ihn zur Hölle.

FAUST:

Unselige Gespenster! So behandelt ihr
Das menschliche Geschlecht zu tausend Malen;
Gleichgültige Tage selbst verwandelt ihr
11490 In garstigen Wirrwarr netzumstrickter Qualen.
Dämonen, weiß ich, wird man schwerlich los,
Das geistig-strenge Band ist nicht zu trennen;
Doch deine Macht, o Sorge, schleichend groß,
Ich werde sie nicht anerkennen.

Luck and ill luck turn to anguish,
In his plenty he must languish;
Be it rapture or dismay,
He will wait another day,
Worry lest the future vanish,
And so he can never finish.

FAUST:

Be still! You cannot thus catch *me!*
I will not have such stupid rant.
Leave me! This wretched litany
Could fool even the wisest with its chant.

CARE:

Should he go, or should he come?
All decision has grown numb;
In the midst of well-paved places
He reels, groping, in half paces.
As he sinks and is more thwarted,
Everything grows more distorted;
Burdening himself and others,
Breathing deeply, he yet smothers;
Not quite smothered, not quite dead,
Not resigned, but full of dread.
Ceaselessly he alternates—
Yields, resenting; must, but hates;
Liberated, then enmeshed,
Barely sleeping, unrefreshed,
He is pinned down in his cell
And prepared to go to hell.

FAUST:

Oh, wretched specters, thus you persecute
The human race with thousand miseries;
Days that might be indifferent, you transmute
Into a monstrous mesh of tangled agonies.
Demons, I know, are hard to drive away,
One cannot break the spirits' iron ties;
And yet your power, Care, creeping and great,
I shall refuse to recognize.

SORGE:

11495 Erfahre sie, wie ich geschwind
Mich mit Verwünschung von dir wende!
Die Menschen sind im ganzen Leben blind,
Nun, Fauste, werde du's am Ende!
(Sie haucht ihn an. Ab.)

FAUST *(erblindet):*
Die Nacht scheint tiefer tief hereinzudringen,
11500 Allein im Innern leuchtet helles Licht;
Was ich gedacht, ich eil es zu vollbringen;
Des Herren Wort, es gibt allein Gewicht.
Vom Lager auf, ihr Knechte! Mann für Mann!
Laßt glücklich schauen, was ich kühn ersann.
11505 Ergreift das Werkzeug, Schaufel rührt und Spaten!
Das Abgesteckte muß sogleich geraten.
Auf strenges Ordnen, raschen Fleiß
Erfolgt der allerschönste Preis;
Daß sich das größte Werk vollende,
11510 Genügt ein Geist für tausend Hände.

GROßER VORHOF DES PALASTS.

Fackeln.

MEPHISTOPHELES *(als Aufseher voran):*
Herbei, Herbei! Herein, herein!
Ihr schlotternden Lemuren,
Aus Bändern, Sehnen und Gebein
Geflickte Halbnaturen!

LEMUREN *(im Chor):*
11515 Wir treten dir sogleich zur Hand,
Und wie wir halb vernommen,

CARE:

Experience it deep in your mind,
As with a curse I now descend!
The human being is, his life long, blind;
Thus, Faustus, you shall meet your end.
(She breathes on him. Exit.)

FAUST *(blinded):*

Deep night now seems to fall more deeply still,
Yet inside me there shines a brilliant light;
What I have thought, I hasten to fulfill:
The master's word alone has real might.
Up from your straw, my servants! Every man!
Let happy eyes behold my daring plan.
Take up your tools, stir shovel now and spade!
What has been staked out must at once be made.
Precise design, swift exercise
Will always win the fairest prize;
To make the grandest dream come true,
One mind for thousand hands will do.

LARGE OUTER COURT OF THE PALACE.

Torches.

MEPHISTO *(in front, as overseer):*

Come here, come here! Come on, come on!
You shaking Lemures,
From tendons, tissues, and from bone,
Patched-up congeries.

LEMURES *(in chorus):*

We come at once, are at your hand,
And we half heard it thus:

Es gilt wohl gar ein weites Land,
Das sollen wir bekommen.

Gespitzte Pfähle, die sind da,
11520 Die Kette lang zum Messen;
Warum an uns der Ruf geschah,
Das haben wir vergessen.

MEPHISTOPHELES:

Hier gilt kein künstlerisch Bemühn;
Verfahret nur nach eignen Maßen!
11525 Der Längste lege längelang sich hin,
Ihr andern lüftet ringsumher den Rasen;
Wie man's für unsre Väter tat,
Vertieft ein längliches Quadrat!
Aus dem Palast ins enge Haus,
11530 So dumm läuft es am Ende doch hinaus.

LEMUREN *(mit neckischen Gebärden grabend):*

Wie jung ich war und lebt und liebt,
Mich deucht, das war wohl süße;
Wo's fröhlich klang und lustig ging,
Da rührten sich meine Füße.
11535 Nun hat das tückische Alter mich
Mit seiner Krücke getroffen;
Ich stolpert über Grabes Tür,
Warum stand sie just offen!

FAUST *(aus dem Palaste tretend, tastet an den Türpfosten):*

Wie das Geklirr der Spaten mich ergetzt!
11540 Es ist die Menge, die mir frönet,
Die Erde mit sich selbst versöhnet,
Den Wellen ihre Grenze setzt,
Das Meer mit strengem Band umzieht.

MEPHISTOPHELES *(beiseite):*

Du bist doch nur für uns bemüht
11545 Mit deinen Dämmen, deinen Buhnen;
Denn du bereitest schon Neptunen,
Dem Wasserteufel, großen Schmaus.

There is to be a spacious land,
And it will be for us.

The pointed stakes, they are all here,
We brought the chain to plot;
But why you asked us to appear,
That we have clear forgot.

MEPHISTO:

This is no time for artistry;
Use your own measure, that suits me.
The longest lie down, stretch out on the ground,
And all the rest can lift the grass around;
As it was our fathers' fare,
Dig out a somewhat oblong square!
From palace to a narrow crate,
That is how stupidly things terminate.

LEMURES *(digging, with mocking gestures):*

In youth, when I would live and love,
Methought that this was sweet;
Where they were gay, sang merrily,
There I would stir my feet.
Now age has come with stealthy steps
And struck me with his crutch;
I stumbled over the grave's door;
Why did it yawn so much!

FAUST *(stepping out of the palace, gropes along the doorposts):*

How the spades' lusty clanking gives me mirth!
It is the throng that slaves for me,
And brings back to itself the earth,
Setting the waves a boundary,
Putting a bond around the ocean.

MEPHISTO *(aside):*

For *us* alone is your commotion,
Your dams and dikes and all your care:
It is for Neptune you prepare,
The Water Devil, a repast.

In jeder Art seid ihr verloren—
Die Elemente sind mit uns verschworen,
11550 Und auf Vernichtung läuft's hinaus.

FAUST:
Aufseher!

MEPHISTOPHELES:
Hier!

FAUST:
Wie es auch möglich sei,
Arbeiter schaffe Meng auf Menge,
Ermuntre durch Genuß und Strenge,
Bezahle, locke, presse bei!
11555 Mit jedem Tage will ich Nachricht haben,
Wie sich verlängt der unternommene
Graben.

MEPHISTOPHELES *(halblaut)*:
Man spricht, wie man mir Nachricht gab,
Von keinem Graben, doch vom Grab.

FAUST:
Ein Sumpf zieht am Gebirge hin,
11560 Verpestet alles schon Errungene;
Den faulen Pfuhl auch abzuziehn,
Das letzte wär das Höchsterrungene.
Eröffn' ich Räume vielen Millionen,
Nicht sicher zwar, doch tätig-frei zu
wohnen.
11565 Grün das Gefilde, fruchtbar; Mensch und
Herde
Sogleich behaglich auf der neusten Erde,
Gleich angesiedelt an des Hügels Kraft,
Den aufgewälzt kühn-emsige Völkerschaft.
Im Innern hier ein paradiesisch Land,
11570 Da rase draußen Flut bis auf zum Rand,
Und wie sie nascht, gewaltsam
einzuschießen,
Gemeindrang eilt, die Lücke zu
verschließen.

You cannot do what you desire:
With *us* the elements conspire,
And ruin reaps your crop at last.

FAUST:

Overseer!

MEPHISTO:

Here!

FAUST:

Feel free to use finesse;
Get throngs and throngs of laborers here,
Spur on with pleasure or severe,
Use ample pay, allure, or press!
And every day inform me how the throng
Has pushed the groove we undertook along.

MEPHISTO *(aside)*:

One talks, if my ears still behave,
Not of a groove, but of a grave.

FAUST:

A swamp still skirts the mountain chain
And poisons all the land retrieved;
This marshland I hope yet to drain,
And thus surpass what we achieved.
For many millions I shall open regions
To dwell, not safe, in free and active legions.
Green are the meadows, fertile; and in mirth
Both men and herds live on this newest earth,
Settled along the edges of a hill
That has been raised by bold men's zealous will.
A veritable paradise inside,
Then let the dams be licked by raging tide;
And as it nibbles to rush in with force,
A common will fills gaps and checks its course.

Ja! Diesem Sinne bin ich ganz ergeben,
Das ist der Weisheit letzter Schluß:
11575 Nur der verdient sich Freiheit wie das
Leben,
Der täglich sie erobern muß.
Und so verbringt, umrungen von Gefahr,
Hier Kindheit, Mann und Greis sein tüchtig
Jahr.
Solch ein Gewimmel möcht ich sehn,
11580 Auf freiem Grund mit freiem Volke stehn.
Zum Augenblicke dürft ich sagen:
Verweile doch, du bist so schön!
Es kann die Spur von meinen Erdetagen
Nicht in Äonen untergehn.—
11585 Im Vorgefühl von solchem hohen Glück
Genieß ich jetzt den höchsten Augenblick.
(Faust sinkt zurück, die Lemuren fassen ihn auf und legen ihn auf den Boden.)

MEPHISTOPHELES:
Ihn sättigt keine Lust, ihm gnügt kein Glück,
So buhlt er fort nach wechselnden Gestalten;
Den letzten, schlechten, leeren Augenblick,
11590 Der Arme wünscht ihn festzuhalten.
Der mir so kräftig widerstand,
Die Zeit wird Herr, der Greis hier liegt im Sand.
Die Uhr steht still—

CHOR:
Steht still! Sie schweigt wie Mitternacht.
Der Zeiger fällt.

MEPHISTOPHELES:
Er fällt, es ist vollbracht.

CHOR:
11595 Es ist vorbei.

MEPHISTOPHELES:
Vorbei! Ein dummes Wort.

This is the highest wisdom that I own,
The best that mankind ever knew:
Freedom and life are earned by those alone
Who conquer them each day anew.
Surrounded by such danger, each one thrives,
Childhood, manhood, and age lead active lives.
At such a throng I would fain stare,
With free men on free ground their freedom share.
Then, to the moment I might say:
Abide, you are so fair!
The traces of my earthly day
No aeons can impair.
As I presage a happiness so high,
I now enjoy the highest moment.

(FAUST *sinks back, the* LEMURES *catch him and lay him on the ground.)*

MEPHISTO:

Fie!
No pleasure sated him, no great bestowment,
He reeled from form to form, it did not last;
The final, wretched, empty moment,
The poor man wishes to hold fast.
He sturdily resisted all my toil;
Time conquers, old he lies here on the soil.
The clock has stopped—

CHORUS:

Has stopped! Like midnight, all life is diminished.
The hand has fallen.

MEPHISTO:

Fallen, it is finished.

CHORUS:

It is all over.

MEPHISTO:

Over! What a stupid name.

Warum vorbei?
Vorbei und reines Nicht, vollkommnes
Einerlei.
Was soll uns denn das ewge Schaffen!
Geschaffenes zu nichts hinwegzuraffen!
11600 «Da ist's vorbei!» Was ist daran zu lesen?
Es ist so gut, als wär es nicht gewesen,
Und treibt sich doch im Kreis, als wenn es
wäre.
Ich liebte mir dafür das Ewig-Leere.

GRABLEGUNG.

LEMUR: *Solo.*
Wer hat das Haus so schlecht gebaut
11605 Mit Schaufeln und mit Spaten?
LEMUREN: *Chor.*
Dir, dumpfer Gast im hänfnen Gewand,
Ist's viel zu gut geraten.
LEMUR: *Solo.*
Wer hat den Saal so schlecht versorgt?
Wo blieben Tisch und Stühle?
LEMUREN: *Chor.*
11610 Es war auf kurze Zeit geborgt;
Der Gläubiger sind so viele.
MEPHISTOPHELES:
Der Körper liegt, und will der Geist entfliehn,
Ich zeig ihm rasch den blutgeschriebnen Titel;
Doch leider hat man jetzt so viele Mittel,
11615 Dem Teufel Seelen zu entziehn.
Auf altem Wege stößt man an,
Auf neuem sind wir nicht empfohlen;

Why over?
Over and pure nothing, it is all the same.
Why have eternally creation,
When all is subject to annihilation?
Now it is over. What meaning can one see?
It is as if it had not come to be,
And yet it circulates as if it were.
I should prefer—Eternal Emptiness.

ENTOMBMENT.

LEMUR *(solo):*
Who has so badly built the house
With shovel and with spade?

LEMURES *(Chorus):*
For you, glum guest in a shroud of hemp,
Too well it has been made.

LEMUR *(solo):*
Who decked the hall in such poor style?
No table and no chair?

LEMURES *(Chorus):*
It was borrowed for a little while;
There are lenders everywhere.

MEPHISTO:
There lies the body; if the soul would fly away,
I shall confront it with the blood-signed scroll.
Alas, they have so many means today
To rob the Devil of a soul.
Our ancient manner is too crude,
The new way does not work too well;

Sonst hätt ich es allein getan,
Jetzt muß ich Helfershelfer holen.

11620 Uns geht's in allen Dingen schlecht!
Herkömmliche Gewohnheit, altes Recht,
Man kann auf gar nichts mehr vertrauen.
Sonst mit dem letzten Atem fuhr sie aus,
Ich paßt ihr auf und wie die schnellste Maus,
11625 Schnapps, hielt ich sie in fest verschloßnen Klauen.
Nun zaudert sie und will den düstern Ort,
Des schlechten Leichnams ekles Haus nicht lassen;
Die Elemente, die sich hassen,
Die treiben sie am Ende schmählich fort.
11630 Und wenn ich Tag und Stunden mich zerplage,
Wann? wie? und wo? das ist die leidige Frage;
Der alte Tod verlor die rasche Kraft,
Das Ob? sogar ist lange zweifelhaft;
Oft sah ich lüstern auf die starren Glieder—
11635 Es war nur Schein, das rührte, das regte sich wieder.
(Phantastisch-flügelmännische Beschwörungsgebärden.)
Nur frisch heran! Verdoppelt euren Schritt,
Ihr Herrn vom graden, Herrn vom krummen Horne,
Von altem Teufelsschrot und -korne,
Bringt ihr zugleich den Höllenrachen mit!
11640 Zwar hat die Hölle Rachen viele, viele!
Nach Standsgebühr und Würden schlingt sie ein!
Doch wird man auch bei diesem letzten Spiele
Ins künftige nicht so bedenklich sein.
(Der greuliche Höllenrachen tut sich links auf.)
Eckzähne klaffen; dem Gewölb des Schlundes
11645 Entquillt der Feuerstrom in Wut,

I used to work in solitude,
Now I must get some help from hell.

In every way, our lot is poor:
Time-honored custom, ancient laws—
Of nothing one can now be sure.
With the last breath it used to quit the house,
I lay in wait and, like a speedy mouse,
Snap! I would hold it in relentless claws.
Now it will linger in the dismal place,
Loathe to forsake the corpse, would rather
smother—
Until the elements which hate each other
Force it at last to quit it in disgrace.
And if I fret and sweat and tear my hair,
The painful question is: When? How? and
Where?
Old death has lost his speed, he is worn out:
And even Whether? gives one cause for doubt;
Often I craved the stiffened members when
It was a sham, they stirred and moved again.

(With fantastic, flugelmanlike gestures of conjuration:)
Come on, increase your speed, don't pause,
Lords of straight horns, lords of the curve,
With ancient devils' grit and nerve,
Be sure you bring along hell's mighty jaws.
Hell, to be sure, has many jaws and swallows
With due regard for rank and worldly station;
The times have changed and, I suppose, it follows
That we, too, can show less consideration.

(The gruesome jaws of hell open up on the left.)
Incisors gape, and from the vaulting throat
The frenzied fire torrents flow,

Und in dem Siedequalm des Hintergrundes
Seh ich die Flammenstadt in ewiger Glut.
Die rote Brandung schlägt hervor bis an die
Zähne,
Verdammte, Rettung hoffend, schwimmen an;
11650 Doch kolossal zerknirscht sie die Hyäne,
Und sie erneuen ängstlich heiße Bahn.
In Winkeln bleibt noch vieles zu entdecken,
So viel Erschrecklichstes im engsten Raum!
Ihr tut sehr wohl, die Sünder zu erschrecken;
11655 Sie halten's doch für Lug und Trug und Traum.
(Zu den Dickteufeln vom kurzen, graden Horne.)
Nun, wanstige Schuften mit den Feuerbacken!
Ihr glüht so recht vom Höllenschwefel feist;
Klotzartige, kurze, nie bewegte Nacken,

Hier unten lauert, ob's wie Phosphor gleißt!
11660 Das ist das Seelchen, Psyche mit den Flügeln,
Die rupft ihr aus, so ist's ein garstiger Wurm;
Mit meinem Stempel will ich sie besiegeln,
Dann fort mit ihr im Feuerwirbelsturm!
Paßt auf die niedern Regionen,
11665 Ihr Schläuche, das ist eure Pflicht;
Ob's ihr beliebte, da zu wohnen,
So akkurat weiß man das nicht.
Im Nabel ist sie gern zu Haus—
Nehmt es in acht, sie wischt euch dort heraus.
*(Zu den Dürrteufeln vom langen, krummen
Horne.)*

11670 Ihr Firlefanze, flügelmännische Riesen,
Greift in die Luft, versucht euch ohne Rast!
Die Arme strack, die Klauen scharf gewiesen,
Daß ihr die Flatternde, die Flüchtige faßt.
Es ist ihr sicher schlecht im alten Haus,
11675 Und das Genie, es will gleich obenaus.

As in the depths, seething in steam, I note
The flaming city in eternal glow.
The crimson surf leaps up and breaks against the
teeth,
The damned seek to escape with failing force,
But the hyena mashes them; beneath,
Crazed with sheer terror, they renew their course.
Much more could be discovered in the nooks,
So much that's worst in the smallest space!
But try to frighten sinners with this place,
They shrug it off like dreams or story books.
(To the fat devils with short, straight horns:)
Now, paunchy rascals with the fiery cheeks,
The hellish sulphur made you red and fat;
Your short block-necks have never turned; you
freaks
Can watch for phosphor glow where once he sat:
That is the little soul, Psyche with wings;
You pluck them out, a nasty worm is left;
I place my stamp on her, and then one flings
Her through the fiery storm into the cleft.
You watch the lower parts with care,
You bloats, and do your duty well!
If she was pleased to dwell down there
Is rather more than we can tell.
And of the navel she is fond:
Be on your guard, that's where she might abscond!
(To the lean devils with long, curved horns:)

You harlequins, gigantic flugelmen,
Clutch at the air, keep trying without pause!
Stretch out your arms and use your pointed claws,
And catch the fluttering fugitive again!
In that decaying house she cannot stop,
And genius always strives straight for the top.

Glorie von oben rechts.

HIMMLISCHE HEERSCHAR:

Folget, Gesandte,
Himmelsverwandte,
Gemächlichen Flugs,
Sündern vergeben,
11680 Staub zu beleben;
Allen Naturen
Freundliche Spuren
Wirket im Schweben
Des weilenden Zugs!

MEPHISTOPHELES:

11685 Mißtöne hör ich, garstiges Geklimper,
Von oben kommt's mit unwillkommnem Tag;
Es ist das bübisch-mädchenhafte Gestümper,
Wie frömmelnder Geschmack sich's lieben mag.
Ihr wißt, wie wir in tiefverruchten Stunden
11690 Vernichtung sannen menschlichem Geschlecht;
Das Schändlichste, was wir erfunden,
Ist ihrer Andacht eben recht.
Sie kommen gleisnerisch, die Laffen!
So haben sie uns manchen weggeschnappt,
11695 Bekriegen uns mit unsern eignen Waffen;
Es sind auch Teufel, doch verkappt.
Hier zu verlieren, wär euch ewge Schande;
Ans Grab heran und haltet fest am Rande!

CHOR DER ENGEL *(Rosen streuend):*

Rosen, ihr blendenden,
11700 Balsam versendenden!
Flatternde, schwebende,
Heimlich belebende,
Zweiglein beflügelte,
Knospen entsiegelte,
11705 Eilet zu blühn!

Frühling entsprieße,
Purpur und Grün;

Glory from the upper right.

HEAVENLY HOST:

Follow, oh holy
Heaven's kin, slowly
In leisurely flight:
Sinners forgive,
Make the dust live;
Bring to all being
As it is seeing
Our host fleeing
A trace of delight!

MEPHISTO:

Discords I hear; a most revolting strumming
Comes from above with the unwelcome dawn;
It is the boyish-girlish bungle-humming
On which the sanctimonious like to fawn.
You know how in the most accursèd hours
We planned destruction for the human race;
The vilest product of our powers
In their devotions has a place.
The dunderheads put on their charms!
But many have been stolen in that wise,
When they were fighting us with our arms:
They, too, are devils—in disguise.
If you lose now, live in eternal shame;
Surround the grave, my hosts, defend my claim!

CHORUS OF ANGELS *(strewing roses)*:

Roses, bright glowing,
Balsam bestowing,
Fluttering and striving,
Secret reviving!
Wingèd stems golden,
Buds are unfolding;
Hasten to bloom!

Spring, do not tarry,
Color the gloom!

Tragt Paradiese
Dem Ruhenden hin!

MEPHISTOPHELES *(zu den Satanen):*

11710 Was duckt und zuckt ihr? Ist das Höllenbrauch?
So haltet stand und laßt sie streuen!
An seinen Platz ein jeder Gauch!
Sie denken wohl, mit solchen Blümeleien
Die heißen Teufel einzuschneien;
11715 Das schmilzt und schrumpft vor eurem Hauch.
Nun pustet, Püstriche!—Genug, genug!
Vor eurem Boden bleicht der ganze Flug.
Nicht so gewaltsam! Schließet Maul und Nasen!
Fürwahr, ihr habt zu stark geblasen.
11720 Daß ihr doch nie die rechten Maße kennt!
Das schrumpft nicht nur, es bräunt sich, dorrt,
es brennt!
Schon schwebt's heran mit giftig klaren Flammen;
Stemmt euch dagegen, drängt euch fest
zusammen!
Die Kraft erlischt! Dahin ist aller Mut!
11725 Die Teufel wittern fremde Schmeichelglut.

CHOR DER ENGEL:

Blüten, die seligen,
Flammen, die fröhlichen,
Liebe verbreiten sie,
Wonne bereiten sie,
11730 Herz wie es mag.
Worte, die wahren,
Äther im Klaren,
Ewigen Scharen
Überall Tag!

MEPHISTOPHELES:

11735 O Fluch! O Schande solchen Tröpfen!
Satane stehen auf den Köpfen,
Die Plumpen schlagen Rad auf Rad
Und stürzen ärschlings in die Hölle.
Gesegn' euch das verdiente heiße Bad!

Paradise carry
Into his tomb!

MEPHISTO (*to the* SATANS):
Why blink and shrink? Are these the devils' habits?
Come, stand your ground, and let them strew!
Back to your places, frightened rabbits!
They seem to think, such flower ballyhoo
Will snow in fiery devils such as you.
It melts before you even grab it:
Just puff at them, puff-heads!—Enough, enough!
Your breath has blighted all that floating stuff.
Whoa! Not so hard! Shut up your snouts and noses!
You blow too hard at those small roses.
Restraint is something you will never learn!
They do not wilt, they char, they burn!
Venomous flames approach. They are not large,
Stand close together and repel their charge!
Their courage fails, their stamina expire:
The devils scent a strange and flattering fire.

CHORUS OF ANGELS:
Bliss-scented flowers,
With fiery powers,
Heavenly love they spread,
Joy from above they spread,
All hearts they sway.
Words of verity
In ether's clarity
Bring hosts of charity
Infinite day.

MEPHISTO:
Damnation! That you are so scurvy!
The Satans have turned topsy-turvy:
The fat ones somersault to hell,
And plunge in, arses uppermost.
Enjoy the hot baths you deserve so well!

11740 Ich aber bleib auf meiner Stelle. –
(Sich mit den schwebenden Rosen herumschlagend.)
Irrlichter fort! Du, leuchte noch so stark,
Du bleibst, gehascht, ein ekler Gallert-Quark.
Was flatterst du? Willst du dich packen!
Es klemmt wie Pech und Schwefel mir im Nacken.

CHOR DER ENGEL:

11745 Was euch nicht angehört,
Müsset ihr meiden,
Was euch das Innre stört,
Dürft ihr nicht leiden.
Dringt es gewaltig ein,
11750 Müssen wir tüchtig sein.
Liebe nur Liebende
Führet herein!

MEPHISTOPHELES:

Mir brennt der Kopf, das Herz, die Leber brennt,
Ein übersteuflisch Element!
11755 Weit spitziger als Höllenfeuer.
Drum jammert ihr so ungeheuer,
Unglückliche Verliebte, die, verschmäht,
Verdrehten Halses nach der Liebsten späht.

Auch mir! Was zieht den Kopf auf jene Seite?
11760 Bin ich mit ihr doch in geschwornem Streite!
Der Anblick war mir sonst so feindlich scharf.
Hat mich ein Fremdes durch und durch gedrungen?
Ich mag sie gerne sehn, die allerliebsten Jungen;
Was hält mich ab, daß ich nicht fluchen darf?
11765 Und wenn ich mich betören lasse,
Wer heißt denn künftighin der Tor?
Die Wetterbuben, die ich hasse,
Sie kommen mir doch gar zu lieblich vor!

But I shall remain at my post.
(Fighting the floating roses.)

Will-o'-the-wisps, away! I loathe your sheen;
Once caught, you turn to filthy gelatine.
You flutter? Will you pack! And quick!
Like pitch and sulphur to my neck they stick.

ANGELS:

What is not part of your sphere
You may not share;
What fills you with fear
You cannot bear.
If the attack succeeds,
We must do valiant deeds.
Love alone leads
Loving ones there.

MEPHISTO:

My heart and liver burn, my head is rent—
A more than devilish element!
Far keener than the flames of hell!
That is why your laments excel,
Unhappy lovers who, despised, still twist
Their necks to see the loved antagonist.

I too? What draws my head that way? What for?
I'm pledged against them to eternal war!
I used to hate this sight, nothing seemed worse.
Has something alien pierced me through and
through?
They are such charming boys, I rather like the
view.
What keeps my tongue tied that I cannot curse?
If I am fooled by such sweet bait,
Who will be called a fool in days to come?
The little villains that I hate
Seem lovely, sweet, and frolicsome!

Ihr schönen Kinder, laßt mich wissen,
11770 Seid ihr nicht auch von Lucifers Geschlecht?
Ihr seid so hübsch, fürwahr, ich möcht euch küssen,
Mir ist's, als kämt ihr eben recht.
Es ist mir so behaglich, so natürlich,
Als hätt ich euch schon tausendmal gesehn;
11775 So heimlich-kätzchenhaft begierlich,
Mit jedem Blick aufs neue schöner schön.
O nähert euch, o gönnt mir e i n e n Blick!

ENGEL:

Wir kommen schon, warum weichst du zurück?
Wir nähern uns, und wenn du kannst, so bleib!
(*Die Engel nehmen, umherziehend, den ganzen Raum ein.*)

MEPHISTOPHELES (*der ins Proszenium gedrängt wird*):

11780 Ihr scheltet uns verdammte Geister
Und seid die wahren Hexenmeister;
Denn ihr verführet Mann und Weib.
Welch ein verfluchtes Abenteuer!
Ist dies das Liebeselement?
11785 Der ganze Körper steht in Feuer,
Ich fühle kaum, daß es im Nacken brennt.
Ihr schwanket hin und her, so senkt euch nieder,
Ein bißchen weltlicher bewegt die holden Glieder;
Fürwahr, der Ernst steht euch recht schön!
11790 Doch möcht ich euch nur einmal lächeln sehn;
Das wäre mir ein ewiges Entzücken.
Ich meine so, wie wenn Verliebte blicken;
Ein kleiner Zugam Mund, so ist's getan.
Dich, langer Bursche, dich mag ich am liebsten leiden,
11795 Die Pfaffenmiene will dich gar nicht kleiden,
So sieh mich doch ein wenig lüstern an!
Auch könntet ihr anständig-nackter gehen,
Das lange Faltenhemd ist übersittlich –

You darling children, let me know:
Do you not also bear Lucifer's name?
You are so handsome, I could kiss you—oh!
I could not be more glad you came.
I feel so natural, such quietude,
As if we'd met a thousand times before;
So stealthily and catlike lewd;
With every glance I like your beauty more.
Come nearer, please; grant me at least a wink!

ANGELS:

We are approaching, but why do you shrink?
We do draw near; remain there, if you can!
(The ANGELS *spread out and occupy the whole space.)*

MEPHISTO *(who is crowded into the proscenium):*

You scold us as damned apparitions,
Though you are witches and magicians;
For you seduce both maid and man.
A curse on this adventure! Shame!
Is this indeed love's element?
The entire body is aflame,
I scarcely feel how my poor neck is rent.—
You hover there, come down: I feel a passion;
Please move your lovely limbs in a more worldly fashion!
There's merit in your serious style;
But just for once I'd like to see you smile!
That would put me in an eternal trance.
I mean the way that human lovers glance;
Just move your lips, that's all—not in disgust!
You, tall one, are the fairest boy I've ever seen;
But what is unbecoming is your popish mien:
Do look at me with just a little lust!
You might be nude and still of decent mind,
The flowing shroud is much too moralizing;

Sie wenden sich – von hinten anzusehen –
11800 Die Racker sind doch gar zu appetitlich!

CHOR DER ENGEL:

Wendet zur Klarheit
Euch, liebende Flammen!
Die sich verdammen,
Heile die Wahrheit,
11805 Daß sie vom Bösen
Froh sich erlösen,
Um in dem Allverein
Selig zu sein.

MEPHISTOPHELES *(sich fassend):*

Wie wird mir! – Hiobsartig, Beul an Beule
11810 Der ganze Kerl, dem's vor sich selber graut
Und triumphiert zugleich, wenn er sich ganz durchschaut,
Wenn er auf sich und seinen Stamm vertraut;
Gerettet sind die edlen Teufelsteile,
Der Liebespuk, er wirft sich auf die Haut;
11815 Schon ausgebrannt sind die verruchten Flammen,
Und, wie es sich gehört, fluck ich euch allzusammen!

CHOR DER ENGEL:

Heilige Gluten!
Wen sie umschweben,
Fühlt sich im Leben
11820 Selig mit Guten.
Alle vereinigt
Hebt euch und preist!
Luft ist gereinigt,
Atme der Geist!

(Sie erheben sich, Faustens Unsterbliches entführend.)

MEPHISTOPHELES *(sich umsehend):*

11825 Doch wie?–Wo sind sie hingezogen?
Unmündiges Volk, du hast mich überrascht,
Sind mit der Beute himmelwärts entflogen;

They turn around—I see them from behind!
The little rogues are all-too-appetizing!

CHORUS OF ANGELS:

Turn toward clarity,
Flames of love, speed!
Those damned by deed
Are healed by verity—
Joyous retrieval
From earthly evil—
They find impunity
In cosmic unity.

MEPHISTO *(recovering self-possession):*

How do I feel! Like Job, with boil on boil,
I see myself, I shudder and recoil;
And yet I triumph, too, when I look deep within
And place my trust in my own self and kin;
Saved are the Devil's noble parts—for sin;
The love spook went no deeper than my skin;
Burnt out are the accursèd flames and done,
And, as is meet and proper, I curse you, every one!

CHORUS OF ANGELS:

Blazes that give
Those they're caressing
Infinite blessing
While they yet live!
Gather up there,
Rise and adore!
Pure is the air,
Breathe, spirit, soar!

(They rise, bearing off FAUST'S *immortal part.)*

MEPHISTO *(looking around):*

But how was that? Where did they fly?
Not yet of age, you took me by surprise,
And with your booty you fled to the sky.

Drum haben sie an dieser Gruft genascht!
Mir ist ein großer, einziger, Schatz entwendet;
11830 Die hohe Seele, die sich mir verpfändet,
Die haben sie mir pfiffig weggepascht.
Bei wem soll ich mich nun beklagen?
Wer schafft mir mein erworbnes Recht?
Du bist getäuscht in deinen alten Tagen,
11835 Du hast's verdient, es geht dir grimmig schlecht.
Ich habe schimpflich mißgehandelt,
Ein großer Aufwand—schmählich!—ist vertan;
Gemein Gelüst, absurde Liebschaft wandelt
Den ausgepichten Teufel an.
11840 Und hat mit diesem kindisch-tollen Ding
Der Klugerfahrne sich beschäftigt,
So ist fürwahr die Torheit nicht gering,
Die seiner sich am Schluß bemächtigt.

BERGSCHLUCHTEN.
Wald, Fels, Einöde.

Heilige Anachoreten gebirgauf verteilt, gelagert zwischen Klüften.

CHOR und ECHO:
Waldung, sie schwankt heran,
11845 Felsen, sie lasten dran,
Wurzeln, sie klammern an,
Stamm dicht an Stamm hinan.
Woge nach Woge spritzt,
Höhle, die tiefste, schützt.
11850 Löwen, sie schleichen stumm-
Freundlich um uns herum,
Ehren geweihten Ort,
Heiligen Liebeshort.

That's why you sought this grave with greedy
eyes!
A peerless treasure, stolen shamefully:
The noble soul that pledged itself to me
They snatched from me, and now they moralize.
To whom could I complain how I am grieved?
Who will enforce the rights that I possess?
Now, in your old days, you have been deceived;
You have deserved it, you are in distress.
At my own bungling I now feel disgust;
A great investment wasted, every shred!
Absurd feelings of love, a vulgar lust
Has turned the tough old Devil's head.
If this affair was childish all-in-all
For one so seasoned to attend,
That foolishness was certainly not small
That overwhelmed him in the end.

MOUNTAIN GORGES
FOREST, ROCK, AND DESERT

Holy Anchorites scattered up the mountainsides, encamped between clefts.

CHORUS AND ECHO:

Forests are coming near,
Towering rocks appear,
Clinging, the roots adhere,
Tree trunks are crowded here.
Wave splashes after wave,
Shelter is found in the cave.
Lions are prowling dumb—
Friendly wherever we come,
Honor the sacred place,
Treasure of love and grace.

PATER ECSTATICUS *(auf- und abschwebend):*

Ewiger Wonnebrand,
11855 Glühendes Liebeband,
Siedender Schmerz der Brust,
Schäumende Gotteslust.
Pfeile, durchdringet mich,
Lanzen, bezwinget mich,
11860 Keulen, zerschmettert mich,
Blitze, durchwettert mich!
Daß ja das Nichtige
Alles verflüchtige,
Glänze der Dauerstern,
11865 Ewiger Liebe Kern.

PATER PROFUNDUS *(tiefe Region):*

Wie Felsenabgrund mir zu Füßen
Auf tiefem Abgrund lastend ruht,
Wie tausend Bäche strahlend fließen
Zum grausen Sturz des Schaums der Flut,
11870 Wie strack mit eignem kräftigen Triebe
Der Stamm sich in die Lüfte trägt:
So ist es die allmächtige Liebe,
Die alles bildet, alles hegt.

Ist um mich her ein wildes Brausen,
11875 Als wogte Wald und Felsengrund,
Und doch stürzt, liebevoll im Sausen,
Die Wasserfülle sich zum Schlund,
Berufen, gleich das Tal zu wässern;
Der Blitz, der flammend niederschlug,
11880 Die Atmosphäre zu verbessern,
Die Gift und Dunst im Busen trug,

Sind Liebesboten, sie verkünden,
Was ewig schaffend uns umwallt.
Mein Innres mög es auch entzünden,
11885 Wo sich der Geist, verworren, kalt,
Verquält in stumpfer Sinne Schranken,

PATER ECSTATICUS *(floating to and fro):*

Blaze of eternal bliss,
Love's glowing precipice,
Seething pangs in the breast,
God's overflowing zest.
Arrows, pierce through me,
Lances, subdue me,
Bludgeons, batter me,
Lightning, shatter me!
Let what is valueless
Fall and evanesce,
My star will shine the more,
Love's everlasting core!

PATER PROFUNDUS *(deep region):*

As the abysses at my feet
Rest on a more abysmal dome,
As myriad gleaming brooks must meet
For the dread fall of flooding foam,
As with an urge to reach above,
The tree thrusts through the air impassioned,
So, too, it is almighty love
By which all things are nursed and fashioned.

Around me sounds a savage roaring,
That shakes the forest and abyss,
And yet the thundering floods are pouring
With love into the precipice,
To bring the valley life and cheer;
And lightning, flashing down in blazes,
Renews the ailing atmosphere
That was consumed by poison hazes:

They are love's heralds and proclaim
What is creative everywhere.
That they would make my insides flame
Where now my spirit dwells in care,
In fetters that dull senses wrought,

Scharfangeschloßnem Kettenschmerz.
O Gott, beschwichtige die Gedanken,
Erleuchte mein bedürftig Herz!

PATER SERAPHICUS *(mittlere Region):*

11890 Welch ein Morgenwölkchen schwebet
Durch der Tannen schwankend Haar!
Ahn ich, was im Innern lebet?
Es ist junge Geisterschar.

CHOR SELIGER KNABEN:

Sag uns, Vater, wo wir wallen,
11895 Sag uns, Guter, wer wir sind!
Glücklich sind wir, allen, allen
Ist das Dasein so gelind.

PATER SERAPHICUS:

Knaben! Mitternachts-Geborne,
Halb erschlossen Geist und Sinn,
11900 Für die Eltern gleich Verlorne,
Für die Engel zum Gewinn.
Daß ein Liebender zugegen,
Fühlt ihr wohl, so naht euch nur!
Doch von schroffen Erdewegen,
11905 Glückliche, habt ihr keine Spur.
Steigt herab in meiner Augen
Welt- und erdgemäß Organ,
Könnt sie als die euern brauchen,
Schaut euch diese Gegend an!

(Er nimmt sie in sich.)

11910 Das sind Bäume, das sind Felsen,
Wasserstrom, der abestürzt
Und mit ungeheurem Wälzen
Sich den steilen Weg verkürzt.

SELIGE KNABEN *(von innen):*

Das ist mächtig anzuschauen,
11915 Doch zu düster ist der Ort,
Schüttelt uns mit Schreck und Grauen.
Edler, Guter, laß uns fort!

Confused and cold, in bitter smart.
O God! relieve all anguished thought,
Illumine Thou my needy heart!

PATER SERAPHICUS *(middle region):*

See the cloud the dawn reveals
Through the spruces' wavering hair?
Can I guess what it conceals?
Infant spirits approach there.

CHORUS OF BLESSED BOYS:

Tell us, father, what we're seeing,
Tell us, please, what we have done,
Who we are, so blesséd: Being
Is so kind to every one.

PATER SERAPHICUS:

Born at midnight on the earth,
Half unsealed spirit and brain,
For their parents lost at birth,
For the angels sweetest gain.
That a loving one is present
You can feel; come to my place!
Of earth's ways, rude and unpleasant,
Happily, you have no trace.
Enter deep into my eyes,
Organs for the earthly sphere,
They are yours to utilize:
Look upon this landscape here!
(He receives them into himself.)

These are trees, and these are rocks,
Thundering torrents, glistening spray
Plunge over tremendous blocks,
Shortening their craggy way.

BLESSED BOYS *(from within):*

What we see is full of might,
But too somber to conceive;
We are shaken with sheer fright.
Noble, good one, let us leave!

PATER SERAPHICUS:

Steigt hinan zu höherm Kreise,
Wachset immer unvermerkt,
11920 Wie nach ewig reiner Weise
Gottes Gegenwart verstärkt.
Denn das ist der Geister Nahrung,
Die im freisten Äther waltet,
Ewigen Liebens Offenbarung,
11925 Die zur Seligkeit entfaltet.

CHOR SELIGER KNABEN *(um die höchsten Gipfel kreisend):*

Hände verschlinget
Freudig zum Ringverein,
Regt euch und singet
Heilge Gefühle drein!
11930 Göttlich belehret,
Dürft ihr vertrauen;
Den ihr verehret,
Werdet ihr schauen.

ENGEL *(schwebend in der höheren Atmosphäre, Faustens Unsterbliches tragend):*

Gerettet is das edle Glied
11935 Der Geisterwelt vom Bösen:
«Wer immer strebend sich bemüht,
Den können wir erlösen.»
Und hat an ihm die Liebe gar
Von oben teilgenommen,
11940 Begegnet ihm die selige Schar
Mit herzlichem Willkommen.

DIE JÜNGEREN ENGEL:

Jene Rosen aus den Händen
Liebend-heiliger Büßerinnen
Halfen uns den Sieg gewinnen,
11945 Uns das hohe Werk vollenden,
Diesen Seelenschatz erbeuten.
Böse wichen, als wir streuten,
Teufel flohen, als wir trafen.

PATER SERAPHICUS:

Rise now to a higher spere,
Growing swiftly all along,
As God's presence, pure and clear,
Makes you and all spirits strong.
For in the celestial field
That becomes the spirits' food:
Timeless loving is revealed,
That unfolds beatitude.

CHORUS OF BLESSED BOYS *(circling around the highest peaks):*

Hand in hand clinging,
Joyously reeling,
Stirring and singing
Of holy feeling,
Divinely inspired,
You may be bold;
Whom you admired
You will be behold.

ANGELS *(floating through the higher atmosphere, carrying* FAUST'S *immortal part):*

Saved is the spirit kingdom's flower
From evil and the grave:
"Who ever strives with all his power,
We are allowed to save."
And if, besides, supernal love
Responded to his plight,
The blessed host comes from above
To greet him in delight.

THE YOUNGER ANGELS:

Loving-holy women gave,
Penitent, the rose to me
That helped win the victory,
Helped the lofty work conclude
And this precious soul to save.
Evil ones fled as we strewed,
Devils yielded as we hit them.

Statt gewohnter Höllenstrafen
11950 Fühlten Liebesqual die Geister;
Selbst der alte Satansmeister
War von spitzer Pein durchdrungen.
Jauchzet auf! Es ist gelungen.

DIE VOLLENDETEREN ENGEL:

Uns bleibt ein Erdenrest
11955 Zu tragen peinlich,
Und wär er von Asbest,
Er ist nicht reinlich.
Wenn starke Geisteskraft
Die Elemente
11960 An sich herangerafft,
Kein Engel trennte
Geeinte Zwienatur
Der innigen beiden,
Die ewige Liebe nur
11965 Vermag's zu scheiden.

DIE JÜNGEREN ENGEL:

Nebelnd um Felsenhöh
Spür ich soeben,
Regend sich in der Näh,
Ein Geisterleben.
11970 Die Wölkchen werden klar,
Ich seh bewegte Schar
Seliger Knaben,
Los von der Erde Druck,
Im Kreis gesellt,
11975 Die sich erlaben
Am neuen Lenz und Schmuck
Der obern Welt.
Sei er zum Anbeginn,
Steigendem Vollgewinn
11980 Diesen gesellt!

DIE SELIGEN KNABEN:

Freudig empfangen wir
Diesen im Puppenstand;

Hell's torments no longer bit them,
Love's pangs sealed their swift disaster;
Even the old Satans' Master
Felt the pain; he, too, retreated.
Jubilate! it is completed.

THE MORE PERFECTED ANGELS:

To carry earth's remains
Still has distressed us:
All earthly things have stains,
Even asbestos.
When every element
Has served the force
Of a strong spirit's bent,
No angel can divorce
Two thus together grown
In close communion;
Eternal love alone
Can part their union.

THE YOUNGER ANGELS:

Misty round rocky height
I now discover,
Stirring in nearby flight
Spirits that hover.
The clouds part and grow clear,
I see a host appear
Of blessed boys;
Freed from the stress of earth,
Their circle comes near,
Full of the joys
Of the new spring and birth
Of our upper sphere.
Let him begin with these
And ascend by degrees
With the blessed boys.

THE BLESSED BOYS:

Gladly receiving
This spirit's chrysalis,

Also erlangen wir
Englisches Unterpfand.
11985 Löset die Flocken los,
Die ihn umgeben!
Schon ist er schön und groß
Von heiligem Leben.

DOCTOR MARIANUS *(in der höchsten, reinlichsten Zelle):*

Hier ist die Aussicht frei,
11990 Der Geist erhoben.
Dort ziehen Fraun vorbei,
Schwebend nach oben.
Die Herrliche mitteninn
Im Sternenkranze,
11995 Die Himmelskönigin,
Ich seh's am Glanze. *(Entzückt.)*
Höchste Herrscherin der Welt!
Lasse mich im blauen
Ausgespannten Himmelszelt
12000 Dein Geheimnis schauen!
Billige, was des Mannes Brust
Ernst und zart beweget
Und mit heiliger Liebeslust
Dir entgegen träget.

12005 Unbezwinglich unser Mut,
Wenn du hehr gebietest;
Plötzlich mildert sich die Glut,
Wie du uns befriedest.
Jungfrau, rein im schönsten Sinn,
12010 Mutter, Ehren würdig,
Uns erwählte Königin,
Göttern ebenbürtig.

Um sie verschlingen
Sich leichte Wölkchen,
12015 Sind Büßerinnen,

We are achieving
Pledge of angelic bliss.
Strip off the lowly,
Earthly cocoon!
Life that is holy
Makes him great soon.

DOCTOR MARIANUS *(in the highest, cleanest cell):*

Here the vision is free,
The spirit exalted.
Women float over me
Where heaven is vaulted.
The glorious one they surround,
Star wreaths attend her,
The heaven's queen is crowned,
I know her splendor. *(Enraptured:)*
Mistress of the firmament!
Let me in the bower
Of the heaven's outspread tent
See thy secret power!
Sanction what so tenderly
Moves men who adore thee,
And with holy loving joy
Carries them before thee.

Courage invincible we feel
If thy glory wills it—
Swiftly tempered is our zeal
If thy glory stills it.
Virgin, beautifully pure,
Venerable mother,
Our chosen queen thou art,
Peer of gods, no other!

Clouds form a garland
Around her splendor
Penitent women,

Ein zartes Völkchen,
Um Ihre Kniee
Den Äther schlürfend,
Gnade bedürfend.

12020 Dir, der Unberührbaren,
Ist es nicht benommen,
Daß die leicht Verführbaren
Traulich zu dir kommen.

In die Schwachheit hingerafft,
12025 Sind sie schwer zu retten;
Wer zerreißt aus eigner Kraft
Der Gelüste Ketten?
Wie entgleitet schnell der Fuß
Schiefem, glattem Boden?
12030 Wen betört nicht Blick und Gruß,
Schmeichelhafter Odem?

(Mater gloriosa schwebt einher.)

CHOR DER BÜSSERINNEN:

Du schwebst zu Höhen
Der ewigen Reiche,
Vernimm das Flehen,
12035 Du Ohnegleiche!
Du Gnadenreiche!

MAGNA PECCATRIX *(St. Lucae VII, 36):*

Bei der Liebe, die den Füßen
Deines gottverklärten Sohnes
Tränen ließ zum Balsam fließen,
12040 Trotz des Pharisäerhohnes;
Beim Gefäße, das so reichlich
Tropfte Wohlgeruch hernieder,
Bei den Locken, die so weichlich
Trockneten die heilgen Glieder –

MULIER SAMARITANA *(St. Joh. IV):*

12045 Bei dem Bronn, zu dem schon weiland
Abram ließ die Herde führen,

People so tender,
Her knees embrace,
Drinking the ether,
Asking her grace.

Thou art undefilable,
But thou art not chiding
When easily beguilable
Women come confiding.

Overwhelmed in weakness' hour,
It is hard to save them;
Who could burst of his own power
Lust's chains that enslave them?
Easily the foot may slip
On the swampy soil:
One is fooled by eye and lip,
Flatteries smooth as oil.
(Mater gloriosa floats into view.)

CHORUS OF PENITENT WOMEN:
Thee we are adoring,
As thou art soaring,
Hear our imploring,
Thou that art divine,
Thou, most benign.

MAGNA PECCATRIX *(Luke 7, 36):*
By the love that washed the feet
Of thy son, as man appearing,
Using tears for balsam sweet,
While the Pharisee was jeering;
By the jar of alabaster
That was spent improvidently,
By the looks that dried the Master's
Venerable limbs so gently—

MULIER SAMARITANA *(John 4):*
By the well that benefited
Abram's herds on ancient trips,

Bei dem Eimer, der dem Heiland
Kühl die Lippe durft berühren;
Bei der reinen, reichen Quelle,
12050 Die nun dorther sich ergießet,
Überflüssig, ewig helle
Rings durch alle Welten fließet –

MARIA AEGYPTIACA *(Acta Sanctorum):*

Bei dem hochgeweihten Orte,
Wo den Herrn man niederließ,
12055 Bei dem Arm, der von der Pforte
Warnend mich zurücke stieß;
Bei der vierzigjährigen Buße,
Der ich treu in Wüsten blieb,
Bei dem seligen Scheidegruße,
12060 Den im Sand ich niederschrieb –

ZU DREI:

Die du großen Sünderinnen
Deine Nähe nicht verweigerst
Und ein büßendes Gewinnen
In die Ewigkeiten steigerst,
12065 Gönn auch dieser guten Seele,
Die sich einmal nur vergessen,
Die nicht ahnte, daß sie fehle,
Dein Verzeihen angemessen!

UNA POENITENTIUM *(sonst Gretchen genannt. Sich anschmiegend):*

Neige, neige,
12070 Du Ohnegleiche,
Du Strahlenreiche,
Dein Antlitz gnädig meinem Glück!
Der früh Geliebte,
Nicht mehr Getrübte,
12075 Er kommt zurück.

SELIGE KNABEN *(in Kreisbewegung sich nähernd):*

Er überwächst uns schon
An mächtigen Gliedern,
Wird treuer Pflege Lohn

By the pail that was permitted
Once to cool the Savior's lips;
By the spring that is still streaming
Hence in pure and bounteous glow,
Overflowing, ever gleaming,
Watering worlds with endless flow—

MARIA AEGYPTICA *(Acta Sanctorum):*

By the church where the immortal
Body of the Master rested,
By the arm that at the portal
Stopped me when I was detested;
By my forty years' repentance
In the lonely desert land,
By the blissful final sentence
That I wrote into the sand—

THE THREE:

Though a woman greatly sins,
Yet she may come near to thee,
And what her repentance wins
Is hers in eternity:
Grant this good soul, too, thy blessing,
That but once herself forgot,
Ignorant she was transgressing;
Pardon her and spurn her not!

UNA POENITENTIUM *(formerly called* GRETCHEN. *Nestling):*

Incline, incline,
That art divine,
Thou that dost shine,
Thy face in grace to my sweet ecstasy!
He whom I loved in pain
Now returns free from stain,
Comes back to me.

BLESSED BOYS *(approaching in circling motion):*

Already his limbs breathe might
And he outgrows us;
Tend him, he will requite

Reichlich erwidern.
12080 Wir wurden früh entfernt
Von Lebechören;
Doch dieser hat gelernt,
Er wird uns lehren.

DIE EINE BÜSSERIN *(sonst Gretchen genannt):*

Vom edlen Geisterchor umgeben,
12085 Wird sich der Neue kaum gewahr,
Er ahnet kaum das frische Leben,
So gleicht er schon der heiligen Schar.
Sieh, wie er jedem Erdenbande
Der alten Hülle sich entrafft
12090 Und aus ätherischem Gewande
Hervortritt erste Jugendkraft!
Vergönne mir, ihn zu belehren,
Noch blendet ihn der neue Tag.

MATER GLORIOSA:

Komm! Hebe dich zu höhern Sphären!
12095 Wenn er dich ahnet, folgt er nach.

DOCTOR MARIANUS *(auf dem Angesicht anbetend):*

Blicket auf zum Retterblick,
Alle reuig Zarten,
Euch zu seligem Geschick
Dankend umzuarten.
12100 Werde jeder beßre Sinn
Dir zum Dienst erbötig;
Jungfrau, Mutter, Königin,
Göttin, bleibe gnädig!

CHORUS MYSTICUS:

Alles Vergängliche
12105 Ist nur ein Gleichnis;
Das Unzulängliche,
Hier wird's Ereignis;
Das Unbeschreibliche,
Hier ist's getan;
12110 Das Ewig-Weibliche
Zieht uns hinan.

All that he owes us.
Early we have returned,
Life scarcely reached us;
This one, however, learned,
And he will teach us.

ONE PENITENT *(formerly called* GRETCHEN*)*:

Amid the noble spirits' mirth,
The newcomer is so engrossed,
He scarcely knows of his rebirth
Before he joins the holy host.
Behold, all earthly ties have peeled,
The old shroud has dropped off at length,
While ether's garment has revealed
The radiance of his youthful strength!
Grant that I teach him; he appears
Still blinded by the new day's glare.

MATER GLORIOSA:

Come, raise yourself to higher spheres!
When he feels you, he follows there.

DOCTOR MARIANUS *(prostrate, adoring)*:

Penitents, behold elated
The redeeming face;
Grateful, be regenerated
For a life of grace.
That all good minds would grow keen
To serve thee alone;
Holy virgin, mother, queen,
Goddess on thy throne!

CHORUS MYSTICUS:

What is destructible
Is but a parable;
What fails ineluctably,
The undeclarable,
Here it was seen,
Here it was action;
The Eternal-Feminine
Lures to perfection.

ABOUT THE TRANSLATOR

Walter Kaufmann (1921–1980) was born in Freiburg, Germany, came to the United States in 1939, and was graduated from Williams College in 1941. During World War II he served first with the U.S. Army Air Force and then returned to Europe with Military Intelligence. In 1947 he received his Ph. D. degree from Harvard and became an instructor at Princeton University, where he was Professor of Philosophy.

He was also visiting professor at Cornell, Columbia, the New School, and the Universities of Michigan and Washington; and, on Fulbright grants, at Heidelberg and Jerusalem. In 1961 he was awarded an international Leo Baeck Prize. He published a dozen books, including *Cain and Other Poems*, *Twenty German Poets*, *The Faith of a Heretic*, *From Shakespeare to Existentialism*, and *Critique of Religion and Philosophy.*